FORGING THE
COLLECTIVE MEMORY

Government and International Historians
Through Two World Wars

Edited by
Keith Wilson

Berghahn Books
Providence • Oxford

Published in 1996 by

Berghahn Books
Editorial offices:
165 Taber Avenue, Providence, RI 02906, USA
Bush House, Merewood Avenue, Oxford, OX3 8EF, UK

Library of Congress Cataloging-in-Publication Data
Forging the collective memory : government and international
historians through two World Wars / edited by Keith Wilson.
    p.   cm.
Includes bibliographical references.
    Contents: Introduction : governments, historians, and "historical engineer-
ing" / Keith Wilson -- The historical diplomacy of the Third Republic / Keith
Hamilton -- The unfinished collection : Russian documents on the origins of the
First World War / Derek Spring -- Clio deceived : patriotic self-censorship in Germany after the Great War / Holger Herwig -- Senator Owen, the Schuldreferat,
and the debate over war guilt in the 1920s / Hermann Wittgens -- History as
propaganda : the German Foreign Office and the enlightenment of American his-
torians, 1930–1933 / E. Evans & J. Baylen -- Austria and the Great War / Ulfried
Burz -- The pursuit of "enlightened patriotism" : the British Foreign Office and
historical researchers during the Great War and its aftermath / Keith Hamilton --
The imbalance of British documents on the origins of the War, 1898–1914 : Gooch,
Temperley, and the India Office / Keith Wilson -- Telling the truth to the people :
Britain's decision to publish the diplomatic papers of the inter-war period / Uri
Bialer -- Appendix : Harold Wilson and the adoption of the thirty-year rule in
Great Britain.
    ISBN 1-57181-862-6 (alk. paper)
    1. Historiography 2. Historians.   3. History--Sources.
I. Wilson, Keith M.
D13.F5945   1996
907'.2--dc20   95-53940
                                                                                      CIP

British Library Cataloguing in Publication Data
A CIP catalogue record for this book is available from
the British Library.

Printed in the United States on acid-free paper

⑤ CONTENTS

Acknowledgements iv

Introduction: Governments, Historians, and 1
'Historical Engineering'
Keith Wilson

1. The Historical Diplomacy of the Third Republic 29
Keith Hamilton

2. The Unfinished Collection: Russian Documents 63
on the Origins of the First World War
Derek Spring

3. Clio Deceived: Patriotic Self-Censorship in 87
Germany After the Great War
Holger H. Herwig

4. Senator Owen, the Schuldreferat, and the Debate 128
over War Guilt in the 1920s
Herman Wittgens

5. History As Propaganda: The German Foreign 151
Ministry and the 'Enlightenment' of American
Historians on the War-Guilt Question, 1930–1933
Ellen L. Evans and Joseph O. Baylen

6. Austria and the Great War: Official Publications 178
in the 1920s and 1930s
Ulfried Burz

7. The Pursuit of 'Enlightened Patriotism': The British 192
Foreign Office and Historical Researchers During
the Great War and Its Aftermath
Keith Hamilton

8. The Imbalance in *British Documents on the Origins*   230
   of the War, 1898–1914: Gooch, Temperley, and the
   India Office
   Keith Wilson

9. Telling the Truth to the People: Britain's Decision to   265
   Publish the Diplomatic Papers of the Interwar Period
   Uri Bialer

   Appendix: Harold Wilson and the Adoption of the   289
   Thirty-Year Rule in Great Britain

   Notes on Contributors   294

   Index   295

Acknowledgements

For permission to reprint certain articles which were first published in
learned journals I would like to thank the editors of *Diplomacy and State-
craft* (chapter 1, 1993), *International Security* (chapter 3, 1987), *Canadian
Journal of History* (chapter 5, 1975), *Historical Research* (chapter 7, 1988),
Historical Journal (chapter 9, 1983). For assistance with translating and
with other matters, I wish to thank Dr Eleanor Breuning (University of
Wales, Swansea), Professor F.R. Bridge (University of Leeds), Dr G.T.
Waddington (University of Leeds), and Professor H. Rumpler (Univer-
sity of Klagenfurt). Mrs Christine Cascarino did the bulk of the necessary
typing, and dealt as efficiently as the developing technology allowed with
certain aspects of the production process. Crown copyright material in the
Public Record Office is reproduced by permission of the Controller of Her
Majesty's Stationery Office.

INTRODUCTION
Governments, Historians, and 'Historical Engineering'

Keith Wilson

Governments have never taken the view that they, and what they regard as their property, the official records of the governance of the state, exist for the sake of historians. If anything, and especially so far as recent international history is concerned, the collective view of governments has been that the situation has been, and must remain, the other way round. This governmental view has generated much tension between historians on the one hand and governments and their officials on the other. On the part of the historians this tension, this incompatibility of interests, may be illustrated by Lord Acton's definition of the problem as 'the enmity between the truth of history and the reason of state, between sincere quest and official secrecy'; by Sir Herbert Butterfield's injunction that 'we must never lose sight of the separate interests of officialdom on the one hand and the academic historian on the other, never allow the situation to be blurred or the tension and conflict between the two to be quietened'; by Professor Owen Chadwick's direct and simple statement: 'The needs of government and the wishes of the historian conflict.'[1] On the part of governments and of officials, it may be illustrated by the remark of the editor in chief of *Die Grosse Politik der Europäischen Kabinette, 1871–1914*, Friedrich Thimme, that as a politician he could not accept the view that the publication of the German documents existed for the study of contemporary history as an end in itself; by the letter of Konstantin von Neurath, German ambassador to the Quirinal, to Gustav Stresemann, of 16 February 1925, which ended: 'The events of the period presently being published [the 1900s] are still of too recent vintage to allow the publication of the pertinent documents according to the criteria of historical research alone

...'; and by Austen Chamberlain's telling G.P. Gooch on 30 July 1926 that as British foreign secretary 'my first duty is to preserve peace now and in the future. I cannot sacrifice *that* even to historical accuracy'.[2]

A.J.P. Taylor became fond of propounding 'Taylor's law', which was that foreign offices know no secrets, and that the patron saint, at least of the British archives, is Joanna Southcott.[3] I would prefer to proceed by advancing a series of multiple propositions. The first of these is that governments and their officials fear historians; that governments of whatever kind take advantage of the fact acknowledged by Sir E.L. Woodward that 'the possibility of investigating at first-hand and not merely discovering by inference the policy of a sovereign state must depend primarily upon the willingness of the state in question to disclose the course and motives of its actions';[4] and that as a result governments try to keep their archives closed, and the work of historians at as great a distance from the present as possible. The second proposition is that governments are well aware of the fact that both the withholding and the releasing of archive material gives them scope for 'historical engineering';[5] and that in debating whether to open their archives to any extent, to the general public or to selected individuals, priority is given to considerations of present and future policy over the study of the past. The third proposition is that governments prefer to see the production of patriotic history; and that they try to ensure that anyone granted (and 'granted' is still the operative word) special access, or the status of 'official' historian or editor of official documents, is a patriotic historian. The fourth proposition is that many historians see it as their duty to write, or to participate in the production of, patriotic history. The final set of propositions is that, despite the series of official documents published in the 1920s and 1930s by the Russians, Germans, Austrians, British, and French, which did so much to promote the development of the study of international history as a branch of history in its own right; despite the post-1945 publications of documents on the inter-war years; and despite the adoption in Britain in the 1960s of the Thirty-Year Rule, the situation has seen, in all the above respects, no real change; that in the forging, or shaping, of the collective memory, the role of governments has always been greater than that of historians, and is likely to remain so.

I

Only in 1957 did the German Foreign Ministry archives covering the Hohenzollern candidature of 1870 see the light of day, and this only as a result of their capture in 1945. In his introduction to his edition of them, Georges Bonnin demonstrated the campaign waged by successive German governments, from 1890 to the Second World War, against historians interested in utilising them in their work. In 1890 the German chancellor Caprivi informed the German historian Heinrich von Sybel, who was producing a history of the founding of the German empire, of his own and Kaiser Wilhelm II's opinion that the time had not yet come for using documentary evidence on the circumstances that preceded the war of 1870. Chancellor and emperor had already agreed that 'the continuation of the publication of the work was to be prevented as far as possible'.[6] When in 1895 Sybel attempted to impress on Caprivi's successor Hohenlohe that he no longer felt bound by the obligation imposed on him by Caprivi of ignoring the secret documents of the Foreign Ministry on the Hohenzollern candidature, he was rebuffed.[7] In 1895 and again in 1897 Hohenlohe and the kaiser intervened to secure the omission of certain documents from a book by the historian Wilhelm Oncken.[8] Also in 1897 the German Foreign Ministry suggested that Colonel von Werthern, who was writing a biography of the Prussian emissary Versen, be told that publication of his chapter relating to Versen's mission to Spain might be considered as 'treason'.[9]

At the beginning of the next century Kaiser Wilhelm II's attitude towards the writing of recent German history was embodied in a letter from Chancellor von Bülow: 'His Majesty considers publications about the said political era as in principle still premature.'[10] A year later, in 1903, the German Foreign Ministry recommended that, in order that the official version of the candidature survive, certain passages in Theodor von Bernhardi's memoirs should be suppressed.[11] Publication was still 'premature' in 1911, when Chancellor Bethmann-Hollweg said, of a manuscript planned by Zingeler, the archivist of the Hohenzollern-Sigmaringen family: 'Under no circumstances must those documents be published.'[12] The treatment handed out to Zingeler was also handed out to Hans Delbrück, who was told that documents which did exist did not exist, to Ernst Marx, and to Erich Brandenburg.[13] After the Great War, in March 1920, Dr Willy Cohn, who wished to consult the reports of Werthern, the Prussian minister to

Munich, was told by the Foreign Ministry that his request must be refused, as other requests had been: it was impossible to depart from the principle that political files could not be made available to historians before their transfer to the state archives.[14] A variation on this theme was played in 1921 regarding a joint request from Professor Platzhoff and Dr Rheindorff, who wished to see the files on the political history of the war of 1870. The Foreign Ministry stated its intention of excluding from files to be communicated material dealing with the candidature, as it did not wish to give historians the proof that Bismarck's statement in the Bundesrat in July 1870 was not true. Bonnin concluded: 'The Platzhoff-Rheindorff incident shows that the Foreign Ministry, with regard to the Hohenzollern candidature, was following the practice of secrecy established before the First World War.'[15] The next victim was the American historian R.H. Lord.[16]

To pursue this theme further, still in relation to Germany but beyond the issue of the Hohenzollern candidature, it was in 1916 that the German Foreign Office ruled that the publication of the political testament of Frederick the Great would be 'inopportune'.[17] Frederick the Great had died in 1786, one hundred and thirty years before. The memory of a church may be longer than that of a state, as Chadwick has said, but the latter runs the former very close. Friedrich Thimme is on record as saying how hard he had to fight in the 1920s to include in *Die Grosse Politik* a chapter on the *Daily Telegraph* interview affair of 1908.[18] Two years into the Second World War, the official archivists of the German Foreign Ministry drew up a catalogue of the papers of Baron von Holstein, who had died in 1909; it read: '(i) Because of their close interconnection with the secret political documents of the Foreign Ministry, the Holstein Papers cannot in future be submitted in their entirety to the examination of private researchers any more than the Secret files themselves. (ii) Certain sections of the Papers can be submitted to private researchers, if at all, only if they form a unity in themselves and if their substantive and formal connection with other parts of the Papers as well as with other previously published literature can be established from the beginning.'[19]

As regards Italy, the same sentiments were expressed, only rather more gracefully. Giolitti, the Italian prime minister, said in 1912 of the papers of Cavour that 'It would not be right to have beautiful legends discredited by historical criticism'.[20] The sentiments of the Italian state were those of Cardinal de Lai, 'first charity and then truth', rather than those of Pope Leo XIII, 'the first law of history is that nothing untrue be said, and nothing true be unsaid'.[21] Italian governments carried this attitude to such an extreme that, alone among the greater powers of Europe, they published during the interwar years no documents at all on the decades immediately preceding the outbreak of war in 1914. It might be noted here in passing, however, that the Spanish diplomatic archives for 1870 were still closed to historians in 1957.[22]

A study of the regulations governing access to the archives of the British Foreign Office also supports the propositions being put forward here. In 1908 no correspondence later than 1780 could be seen without restriction and censorship; correspondence between 1780 and 1850 was open to inspection, and could be copied, but only under special permit issued by the secretary of state, and these permits imposed certain restrictions on the use to be made of any notes taken or abstracts or copies made. The regime obtaining was as follows:

> On presentation of such permits, the papers are ... produced in the Government Search Room of the Record Office. The officer in charge of this room reads all copies and notes made by the holders of permits, with a view of ascertaining whether these papers contain anything of which the publication might be regarded as objectionable. They are then forwarded, with a report, to the Secretary of State for approval. In the Foreign Office they are subjected to fresh examination by the Librarian and his staff ... Occasionally passages to which objection is taken are deleted, and sometimes portions of the papers are held back.[23]

There was thus, as Sir E.A. Crowe described it, 'a double system of censorship'. Crowe was at this time the representative of the Foreign Office on the Committee on Public Records which had been considering the question of access and was about to make certain recommendations. Crowe wanted to know how far these recommendations would meet with the general approval of the secretary of state. He made it clear at the outset that the secretary of state 'will, of course, in any case, not be definitely bound by what the Committee may recommend to be done'. The most important of the recommendations was that the correspondence of all government departments should be opened to 1837, the year of the accession of Queen Victoria. This 'opening' was to be accompanied, however, by 'stricter rules of admission ... sufficient to ensure that something be known of every person entering the Search Room'.[24] The adoption of these proposals would mean that special permits issued by the secretary of state as regards Foreign Office correspondence would be required only for papers for the years 1837 to 1850.

Crowe was not anxious that the system of censorship be removed, but did believe it could be completed in one stage instead of two. He had told the Committee that, 'if the kind of information which, if published, might give rise to objections, be indicated with sufficient precision, the Record Office can be relied on to exercise a proper discretion in the matter of bringing all doubtful cases to the notice of the Secretary of State'. He thought that an existing list of sensitive material could be expanded by the Foreign Office Librarian's Department for the guidance of the Record Office. He also thought that 'power ought to be retained so as to withhold any particular volumes or documents, whether relating to the period before or after 1837'. He had opposed a suggestion that a rule should be made under which after a specified number of years (say ten) the period over which unrestricted access was allowed to all records should be automatically advanced by the same number of years. To this he objected on the ground that a rule depriving the secretary of state of any power in future to have a voice in a matter of such importance 'might become very inconvenient'. As a result, the Committee had agreed 'merely to recommend that any rules to be made now ... should be reconsidered ten years hence'. Whilst he personally professed to be prepared to open down to 1861, the year of the death of Prince Albert, the papers that could be seen under the system of special permits (having convinced himself 'that nothing not hitherto known that could be published from our archives relating to the Crimean War, could possibly have any political effect on our present relations with Russia') he was very much concerned to stop well short 'of what may be described as the Bismarck era in foreign politics, to which we are still so close in point of time and interest as to justify a special measure of caution and reserve'.[25]

Crowe had the impudence to end his memorandum with the following sentence:

> It is a great pity that so little original historical work is at present done in this country, and any encouragement which could be offered in this direction by the Secretary of State would, I feel sure, be a benefit to this country and to the world at large.[26]

The suggestion he made in his final paragraph, that certain historians of British nationality might obtain as 'a personal privilege accorded by the Secretary of State, and under specially devised rules and safeguards', access to papers for, presumably, the period between the death of the Prince Consort and the beginning of the 'Bismarck era', was hardly designed to remedy this situation. It was, moreover, heavy with conditions: 'provided it be understood that the actual text of anything proposed to be published must be submitted for the censorship of the Secretary of State and that on publication being authorised, the original notes, abstracts or copies, of Foreign Office papers are handed over to him'.[27]

What Lionel Curtis called 'the inveterate hostility of Crowe' was still in evidence at the end of the Great War.[28] It was displayed in connection with the establishment of an institute of international affairs, whose proponents looked forward to creating a forum where officials and academics interested in the study of recent and contemporary international affairs might meet. Crowe immediately raised the difficulty of the cooperation of officials and the question of official secrets. His views were shared by Lord Curzon, already designated to succeed Balfour as foreign secretary, and by Lord Hardinge, the permanent under-secretary.[29]

Only in 1919 were Foreign Office records opened from 1850 to the end of 1860. In May 1920 the conditions of access to correspondence for 1861 to 1885 were that

(a) all notes, extracts and transcriptions of correspondence shall be inspected and approved by Foreign Office officials;
(b) prior to publication, proofs of the parts based on information and material derived from the Foreign Office archives shall be submitted to the Foreign Office for inspection and approval.[30]

At the end of 1924 the 'open' period was extended from the end of 1860 to the end of 1878. The cutoff point was rigorously enforced: when E.L. Woodward, who had been recruited to the staff of the Political Intelligence Department in the final year of the war, during which time he had used restricted documents to write a monograph on the Congress of Berlin which he had then been forbidden to publish, asked in December 1924 if he might now publish it, he was told that if any references were made to papers later than 1878, they must be omitted.[31]

Former officials were treated far more leniently than professional historians, as a memorandum of 1923 makes clear:

> As regards ex-officials ... the practice is similar to that which is pursued as regards historians generally, with the difference, *of course*,

that much greater latitude is given to the former as regards access to papers.[32]

Even so, in that year (1923) the account in the memoirs of the former ambassador to Rome Sir Rennell Rodd of his role in frustrating French policy towards Egypt and the Upper Nile was censored: 'It reveals', wrote Crowe, now permanent under-secretary, 'a piece of history which it would be far better not to give the world as yet'.[33] In his memorandum of November 1908 Crowe had stated that much important and confidential Foreign Office material had remained in the private possession of secretaries of state and heads of diplomatic missions, and that many documents had found their way, under deed of gift, to the British Museum, 'where they may be freely consulted'. That this was tendentious if not absolutely misleading is revealed by the first section of R.C. Dickie's memorandum of March 1923, 'Foreign Office Confidential Papers and Information: Control over Unauthorised Publication', which catalogues the efforts made by the Foreign Office since the 1860s to retrieve as much of this material as came to its attention, and the arrangements it insisted on both as regards papers in private hands (those of Lord Granville and Sir Robert Morier, for instance) and with the trustees of the British Museum in the cases of the papers of Sir Robert Peel, Sir Henry Layard and others, that these papers should on no account be freely consulted or published. Some pieces of history the Foreign Office was determined to keep from the world forever: in the autumn of 1924 the Foreign Office librarian raised no objection to the destruction of the archives of the Foreign Trade Department of the Foreign Office, saying, 'I think that the time has now passed when they can ever be wanted for any very serious purpose'.[34]

This being the mentality of the British Foreign Office, it comes as no surprise that, in the 1930s, the British government requested the government of the United States not to publish certain documents in its supplement to *Foreign Relations of the United States 1917*; nor that during the Second World War the British government requested the United States government not to publish certain entire volumes, even though they had already been printed, of the series commenced in 1942 of documents on the Paris Peace Conference of 1919.[35] The Americans complied, as under the statement of principles for the editing of *FRUS*, approved by Secretary of State Frank B. Kellogg in March 1925, they were bound to do.

According to this, certain omissions were recognised as legitimate and necessary:

(a) Matters which if published at the time would tend to embarrass negotiations or other business;

(b) To condense the record and avoid needless details;

(c) To preserve the confidence reposed in the Department by other governments and by individuals;

(d) To avoid needless offence to other nationalities or individuals by excising invidious comments not relevant or essential to the subject; and

(e) To suppress personal opinions presented in despatches and not adopted by the Department. To this there is one qualification, namely, that on major decisions it is desirable, where possible, to show the choices presented to the Department when the decision was made.

... when a foreign government, in giving permission to use a communication, requests the deletion of any part of it, it is usually preferable to publish the document in part rather than to omit it altogether ...[36]

At least the United States made public (although not until 1928) the guidelines that applied to *FRUS*, which since the 1860s had been their, annual, equivalent of the much more spasmodic British Blue Book, of which C.K. Webster told the American Historical Association in December 1924: 'Though large measures of papers were laid before Parliament, their bulk increasing as the [nineteenth] century progressed, yet these were often written as much to obscure as to reveal the real aims of the statesmen',[37] and of which Headlam-Morley, when assistant director of the Political Intelligence Department in 1919, had written: 'Although the information contained in many of the Foreign Office Blue Books is obviously of the highest importance, the form in which it is presented to the public is such that it can often only be used by those who have special knowledge and can devote a good deal of time to finding their way through a tangled correspondence. The method of publication is also such that it is in fact not easy for those outside official circles even to get knowledge of their existence'.[38] The British quandary, at least, was well stated by Sir Edward Grey in December 1911, in reply to accusations of secrecy:

This is an age of inventions, and perhaps some day something will be invented by which it is possible to publish Papers in the House of Commons which shall not be known elsewhere. I can assure the House that the motive for secrecy in ninety-nine cases out of a hundred is not to withhold information from the House, but is the difficulty of giving information to the House without giving it to the world at large; and the knowledge we give to the world at large may cause difficulties abroad which are unnecessary ...[39]

In respect of keeping historians, and the past, at a distance, the United States government differed from the British, and from those of the other major powers, and overcame, apparently, what C.K. Webster called the 'instinctive and intense distrust' with which the academic expert had to contend. For in 1924 professional historians were recruited to edit *FRUS*, hitherto edited by members of staff in the State Department. However, this was less of a breakthrough for the historical profession than it might seem, for the identity of those selected was not disclosed. Since they were chosen by the chief of the Division of Publications in the State Department and worked under his direction, and since the Kellogg guidelines were in force throughout, realistic doubts have been expressed that the freedom given to the editors in the selection of material for publication was far from complete.[40]

II

In December 1918 Dr Solf, foreign minister in the republican administration of Prince Max of Baden, sent the following communication to the governments of Britain, France, and the United States:

> For the purpose of bringing about universal peace, of insuring lasting guarantees against future wars and of restoring the peoples' confidence in one another, it seems imperatively necessary to throw light on the events which brought on the war, in all the belligerent States and in all their particulars. A complete truthful account of the world conditions and of the negotiations among the powers in July 1914 and of the steps taken at that time by the several Governments could and would go far toward demolishing the walls of hatred and misconstruction erected by the long war to separate the peoples. In a correct appreciation of the course taken by friend and foe lies the augury for the future reconciliation of the peoples, the one possible foundation for lasting peace and a league of peoples.
>
> The German Government therefore proposes that a neutral Commission be organised to probe the responsibilities for the war, which should be composed of men whose character and political experience will guarantee a true verdict. The Governments of all

the belligerent powers should declare their readiness to place at the disposal of such a Commission all of their records ...[41]

It might seem, from what has been said in the preceding section, that Solf's demand, which was immediately rejected by the governments to which it was sent, was an aberration. It was not. It was a political act, designed to advance the present and future objectives of the German state. It was not an example of disinterested interest in the development of scholarship. Thimme has already been quoted as saying that he could not accept the view that the publication of the German documents existed for the study of contemporary history as an end in itself. What he went on to say serves as the most appropriate motto in this connection: 'The political end, to which the documents also owe their existence, stands higher. And whenever contemporary documents are being published, one does well to suspect political ends.'[42] Professor Ernest R. May's speculation that the declassification by Henry Kissinger of NSC 68 in February 1975 was designed to revive the nomination of Paul Nitze for the post of assistant secretary of defense for international security affairs by removing from Nitze's reputation any disposition towards unilateral disarmament, is but the most recent example which the present writer has encountered.[43]

The German Foreign Ministry left itself in no doubt as to the purpose of Die Grosse Politik. In a memorandum of 7 May 1921, produced in Department IX D, it was stated: 'The great document publication is not being prepared so that its volumes ... might only gather dust in archives or be studied by isolated historians with effects which will be apparent only after years.'[44] In August 1924 the German chancellor Wilhelm Marx wrote to the British prime minister and foreign secretary Ramsay MacDonald, and told him that once Die Grosse Politik was completed, Germany would challenge the victorious powers to convene an international court of arbitration to inquire into the causes of the Great War and pass an impartial judgment. He followed this up in an article in Foreign Affairs in 1926, which attacked the policy of Russia and France before concluding that only a condemnation of the Treaty of Versailles could insure the future happiness of humanity.[45] It was noticed by the French that Stresemann and others, in interviews, declared that the published documents 'sont de nature à prouver la volonté de paix de l'Allemagne', which they took as a contradiction of what Rathenau had said in the Reichstag on 13 June 1922 to the effect that Die Grosse Politik would contribute 'à

l'apaisement moral du monde'.[46] When in February 1925 Neurath
passed on to Stresemann certain Italian complaints regarding *Die
Grosse Politik*, Stresemannn instructed him to explain that the publication was an act of self-defence on the part of the German people; the Italian government could be assured that all volumes were
examined by a former diplomat before printing in order to avoid
any unnecessary offence being given to any statesman still alive,
and in future the material relating to Italy would receive special
attention.[47] That this was followed through is the explanation for
Thimme's memorandum of 10 May 1925, in which he admitted
that it would not be in the interests of German foreign policy if her
own statesmen were unnecessarily compromised by the publication, and in which he stressed that in the selection of documents
and in the footnoting the editors were very circumspect as regards
foreign statesmen who might still be important in the shaping of
future relations with Germany.[48] His coeditor, Professor Bartholdy,
put the main point quite bluntly in *Europäische Gespräche* in July
1926: 'our document collection is indeed intended to serve the
future, not the past'.[49]

The same consideration was applied by the governments which,
at the end of 1918, had rejected Solf's demands. In August 1924
Ramsay MacDonald attempted to dissuade Chancellor Marx from
pursuing the course of action which he had outlined, on the
grounds that it would be counterproductive:

> I should strongly advise you not to raise this question at present. It
> has now become a matter for the historian. The life of nations goes
> on in defiance of these hasty verdicts and, in the end, the truth is dis-
> covered and everybody agrees to forget falsehoods and errors. Were
> I in your position, I should content myself and wait for the verdict.[50]

This was richly disingenuous, given that MacDonald had decided
several months earlier *not* to leave matters alone but to authorise an
official publication of British documents mainly in order to combat
the impression that *Die Grosse Politik* was making and was considered, when complete, likely to make, to the prevailing verdict on
responsibility for the Great War. He was not 'content' to 'wait for
the verdict' – he intended to manipulate that verdict. He *was* prepared, as in his letter to Marx he professed not to be, to 'baffle' German attempts to clear themselves. He was one of those in whose
keeping 'justice' was. At that very time he was engaged in a search
for the British historian that this would be a matter for; in September 1924 he authorised the Treasury to release the necessary funds.

Also disingenuous was the introduction penned by the historical adviser to the Foreign Office to the four-volume English translation, by E.T.S. Dugdale, of the fifty-seven volume German publication. 'The object', wrote Headlam-Morley, 'is not propaganda, not defence of the British Government, but to provide students of our foreign policy with material which it is essential that they should be acquainted.'[51] This was the reverse of the truth. Dugdale's edition was, like *Die Grosse Politik*, like *British Documents on the Origins of the War*, like *Documents Diplomatiques Français*, all part of Schwertfeger's 'world war of documents'.[52]

The French government, at the beginning of the 1920s, had resisted requests for documents with Poincaré's argument that to produce any would be to imply 'une attenuation de l'aveu des responsabilités allemands'.[53] At the end of the decade Poincaré is to be found putting pressure on the former diplomat and official Maurice Paléologue to release material. The sort of posthumous publication preferred by Paléologue in order to avoid the grave political dangers of an 'exhibition générale', argued Poincaré, 'would come too late to wash from France the calumnies of the world'.[54] Barthou, the French minister for foreign affairs, was even more explicit in May 1934: *Documents Diplomatiques Français* was 'de portée essentiallement politique'.[55]

What was for the French, Germans and British 'de portée essentiallement politique' was for the Russians 'de portée essentiallement idéologique'. This is clear from the introduction written by Professor Pokrovsky, the chairman of the commission set up by the Soviet government to edit documents covering the years 1878 to 1917. Pokrovsky wrote:

All these 'fatal days' and 'fatal weeks', to which the bourgeois historians and editors of documents attach such great importance, are for us considerations of the third order, in so far as we know that the war was not the work of the evil intentions of individual persons and individual groups, but resulted of iron necessity from the economic system of the last decades, the system of monopolistic capitalism. But it certainly does not in consequence follow, as many naive persons think, that 'there are no guilty ones', and that it is not worth seeking for them. The grasping appetites of all imperialistic governments made for war: but none of them acknowledged this nor does so now; they were all, so they say, the victims of the grasping of others. To prove the mania of all imperialistic governments and groups for grabbing, and that not only *a priori* on the basis of the hypothesis that they must be grasping, but on the basis of documentary material that is unimpeachable and possesses validity for all, is to solve a problem of enormous importance. For the struggle against imperialism, we must know surely and quite exactly how it acts, of what sort are its procedure and methods. And if the grasping activity of imperialists is irrefutably established by a series of incontestable documents, we shall naturally have a bill of indictment – but a bill of indictment not against a single person or even against a single country, but against a *class*, and that class the one which in 1914 held power in its hands in all great countries and in most of them still holds it.[56]

When governments withhold documents, they do so for present 'political reasons'.[57] The same reasons dominate the making available of documents. Just as keeping the archives closed prevents harm being done to 'the accredited legend', as Caprivi described one of these in 1890,[58] so opening the archives provides governments with the opportunity to manufacture new ones, all the more so as, given the regulations which they devise and enforce, they remain able to control both access to and selection of the source materials.

III

For governments, patriotic history is the only legitimate kind of history. The director of the archives of the French Foreign Ministry, Faugère, reminded French historians in 1879 that it was their duty to 'ménager l'honneur' of France and French governments in any revelations based on the official archives.[59] In 1875 he had considered that the patriotic sentiments of the historian Legrelle sufficiently guaranteed his proper usage of the documents.[60] Heinrich von Sybel, commissioned by Bismarck in 1881 to write a history of Prussia for the years 1850 to 1870, had written in 1878 that there was 'no better propaganda for the reputation of Prussia in the world than the authentic knowledge of Prussian history'.[61] Herman Hesselbarth, who in 1913 had escaped the net and published on the Hohenzollern candidature using sources not under the control of the German government, found himself strenuously opposed by the Foreign Ministry when in 1924 he wished to make further revelations.[62] Karl Kautsky, having completed an edition of German documents on the outbreak of war in 1914 commissioned by one government, found the Foreign Ministry under its successor labelling his work as treasonable and opposing and delaying its publication.[63] Thimme, having completed *Die Grosse Politik*, was sufficiently 'unpatriotic' in 1931 as to publish a volume of replies by diplomats to the memoirs of Prince von Bülow. He was immediately denied any further access to the documents he had edited.[64]

The official British attitude to history was revealed in an exchange in the House of Lords, in July 1907, between Viscount Esher and the lord chancellor, Loreburn. Esher had asked 'whether written communications on official business of State between the Sovereign and members of the Cabinet, the Viceroy of India, and British Ambassadors to Foreign Courts, as well as between members of the Cabinet themselves, are protected under the Official Secrets Act, or are in any way safeguarded against unauthorised publication'. He claimed that he had 'no wish to curtail in any way reasonable freedom of authors to write biographies or of the public to read them'. He went on, however, to make a case for the extension of the Official Secrets Act to cover precisely this material. Loreburn agreed that a case had been made and, in summing up, defined 'freedom' as 'patriotic freedom': 'I believe it is well worthy of our consideration whether some further safeguard should be imposed, without in the slightest degree restricting any honest freedom – such honest, patriotic freedom as I feel sure would be fairly exercised by the great majority of the press of this country.'[65]

Because it was 'a defence of British foreign policy down to 1870–1' that John Holland Rose wished to undertake in 1915, Balfour raised no objection to Rose's seeing the archives.[66] Because Lawrence Steefel might produce on the Schleswig-Holstein question of the 1860s a book with a strong anti-British bias, Crowe in 1920 opposed his being given access to them.[67] Headlam-Morley, in the same year, was afraid that G.P. Gooch, in his chapter for the *Cambridge History of British Foreign Policy*, would not state the British case 'strongly and firmly' as the Foreign Office wished to do; that on the contrary what Gooch would write would 'be on the whole unfavourable to the conduct of foreign affairs during the years that he deals with', and would leave people feeling 'that after all it was errors in judgment by Sir Edward Grey that were very largely responsible for the state of things out of which the war inevitably arose'.[68] Gooch's prewar criticisms of Grey's policy, his connection with the Union of Democratic Control and his sympathy for a negotiated peace, did not recommend him to the Foreign Office. Harold Temperley also disapproved of Gooch. Writing to the former diplomat Sir Ernest Satow in May 1924, Temperley said: 'Gooch is a little wrong, I always think, being not wholly practical in his views, and inclined to say the best for Germany – with every disposition to treat her fairly.'[69] There is no doubt as to where Temperley stood: 'I don't much care for [Germany] as "the lamb", which is where Gooch usually wants to put her';[70] in 1925, having been exposed to S.B. Fay's revisionist views at the American Historical Association, Temperley wrote: 'I must get in to Fay. I wish I had seen it before. His attitude struck me at Richmond as much worse than his writings.'[71] The Foreign Office approved of Temperley, and welcomed his appointment as one of the editors of *British Documents on the Origins of the War*: as Crowe put it, 'He has worked with and for us before, and earned general respect and satisfaction'.[72]

On the other hand C.K. Webster was in Crowe's eyes 'a terror', to be avoided at all costs.[73] Webster had blotted his copybook with the Foreign Office by maintaining, in his inaugural lecture delivered in 1923, that 'Almost all accounts of foreign politics are disfigured by a national bias that is so common that it has come to be expected almost as a matter of course', and that '[History] has tended to be in all the schools of the world a glorification of the national prejudices'. He blotted it still more by taking up these themes again in a memorandum which in April 1924 Harold Laski of the London School of Economics and Political Science sent in to the Foreign Office. Webster's Notes on Public Access to the Foreign Office records began: 'Access to the Foreign Office Records is a vital consideration in all attempts to make Foreign Policy depend on the popular will. The History of past Diplomacy is essential to a proper understanding of the present. If British Foreign Policy is really to represent the wishes of the people it can only be successful if the people are adequately instructed and informed; and no text-book or pamphlets will supply the necessary information unless the preliminary work of scientific investigation can be also adequately carried out.' Webster finally burned his boats with the Foreign Office by converting this into an article which was published in June 1924 in *The Nation and the Athenaeum* under the title 'The Labour Government and Secret Diplomacy'. It was bad enough to mention in private the existence of signals intelligence, ciphers, and spies; to mention them in public was almost treasonable – it was, said the librarian of the Foreign Office, Gaselee, 'very wrong'. The legal adviser reacted by recommending that if Webster was currently the recipient of any special facilities, they should be withdrawn immediately: 'After this exhibition ... we shall be justified in denying him access to everything which is not freely available to the general public.' The permanent under-secretary, Sir Eyre Crowe, agreed: 'This should certainly be done.' The inveterately hostile Crowe, who had already resisted Webster's modest proposal that 'the public papers should be the property of the public, and it is suggested that after forty years no possible harm could result' with the remark 'This is not a sound proposition', had made a point of speaking personally to the Prime Minister about what he called 'this regrettable case'.[74]

IV

To those who called for a new and more open diplomacy the doors of Foreign Offices remained closed. There were many historians, however, who *were* prepared to provide the sort of patriotic history that governments preferred, who were prepared to submit to the constraints imposed upon them by the governments which retained the keys to their source material, who were willing to place themselves at the service of the state, and to put the interests of the state, as defined by the state, before the interests of history, to put the present and the future, as defined by the state, before the objective and neutral study of the past. Georges Bonnin believed that Bernhardi's son may have censored his father's manuscript himself before submitting it in 1913 for further censorship.[75] In the course of the setting up of the Royal Institute of International Affairs in 1919 Lionel Curtis, one of the moving spirits, assured the Foreign Office that the new organisation would be developed only on lines helpful to the Foreign Office and that it would have no embarrassing features. He promised that a copy of the history of the Paris Peace Conference would be sent to the Foreign Office before publication so that all material not in the public interest might be removed.[76] It did not disturb Temperley, who was in overall charge of this large project, that in certain instances, as he put it, 'We cannot, of course, tell the whole truth'.[77] Thimme, whilst editing *Die Grosse Politik,* asked in 1922 to see certain files of the period 1862 to 1890 in connection with another publication. He gave his assurance that he would as a matter of course retain for publication only those documents which politically would not be open to objection.[78] Professor John D. Fair, in a masterly biography of Temperley, has demonstrated the 'patriotic' credentials of one of the editors of *British Documents on the Origins of the War*, who deliberately played down, for instance, the extent to which his work on the Peace Conference and Treaty of Versailles was of an official nature.[79] (A question mark hangs even over G.P. Gooch, in the sense that, when mentioning in 1927 Thimme's article in *Archiv für Politik und Geschichte* of June 1924, he forbore to quote the damning sentiments there expressed, and already quoted above: 'The political end ... stands higher [than the study of contemporary history as an end in itself]. And whenever contemporary documents are being published, one does well to suspect political ends.'[80]) In the third section of their report of March 1924 on the secret documents on the Hohenzollern candidature for the Spanish throne, Rheindorff and Platzhoff wrote:

> From the standpoint of historical studies the publication of the secret files would without doubt be in the highest degree desirable. For thereby all guessing about the course taken by the Hohenzollern candidature would be brought to an end once and for all – and investigation at last established on a firm basis of fact. In spite of this the undersigned feel it their duty – however much as historians they deplore the renunciation – strongly to deprecate any such publication on weighty political grounds.[81]

In Germany, the prevalence of such attitudes was epitomised by a remark made several decades later by a leading German historian as regards Fritz Fischer's *Griff nach der Weltmacht*: 'We had really fixed it all so well, and then this stupid ass must come along and spoil it.'[82]

V

The reasons why governments and officials fear historians, and especially those historians whose field is the study of recent or contemporary history, are the same now as they have always been. In 1889 Lord Salisbury remarked: 'We live no longer, alas, in Pitt's time; the aristocracy governed then ... Now democracy is on top, and with it the personal and party system, which reduces every British government to absolute dependence on the aura popularis.'[83] Salisbury renewed this lament at the turn of the century: 'In our time the organised governments are distinctly losing force, and public opinion is distinctly gaining ground in power'; the actions of governments were 'always liable to be superceded by the violent and vehement operations of mere ignorance. We cannot be certain that any government will not yield its powers to the less educated and less enlightened classes'.[84] He once said, 'It is very hard to have to conduct a great public department dealing with a difficult question, with something like a huge lunatic asylum at one's back'.[85]

In the House of Lords in July 1907 it was made clear what the fundamental problem was: Esher spoke of 'the penalty commonly exacted from any Minister who fails to respond to the hot fit of the people of this country when they are in a passion ...', and Loreburn understood him to mean 'that at a time when public feeling is inflamed there may be most disastrous results from the undue or careless publication of some State documents'.[86] Lord Cromer, one of those whom Esher was at pains to protect, wrote that what he most feared, as a proconsul, 'was not deliberate action taken by the diplomacy of any nation, but rather the occurrence of some chance incident which would excite a whirlwind of national passion, and which, being possibly manipulated by some skilful journalist who would focus on one point all the latent hysteria of France or England, would create a situation incapable of being controlled by diplomacy'.[87] Prince von Bülow had the same problem: in his *Memoirs* he recounted an encounter with Professor Ernst Hasse, the president of the Alldeutscher Verband, during the Boer War:

> I had pointed out how difficult he was making it for me to create any real understanding between the German people and the English, by his tactless and ill-regulated press campaign in favour of the Boers. The good Hasse answered that he considered it both his duty and his right to express what the German people were feeling: my business as Minister was to see to it that our diplomatic relations with England were not prejudiced by anything he might say![88]

Crowe had a similar problem twenty years later, when he refused to allow documents to be used to refute certain allegations that had been made: great caution was necessary, he maintained, 'in discussing with these wild (*Daily*) *Herald* people and similar crooked minds what are the internal affairs of this office'.[89] The stakes, in his view as in Lord Salisbury's, could not be higher. When opposing the establishment of the Royal Institute of International Affairs in 1919 he put it as follows:

> The manner in which the foreign policy of the government should be presented to the country, and public opinion educated truly to

appreciate it, is so important a factor in the conduct of foreign affairs, that only the Secretary of State himself – or some one specifically authorised by him to this effect, is really able to discharge this difficult duty without risk of embarrassment to the government. Discussions of foreign affairs require to be approached with every kind of special precaution. It may be desirable in regard to some particular matter, to take the public into the fullest confidence. At other moments such a course might be highly dangerous and even lead to war ...[90]

Because governments and officials fear and distrust the public, and because historians are, or could be, intermediaries between governments and the public, governments and officials fear and distrust historians. A public opinion or a collective memory of the very recent past created by historians whose first and only allegiance was to the truth, rather than by governments and officials, is a public opinion or a collective memory which governments and officials think they can well do without. C.K. Webster gave one example of what, from the point of view of governments and officials, was a worst-case scenario:

> If the British and the German peoples had known of the negotiations for alliance that were proceeding between their governments at various times between 1895 and 1902, or if they had known exactly the obligation which bound Britain to France, might not the final issue have been different?

Another worst-case scenario would have followed from the publication of documents revealing the extent to which King Edward VIII, later Duke of Windsor, tried to betray his country. When in 1957 *Documents on German Foreign Policy 1918–1945* reached mid-1940, the British government, in a damage limitation exercise, accompanied volume X of Series D with the following *démenti* :

> The Duke was subjected to heavy pressure from many quarters to stay in Europe, where the Germans hoped that he would exert his influence against the policy of His Majesty's Government. His Royal Highness never wavered in his loyalty to the British cause or in his determination to take up his official post as Governor of the Bahamas on the date agreed. The German records are necessarily a much tainted source. The only firm evidence which they provide is of what the Germans were trying to do in this matter, and of how completely they failed to do it.

German documents not published in that series demonstrate the disloyalty of the duke. What is left of the relevant *British* documents

will remain closed until 2044, unless the successors of those who
have known these secrets all along have a sea-change of mind and
decide to share them, and the truth, with the country as a whole.[91]

———◦———

It was to the fact that history was a subject with a political nature
that governments and officials objected. The fact that it was also a
popular subject, that there was a 'deep longing of the human soul
to understand its own experiences' and that this 'always led it
back to a study of the past',[92] only made the situation, from the
point of view of governments and officials, worse. What J.A.R.
Marriott said in 1918, about the passing on of knowledge and the
avoidance of pitfalls; what Webster said in 1923 about the learning
of lessons and the elucidation of present-day problems; what G.B.
Henderson said in 1941 about the drawing of balanced conclusions and the making of judgements,[93] is anathema to governments
and officials, and the more recent the subject of the knowledge, the
more repugnant it is. Governments and officials equate 'knowledge' with 'embarrassment', 'pitfalls' with the revelation of their
own mistakes, 'judgements' with a verdict of guilty or incompe-
tent upon their handling of public, and the public's, affairs. Unaccountability, and being 'economical with the truth', are amongst
the aphrodisiacs of power; governments and officials have no
wish to share power, via historians and/or journalists, with the
public they claim to serve.

Being unaccountable is important to the official mind because it
allows the official mind to operate upon a different plane from the
mind of the public. Unaccountability allows the official mind to
indulge a different set of moral standards. Crowe wrote of G.P.
Gooch in 1920: 'when history merges into politics, his judgment
becomes rash and nebulous'. Headlam-Morley was more explicit:
having said in May 1920, 'I entirely distrust his judgment; he has
no real sense of the realities of things', he went on in July to say,
'Mr Gooch ... is primarily a student with no real grasp of the
nature of the responsibilities which fall upon a man of action; he is
therefore constitutionally unable to understand or sympathise
with a statesman who may have deliberately to do a minor injustice or adopt a course of action which obviously has many incon-
veniences attending on it in order not to sacrifice greater and more
important objects ...'.[94] Behind such patronising remarks lay a

recognition that the standards of the few 'public servants' would always be at variance with the standards of the many, that *raison d'état* would never be acceptable to the majority of the population. Gooch himself wrote, in the foreword to the book by Georges Bonnin so frequently cited here:

> 'If we did for ourselves what we do for our country', exclaimed Cavour, 'what rascals we should be.' The Iron Chancellor agreed with the Piedmontese Premier in regard to the difference between public and private morality, for *raison d'état* has always been a religion of the majority of statesmen.[95]

Here Gooch was at one with Lord Acton: 'What people conceal is not their best deeds and motives but their worst. What archives reveal is the wickedness of man. It [*sic*] destroys idols and scatters theories'; 'The one constant result is to show that people are worse than their reputation'.[96] It was the idols' certainty that they would be discovered to have feet of clay that accounts for the premium they put on secrecy, selection, manipulation, and control.

In 1963, in an effort to persuade the British authorities to be more liberal in their attitudes, D.C. Watt published an article in which he claimed that 'The historian is among other things the custodian of the national memory'.[97] The thrust of this introduction, and of much of what it introduces, is that historians are the custodians only of such knowledge as governments allow them to acquire, and that the 'national memory' is primarily the product of governments and officials, even where it seems to be the product of historians.

F.W. Pick, writing in 1946, pointed out the danger that 'the State, holding the key to the evidence, might choose the editors not for their worth as historians but for their usefulness as servants of the State'.[98] A.J.P. Taylor, writing in 1947 that editors 'must regard themselves as watchdogs of the public, not as employees of the Foreign Office', was not at all sure that the editors of *Documents on British Foreign Policy 1919–1939* had not subordinated their independence to a government department.[99] Sir Herbert Butterfield, writing in 1948, said that 'Nothing could be more subtle than the influence upon historians of admission to the charmed circle'.[100] Admission to the charmed circle, whether by the route recommended by Crowe in November 1908 – 'young historical talent vouched for by some recognised authority ... obtaining, as a personal privilege accorded by the Secretary of State ... access to our papers', or by any other route, risks the striking of a faustian bargain. Pick and Butterfield were right, and Conyers Read, like Taylor, did well to suspect E.L. Woodward, in his turn, of a certain degree of patriotic self-censorship.[101]

Pick recommended that writers of contemporary history 'must fortify themselves with an extra dose of anti-governmental or at least supra-governmental conscience; they must make very sure that they will not be influenced in any way by the pleasing fact that they have been chosen editors of official despatches, have become the chosen instrument of a governmental scheme; that they see papers which their colleagues will either not see at all or only by means of the publication eventually selected by them, the favoured ones'.[102] In 'The Dangers of History', Butterfield was more pithy: '... the more the historian seeks to please his generation or serve his government or support any cause save that of truth, the more he tends to confirm his contemporaries in whatever they happen to want to believe, the more he hardens the age in its favourite and fashionable errors.'[103]

My own view is that the true role of the historian, and the true internationalism of the international historian, is to be found in being objective enough not to write 'national' history. This is a challenge which has not diminished. I end with a quotation from Butterfield's 'Reconstruction of an Historical Episode – The History of the Enquiry into the Origins of the Seven Years' War':

> The publication of diplomatic documents fails to bring historians to the heart of the problem, and even may carry the student further away from the truth, if the secret and central documents, particularly the policy-making ones – the ones which really reveal a government's purposes, are not open to the free play of scholarship.[104]

Notes

1. D. McElrath, ed., *Lord Acton: The Decisive Decade, 1864–74* (Louvain, 1970), p. 131; H. Butterfield, 'Official History: Its Pitfalls and Criteria', in *Studies* vol. 38 (1948–9), pp. 132–3; O. Chadwick, *Catholicism and History: The Opening of the Vatican Archives* (Cambridge, 1978), p. 1.
2. Fritz T. Epstein, 'The Accessibility of Source Materials Illuminating the History of German Foreign Policy. The Publication of Documents of the German Foreign Ministry After Both World Wars', in Robert F. Byrnes, ed., *Germany and the East* (Bloomington, 1973), pp. 174, 177; J.D. Fair, *Harold Temperley: A Scholar and Romantic in the Public Realm* (Toronto, 1992), p. 199.
3. A.J.P. Taylor, 'The Rise and Fall of Diplomatic History', in *Englishmen and Others* (London, 1956), pp. 81–87.
4. E.L. Woodward, 'The Study of International Relations at a University', inaugural lecture at the University of Oxford, 17 February 1945, (Oxford, 1945), p. 14.
5. The phrase is Noam Chomsky's: see *World Orders, Old and New* (London, 1994), p. 270, and *Necessary Illusions* (London, 1989), p. 197.
6. G. Bonnin, *Bismarck and the Hohenzollern Candidature for the Spanish Throne: The Documents in the German Diplomatic Archives* (London, 1957), pp. 13–16.
7. Ibid., p. 16.
8. Ibid., pp. 16–17.
9. Ibid., p. 18.
10. Ibid., p. 19.
11. Ibid.
12. Ibid., p. 20.
13. Ibid., pp. 21–22.
14. Ibid., p. 25.
15. Ibid., pp. 25–6.
16. Ibid., p. 26.
17. Chadwick, pp. 133, 139.
18. F.W. Pick, 'Contemporary History: Methods and Men', *History* 31, (1946), p. 36.
19. N. Rich and M.F. Fisher, *The Holstein Papers* vol. 3 (Cambridge, 1961), p. xiii.
20. D. Mack Smith, *Victor Emmanuel, Cavour, and the Risorgimento* (London, 1971), pp. ix-x.
21. Chadwick, pp. 126, 101.
22. Bonnin, p. 5.
23. Memorandum by Crowe, 17 November 1908, F.O. 370/16, para. 5.
24. Ibid., para. 3.
25. Ibid., paras. 7, 14, 19, 21, 22.
26. Ibid., para. 23.
27. Ibid.
28. Curtis to Temperley, 12 April 1920, Royal Institute of International Affairs mss., PPC 16/2a.
29. M.L. Dockrill, 'The Foreign Office and the "Proposed Institute of International Affairs 1919"', *International Affairs* 56 (1980), pp. 667, 669–70.
30. Note by Headlam-Morley, May 1920, F.O. 370/116/L5.
31. Montgomery to Woodward, 16 December 1924, F.O. 370/203/4731.

32. Memorandum by R.C. Dickie, 'F.O. Confidential Papers and Information: Control over Unauthorised Publication', 2 March 1923, F.O. 370/203/L2308, para. 44, my italics.
33. Minute by Crowe, 5 June 1923, F.O. 370/190/L2350.
34. Minute by Gaselee, 26 September 1924, F.O. 370/203/L3837.
35. *Foreign Relations of the United States, 1917* (Supplement 2) iv (Washington, 1932); F.W. Pick, 'The European Settlement of 1919', *Journal of Central European Affairs* vol. 4, no. 4 (1945), also in Pick, *Contemporary History* (Oxford, 1949), p. 60.
36. Preface to *FRUS, 1914 Supplement* (Washington, 1928), pp. iii-iv.
37. C.K. Webster, 'The Study of British Foreign Policy (Nineteenth Century)', *American Historical Review* vol. 30 (1925), p. 729.
38. Memorandum by Headlam-Morley, 28 October 1919, F.O. 371/4382.
39. *Hansard*, 5th series, xxxii, cols. 2610–2613; see also H.W.V. Temperley and L.M. Penson, *A Century of Diplomatic Blue Books 1814–1914* (London, 1938); and K.M. Wilson, '"Refuse in the Usual Terms": The Old Foreign Office, the Press, and the Distribution of Blue Books 1887–1905' in *Empire and Continent* (London, 1987) ch. 2.
40. C.K. Webster, 'The Study of International Politics', inaugural lecture at the University College of Wales, Aberystwyth, 23 February 1923 (Cardiff, 1923), p. 10; R. Humphrey, 'The "Official" Scholar: A Survey of Certain Research in American Foreign Policy' in Norton Downs, ed., *Essays in Honour of Conyers Read* (Chicago, 1953), p. 36; Conyers Read, 'Recent U.S. and British Government Publications on the London Naval Conference of 1930' *American Historical Review* vol. 54 (1948–9), p. 308. For an example of how material was kept out of *FRUS* at the turn of the century, see Marilyn B. Young, *The Rhetoric of Empire: American China Policy 1895–1901* (Cambridge, Mass., 1968), p. 259, note 1 to ch. 5.
41. *FRUS, The Paris Peace Conference, 1919* vol. 2 (Washington, 1942), p. 71.
42. Epstein, p. 174.
43. E.R. May, ed., *American Cold War Strategy: Interpreting NSC 68* (New York, 1993), pp. 16, 19 (note 31).
44. Politisches Archiv des Auswärtigen Amtes, Akten betr. Herausgabe der amtlichen Dokumente zur Vorgeschichte des Krieges I: vom Januar 1921 bis 30 Juni 1922.
45. Marx to MacDonald, 16 August 1924, ibid. Büro Staatssekretär, Akten betr. Kriegsschuldfrage I: Aug. 1924 bis Oktober 1926, 4519 H/E 134072–4; Marx 'The Responsibility for the War', *Foreign Affairs* 4 (1926), pp. 177–94.
46. Avertissement by A. Aulard to vol. 1 of French translation of *Die Grosse Politik* (Paris, 1927). In their translation, the French reorganised the German documents and placed them in a strictly chronological sequence. Of the original German arrangement of the documents selected into chapters, devised by the editors, as Thimme put it, so that the documents 'should be quickly understood and have their effect', A.J.P. Taylor was later to write: '... the *Grosse Politik*, by its selection of documents and still more by the arrangement of them, gave a false impression of the harmlessness of German policy and of the malignancy of Germany's opponents. For instance, the documents relating to the Morocco crisis of 1905 are in one volume; the documents concerning the abortive Russo-German alliance of 1905 (the Treaty of Björko) are in another. Thus it remains obscure that the object of Germany's Moroccan policy was to force France into a continental bloc under German leadership. Or again, the

German attempt to extract from Great Britain during the negotiations over naval limitation some promise of neutrality appears relatively harmless until the reader discovers, at some volumes' distance, that this promise was being sought in order to discredit the British in Russian eyes and that a similar promise was being sought from the Russians for a similar purpose.' See 'The Secrets of Diplomacy' in *The Times Literary Supplement*, 12 April 1947.

47. Epstein, pp. 177–8.
48. Ibid., pp. 172–3.
49. Bartholdy, 'Kleine Missverständnisse über eine grosse Publikation', *Europäische Gespräche* iv no. 7 (July 1926), p. 387.
50. MacDonald to Marx, 22 August 1924, as for note 45, H/E 134077–9.
51. 'Historical Introduction', by Headlam-Morley, to vol. 1 of E.T.S. Dugdale, ed., *German Diplomatic Documents* (London, 1928), p. xii.
52. Epstein, p. 175.
53. See ch. 1, note 76.
54. Poincaré to Paléologue, 27 December 1929, part of an exchange printed as an Annexe to P. Renouvin, 'Les documents diplomatiques francais 1871–1914', *Revue Historique* 226 (1961), p. 149.
55. See ch. 1, note 81.
56. For this and further quotations from Pokrovsky see B.E. Schmitt, 'Russia and the War', *Foreign Affairs* 13 (1934–5), pp. 133–153.
57. Bonnin, p. 22.
58. Ibid., p. 14.
59. See ch. 1, note 107.
60. See ch. 1, note 105.
61. See ch. 1, note 41.
62. Bonnin, pp. 24–25, note 5.
63. See ch. 3, note 8.
64. Pick, 'Contemporary History', p. 36–7.
65. *Hansard*, 4th series, clxxix, House of Lords, 30 July 1907, cols. 716–721.
66. F.O. 370/73/L38322.
67. F.O. 370/116/L758.
68. Minute by Headlam-Morley, 21 July 1920, F.O. 370/116 f.27.
69. Fair, p. 192.
70. Ibid.
71. Ibid., p. 196.
72. Ibid., p. 192.
73. F.O. 370/202/L3140.
74. Webster, 'The Study of International Politics', pp. 21, 24; Webster, 'Notes on Public Access to the Foreign Office Records' April 1924, F.O. 370/203/L1484; *The Nation and the Athenaeum*, 21 June 1924, pp. 371–2; minutes by Gaselee, Bland, and Crowe, 25, 27 June, 4 July 1924 F.O. 370/203/L2571. The patriotic motive behind MacDonald's decision is implicit in his initial wish, which was to have published 'some *histories* about the events leading up to the war, and so displace the pamphleteering rubbish that some so-called historians palmed off upon us': F.O. 370/202. In 'FCO Records, Policy, Practice and Posterity 1782–1992' (Historical Branch no.4, August 1992), p. 12, only the first sentence of Webster's 'Notes' is quoted. As a result the arguments and attitudes of the Foreign Office are disguised just as those of Webster are distorted.
75. Bonnin, pp. 19–20.

76. Dockrill, pp. 671–2.
77. Temperley to Shotwell, 26 February 1920, PPC 16/2a.
78. Bonnin, p. 35.
79. Fair, p. 193; see also pp. 192, 298.
80. G.P. Gooch, *Recent Revelations of European Diplomacy* (London, 1927), p. 4.
81. Bonnin, p. 33.
82. F.L. Carsten, 'Living with the Past: What German Historians Are Saying', *Encounter* xxii no. 4, (April 1964), p. 110.
83. Herbert Bismarck to Bismarck, 22 March 1889, printed in C.J. Lowe, *The Reluctant Imperialists* (London, 1967), pp. ii, 65.
84. *Quarterly Review* vol. 196 (October 1902), p. 666.
85. Sanderson to Grey, 9 September 1908, Grey MSS F.O. 800/111.
86. As note 65 above.
87. Lord Cromer, *Political and Literary Essays*, second series (London, 1914), p. 290.
88. B. von Bülow, *Memoirs* (London, 1932), pp. iii, 308.
89. F.O. 370/171/L3627.
90. Minute by Crowe, 26 June 1919, F.O. 608/152.
91. Webster, 'The Study of International Politics', p. 25; see review in *The Times*, 1 August 1957, p. 9 (by Iverach McDonald; and the articles by Richard Norton-Taylor, Jill Jolliffe, Richard Brooks in *The Observer*, 12 November 1995 ('House of Windsor's Nazi Shame') and *The Guardian*, 13 November 1995 ('Kaiser Edward'); more light will be shed on this matter by my colleague G.T. Waddington's forthcoming study of Ribbentrop, to be published by Cambridge University Press in 1997.
92. Ibid., pp. 8, 9.
93. J.A.R. Marriott, 'Modern Diplomacy', in *Quarterly Review* vol. 229 (1918), pp. 222–5; Webster, pp. 17, 19; Henderson, 'A Plea for the Study of Contemporary History', *History* 26 (1941), p. 53. See M. Beloff's reply to Henderson, 'The Study of Contemporary History: Some Further Reflections', *History* 30 (1945), pp. 75–84.
94. Minutes by Crowe and Headlam-Morley, F.O. 370/116/L5, L678.
95. Bonnin, p. 11.
96. Chadwick, p. 141; H. Butterfield, *Man on His Past* (Cambridge, 1955), p. 84, note 2.
97. D.C. Watt, 'Foreign Affairs, the Public Interest and the Right to Know', *Political Quarterly* 34 (1963), p. 123.
98. Pick, 'Contemporary History', p. 36.
99. See note 46 above.
100. Butterfield, 'Official History', p. 136.
101. Read, p. 309.
102. Pick, p. 45.
103. Butterfield, 'The Dangers of History' in *History and Human Relations* (London, 1951), p. 163.
104. Butterfield, *Man on His Past*, p. 169.

 Chapter 1

THE HISTORICAL DIPLOMACY OF THE THIRD REPUBLIC

Keith Hamilton

> Our Archives – it cannot be repeated too often – are a sort
> of gun powder which can, in certain cases, explode and
> cause damage, when it ought to be used only to defend
> ourselves against our enemies.
>
> *Baron de Courcel, 8 May 1907*[1]

Diplomatic archives are the raw material of international history.
They are also an invaluable asset for those charged with the
administration and conduct of foreign policy. Besides providing
enlightenment on past developments and precedents for current
and future negotiations, they usually contain material for education and propaganda.[2] During the Weimar era the officials of the
Wilhelmstrasse in Berlin sought through the publication of their
prewar records to exculpate Germany from the 'war guilt' attributed to her by the victorious Allies.[3] Other governments responded
by sanctioning and sponsoring similar documentary publications,
and in the 1920s archivists, historians and librarians were har-
nessed to a diplomacy which was both open and retrospective.[4]
However, long before the First World War history had been utilised for diplomatic ends. After Napoleon's return from Elba the
French Foreign Ministry had, for example, begun work on a study
which was intended to demonstrate the essentially defensive origins of the emperor's previous conquests.[5] And following France's

defeat in the Franco-Prussian War a sustained effort was mounted in Paris to make the Quai d'Orsay's archives serve the foreign policy needs of the nascent and isolated Third Republic. A Commission des Archives Diplomatiques was established in 1874, and during the next forty years it became an effective, if not always very efficient, instrument for the pursuit of what might best be called historical diplomacy.

Neither under the restored Bourbon monarchy of 1814–30, nor for long periods during the First and Second Empires, had historians enjoyed ready access to France's diplomatic records. Unlike those of the Foreign Office in London and the Auswärtiges Amt in Berlin, they were at no stage transferred to national or state archives. The officials of the Foreign Ministry regarded their records as departmental property which a few privileged and carefully supervised researchers were occasionally permitted to peruse. As *directeur* responsible for the archives Pierre Faugère was simply reiterating a well-established principle when in 1874 he observed in a letter to *l'Univers:* 'The archives are not for public use; they are intended only for the internal use of the ministry.'[6] The Ministry's archives were indeed regarded by some historians as a veritable Bastille. Even a recommendation from Fouché, Napoleon I's notorious minister of police, had not sufficed in 1808 to secure access for one would-be researcher. He was informed that he must first obtain the authority of the emperor.[7] There were of course occasions when eminent scholars did succeed in penetrating the darker recesses of the archives. One obvious example is that of Leopold von Ranke, who took advantage of the less restrictive conditions that prevailed during the reign of Louis-Philippe in order to consult French diplomatic correspondence of the sixteenth and seventeenth centuries.[8] Access to the archives nevertheless seemed often to depend upon the arbitrary whim of the *directeur des archives.* And although the appointment of Faugère as *directeur* in 1866 was seen as heralding a more liberal régime, there were still no fixed rules to which researchers could appeal. It was thus only after having gained the support of Bismarck and Napoleon III that Heinrich von Sybel, the founder of the *Historische Zeitschrift* and future director of the Prussian state archives, was able to make use of the Foreign Ministry records for his seminal study of the French Revolutionary era.[9]

Ironically, the results of Sybel's researches were much resented in France. A patriotic historian, Sybel placed his literary talents at the service of the Prussian state, and after the Treaty of Frankfurt he lost no time in defending the restoration of Alsace-Lorraine to German rule. But what also offended the susceptibilities of French academics was the way in which he had deliberately set out in his five-volume *Geschichte der Revolutionenzeit* to dissipate the halo of heroism which European liberals had previously attached to the French Revolution.[10] To French historians 'this enormous war machine in five compact volumes' was evidence of Sybel's hostility towards France,[11] and at a later date criticisms made of Sybel during a session of the Commission des Archives were judged so strong that they were cut from the Commission's minutes.[12] Moreover, Faugère never seems to have tired of retelling how he had uncovered an attempt by Sybel to falsify history. Apparently Sybel, who like other researchers was required to submit his notes to the scrutiny of the *directeur*, had taken notes only on such extracts of a particular document as revealed France in a poor light. Faugère had therefore substituted for Sybel's notes a full copy of the document. He had subsequently received Sybel's thanks and the explanation that his French had not been good enough to appreciate the significance of the omitted passages. This in Faugère's estimate was a lame excuse.[13] It is, however, probable that Faugère told the story in his own defence, for at a time when access to the Quai d'Orsay's archives was still very restricted, Sybel used the preface of his *Geschichte* to praise the *directeurs* of the various French archives to which he had been admitted. Faugère thereby found himself open to the accusation of having collaborated with the enemy *outre-Vosges*.[14]

Much more was involved in this matter than the national animosities bred by the recent war. Sybel's achievement in writing one of the first accounts of the Revolutionary period on the basis of archival sources and the French reaction to it were both symptomatic of the malaise then afflicting the historical fraternity in France. Overshadowed and very often outclassed by German scholarship, French historians shared with many of their fellow-countrymen a sense of national inferiority.[15] In the words of Gabriel Monod, an admirer of the discipline, industry and scientific methodology of German scholars, Germany could be compared to 'a vast laboratory of history where all efforts are concentrated and coordinated and no effort is wasted'.[16] By contrast, some of the most noteworthy of France's historians of the previous half-century had seemed to attach relatively little importance to archival research. Gabriel Hanotaux, who in 1878 was admitted to the Foreign Ministry archives to begin his work on Richelieu, included amongst these Chateaubriand, Augustin Thierry and, somewhat surprisingly, Jules Michelet, who in 1831 had been appointed chief of the historical section of the Archives Nationales. 'A powerful imagination, a superior ability to synthesise, and exceptional stylistic gifts had', Hanotaux recalled, 'been the means by which their great works had been achieved.'[17] There had certainly been a neglect of diplomatic history in France. When the École Libre des Sciences Politiques opened in January 1872 the subject was not taught in any French university, and Albert Sorel, who took leave from his post at the Quai d'Orsay to lecture at the school on the diplomacy of the French Revolution, found that he had to 'crosscheck the numerous texts which had been published on the same subject in Germany, based on documents in the archives of Vienna and Berlin'.[18]

A growing number of intellectuals and publicists found in this failure to pay more attention to the systematic study of modern history a reason for the disasters that had befallen France in 1870–71. If Germany's victory could be attributed to the virtues of the Prussian schoolmaster, then France's defeat could equally well be blamed on the shortcomings of French universities. The École Libre was indeed founded to remedy this deficiency by educating an élite and through it encouraging a more thorough and mature understanding of domestic and international politics. Émile Boutmy, the school's first director, told an audience of subscribers in July 1872 that he and his colleagues had been struck by the ignorance and recklessness with which opinion in France had pronounced itself in favour of the adventurism of Napoleon III. He added:

> We wondered if it might not be possible to make the next generation understand the complexity of, and difficulty with, political questions, to put it on its guard against the conclusions of a frivolous journalism, to furnish it with a number of exact concepts, which its parents lacked, and to add some ballast to that flag-bedizened cockleshell of brilliant generalisations which men call the French intellect.[19]

It was in similar vein that in 1876 Monod introduced the first volume of the *Revue Historique* with the warning that it was necessary for historians to reawaken in the soul of the nation 'an awareness of itself through the better knowledge of its history'.[20] Historians thus accredited to themselves a vital role in the process of *recueillement* (contemplation) and in the rebuilding and strengthening of

France. 'The whole period weighed upon us, inspired us, exalted us', Hanotaux observed, 'new politics demanded new history.'[21]

A new history also required new documents or, to be more precise, freer access to old ones. Armand Baschet, the author of a history of France's diplomatic archives which appeared in 1875, was at one with a younger generation of French historians when he complained in his preface that while of late researchers had received 'a welcome which was certainly less reserved' at the Foreign Ministry, this was still 'inadequate'.[22] But few historians were better placed to influence government policy towards the archives than Sorel who, in 1873, returned to the Quai d'Orsay to become private secretary to Élie, Duc Decazes, the Orléanist foreign minister in President MacMahon's *cabinet des ducs*. Given Sorel's recent experience at the École Libre, his commitment to archival research, and his belief in history as a means of rejuvenating and revitalising France, it is more than likely that he played at least some part in persuading Decazes to refer the administration and regulation of his ministerial archives to a special commission. The ministerial decree of 21 February 1874 which constituted the first Commission des Archives Diplomatiques seems in any event to have been in accord with Sorel's thinking on this matter. Composed of eleven members, including archivists, diplomats, historians and librarians, the Commission was charged with three tasks: the determination of the conditions under which researchers might have access to the archives; the recommendation of the mode of publishing such correspondence and other documents 'whose bringing to light would truly be of interest from the point of view of our national history and diplomatic traditions'; and the examination of what could be done to ensure the conservation of records in France's missions overseas and the recovery of papers retained by former agents and their heirs.[23]

By 9 May the Commission, which met under the presidency of a former diplomat, the Baron de Viel-Castel, had completed its proposals. These, which were accepted by Decazes, were hardly generous when it came to offering access to the archives. Two open periods were established: the first up until the Treaty of Utrecht (1713), and the second extending to the death of Louis XV (1774). The distinction between the two was that scholars admitted to the latter period still had to submit any notes they might take to the *Direction des Archives*. Post-1774 papers could be communicated to researchers 'à titre exceptionnel' and with special conditions attached, but at the same time the Ministry reserved to itself the right to withhold any material from the open periods whose revelation might cause serious inconvenience. On these matters and the rules governing the retention and return of departmental papers by diplomats, the Commission seems to have found it relatively easy to reach a decision. Where, however, the question of advising on the publication of records was concerned, the commissioners were less sure of their mandate.[24] The department had in the past contributed to the Ministry of Public Instruction's series, Les Documents inédits sur l'Histoire de France,[25] and papers relating to current issues had been released for parliamentary and propagandistic purposes. The commissioners were therefore formalising rather than extending existing practises when they stipulated in their draft règlement for continued collaboration with the Ministry of Public Instruction, and for the publication of historical documents, either directly by the Quai d'Orsay itself, or by independent editors acting under its auspices.[26] There was, nevertheless, a good deal of uncertainty over whether it was up to the Commission to suggest what might be published.[27]

Faugère, who as directeur des archives was one of the most active and influential members of the Commission, felt that this matter had best be left to a permanent committee. He had initially assumed that the sole function of the Commission was to draw up a set of regulations for the archives and that once this was done it would be dissolved. There were in any case obvious difficulties in the way of its attempting to decide on the substance of publications. As Faugère indicated to his fellow-commissioners on 22 March, while the department possessed analytical tables of its diplomatic correspondence, it had no proper catalogues, and a search for suitable manuscripts seemed therefore bound to be a wearisome and time-consuming business.[28] This, however, did not satisfy Decazes. He wrote to Viel-Castel on 3 April that he had counted on the Commission enlightening him on the nature and importance of the documents in the archives, and on which of these would be of most historical interest and of most advantage to the study of diplomatic questions. His concern, he stressed, was not simply with satisfying historians and politicians, but with publications which would encompass a 'real diplomatic education'. He concluded:

> In thus furnishing the servants of France with the means to fathom the details and processes of that policy which has created and consolidated our greatness, we shall give them, not only models to follow, but also the possibility of taking up again a task

which has for too long been abandoned, or, at least, a tradition for too long interrupted.[29]

This was as clear a definition as any French statesman was to give of the primary purpose of the Third Republic's historical diplomacy. Published documents were in this instance required not for propaganda, but for education. The leaders of the France that emerged from what Hanotaux described as 'the great and double Napoleonic disillusion' hoped that the study of the experiences, methods and manners of the master diplomats of the past would assist them in regaining for France her former stature in Europe.[30]

To this end Decazes asked the Commission des Archives to remain in existence in order to fulfil the functions that Faugère had wanted to attribute to a permanent committee.[31] Yet during the next six years the commissioners made little if any progress towards the sponsoring of documentary publications. A preliminary search of the archives by Faugère and his *sous-directeur,* and a subsequent investigation by a *sous-commission* made up of three historians, Matthieu Geffroy, Camille Rousset, and Jules Valfrey, revealed a number of texts that might be worth publishing.[32] And Sorel, who in May 1874 became assistant secretary to the Commission, offered to prepare a work on the seventeenth-century diplomat, Hugues de Lionne.[33] Doubts were, however, soon being expressed about how the projected publications were to be funded.[34] The commissioners were uncertain about cooperating with the Ministry of Public Instruction, and Faugère thought it unlikely that parliament would provide money for what might be called the *Documents inédits du Ministère des Affaires Étrangères.*[35] Moreover, hardly had Valfrey begun work on editing the memoirs of Nicholas de la Motte Goulas, than he discovered that Charles Constant was already preparing a similar volume for the Société de l'Histoire de France.[36] Sorel had in the meanwhile become absorbed in researching his history of Europe and the French Revolution, and it was Valfrey who, with the encouragement, but not the assistance, of the Commission, completed in 1877 a study of Lionne's embassies in Italy.[37]

A more constructive and urgent approach towards the pursuit of historical diplomacy had to await the electoral triumphs of the opportunist republicans. Thus the appointment in December 1879 of Charles de Freycinet both as president of the Council of Ministers and as foreign minister was followed in February 1880 by a

general administrative reform which resulted in the reconstitution of the Commission des Archives. The new Commission, which
met under the presidency of the republican senator and historian,
Henri Martin, was almost twice the size of its predecessor. Geffroy
and Rousset were once more members, as also was Alfred Maury,
the *directeur-général* of the Archives Nationales. But amongst the
newcomers were Boutmy, Monod, Sorel, and Alphonse, Baron de
Courcel, a career diplomat whom Freycinet made his *directeur des
affaires politiques*. Courcel was especially eager that the Quai
d'Orsay's archives should be fully exploited for diplomatic ends.
'I would like to see regular use made of the precious resources of
our archives in works which', he explained to Freycinet, 'regularly produced in the manner followed by specialists, would
provide most useful assistance to the study and discussion of
questions of contemporary policy'.[38] Moreover, Courcel was to
help foster the career of Hanotaux who, after having been invited
by Faugère to join his staff, became a paid attaché in the Direction
des Archives in 1880, and served subsequently as assistant, and
then principal, secretary to the Commission. Always more richly
endowed with historical enthusiasm than political common
sense, Hanotaux was after becoming foreign minister in 1894 to
display an almost platonic reverence for the philosopher kings of
the Commission.

Before any recommendation could be made on how best to
make use of the extensive records of the Ministry, Freycinet's
reconstructed Commission had, like its predecessor, to determine
the exact contents of the archives. Particular concern was shown
over the series usually referred to as *Mémoires et Documents*, which
included a massive collection of personal and state papers, some
of which were of little or no relevance to France's foreign relations. A *sous-commission* was therefore established to supervise the
preparation of a catalogue, and to consider the form and subject
matter of possible publications.[39] And on 6 April 1880 three of its
members, the historians, Georges Picot, Monod, and Sorel, reported
respectively on the inventory of the *Mémoires et Documents*, foreign
archival publications and what might be published from the Foreign Ministry's records.[40]

Monod once more found inspiration in Germany, and in particular in the *Publicationen aus den königlichen Preussischen Staatsarchiven*, a monumental series which the Prussian Landtag had
agreed to fund in 1873. He thus wholeheartedly endorsed Sybel's
claim in his preface to the collection:

A people which knows not from whence it comes, also knows not whither it goes. Its political education will only be effected in a sound manner if it is tied to a living consciousness of its historical development, and this is not imaginable so long as original documents remain inaccessible.

But Monod significantly omitted any reference to Sybel's equally confident assertions that the interests of the state and scholarship were one and the same, and that there was 'no better propaganda for the reputation of Prussia in the world than the authentic knowledge of Prussian history'.[41] Moreover, whilst he sympathised with the educational objectives of Sybel's work, Monod recommended that in the long run the Quai d'Orsay should follow the British example and set about publishing material in a form similar to the *Calendars of State Papers:* the catalogues of documents with introductions and historical notes, which, with the assistance of subventions voted annually by parliament, were prepared under the auspices of the deputy keeper of the public records and the master of the rolls. On a similar basis and with the assistance of a publishing house and the *Imprimerie Nationale*, Monod reckoned that a catalogue and three volumes of documents might be produced each year.[42]

It was partly with a view to securing parliamentary backing for such a work that Sorel proposed the publication in a series of volumes of the instructions given to France's resident envoys at the outset of their missions during the period between the Peace of Westphalia (1648) and the Revolution of 1789. He anticipated that the first volumes of this *Recueil des Instructions* – those issued to France's ambassadors and ministers in Austria, England, and the Netherlands – could be ready within a year, that their value would be quickly recognised, and that the scheme would then attract further funding from the chambers. Since the *Instructions* were in themselves 'veritable introductions to the history of the political relations between France and the state to which the envoy is accredited', Sorel presumed that there would be no need for extensive prefaces, and that the editing might be limited to introductions giving a précis of the previous state of relations between France and the host country, and explanatory notes and appendices based upon diplomatic correspondence.[43] His colleagues accepted this format and recommended the eventual publication of some twelve to fifteen volumes.[44] Freycinet also concurred and on 5 July 1880 he invited Armand Baschet to edit the volume relating to England. Meanwhile, work began on preparing for publication a catalogue

of the *Mémoires et Documents*, and exploratory talks were entered
into with publishers as to the terms of possible contracts.[45]

The commissioners had not, however, reckoned with either the
ministerial instability or the interdepartmental rivalries of the
republic. In September a new government was formed under Jules
Ferry, and Freycinet was replaced at the Quai d'Orsay by Barthél-
emy-Saint-Hilaire. The latter was altogether more cautious than
his predecessor about the prospects of parliament making provision in the Foreign Ministry's budget for the proposed publications, and was insistent that he should have time to reconsider the
matter.[46] Moreover, Ferry, who as minister of public instruction
had already identified educational reform with the promotion of
republican virtues, seems to have been determined that his department should supervise all publications from administrative
archives. As a result, meetings of the Commission des Archives
were suspended in January 1881, and two of its members, Sorel
and Girard de Rialle, were appointed to a commission which was
instituted to mediate between the Education Ministry's Comité
des travaux historiques and other ministries on the publication of
historical records.[47] This body seems to have made little progress.
Nevertheless, it was only after the return of Freycinet to the Quai
d'Orsay on 30 January 1882 that the Commission des Archives
resumed its work. Its members lost no time in making clear their
unanimous opposition to what they saw as an attempt to deprive
them of their primary functions. They were also determined that
in future they should meet at fixed regular intervals.[48]

What was particularly galling for Sorel was that whilst the
preparation of the proposed *Recueils* had been delayed by an
administrative wrangle, Paul Bailleu, a German historian, had
under Sybel's direction published a new volume of diplomatic
correspondence, *Preussen und Frankreich von 1795 bis 1807*, which
drew upon French as well as Prussian sources.[49] At a meeting of
the Commission des Archives on 10 February 1882 Sorel complained that while Frenchmen had been deliberating over what to
publish Bailleu had made use of the Quai d'Orsay's archives and
had included in his work 'the pick of our documents'. Sorel also
insisted that a distinction be made between the works published
by the Ministry of Public Instruction and the 'compact practical
works, in a handy format and suitable for the use of diplomats'.[50]
As Hanotaux later recalled, the projected *Instructions* were
intended to serve 'the practical education of our young diplomats
and to acquaint them with the traditional policy of France'.[51]

Other members of the Commission were of the same opinion and were unanimous in rejecting any notion of the Comité des travaux historiques having any say in what were understood to be professional publications.[52]

The Ministry of Public Instruction finally conceded that the Commission des Archives could publish 'documents techniques' without trespassing on the prerogatives of the Comité des travaux historiques.[53] And in his annual report for 1882 Henri Martin reaffirmed the educative function of the intended publications. An ardent nationalist who believed that France could never renounce 'what it could not recover peacefully', he emphasised the patriotic objectives of the collection and in particular the value of producing for French diplomats and historians 'a sort of manual of the political traditions of France'.[54] Progress with the work was, however, also dependent upon the efficiency, energy and enthusiasm of individual editors. Thus Baschet, who had been expected to initiate the series, seems to have been impeded by old age and failing health, and despite repeated assurances that his manuscript was nearly complete, he failed to submit anything to the Commission before his death in 1886.[55] As a result, the first volume to appear was that assembled by Sorel on the instructions to France's envoys in Austria – a tome which was published in 1884. Ferry had by then exchanged his education portfolio for that of foreign affairs, and he was well pleased with a project which had for its object 'to make our democratic society aware of the true French tradition'.[56] As one of those responsible for what Eugen Weber has characterised as the transformation of peasants into Frenchmen,[57] he was evidently pleased with the prospect of moulding democrats into diplomats.

Sorel's volume was soon followed by others. But the notion of limiting the collection to twelve or fifteen volumes proved quite unrealistic. Indeed, the work was still incomplete in 1939, and has continued since the Second World War under the auspices of the Centre national de la recherche scientifique. Some of the volumes also raised problems with regard to editorial freedom. The trouble was that published documents, even when they were intended to demonstrate the skills of France's former diplomats, could reveal truths embarrassing for current French diplomacy. One such instance was the volume of instructions to France's ministers in Tuscany, Modena, and Genoa, which was prepared by Edouard Driault and presented in draft to the Commission in April 1911. Such a *Recueil* hardly seemed likely to contain anything that might

injure the international standing of the Third Republic. Nevertheless, Monod, who acted as *rapporteur* for the manuscript, drew
his colleagues' attention to the fact that it contained a proposal,
made in September 1762 by the French agent at Genoa, to the
effect that France should encourage the Genoese to cede Corsica
to the Savoyard rulers of Sardinia in return for frontier rectifica-
tions favourable to France and Genoa. Might it not be inconvenient, Monod speculated, to reveal that a French diplomat had
considered abandoning Corsica to the power that had since become
the kernel of a united Italy?[58]

Despite the doubts expressed by Monod, Driault's volume was
sanctioned by the Commission. There was, after all, as Monod
himself explained, a real interest in showing how in 1762 a French
diplomat viewed the situation in northern Italy, 'very differently
from what it would appear today to have really been'.[59] But it was
the editorial rather than the documentary contents of volumes
which tended to give the commissioners most cause for concern.
This was particularly true of the introductions which sometimes
went far beyond the brief prefaces originally envisaged by Sorel.
Thus the eminent publicist, Joseph Reinach, who was charged
with editing the volume relating to Naples and Parma, took the
opportunity to introduce the documents with an account of his
personal interpretation of Franco-Italian relations during the previous three hundred years. In consequence, his manuscript, which
was presented in proof to the Commission in January 1893, contained an introduction which, though it barely mentioned Parma,
sought to demonstrate how France's transalpine ventures had
awoken, stimulated and eventually frustrated Italian national sentiment.[60] Even after protests from commissioners, who insisted on
its amendment, the volume was published with an 181-page introduction.[61] Complaints over Reinach's extensive theorising, however, hardly bore comparison with the heated discussions that
arose in the autumn of 1910 over the instructions to France's
envoys to the imperial German diet at Ratisbon: a volume which
was diligently prepared by Bertrand Auerbach, the dean of the
arts faculty at Nancy.

Almost any collection of diplomatic documents dealing with
France's relations with the German-speaking world seemed bound
to touch upon sensitive issues. This was made plain when in June
1909 the Commission considered the production of a volume of
instructions to France's representatives at the lesser German
courts. As one commissioner, Boulay de la Meurthe, explained,

such a work could not fail to 'revive in Germany certain feelings towards us'. Courcel, who had served as French ambassador at Berlin from 1881 to 1886, likewise warned his colleagues that any treatment of France's age-old activities in Germany, and particularly in the Rhineland, demanded 'great prudence, and this prudence is all the more necessary as it is a question of an official publication'.[62] And it was evidently in this sense that Courcel, as commissioner responsible for overseeing Auerbach's volume, advised the historian of the delicate nature of his task and of the propriety 'of looking only at certain questions which remain in the tradition of French policy'. The trouble was that Auerbach not only lacked the necessary 'grande prudence', but also had a very different conception of what constituted France's political tradition. In any event, his manuscript did not conform to his limited editorial remit, and he chose to supplement the documents with chapters in which he endeavoured to trace the evolution of a German national spirit within the diet and in reaction to French meddling in German affairs. Germany was thereby made to appear the victim of the ambitious intrigue, violent usurpations, insolence and corruption of the French, and the Westphalian treaty which ceded Alsace to France was, in Courcel's words, portrayed as 'a dubious transaction conducted in bad faith, temporarily torn from the German consciousness'. It was not an interpretation which was calculated to appeal to French patriots who were accustomed to regard their nation as the injured party of 1871. Nor in Courcel's estimate could its appearance in an official publication serve France's diplomatic ends. It would, he argued, give rise to further polemics against France in Germany.[63]

Courcel's objections were supported by his fellow commissioners, and on 9 November 1910 they decided to suspend work on Auerbach's manuscript.[64] But there were complications. Courcel had not been able to decipher Auerbach's handwriting, and in consequence his final draft had been sent directly to the printers and was already largely in proof. Moreover, Auerbach had not been the first author in the series to stray beyond his editorial mandate.[65] There was therefore, as Monod subsequently indicated, a case for asking Auerbach simply to revise his manuscript by extracting the offending chapters and extending his explanatory preface. Auerbach was ready to comply. At the same time, however, he sought permission to use in a personal and separate publication the omitted portions of his volume. This posed a dilemma for the Commission since it seemed almost inevitable that readers would assume a correlation between the official documents and the conclusions reached in Auerbach's unofficial but parallel monograph.[66] Nevertheless, while the commissioners were reluctant to abandon altogether the projected volume of instructions, they doubted their competence to prevent Auerbach from publishing the results of his research. In the end they agreed to Auerbach's plea on condition that he respected 'in an unofficial and friendly capacity the particular feelings of the commission'.[67] The outcome was not wholly displeasing from Auerbach's point of view. His somewhat reduced *Recueil* was completed in December 1911,[68] and in the following year he published his seminal study, *La France et le Saint-Empire germanique depuis la paix de Westphalie jusqu'à la Révolution française.* He therein reiterated his views on the emergence of a German national consciousness in response to French interventions in Germany. Yet he was careful to add that France had also benefited Germany insofar as she had defended German liberties and upheld the federal order.[69] He was thus as diplomatic as any honest French historian could be in explaining how during two centuries the Bourbon monarchy had encouraged and exploited the disunity of its neighbours.

Franco-German relations also played a large part in determining the form and content of two further collections of Foreign Ministry documents: *Les Origines diplomatiques de la Guerre de 1870–1871 (OD)*, and *Les Documents diplomatiques français 1871–1914 (DDF)*. Both of these were, however, prepared under the auspices of commissions which, though they drew some of their membership from the Commission des Archives Diplomatiques, were administratively separate from it.[70] When they began their work they were also concerned with documents which were otherwise closed to historical researchers. The first of the commissions, that which dealt with the origins of the Franco-Prussian War, was initiated in March 1907 by Stephen Pichon, Clemenceau's foreign minister.[71] But its establishment was probably more closely related to the political evolution of the Third Republic than to any change in France's international position. This at least was implied by Joseph Reinach, who in February 1908 became president of the relevant commission, and who subsequently claimed credit for having urged the advantages of such a project upon Léon Bourgeois, Pichon's immediate predecessor. Reinach, a passionate Dreyfusard who had once been Gambetta's *chef de cabinet*, appears to have seen in the publication a means of distancing the republic from the shortcomings of the Second Empire and its supporters.

He was particularly anxious to combat the one-sided interpretation placed upon the occult diplomacy of Napoleon III by the emperor's last premier, Émile Ollivier, who had been allowed access to the Quai d'Orsay's archives, and who in 1907 published the tenth volume of his eighteen-volume *l'Empire libéral*.[72] At the same time there was still a desire to learn from past mistakes, and as Pichon explained to the president of the republic, the proposed collection of documents would constitute 'a collection of verified and cross-checked facts from which enduring lessons would emerge for historians and for our country'. A democracy had the right, he added, to be truthfully instructed so that it might judge the men whose actions had so profoundly affected its destiny.[73]

Work on the *OD* was hindered by the outbreak of war in 1914, a lengthy legal dispute with the original publishers of the series, and official parsimony.[74] In addition, the volumes incurred the wrath of those on the political right who found in their editing fresh evidence of a Jewish-inspired plot to besmirch France's honour and international credibility. It was thus not until 1932 that the final volume of the collection, the twenty-ninth, appeared in print. Meanwhile, the decision had been taken to proceed with the *DDF*, three series of documents, whose format resembled the *OD* insofar as the documents were assembled by historians in strictly chronological order, but whose prime purpose was quite explicitly diplomatic. The Commission de Publication des Documents relatifs aux Origines de la Guerre de 1914–1918 was constituted in response to the prewar documents published from the Austro-Hungarian, German and Russian archives, with the assistance of which the Wilhelmstrasse had waged an effective public campaign against Article 231 of the Treaty of Versailles and the 'war guilt' it attributed to Germany. The appearance during the early 1920s of German diplomatic correspondence in the form of *Die Grosse Politik der europäischen Kabinette, 1871–1914*, and the Wilhelmstrasse's sponsorship of such reviews as the *Kriegsschuldfrage*, had already led to appeals from French diplomats for positive action on the part of the Quai d'Orsay to combat what was regarded as German propaganda. Indeed, in January 1922 the *direction politique* of the Foreign Ministry did indicate a readiness to provide French missions with copies of authentic documents relating to the war crisis of 1914.[75] But there was also a reluctance on the part of officials and politicians to participate in any discussion which might tend to undermine the basis of France's reparations claims. This was made quite clear by Raymond Poincaré, who had been president of the republic between 1913 and 1920 and who formed his first postwar cabinet in January 1922. The French government, he insisted in a despatch of 2 February 1922, wanted to do nothing that could imply 'a weakening of the acknowledgement of German responsibilities'.[76]

Similar sentiments were expressed in the Foreign Ministry with regard to the publication of the *British Documents on the Origins of the War*. French officials were far from pleased with the proofs of the first volume of this collection (that which concentrated upon the events of the summer of 1914), which they received from the Foreign Office early in 1926. The Quai d'Orsay objected to its contents and in a note of 23 February 1926, which listed the amendments it desired, it concluded that it would be inopportune 'at the moment when Germany was about to join the League of Nations, that so important a publication ... should remain silent about some of the most notorious facts establishing the responsibility of Germany and its allies in regard to the world war'.[77] Moreover, much to the irritation of the editors of the *British Documents*, French objections to subsequent volumes were to delay their publication.[78]

It was, however, evident to France's representatives abroad that in an era of open diplomacy they could neither halt nor win an historical debate by adopting a purely negative approach. Pierre de Margerie, who had been *directeur politique* at the Foreign Ministry in 1914, and who had since become France's ambassador at Berlin, was, despite his close association with the 'old diplomacy', fully aware of the implications of the 'new'. And like Sorel and Hanotaux before him, he understood the inconvenience of allowing Germans to monopolise historical publications. In a despatch of 3 March 1926 he warned the then foreign minister, Aristide Briand:

> There can be no doubt that under the influence of the enormous quantity of documents that the Wilhelmstrasse has thrown on to the historical market, world opinion has already begun to change to our disadvantage. The rapid publication of the documents in our archives relating to the events of 1914, thus demonstrating, particularly to Anglo-Saxon opinion, that we have nothing to fear from the judgements of posterity, would be desirable.[79]

But administrative decision making was a slow process in France, and it was not until January 1928, almost two years after the publication of the final volume of *Die Grosse Politik*, that Briand was moved to establish the Commission de Publication by ministerial decree.

The new commission was a large and unwieldy body, presided over by Sébastien Charléty, the rector of the Académie de Paris. It had fifty-six members, including historians, other academic specialists, and former and serving diplomats. Its role was, however, essentially supervisory, and much of the real work of editing was done by its *bureau*, a permanent editorial board which met at regular intervals, and four *équipes de travail*, each of which was made up of a *collaborateur* and a *commissaire*, whose task was to make a preliminary selection of documents from set chronological periods. Auerbach was, for instance, the *collaborateur* responsible for the initial search of the archives for the years 1901–1905, and Pierre Renouvin, who was also a secretary of the commission, was *commissaire* for the third series covering the years 1911–1914. The editors' mandate was a broad one. The commission was, according to Charléty, required 'to produce works of history, leaving out of account all considerations whatsoever alien to this purpose', and to this end Briand and Poincaré, the president of the council, decreed that its *collaborateurs* should have free access to all documents, whether they be in the Quai d'Orsay or other ministries.[80] But like the editors of the *OD*, their endeavours were impeded by a world war and administrative wrangling. Hardly had they begun their work before they came up against the budgetary constraints of an impecunious republic. Indeed, an attempt by the Finance Ministry in 1934 to impose economic cutbacks upon the Quai d'Orsay threatened to deprive the commission of three members of its editorial staff, Professors Appuhn, Auerbach, and Salomon, and Louis Barthou, the foreign minister, felt compelled to defend their work on the grounds that the *DDF* was 'of an essentially political significance'. Its aim, he observed, was 'whilst in maintaining the fullest historical objectivity, to counterbalance the campaign launched by Germany following the Treaty of Versailles, and to reaffirm to the world the truth about the events which brought about the war'.[81] Another twenty-three years was nonetheless to elapse before the collection was completed in 1957. By then the passage of time and developments elsewhere had made it more a work of academic enlightenment than historical diplomacy.

Whatever may have been the educational and propagandistic value of the *OD* and the *DDF*, such publications were primarily of interest to historians. It was they who were in the main responsible

for charting and interpreting the past actions of French diplomats and statesmen. But they too were dependent upon the
Commission des Archives Diplomatiques for access to the authentic records of the Foreign Ministry. Ever since its foundation the
Commission had been concerned with advising the minister on
what categories of documents might be made available for public
consultation, and what conditions should be attached to their
communication. At the request of Decazes it had also taken on the
task of vetting the applications of individual scholars for admission to the archives.[82] The attitude of the first Commission – that
established in 1874 – was by modern standards undoubtedly restrictive. However, after its reconstitution the regulations governing
research in France's diplomatic archives were brought more or
less into line with those prevailing in other European capitals.
Thus in 1880 general access was granted up until the proclamation
of the republic in September 1791, and conditional access was permitted up until the Treaty of Paris of May 1814. Then in December
1891 the Commission recommended the extension of the second
period to the fall of the Bourbon monarchy in July 1830.[83] Yet by
the beginning of the twentieth century the Quai d'Orsay was
lagging behind the other foreign ministries in the freedom it
allowed to historians. Early in 1905 the Haus-, Hof- und Staatsarchiv in Vienna was opened to the end of 1847, and in 1909, the
year in which Pichon made the Foreign Ministry archives available to 1848, the Foreign Office gave scholars access to its
archives up until 1860. Historians had to wait until 1917 before
French nationals were permitted to inspect France's diplomatic
archives of the years 1848–51,[84] and it was another ten years
before Briand announced their opening until 1871.[85] The Austrian
archives were by then open to 1894 and the British to 1878.

In deciding which periods should be open to archival research
the Commission was above all influenced by the wish to avoid
communicating material that might adversely affect France's foreign relations. It was essential to separate history from contemporary politics. This was easier said than done. Even in 1880 Sorel
insisted that the archives should be open only until 30 May 1814
because the Congress of Vienna constituted 'the prologue of modern policy which it was desired not to reveal'. Moreover, when
Monod then had the audacity to suggest the release of documents
up until 1830, he was reminded by Courcel of the inconvenience
of allowing access to a period in which French diplomacy had
been particularly active, and which could be regarded as setting

precedents for current affairs.[86] A similar argument was employed in April 1927 by Victor Bérard, a member of the Commission who opposed the extension of the open period until 1871. Evidently with German reparation payments in mind, he contended that there would be 'in some instances a grave danger in opening the archives of the Second Empire and that before doing so it would be advisable to await, at least, the complete carrying out of the Treaty of Versailles'. But Bérard protested in vain. So too did Émile Bourgeois, who feared lest the availability of documents for the whole of the Second Empire devalue the work of the editors of the *OD*, the latest volumes of which were still awaiting publication.[87]

It has also to be remembered that France's diplomatic archives were regarded by their guardians both as a departmental asset and as a political instrument. They were, in the language of Courcel and Sorel, an 'arsenal',[88] to which the public were admitted more as a privilege than as a right, and any suggestion that they might be transferred to the Archives Nationales was stoutly resisted by the Commission.[89] This meant that their administration was dependent upon the limited financial resources of the Quai d'Orsay, and that in consequence the facilities provided for researchers were barely adequate. In 1880 there were only twelve spaces available in the Salle de Communication, to which researchers were admitted between midday and 4 P.M.[90] The manner in which French diplomatic correspondence was bound in volumes according to country, and irrespective of the significance or sensitivity of individual documents, likewise encouraged the Commission to adopt a cautious attitude towards advancing the open period. Courcel was under the erroneous impression that the British Foreign Office's method of filing its records allowed it to be more liberal than the French in this respect. He thus explained in a Commission meeting of 14 March 1880 that since most of the Foreign Office's correspondence was printed on paper whose colour varied according to the importance of the document, this facilitated the withholding of anything the government might wish to keep a secret.[91] In French eyes Albion's archivists were apparently every bit as perfidious as her diplomats.

The Commission had, however, its own very effective means of vetoing historical research. All scholars seeking admission to the archives had first to apply to the Quai d'Orsay, and the Commission usually required from them a very specific definition of their intended research. The vast majority of those desiring access to documents in the open periods were thereby admitted on the recommendation of the Commission. But there were some notable exceptions. Generally speaking, the Commission was reluctant to sanction the communication of three categories of documents: (1) those whose revelation might be embarrassing or inconvenient to the government or individuals because of recent economic, political, or social developments;[92] (2) those which related to France's frontiers;[93] and (3) those which dealt with issues which were either subject to, or likely to be subject to, litigation.[94] Certain manuscript collections were also closed to public consultation for exceptionally long periods. These included France's consular archives and the *Fonds Alsace*. The former, which had originally belonged to the Ministry of Marine, were still unbound and uncatalogued in 1909, and were considered particularly sensitive since they frequently dealt with matters of private interest – an argument which, as the *sous-directeur des archives* admitted in 1909, was patently absurd where seventeenth- and eighteenth-century consular records were concerned.[95] The latter consisted of some sixty volumes of documents relating to the administration of Alsace, which dated from pre-Revolutionary times when it had been customary for all secretaries of state, including those charged with foreign affairs, to share responsibility for provincial government. What the Commission feared was that Alsace's German rulers might, if they learned of their presence in the Foreign Ministry, claim that the volumes were rightly theirs. It was therefore thought best to make no reference to them, and when in 1910 a student of the University of Strassburg applied, with the backing of the German embassy, to see seventeenth-century papers relating to France's representation in Strassburg, the Commission concluded in Orwellian terms that the volumes he wished to consult were 'inexistants'.[96]

Even after France's military reoccupation of Alsace in 1919, the Commission was of the opinion that precautions would have to be taken with regard to the communication of these documents 'and that, without keeping the archive closed, it would be well to consider carefully the applications that will be made'.[97] What, however, was judged politically inconvenient naturally varied according to circumstances. One of the earliest decisions by the Commission was to reject an application related to what was an essentially religious matter. Access was thus denied to a well-known ultramontane who in August 1874 wished to consult French diplomatic correspondence with Rome for the years 1675–95, because, at a time when church-state relations were so strained elsewhere in Europe, it was considered unwise to allow the archives to be utilised for religious polemic.[98] Two years later, in June 1876, doubts were expressed by Faugère about admitting two researchers who were interested in the activities of Lafayette and Vergennes at the time of the American War of Independence. Both were allowed to pursue their researches. But Faugère told his colleagues that he regretted the possibility of the archives being used in any way which might weaken the debt of gratitude which Americans felt towards France.[99] The French role in assisting the thirteen colonies to achieve their independence had acquired a near legendary status, and an isolated France needed to maintain all those legends which might encourage other powers to sympathise with her predicament.

Almost half a century later relations with the United States still figured large in the Commission's decision making. The French hoped in the aftermath of the First World War to retain the friendship and support of the United States, and there was perhaps some advantage to be derived from facilitating the researches of a growing number of American scholars (one in 1920, twelve in 1924 and ten in the first quarter of 1925) who applied for access to the Foreign Ministry's records.[100] There was, however, also the danger that an untimely revelation might weaken rather than strengthen the increasingly strained relationship between France and her former wartime associate. In these circumstances the Commission rejected a request made in 1924 by Jean Ingram Brookes of the University of Chicago for permission to use documents concerning France's colonial expansion in the Pacific Ocean during the years 1814–48. The new *chef du service des archives* thought it 'inopportune in view of the interpretations and even passions to which the study of the question might give rise in America as well as the Pacific'.[101] And Jules Cambon, a former ambassador at Washington, warned his fellow-commissioners that the American press would eventually use any information resulting from this research in a sense hostile to France.[102] Similarly in 1925 and 1926 the Commission opposed the applications of W.A. Dunham, a professor of history at Yale, and Charles Webster, the professor of international politics at Aberystwyth, to have access to papers relating to the negotiation and consequences of a treaty concluded in July 1831 for the mutual settlement of French and United States claims resulting from the seizure, sequestration, and destruction of shipping during the Revolutionary and Napoleonic wars. The French parliament had declined to ratify the treaty, and in consequence France had defaulted on a twenty-five million franc debt to the

United States. There was thus an all too obvious and uncomfortable parallel between France's attitude then and that adopted by French legislators towards the war debt payments due to the Americans since 1919.[103] Just as the Commission was reluctant to dispel those myths which seemed to enhance France's reputation, so was it averse to reminding the world of some of the more enduring, though less endearing, mores of French diplomacy.

There were, nevertheless, occasions when the Commission considered that France's interests might best be served by offering positive encouragement to researchers. One obvious example is that of Sorel who, in 1875, was admitted 'à titre exceptionnel' to papers outside the open periods in order to prepare his study of European diplomacy and the French Revolution. Such a work, it was predicted, would 'rectify errors harmful to our country'.[104] For similar reasons, the majority of the commissioners were sympathetic towards Legrelle, the author of *la Prusse et la France devant l'histoire*, who wished to complete and verify the accounts of historians, such as Ranke, of Louis XIV's seizure of Strassburg in 1681. In this instance Faugère thought that the patriotic sentiments by which Legrelle was motivated were a sufficient guarantee of his proper usage of documents.[105] In the same year, 1878, the Commission was also prepared to allow a German scholar, Professor Hüffer of the University of Bonn, to continue researches first begun in 1867 into the Quai d'Orsay's records of the diplomacy of the Revolutionary era. Hüffer had previously assured Faugère that he intended to contradict on many points 'the assertions and judgements of M. de Sybel', and in the opinion of another member of the Commission 'it would be good policy to provide this author with weapons against another historian so notoriously hostile to France'. The very fact that Hüffer wanted to make a defence of Bernadotte's embassy at Vienna was also regarded by Viel-Castel as proof of his impartiality.[106] This was a quality which foreigners were rarely supposed to possess when it came to writing about French history and politics. Even Frenchmen were sometimes found wanting, and Faugère thought it necessary to remind French historians in January 1879 of their duty to 'ménager l'honneur' of their country and government in any revelations they made from the diplomatic archives.[107]

This also helps explain the Commission's attitude towards the copying of manuscripts or whole series of documents. Its regulations, drafted in 1874, were quite clear on this point: the authorisation to carry out research did not according to Article vi imply

'the right to make full copies with a view to their subsequent publication either as a continuous text, such as a collection of letters,
or as a series of documents or diplomatic despatches'. This required
a special sanction.[108] But prior to the drafting of the *règlement* permission had already been granted to historians and learned societies to make copies in the archives. In 1872, for instance, the
Imperial Russian Historical Society had been authorised to begin
making textual copies of the reports of France's agents in Russia
during the eighteenth century, and in the process some eighty documents were photographed.[109] Moreover, scholars were usually
permitted to take detailed notes, though these might have to be
submitted to inspection. Hanotaux recalled in his memoirs how
the British historian, Samuel Lawson Gardiner, having been denied
the right to take notes, used to memorise portions of the seventeenth-century documents he was researching in the Quai d'Orsay
and then rush out to the bar on the corner of the rue de Bourgogne
where he would write down all that he could remember.[110] The
story is not, however, entirely accurate. When Gardiner applied in
1876 to see papers relating to his work on Stuart England no special conditions were attached to his research which might have
inhibited his notetaking, and a more likely explanation of his conduct was that he was simply trying to secure full copies of manuscripts without previous authorisation.[111]

There was in any case, as Faugère explained in March 1878, generally no objection to the publishing of individual documents.[112]
But the Commission did insist that its permission was required
where a whole series of manuscripts was concerned, and in
November 1880 Sorel, with Courcel's backing, opposed a request
from a Swiss historian to be allowed to prepare an inventory of the
despatches of French envoys in Switzerland from the earliest times
until 1803. There was a reluctance to shed light upon frontier
issues that could still upset Franco-Swiss relations. In addition,
however, Sorel feared that by communicating so many documents
to a foreigner the Commission might set a precedent that other
governments would invoke. 'Thus', he observed, 'our arsenal
would soon be empty.'[113] The metaphor was much favoured by the
commissioners. And when in April 1889 Monod suggested that it
was not necessary to mix 'questions of patriotism with archival
questions', he was curtly reminded that 'you do not trespass on the
rights of history merely because you refuse to allow a foreigner to
publish certain documents'.[114] Similar issues were raised twenty
years later in connexion with requests emanating from Germany

and Canada. Thus in June 1909 the Hamburg Senate sought to reconstitute archives destroyed in a fire by obtaining copies of seventeenth- and eighteenth-century French diplomatic correspondence, and in the following November the Canadian Office of Manuscripts asked permission to make a summary of Quai d'Orsay documents relating to the history of Canada up until 1763. The Commission was sympathetic towards Hamburg's plight and agreed to the Canadian project.[115] Nevertheless, in the ensuing debate Edmond Bapst, the *directeur politique*, raised the question of whether compensation should be required for the state abandoning property rights over its papers. The idea was strongly supported by Courcel, and in December 1909 it was finally resolved that when in future such applications were made by foreign states or bodies 'it will be advisable ... to grant authorisation only after having negotiated, as far as possible, *reciprocal advantages* for our nationals'.[116]

Foreign archivists and librarians were usually prepared to reciprocate. The United States Library of Congress did so when in 1923 the Commission agreed to let its representatives begin the copying of diplomatic documents relating to North America and the West Indies up until September 1791.[117] Nevertheless, during the 1920s members of the Commission became increasingly concerned about the extent of copying being done on behalf of American institutions and scholars by agents funded by such bodies as the Carnegie Institute. They were also disturbed by the increased use of photography, which seemed to make it all the more difficult to keep a check on what was being copied. And when in December 1927 the Library of Congress sought authorisation to photograph all the Quai d'Orsay's diplomatic correspondence concerning the United States up until 1871, the Commission's secretary spoke out vehemently against this possible alienation of the property of the French state.[118] Jusserand argued that in American hands such papers might be used against France, and although subsequent enquiries revealed that the Public Record Office was prepared to allow the photographing of any of its documents that were already open to researchers, the Commission maintained that nothing could be photographed beyond January 1814.[119] Samuel Bemis, the American historian responsible for directing the Library of Congress's project, found this decision incomprehensible. It was also very frustrating because John D. Rockefeller, the American millionaire who had provided money for the work, had set a time limit for its completion. American protests were, however, of no avail. Was it necessary, asked Émile Bourgeois, a long-standing member of the Commission, for the French state to bend 'its age-old laws and its requirements to suit the convenience of an American millionaire'?[120]

The practitioners of France's historical diplomacy rarely questioned either the value of their weaponry or the importance of their task.[121] Their function was not simply to safeguard sensitive material whose revelation might damage France's national interest, but to assist in educating their fellow-countrymen in the art and practice of diplomacy. Hanotaux, the longest serving member of the Commission between 1874 and 1939, was confident that the study of the past was vital for the conduct of foreign policy. On 3 June 1894, shortly after becoming foreign minister, he told the commissioners that he intended to preside over their meetings as often as possible because he could only gather useful inspiration for current policy in coming to listen to men who for him had been and would always be the masters. He went on to recall:

> When I was secretary of the Archives Commission and I was a silent witness of your deliberations, I often dreamed of seeing the minister responsible for our external interests coming to learn from the profound and varied experience each of you has gained from the study of the past, legal knowledge and administrative activity, and which makes of the Commission a sort of high court watching over our traditions and national sentiments.[122]

Seldom can a foreign minister's historical advisers have been the recipients of such praise.

The commissioners were, however, hardly the most modest of men. That reawakening of French nationalism on the eve of the First World War, which was associated with the appointment of Poincaré as premier and foreign minister in January 1912 and his elevation in the following year to the presidency of the republic, was thus portrayed by Courcel as a by-product of the Commission's work. Poincaré had for some time been a member of the Commission, and in January 1913 Courcel told his colleagues that the Commission could feel itself all the more proud in being able to claim its part in the 'mouvement national' that had brought about his election. He further explained:

> In having, in effect, for nearly forty years fostered the study of our political traditions, in causing the present generation to draw from the living sources of history an ever clearer understanding of past endeavours, of the underlying and permanent interests, the

Commission may pride itself on having contributed to the development, strengthening and enhancing in France of the public consciousness; and it is the alerting of opinion to our diplomatic actions which, in the present crisis, has conditioned the Congress's choice of the foreign minister [as president], by reason of the dignity of his conduct and the way in which he has articulated the action of France in Europe.[123]

And by November 1919 Hanotaux, who was once again a nonpolitical member of the Commission, had little doubt that his fellow historians had played a significant role in reversing France's fortunes. The Commission had instructed the fledgling democracy in France's traditions 'in providing it, along with a sense of continuity which conforms to the underlying interests of the country, with all consciousness of the perspectives opening up before it'.[124]

Within barely half a century Hanotaux had witnessed France's emergence from her diplomatic isolation, her territorial expansion in Africa, her participation in a triumphant military coalition against imperial Germany, and finally the restoration of her lost provinces. He evidently felt that this was at least in part due to that relearning of France's diplomatic traditions that the Commission had tried to promote. It was equally natural that he should have looked towards history to assist in halting France's relative decline in the years between the world wars. On 12 May 1937, at the age of eighty-four, he used his position as president of the Commission to make an impassioned plea for the opening of the Quai d'Orsay's archives until 1896. He was particularly anxious that scholars should be encouraged to make use of the Ministry's commercial correspondence. After all, he argued, 'economic and commercial policy' had for more than fifty years been 'the great pivot of French policy', and a better understanding of the basis of France's past prosperity might hasten the finding of a solution to France's current economic predicament. Hanotaux's main concern was, however, with the 'need to make known, to Frenchmen and foreigners alike, what French policy really is'. Otherwise, he feared that if historians were denied access to France's archives they would come to rely on foreign sources and the history of France would be written against France. Austria, Britain, Germany and Russia had already made a mass of documents available to historians. By contrast, the French government had limited itself to a single official publication and that relating to the preparation for war. Yet, Hanotaux, protested, France had nothing to hide: 'the history of France is always honorable'.[125]

This last contention would have to await the judgement of another generation of historians. In the meantime, those present on 12 May hastened to disabuse Hanotaux of the notion that the *DDF* would be limited to the purely political origins of the war. The publication, they explained, would encompass all France's 'politique générale' between 1871 and 1914, 'which no country had done on such a scale'.[126] Hanotaux's strictures were nonetheless not wholly misplaced. During the 1920s the French had responded in a tardy fashion to the archival initiatives of the Wilhemstrasse. France's diplomats were perhaps the victims of their own success. The Quai d'Orsay had emerged from the First World War with enhanced prestige, and its officials had not been under the same pressure as those in the Foreign Office and the Wilhelmstrasse to defend themselves against their domestic critics and bureaucratic rivals. There was indeed a certain irony in the fact that the *OD*, the one published series of French diplomatic documents which was completed before its German counterpart, served less to demonstrate the culpability of the republic's external foes than the fallibility of a former régime. Economic constraints had, however, also slowed the pace of France's historical diplomacy. Even before 1914 the administration of the diplomatic archives had been underfunded, and work on both the *OD* and the *DDF* was impeded by financial stringency.[127] Moreover, the short-staffing of the Service des Archives meant that it was unable to undertake the kind of preliminary examination of documents that was considered necessary for the release of papers of a more recent date. The situation seemed unlikely to improve. Only bound volumes were usually communicated to researchers. But, as Hanotaux lamented, none of the Ministry's political and commercial correspondence had been bound since 1897.[128] Unless drastic action were taken the prospects for diplomatic historians of twenty, thirty or forty years hence would remain distinctly dim.

There was, however, another and more fundamental flaw in the work of the Commission. This lay in its frequently all too narrow conception of how history could be used for diplomatic ends. In November 1906 Courcel summarised the functions of the Commission in the following terms:

> The management of our work is sometimes a delicate task; stemming from a twofold impulse, it involves at one and the same time the revealing of what the documents have to say, and great caution in the selection of documents. These are, so to speak, weapons apt for use in the defence of our country's interests: it is advisable not

to allow them to be employed other than sparsely and with dis-
cernment. As has been rightly said, this archive is a museum, but,
above all, an arsenal. Our Commission has been formed precisely
to watch over it in its latter guise.[129]

And just six months later he warned his fellow-commissioners that
the Ministry's archives constituted 'a sort of gunpowder' which
must serve and not injure the interests of France.[130] The resulting
historical diplomacy mirrored that of Prussia, sharing many of its
virtues and defects. The Recueils des instructions were thus a considerable scholastic achievement, and the OD was a pioneering
enterprise in the publication of nineteenth-century diplomatic documents which was unrivalled until after the First World War. But
the Recueils were intended not so much as aids to an understanding
of the past, as guides to future conduct. History was meant not
simply to enlighten, but to teach. Moreover, although the Quai
d'Orsay was hardly less liberal than other European foreign ministries in the restrictions it imposed upon researchers, the commissioners seemed sometimes to suffer from diplomatic myopia when
it came to assessing the likely effect of archival revelations upon
France's current policies and interests. The goodwill generated by
a more benevolent response to the requests of American scholars in
the 1920s might, for instance, have outweighed any temporary
embarrassments caused by the news that Frenchmen had not
always acted in the spirit of Lafayette.

    In the aftermath of the Paris Peace Conference, and in a decade
in which Franco-German relations were dominated by matters
relating to the liquidation of the war, French diplomats grew
increasingly aware of the importance of seeking to influence academic and ultimately public opinion abroad through the publication of diplomatic documents. They could not afford to ignore the
warning delivered by the German historian Alfred von Wegerer in
December 1925 that in the United States all propaganda on the
war-guilt issue would be not only useless, but harmful, because
the evolution of American opinion was above all dependent upon
the works of American scholars.[131] Nevertheless, by the time of the
publication of the first volume of the DDF in 1929 the Wilhelmstrasse's case was already well established, and the appearance of
subsequent volumes of the French documents was to have little
impact upon international relations. The historical diplomacy of
the Third Republic was of doubtful relevance in a Europe about to
fall prey to the hysterical diplomacy of the Third Reich. Moreover,

between 1940 and 1944 France's diplomatic arsenal, *les archives diplomatiques*, was sadly to suffer the depredation of war. When on 23 May 1946 the Commission reassembled for the first time in seven years, its members were faced with the awesome task of deciding how to begin the work of restitution and restoration. Fortunately, Georges Bidault, the foreign minister who would bear the responsibility for finding the money for this project, was fully alive to the value of the archives for France's diplomacy. In his address to the Commission he observed that the Quai d'Orsay's archives and its library existed to assist in the making of foreign policy. But, he added, there was 'something else as well ... there is the world at large, upon which crude propaganda has of late made too deep an impression, but on which the propaganda of truth, the publication of documents, also exerts its influence and makes its mark'. It was a message that Courcel, Hanotaux, Monod, Sorel, and very probably Sybel, would each have appreciated and endorsed.[132]

Notes

The opinions expressed in this paper are the author's own and should not be taken as an expression of official government policy. I should like to thank M Jean Batbedat, the Directeur des Archives et de la Documentation of the Ministère des Affaires Étrangères at Paris, for his kind assistance in drawing my attention to the Archives des Archives and other records cited in this paper. I am also grateful to my colleague, Dr Eleanor Breuning, for her advice and encouragement, and to the British Academy for the award which it made me from its Small Grants Research Fund in the Humanities.

1. All documentary sources cited in this paper are, unless otherwise stated, to be found in the series Archives des Archives of the archives of the Ministère des Affaires Étrangères (MAE), Paris. Procès-verbaux de la Commission des Archives Diplomatiques (hereafter cited as CAD), vol. ii, 8 May 1907.

2. The Quai d'Orsay's archives were, according to their relevant service, 'appelées à fournir au Ministre et ses Services les précédents nécessaires à la conduite des affaires, à la défense des droits et des intérêts du pays en attendant qu'ils soient un jour le source à notre histoire nationale'. Anciens fonds, AR 13, série 4–4–1, Projet de note pour le Ministre, 23 May 1938.

3. Holger H. Herwig, 'Clio Deceived: Patriotic Self-Censorship in Germany after the Great War', ch. 3.

4. See for example: K.A. Hamilton, 'The Pursuit of "Enlightened Patriotism": The British Foreign Office and Historical Researchers During the Great War and Its Aftermath', ch. 6.

5. Centre National de la Recherche Scientifique, *Les Affaires Étrangères et le Corps Diplomatique Français* (2 vols., Paris, 1984), i, p. 524.

6. Gabriel Hanotaux, *Mon Temps* (4 vols., Paris, 1935–47), ii, pp. 11–12.

7. Ministère des Relations Extérieures, *Les Archives du Ministère des Relations Extérieures depuis les Origines* (2 vols., Paris, 1984–85), i, p. 251.

8. Ibid., p. 256.

9. Faugère told the Commission des Archives Diplomatiques in March 1874 that prior to his appointment 'la doctrine constamment maintenue' had been 'le refus était la règle et l'admission l'exception'. CAD., i, 18 March 1874. Armand Baschet, *Histoire du Depôt des Archives des Affaires Étrangères* (Paris, 1875), p. 547; Antoine Guilland, *L'Allemagne nouvelle et ses historiens* (Paris, 1899), p. 162.

10. H. von Sybel, *Geschichte der Revolutionenzeit von 1789 bis 1800* (5 vols., Düsseldorf, 1853–70).

11. Guilland, p. 161.

12. CAD, ii, 3 Nov. and 1 Dec. 1909.

13. See for instance: CAD, 1, 10 June 1876 and 23 April 1878.

14. v. Sybel, *Histoire de l'Europe pendant la Révolution française*, vol. i (Paris, 1869), p. vi.

15. Claude Digeon, *La Crise allemande de la Pensée française 1870–1914*, (Paris, 1959), pp. 372–3.

16. Gabriel Monod, 'Du progrès des études historiques en France depuis le XVIᵉᵐᵉ siècle', *Revue Historique*, i (1876), p. 28.

17. Hanotaux, ii, p. 5.

18. CAD, i, 28 April 1875. See also: Jacques Bariéty, 'Albert Sorel: l'Europe et la Révolution française, 1885 – 1904', *1889: Centenaire de la Révolution Française: Réactions et Representations Politiques en Europe*, ed. J. Bariéty (Berne, 1992), pp. 129–44.

19. Jean Albert Sorel and V.C. Pichois, 'Albert de Gobineau et Albert Sorel: correspondence inédite (1872–1879)', *Revue d'histoire diplomatique (1977)*, p. 229.

20. Monod, 'Du progrès', p. 38.

21. Hanotaux, ii, p. 8.

22. Baschet, p. 547.

23. The Commission met for the first time on 15 March 1874. CAD, i, 15 March and 9 May 1874.

24. Ibid.

25. The rules drafted by the Commission expressly stated that the Foreign Ministry should continue to contribute to this series. CAD, i, 29 March 1874.

26. CAD, i, 22 March 1874.

27. CAD, i, 4 April 1874.

28. CAD, i, 22 March 1874.

29. Decazes's letter was communicated to the Commission by Viel-Castel. CAD, i, 4 April 1874.

30. Hanotaux, ii, p. 3.

31. CAD, i, 27 April 1874.

32. CAD, i, 14 Aug. 1764.

33. CAD, i, 30 May 1874.

34. CAD, i, 12 Dec. 1874.

35. CAD, i, 28 April 1875.
36. CAD, i, 22 March 1876.
37. J. Valfrey, *La diplomatie française au XVIIeme siècle: Hugues de Lionne, ses ambassades en Italie, 1642–1656 d'après sa correspondance conservée aux archives du ministère des affaires étrangères* (Paris, 1877).
38. CAD, i, 17 March 1880.
39. CAD, i, 17 March 1880.
40. CAD, i, Sous-Commission du Catalogue et de la Publication, 6 April 1880.
41. Ibid. *Publicationen aus den königlichen Preussischen Staatsarchiven*, vol. i, *Preussen und die Katholische Kirche seit 1640* (pt. i, 1640–1740), ed. Max Lehmann (Berlin, 1878), pp. v–vi.
42. CAD, i, Sous-Commission du Catalogue et de la Publication, 6 April 1880.
43. Ibid.
44. Ibid., 30 June 1880.
45. CAD, i, Rapport addressé à la Commission des Archives Diplomatiques, 9 Feb. 1882.
46. CAD, i, 12 Jan. 1881 (incorrectly amended to 1882).
47. CAD, i, 10 Feb 1882; Rapport, 9 Feb. 1882.
48. CAD, i, Resolutions, 10 Feb. 1882.
49. *Publicationen aus den k. Preussischen Staatsarchiven*, vol. viii, *Preussen und Frankreich von 1795 bis 1807: Diplomatische Correspondenzen*, ed. Paul Bailleu (Leipzig, 1881).
50. CAD, i, 10 Feb. 1882.
51. CAD, i, Sous-Commission des Archives Diplomatiques, 8 March 1882.
52. CAD, i, 18 Feb. 1882.
53. CAD, i, 1 March 1882.
54. Hanotaux, ii, pp. 370–1. *Recueil des Instructions données aux Ambassadeurs et Ministres de France depuis les traités de Westphalie jusqu'à la Révolution Française. Autriche*, ed. A. Sorel (Paris, 1884), pp. i–iii.
55. CAD, i, 8 March 1882 and 3 Feb. 1886.
56. CAD, i, 9 Jan. and 2 July 1886.
57. Eugen Weber, *Peasants into Frenchmen: The Modernization of Rural France* (Stanford, Calif., 1976).
58. CAD, iii, 5 April 1911.
59. Ibid.
60. CAD, ii, 7 Dec. 1892 and 3 Jan. 1893.
61. *Recueil*, vol. x, *Naples et Parme*, ed. J. Reinach (Paris, 1893). CAD, ii, 1 Feb. 1893.
62. CAD, ii, 9 June 1909.
63. CAD, iii, 9 Nov. 1910.
64. Ibid.
65. There was also the danger, as one commissioner pointed out, that if the volume were suppressed a legend would be created in Germany regarding it, and that the affair would have a gravity that the Commission would wish to avoid. CAD, iii, 7 Dec. 1910.
66. CAD, iii. 11 Jan. 1911.
67. CAD, iii, 1 Feb. 1911.
68. CAD, iii, 6 Dec. 1911. *Recueil*, vol. xviii, *Diète Germanique*, ed. Bertrand Auerbach (Paris, 1912).
69. Auerbach, *La France et le Saint-Empire depuis la Paix de Westphalie jusqu'à la Révolution Française* (Paris, 1912), p. 467.

70. The commission responsible for the *OD* was in fact wholly composed of members of the Commission des Archives Diplomatiques. Its first president was Pierre Deluns-Montaud, the Chef de la Division des Archives at the Quai d'Orsay. *OD*, vol. i (1910), p. iv. Hanotaux had expected to be named president. Hanotaux, *Carnets (1907–25)* (Paris, 1982), p. 15.

71. *OD*, i, pp. i-iii.

72. AR 70, série 20–14, extract from *l'Echo de Paris*, 24 July 1910; 'Die diplomatischen Ursachen des Krieges von 1870/71 in französischer Beleuchtung', *Illustrierte Zeitung*, 24 Aug. 1910.

73. *OD*, i, pp. i-iii.

74. AR 68, série 20–14, Aulard and Bourgeois to Poincaré, 29 March 1922. CAD, iii. 2 Feb. 1927.

75. AR 73, série 20–15, note for the *directeur des archives*, 21 Jan. 1922.

76. Ibid., Poincaré to Christiania, 2 Feb. 1922.

77. PRO (London), FO 370/239, L1483/24/402, Note from the French embassy, 23 Feb. 1926. The Count de Saint-Aulaire, France's ambassador in London, warned the Quai d'Orsay in April 1924 that the German historian, Professor Kantorowicz, was attempting to develop the thesis that neither Britain nor Germany were responsible for the First World War, which was entirely due to France and Russia: a view widely held by an important section of English public opinion. De Saint-Aulaire suggested that the Quai d'Orsay should publish material in order to counter this 'mensonge', AR 73, série 20–15, despt. 222, Saint-Aulaire to MAE, 5 April 1924.

78. Hamilton, 'The Pursuit of "Enlightened Patriotism"', note 117.

79. AR 73, série 20–15, despt. 294, Margerie to Briand, 3 March 1926.

80. AR 72, série 20–15–4, COG 14, 15 March 1928.

81. AR 72, série 20–15–4, Barthou to Martin, 3 May 1934.

82. CAD, i, 27 April and 14 Aug. 1874.

83. CAD, ii, 2 Dec. 1891.

84. The opening of the Foreign Ministry archives until 1848 followed requests from individual historians, the Historical Congress at Rome and the budget commission of the Chamber of Deputies. CAD, ii, 2 July 1902; 5 April, 3 May and 7 June 1905; 19 May 1909. In 1917 the Commission was faced with a request from the minister of education for the opening of the archives until September 1870. But the commissioners were reluctant to make such a concession and expressed their concern over the 'grands inconvénients' which could arise from 'l'étude de certains sujets délicats, de problèmes politiques dont la solution interviendra seulement à la conclusion de la paix', CAD, iii, 12 Dec. 1917.

85. CAD, iii, 1 June 1927.

86. CAD, iii, 17 March 1880.

87. CAD, iii, 6 April 1927.

88. CAD, iii, 17 March 1880.

89. CAD, iii, 5 Feb. 1908.

90. CAD, i, 17 March 1880. In 1912 the Salle de Communication was enlarged to accommodate forty-four researchers. CAD, iii, 3 July and 6 Nov. 1912.

91. CAD, i, 17 March 1880.

92. There was also a reluctance to allow the diplomatic archives to be used for polemic. The commissioners had, for instance, grave doubts in 1878 about admitting two Poles who wished to consult documents relating to French

diplomacy and Poland since 1796. One commissioner remarked that 'à l'histoire de Pologne se rattachent des questions qui n'ont pas cessé d'être le sujet de polemique et sont toujours brûlantes': there was a danger that Polish researchers would substitute 'à une étude historique les thèmes d'une polémique passionnée'. CAD, i, 23 April 1878. There was, however, a certain irony in the fact that in June 1914 the Sous-Commission des Archives, with the backing of the CAD, recommended that the Serbian historian, Gregoire Yakschitch, be denied permission to see papers relating to the encouragement given by the Second Republic in 1848 to South Slav aspirations for a Greater Serbia because of the possible impact of his revelations on Franco-Austrian relations. CAD, iii, 3 June 1914.
93. See for example: CAD, ii, 7 Feb. 1907.
94. The latter category also included matters in dispute between other states. Thus in 1912 the Commission refused the communication to Professor Palmer Briggs of the University of California of papers relating to the Falkland Islands in the period 1764–72. CAD, iii, 5 June 1912.
95. CAD, ii, 19 May 1909.
96. CAD, iii, 20 July and 9 Nov. 1910.
97. CAD, iii, 4 June 1919. Even in 1932 a student wishing to consult documents regarding the mission of Hérault de Séchelles to Alsace and the projected annexation of Mülhausen in 1793 was invited to 'user prudemment des documents consultés'. CAD, iv, 6 April 1932.
98. CAD, i, 14 Aug. 1874.
99. CAD, i, 10 June 1876.
100. The Commission's minutes also recorded in June 1925 that hardly a single request had emanated from a German since the war 'alors qu'ils venaient assez nombreux, avant 1914, travailler dans nos Archives'. CAD, iii, 1 July 1925.
101. CAD, iii, 9 April and 4 June 1924.
102. CAD, iii, 1 July 1925.
103. CAD, iii, 14 April 1926.
104. CAD, i, 28 April 1875.
105. CAD, i, 3 Jan. 1875.
106. CAD, i, 23 April 1878.
107. CAD, i, 28 Jan. and 26 March 1879.
108. CAD, i, 19 March 1874.
109. CAD, i, 3 March 1875.
110. Hanotaux, ii, pp. 10–11.
111. CAD, i, 12 Jan. 1876.
112. CAD, i, 16 March 1878.
113. CAD, i, 30 Nov. 1880. Documents regarding Franco-Swiss relations were invariably regarded by the Commission as being of a particularly sensitive nature. This was mainly because of their bearing on the customs free zones in Savoy which had been conceded to Switzerland in 1814–15 and in the 1860s. Prior to France's annexation of Savoy in 1860 the French had tended to support the Swiss in their quarrels with the rulers of Savoy, and the commissioners were worried lest through the opening of the archives they should provide the Swiss with diplomatic and legal ammunition that could henceforth be used against France. CAD, iii, 3 June and 1 July 1914, 7 Nov. 1923. See also: D.J. Grange, 'La question frontalière franco-genevoise depuis 1945', *Relations Internationales*, 63 (1990).

114. CAD, ii, 9 June 1909.
115. CAD, ii, 3 Nov. 1909.
116. CAD, ii, 1 Dec. 1909.
117. CAD, iii, 6 June and 7 Nov. 1923.
118. CAD, iii, 7 Jan. 1923.
119. CAD, iii, 11 Jan. 1928.
120. Ibid. The Library of Congress renewed its request in March 1934 only to have
     it rejected again. CAD, iv, 7 March 1934.
121. Courcel spoke in December 1906 of 'les documents de nos archives étant des
     armes qu'il convient de n'utiliser qu'avec prudence et expérience'. CAD, ii, 5
     Dec. 1906.
122. CAD, ii, 8 June 1894.
123. CAD, iii, 22 Jan. 1913.
124. CAD, iii, 5 Nov, 1919.
125. CAD, iv, 12 May 1937. From 15 June 1937 the Quai d'Orsay's archives were
     officially open until 1877.
126. Ibid.
127. CAD, ii, 4 Nov. 1903, 5 Feb. and 4 March 1908. The Commission's work was
     so underfunded that in 1909 the Société d'Histoire Diplomatique felt obliged
     to offer financial assistance to support its publications. CAD, ii, 20 Jan. and 10
     Feb. 1909.
128. CAD, iv, 12 May 1937.
129. CAD, ii, 7 Nov. 1906.
130. CAD, ii, 8 May 1906.
131. AR 73, série 20–15, despt. 542, Laboulaye to Briand, 11 Dec. 1925.
132. AR 13, série 4–4–2, CAD, 23 May 1946.

Chapter 2

THE UNFINISHED COLLECTION
Russian Documents on the Origins of the First World War

Derek Spring

The imperial Russian Ministry of Foreign Affairs had not been in the habit of regularly publishing correspondence about its activities comparable to the British Foreign Office Blue Books. In the second half of the nineteenth century there was only one near contemporaneous publication. This consisted of 155 documents from the Anglo-Russian correspondence about central Asia published in 1886 to give the Russian government's view of the recent crisis and its background.[1] A public opinion was certainly emerging in Russia in this period, but in an autocratic political system in which the public did not have formal channels by which they could influence foreign policy, such publications were not considered a priority.

The establishment of the Duma in 1906, however, gave a role to elements of the Russian public in political life. Even though the Duma did not exercise powers formally over foreign policy, the views expressed there, in the moderate political parties and in the press, were undoubtedly influential in the formation of foreign policy.[2] Already in 1905 a Press Office was established in the ministry, and the reform of the ministry set in motion by Foreign Minister Alexander Izvolsky was intended to adapt it more effectively to these post-1905 conditions. Amongst other aspects of this trend was the publication of collections of recent diplomatic correspondence on issues of the day. Already in 1905 the Committee on Far

Eastern Affairs, representing the nonministerial advisers under Admiral Abaza who had done so much to precipitate the Russo-Japanese War, published documents to clarify their role on the eve of the war.[3] Only four hundred copies of this 'Crimson Book' were published, but they reached the British press and the Russian emigration. Lamsdorf for the Foreign Ministry challenged their version of events and successfully advised the tsar to impound all obtainable copies. Reluctant to adapt to the new conditions, the minister thought it appropriate that his collection should be published only in a limited edition for official circulation rather than for sale.[4] But soon new habits prevailed. Official 'Orange' books were published by the Ministry of Foreign Affairs on many aspects of Russian diplomatic activity. These began with the publication on the reforms in Macedonia in cooperation with Austria-Hungary from 1902, and continued with those on the negotiation of a fishing convention with Japan in 1906, on Persian affairs (seven issues covering 1906 to 1911), on Balkan affairs 1911–13, on Mongolia 1912–13 and on Armenia 1913–14 before the collections on the outbreak of the wars with Germany and with Turkey in 1914.[5] The publications showed the ministry's awareness of the need to defend its activities both before the domestic and the international community. But of course, as later publications have revealed, the documents they published at the time were very selective, often much truncated, with omissions and stylistic alterations.

In November 1917, however, the Bolshevik Party came to power with a commitment to abolish secret diplomacy which it saw as a conspiracy against the peoples. Their first task, as stated in the Decree on Peace of 8 November 1917, was to publish all secret treaties made or confirmed by the Russian government 'between February and 25 October 1917' in order to discredit the provisional government as being committed to the continuation of the policies of the tsarist regime. But first of all they had to obtain access to the archives of the ministry. Trotsky, the new commissar for foreign affairs, declared that his job was simply 'to publish a few proclamations and then shut up shop' as the whole character of international relations would be changed by the imminent world revolution. The new commissar was therefore slow in taking over full control of the ministry. It was left to the long-time Bolshevik and émigré I.A. Zalkind (1855–1928), appointed assistant commissar, and the sailor N.A. Markin (1893–1918), a delegate to the second All Russian Congress of Soviets and secretary to the commissar, to bring the staff of the ministry to order after their strike against the new regime. The stalemate lasted for ten days after the Bolshevik seizure of power. A.A. Neratov, the former assistant minister (since 1910), resisted for a few days longer but was eventually found, brought to the ministry and forced to give up the keys to the inner sanctums and safes of the ministry's Secret Archive.[6]

At the beginning of the war in 1914 all the ministry's files had been packed up ready for transport in the expectation of the evacuation of St. Petersburg. But it was only in September 1917 that the Kerensky government loaded the five hundred packing cases of files on to a barge and moved them to the Kirillo-Belozersky monastery in Novgorod province.[7] So Zalkind and Markin were left with the Secret Archive and wartime correspondence in the ministry in Petrograd. From these the Bolsheviks were committed to finding and publishing urgently some striking revelations. Already on 21 November Lenin was enquiring after the first package of documents.[8] Markin, a man of little education, remarkably managed to select some significant items from the papers. Between 23 November and 6 December *Pravda* published documents dating from 1915 to 1917 including the wartime agreements of the Allies on the Straits, Alsace-Lorraine, and Persia. Publication continued in other newspapers up to 21 February 1918. Less ephemeral were the seven booklets of documents published by Markin for the new commissariat between November 1917 and February 1918, which contained over a hundred documents and treaties.[9] In February 1918, with the crisis at the front, Markin was detailed to other duties, and publication was suspended. He was subsequently killed in October 1918 fighting against the Whites in an incident on the Kama river.[10]

Among the one hundred and thirty documents published by Markin were some significant revelations of the texts of treaties and agreements made by the tsarist government. These included the Three Emperors' alliance of June 1881, the Franco-Russian military convention of 1892, the Russo-Bulgarian military convention of 1902, the Björkö treaty of 1905, the Russo-German treaty on the Baltic of October 1907, the Russo-Japanese treaty of July 1907, and the Russo-Bulgarian treaty of 1909. But the publication also contained documents which were already well known to the initiated, such as the Anglo-Russian convention of 1907 and the Anglo-French agreement of 1904 on Egypt and Morocco, which had already been published. Apart from the treaties, almost all of the documents were from the wartime period,

including correspondence on Rumania's entry into the war and
the Russo-Rumanian military convention of 1915, the Russo-
Japanese agreement of 3 July 1915 against any third power attempting to achieve dominance in China, and material on the Straits
question during the war. Treaties of foreign powers discovered in
the secret archive and published included the Serbian-Bulgarian
treaties of 1904 and of 1912. It included quite a lot of material from
the period of the provisional government with the immediate
political objective of discrediting it and associating it with the war
aims of the imperial regime and showing the involvement of foreign diplomats in the Kornilov affair of August 1917. Markin also
could not resist the urge to publish merely informational reports
from Russian representatives abroad about revolutionary discon-
tent and disturbances in other countries, such as the dossier of
material in 1917 from the ambassador in Madrid. A.A. Neratov,
while not discounting the validity of the documents, rightly
warned against taking all that was published as having been the
considered policy of the imperial government. Many items published were undated, unsigned or without any heading to determine their origin.[11]

With the onset of the civil war the question of publication of
documents from the former Ministry fell into the background. The
archive of the ministry itself was scattered in several centres and
in no condition for study and analysis. In the course of 1919 the
Soviet government ordered the transfer of the archive from the
Kirillo-Belozersky monastery to Moscow. Unfortunately, there
was an accident with the barge onto which the material was being
loaded. Many of the boxes were broken and files lost; the rest were
left at the monastery until the summer of 1921 when they were
finally moved to Moscow. Meanwhile, the papers which had
remained in Petrograd in 1917 were transferred to Moscow with
the government in the spring of 1918. They were scattered over
three different sites and no definite decision was made as to which
commissariat should control them. Serious work was not begun
until the transfer of the main part of the archive from the monastery in the summer of 1921. The officials of the Commissariat of
Enlightenment had scarcely begun to unpack the files when it was
decided to bring the archive together with other foreign policy
files in a single building. In October and November 1924 it was
finally packed up and moved again to the building on Serpuk-
hovskii Street where it is still situated. In spite of this confusing
process over ten years from 1914 to 1924 it was claimed that only

a few documents of primary importance were lost. Systematic ordering of the archive began in April 1922 but proceeded very slowly with only seven permanent and three temporary staff. In 1922 two hundred boxes were opened and the files indexed and made available to readers; in 1923 a further three hundred boxes were dealt with, so that by then a total of 400,000 files were available for consultation.[12]

Already in early 1918, M.N. Pokrovsky, the only Russian Marxist historian of any standing, had urged the centralisation of control of historical documents in a state archive so they could be used in the interests of the new regime. In the same year he was appointed to a commission for the study of the origins of the war on the basis of the diplomatic documents.[13] The commission was apparently engulfed by the civil war but Pokrovsky did manage to publish three important documents on prewar interministerial Special Conferences from 21 January 1908 (OS dates) on the crisis in relations with Turkey, from 31 December 1913 on the Liman von Sanders affair, and 7 February 1914 on preparations for the seizure of the Straits, all of which shed important light on the objectives of the Russian government.[14]

It was not until 1921 that Pokrovsky was able to put his plans fully into effect when he was appointed head of the new *Tsentrarkhiv* – the central archive. He immediately initiated the publication of a new journal, *Krasnyi Arkhiv,* which in 106 issues from 1922 to 1941 was to be the major focus of publication of material on all aspects of late tsarist Russia. It set as its basic task 'to expose the secrets of imperialist policy and diplomacy'.[15] The major part of the first volume was a collection of documents on Russo-German relations, mostly from the Secret Archive of the Foreign Ministry. It included the texts of the conventions forming the Three Emperors' alliance of 1873, the Russian versions of the Reichstadt agreement of 1876 and the Budapest convention of 1877, Saburov's reports on Bismarck's views in 1879, the Three Emperors' alliance agreements of 1881 and 1884, the text of the reinsurance treaty with Shuvalov's report of the discussions with Bismarck, correspondence relating to the 'project to seize the Bosphoros' in 1897, and finally fifty-six documents from 20 July to 1 August 1914 either unpublished in the Russian Orange Book on the July crisis or published only in part or altered text. Pokrovsky particularly focused on those documents relating to the Straits, the seizure of which was taken to be the consistent aim of Russian foreign policy in the nineteenth century. Where documents did not seem to confirm this, he considered it to have been simply a 'mistake' of Russian diplomacy.

Krasnyi Arkhiv continued to publish material relating to foreign policy, amongst many other aspects of prerevolutionary Russia. But while not denying the value of each collection of documents, it is noticeable that the themes were selected rather haphazardly and gave no full coverage of any particular period. Some items included many extracts rather than complete documents, or the articles were cut short or promised 'continuations' failed to appear. For instance, the collection on the First Balkan War did not contain anything after 19 November 1912 (OS),[16] on the Young Turk Revolution and on policy on the eve of the Russo-Japanese War the promised continuations never appeared.[17] Amongst the foreign policy material there was also quite a lot which shed light on the internal situation in foreign countries in ambassadors' reports, rather than the making and direction of Russian foreign policy in documents such as instructions from the ministry in St. Petersburg.[18]

Amongst the more substantial publications of documents of Russian foreign policy relating to the period before and during the First World War were the diary of Kuropatkin before the Russo-Japanese War, correspondence relating to the Björkö agreement and the Algeciras conference, the Portsmouth peace negotiations, Sazonov's reports to the tsar on his foreign visits from 1910 to 1912, the preparation for the First Balkan War and correspondence during it, the Chinese revolution, Russia and Mongolia in 1913–1914, the diary of the Ministry of Foreign Affairs for July 1914, the correspondence of Sukhomlinov and Yanushkevich, and of military headquarters (Stavka) with the Ministry of Foreign Affairs during the war.

At the same time that Pokrovsky was active with *Krasnyi Arkhiv*, other publications appeared, mostly with his help. In 1922 a volume of documents on Franco-Russian relations from 1910 to 1914 was published in Russian by the Commissariat of Foreign Affairs.[19] Essentially the same documents appeared in French translation in Paris as the *Livre Noir* as a result of the work of the French Communist journalist René Marchand in the archives with the cooperation of Pokrovsky.[20] These publications contained much valuable material, for instance, the protocols of the Franco-Russian military conversations. But they were rather unsystematic and based mainly on a selection from the files of correspondence from the Paris embassy and contained much that had little relevance to

Franco-Russian relations. They were very heavy on the dispatches of Izvolsky from Paris and less revealing of the instructions of the ministry from St. Petersburg.

At the same time the People's Commissariat of Foreign Affairs began to publish documents in their hands from the period of the war itself. The first of these was on the Greek question during the war.[21] This also suffered from a lack of system and was incomplete. There were no internal memoranda, no reports to the tsar on the Greek question nor material from Serbia and Bulgaria, whose governments' views were relevant; and only three telegrams from Sazonov as the responsible minister were included.[22] Further volumes appeared on the wartime diplomacy of the entente powers regarding the partition of Asiatic Turkey, based on a prepared dossier of material in the minister's archive. But it did not include material from the Second (former Asiatic) Department where a dossier had also been compiled on this theme.[23] Further volumes on Constantinople and the Straits question also relied on well-prepared dossiers of material in the Secret Archive of the ministry.[24] But the twenty-one thematic chapters artificially divided the subject into the themes in the ministerial dossiers, obscuring interrelationships between them. A number of the documents were reproduced in both publications as the themes overlapped. If further volumes had been produced on the entry into the war of Bulgaria, of Rumania, or of Italy, there would have had to have been a considerable amount of duplication. All these volumes were produced in very small print runs of about one thousand copies which illustrated the limited means and priorities of the time.

Apart from the Foreign Commissariat, Pokrovsky's *Tsentrarkhiv*, in a flurry of activity in the course of the 1920s, published numerous volumes of documents and diaries relating to Russian foreign policy as well as to internal affairs. Among those of interest here were the correspondence of the kaiser and the tsar (1923);[25] the diary of Kuropatkin on the eve of the Russo-Japanese War (1923); further extracts from the diaries of Kuropatkin and Linevich and other materials on the Russo-Japanese War (1926), from the diary of Polivanov (assistant war minister 1907–16), and, most importantly for foreign policy, the first volume of the diary of V.N. Lamsdorf for 1886–1890.[26] Pokrovsky added to these in 1926 with his own publication of nearly five hundred documents on Russia's relations with Turkey, Bulgaria, Rumania and Italy in the world war.[27] An important collection was published in 1925 on Russia's international financial relations in the crucial period of

1904–1906, edited by E.V. Preobrazhensky, a bolshevik close to Trotsky at this time.[28] The volume was published in a print run of nine thousand copies, surprisingly large for such a specialised publication, and several documentary articles appeared simultaneously in *Krasnyi Arkhiv* on the same theme.[29] Their aim was evidently to show, for the sake of the ongoing negotiations about the settlement of tsarist debts, that the loans of 1904–06 had been in support of the tsarist system and not for the needs of the people. The former general turned historian A.M. Zaionchkovsky also wrote a study of Russia's road to the Great War which included important unpublished documents, particularly from the Bosnian crisis.[30] It was not until I.V. Bestuzhev's publication in 1962 of documents on Russian policy in the Bosnian crisis that much further light was shed on it.[31]

As early as 1924 Pokrovsky expressed impatience with the limited publication of diplomatic documents from the Russian archives: 'In the whole world we are the sole guardians of the secrets of the imperialist war in so far as they are reflected in the Russian Foreign Ministry.' And in answer to his question 'How have they been used?', he replied 'Extremely badly ... Nothing prevents us from using this material from our class point of view ... We should do it, and not on such a microscopic scale as we do in the pages of *Krasnyi Arkhiv* but considerably more extensively'.[32]

The Russians were at some disadvantage in comparison with other powers as they could not control the publication of tsarist diplomatic documents which had remained abroad either in the former imperial embassies or in private hands of former Russian diplomats. A major 'leakage' occurred through the embassy in London. In 1921 Benno von Siebert, former secretary at the Russian embassy, published material from the correspondence of the ambassador Benckendorff for 1909–14 which touched on worldwide issues of Russian policy.[33] Later, in 1928, this collection was to be more systematically assembled with some additions into the Benckendorff correspondence for 1907–14.[34] Other documents from the London embassy had also been published outside Soviet control. With the permission of A.A. Sablin, the last imperial Russian chargé d'affaires at the embassy before the new Soviet government was recognised, the historian and East European specialist R.W. Seton-Watson was able in early 1924 to copy documents on the Balkan crisis of 1875–78, which immediately began to appear in the British *Slavonic Review*.[35] As a result of the same arrangement Alexander Meyendorff was able in 1926 to publish the diplomatic correspondence of Baron de Staal, Russian ambassador in London from 1886 to 1900.[36] And in 1925 Friedrich Stieve, pursuing the theme of the responsibility of Izvolsky for the world war, published his four-volume collection in German translation. This included most of the material in the Soviet 1922 volume on Franco-Russian relations and in volumes 1 and 2 of *Livre Noir*, but also contained some as yet unpublished documents which appear to have come from the Russian embassy in Paris.[37]

The stimulus for the planning of a Soviet publication of a systematic and comprehensive collection of documents from the imperial Russian Foreign Ministry was the initiatives taken in Germany and Britain. The German *Die Grosse Politik* had been planned since 1919 and appeared between 1922 and 1927 in forty volumes covering the years 1871 to 1914. The approval for the publication of a British collection was given in the summer of 1924, and by 1927 three volumes had already appeared. Work on the Austro-Hungarian collection began in summer 1926. These substantial publications put in question the Soviet claim to be the only power able to reveal the secrets of the Great War. They threatened to make the publication efforts of the Soviets look partial and haphazard. These inadequacies were evident to Pokrovsky. He wanted the Russians to fulfil their original promise to reveal the iniquities of the secret diplomacy of the imperialist powers. But how could they make a distinctive contribution appropriate to the special understanding which their Marxist outlook gave them? In an article in the journal of Soviet archivists in January 1927, Pokrovsky noted that the German and British publications were focused on the origins of the war and not on the war itself. He deeply regretted that while the Soviets had material on all the diplomatic secrets of the period of the war itself, yet 'in this battle by means of archive documents, we are not taking any part at all'. By the publication of a scholarly edition of the Russian documents 'we would explode a magnificent bomb, we would intervene in the debate and probably would force the review of a whole series of purely practical, as well as historical and theoretical questions. One should not forget that our publications laid the foundation for all the later ones'.[38] Already in May 1927 a new commission was established in the Communist Academy to consider the question.[39] Debate centred around what would be the most appropriate model, and a scheme was drawn up for a publication on the thematic principle in the same format as the German collection and with much the same chronological compass.[40]

In the autumn of 1927 Pokrovsky returned to the issue in an article in *Pravda* (28 November 1927). Recalling the publication of secret documents in 1917–18, he still regretted that 'Ten years have gone by and how little we have used this sharpest of weapons' – the archival document. 'We have published a great deal, but we still do not have a systematic collection of the documents of secret diplomacy of the imperialistic war. Yet it is precisely in that area that we could once again say a new word: the prewar documents are already so well known that one cannot expect any great revelations there. But the bourgeoisie are still carefully hiding the wartime diplomacy in their safes, understanding full well that this weapon is incomparably sharper. It is time for us to draw it from its scabbard.'[41] Pokrovsky explained in his introduction to the first volume in the series eventually published in 1931, that, 'for the struggle against imperialism we need to know definitely and exactly how it operates, what are its ways and means. And when the expansionist activity of the imperialists is unequivocally established by a series of irrefutable documents, we will have of course an indictment but not against an individual or even against an individual country but against a class – that class which held power in all the great powers in 1914 and which still holds power in most of them'.[42]

It is evident from Pokrovsky's comment in November 1927 that at that time no decision had been made about a competing Russian collection on the world war. But by the autumn of 1928 the issue was clearer. His colleague Maksakov was able to forecast that 'a series of diplomatic documents on the world war edited by M.N. Pokrovsky will undoubtedly have a world historical significance, and this will not only be for scholarship but it will also have a huge political significance'.[43]

Pokrovsky's emphasis as late as 1927 on the publication of the documents of the war period was curious as so much of the Soviet effort so far had been focused on those years in the publications of the Commissariat for Foreign Affairs and Pokrovsky's own volume, *Tsarist Russia in the World War*. It was evident that under the influence of the appearance of the German and British series, Pokrovsky had in mind a substantial systematic collection including the prewar diplomacy. But still the emphasis was to be the year 1914 and the period of the war itself as a first priority to make clear its imperialist character, even if the material would convincingly show this only on the entente side. The emphasis on the wartime period in Soviet publications had several causes. From the beginning the concern of the Bolshevik government had been to argue that the war was being fought not for the defence of small nations against German militarism, but for imperialist booty. The publication of documents on the wartime diplomacy and agreements in which the imperial government had participated would show this most graphically and would also condemn the provisional Russian government of 1917 for its failure to convincingly renounce them. To begin with the 1870s, as the German series did, would have reduced the impact of the Soviet publication on the ongoing debate in the late 1920s about the nature and origins of the war in which the Soviet historians (and government) wished to participate.

The Soviet historians evidently did not expect that adequate resources, staff and time could be devoted to the project to produce quickly a series comparable in scope to *Die Grosse Politik*. This and the political imperatives required the selection of some period as a priority. In the event, the volumes of the eventual Soviet third series (January 1914 to November 1917) did not produce so dramatic an impact, in spite of the absence of wartime material from the other powers. An unforeseen result was that the more lengthy second series (1900 to December 1913) was never finished, and we are thus left with only a fragment (though substantial) of a systematic publication of documents from the imperial Russian Foreign Ministry on the origins of the war.

In spite of their preconceived opinions about the war, Pokrovsky and his fellow-editors were determined that their publication of documents should be recognised also in the capitalist world as meeting the highest standards of scholarship. They should not lay themselves open to criticism by bourgeois historians. In early 1929 A.L. Popov subjected the German and British collections, as well as the earlier Soviet publications and the proposals of 1927, to a critical scrutiny in order to determine what would be the most effective and scholarly principles for the proposed publication. He concluded that the most appropriate format was the strictly day-to-day chronological one rather than the thematic approach used in the British and German documents. The allocation of a particular document to a particular date should depend on the date of reception in or despatch from the ministry. Within the correspondence for each day he established a hierarchy to determine the order of publication. The whole collection would be supplemented with full indices giving lists of documents relating to particular subjects and to particular countries to ease cross-referencing. This approach, which was put into effect in the Soviet series, allows the historian to see the complex interrelationships between different issues which were being dealt with by the ministry at any one point in time.[44] While most of the documents subsequently published in the Soviet series were from the archive of the Foreign Ministry, related material was also published from other archives such as that of the Council of Ministers, War Ministry, General Staff, and Finance Ministry, in contrast to some of the other publications on the origins of the war.

That the focus on the war years would reveal the secrets of only one of the opposing blocs was no problem for Pokrovsky, who considered the imperialism of the entente powers mainly responsible for the war. While the question of a documentary collection was being discussed in 1927 and 1928, Anglo-Soviet relations passed through a particularly tense period, even arousing a war scare in Moscow. In the autumn of 1928 Pokrovsky fiercely attacked the 'ententophilism' of the non-Marxist historian E.V. Tarle for suggesting a more general responsibility of the Great Powers for the war.[45] Towards the end of his life Pokrovsky came to recognise to some extent that the material he had used had produced a one-sided emphasis in his analysis, and he had been too soft on the Central Powers. And this was one of the accusations laid against him in the bitter attacks on him and his 'school' in the late 1930s, when war with Germany again threatened.[46]

It was evidently a struggle for Pokrovsky to bring his idea to fruition. Writing in mid-1928, Maksakov considered that the main obstacles had been overcome, but noted the difficulties which Pokrovsky had had to face, which he defined as 'financial, formal organisational and bureaucratic problems'.[47] For the impoverished Soviet state a case needed to be made for the allocation of limited financial resources and paper to such a project; the responsibility for the project was also a problem – should it be in the hands of the Commissariat for Foreign Affairs or some other commissariat? In January 1928 the French government had followed the lead of other powers and established a commission for the publication of French documents on the origins of the war covering the same lengthy period as *Die Grosse Politik*. Russia was left as the only major participant in the war without a systematic project for publication. During the course of the first half of 1928 it seems that the matter was decided in principle, but it was not until 22 June 1929 that the Presidium of the Central Executive Committee of the Congress of Soviets of the U.S.S.R. issued a resolution recognising as 'necessary' the publication of documents on the history of Russian foreign policy from 1904 to 1917 and initially on the war years. A Commission for Publication of Documents of the Epoch of Imperialism was established, chaired by Pokrovsky and directly subordinated to the Central Executive Committee rather than to any particular commissariat.[48]

The contemporary situation exercised an influence on the project in another way. The isolation of the Soviet state demanded the fullest possible development of the Rapallo policy towards Germany, including the expansion of cultural ties. This met a response on the German side because of Pokrovsky's outlook on the origins of the world war and the expectations that publication of documents from the Russian archives by a regime which was hostile to the tsarist government and to the entente would add to the weight of evidence against Germany's exclusive 'war guilt'. The Germans were already translating the earlier volumes published by the Commissariat for Foreign Affairs on the wartime diplomacy of the Allies as well as Pokrovsky's own volume.

In 1925 a delegation of German scholars visited Moscow and Leningrad for the two-hundredth anniversary of the Academy of Sciences. Within the pro-Russian camp on the German political scene an important role in the development of cultural relations was played by the Deutsche Gesellschaft zum Studium Osteuropas, led by the historian and nationalist politician Otto Hoetzsch, who had also been close to official circles as a Russian expert before 1914 and during the war. In 1925 he declared his opposition to Locarno and sought to encourage the expansion of cultural links between Germany and the U.S.S.R. With this in mind, a small exhibition of new Soviet literature was planned to mark the occasion of (though not to celebrate) the tenth anniversary of the Bolshevik Revolution. To prepare for this, the secretary of the association, Dr Schmidt-Ott visited Moscow in November 1927. There he met Lunacharsky and Pokrovsky (who amongst his many other responsibilities was a deputy commissar in the Commissariat of Enlightenment), and they persuaded him that a larger event would be appropriate in order to introduce German and Soviet historians to each other and lay the basis for their cooperation. Pokrovsky sought to establish an agreement for the exchange of archival material and for mutual cooperation in the use of each others' archives. The State Printing House promised to let the Osteuropa Gesellschaft know of planned historical publications, particularly of documents, and to let them have copies. Schmidt-Ott was impressed

with the standing of the Deutsche Gesellschaft zum Studium
Osteuropas amongst prominent political and scholarly figures in
Moscow. Its value for cementing multifaceted ties between Ger-
many and the new Russia was clearly appreciated.[49]

The result of Schmidt-Ott's visit was the Russian Historical
Week in Berlin, 7–14 July 1928. Here Hoetzsch met Pokrovsky,
who was already seriously ill and under medical treatment.
Pokrovsky suffered from bladder cancer from which he died in
April 1932. One consequence of this was that he was frequently in
Berlin for treatment during the following years when the documentary publication was being planned and was able to keep in
contact with Hoetzsch. In spite of Pokrovsky's Marxism, his per-
sonality, energy and scholarly credentials strongly impressed
Hoetzsch.[50] At the meeting in Berlin in July 1928 Pokrovsky
revealed to the German historians the Soviet plan for the publication of diplomatic documents on the war period. In order to give
them a more international impact, Pokrovsky proposed to Hoetzsch that the Russian documents should appear in a simultaneous
German translation. They returned to the issue on a further visit of
Pokrovsky to Berlin in July 1929. The negotiations were evidently
complicated. Hoetzsch and Hans Jonas visited Moscow in 1929
and 1930, and only on 6 June 1930 was an agreement concluded
between the Soviet Commission on the one hand and Hoetzsch
and Hans Jonas for the Deutsche Gesellschaft zum Studium Osteuropas on the other whereby the eleven volumes of Russian documents from January 1914 to November 1915 (to the entrance of
Bulgaria into the war) would be published in a more or less simultaneous German translation, beginning with five volumes on January to August 1914.

It cannot be said that without agreement with the Germans the
project would never have come to fruition. But the content of the
agreement, as well as the limitations of Soviet resources at the
time and the strategy of the Soviet government towards Germany, suggest that it was of more than incidental significance.
The Osteuropa Gesellschaft were given all rights for publication of
the German and of any other non-Russian edition of the documents. There was to be close correlation between the publication
of the Russian and the German editions, and the Soviet editing,
footnotes, and introductions were not to be tampered with in the
German translation. Hoetzsch had to see to the translation of the
documents and could add further separate footnotes as necessary
for the German reader. But the printing of both editions would be

in Germany. In illustration of the paper and printing problems in Soviet Russia at the time, even for the Russian edition the State Printing House was to supply the matrices but the Germans would supply the paper and the printing capacity at the Hartung press in Königsberg. And it was agreed that the Russian edition of each volume would not appear before the German, as the Soviet Union was not a signatory of the Berne Copyright Convention of 1886.[51]

Between 1931 and 1934 the first five volumes appeared of *Mezhdunarodnye Otnosheniya v Epokhu Imperializma. Dokumenty iz arkhivov tsarskogo i vremennogo pravitel'stv* (International Relations in the Age of Imperialism. Documents from the Archives of the Tsarist and Provisional Governments). These were to cover the first seven months of 1914 in the Soviet series III for 1914 to November 1917. The volumes contained more than 2,200 documents in simultaneous Russian and German editions printed in Königsberg. For the first volume covering January to March 1914, published in 1931, Pokrovsky wrote a substantial analytical introduction. He recognised that 'to be precise in this first volume there are relatively few large documents which have not been published before' but that subsequent volumes would make up for this. But by the summer of 1932 Pokrovsky was too ill to work and unable to contribute his views on the expanding collection, and later volumes lacked any similar introductory commentary.[52]

In Germany, Hoetzsch and the Foreign Ministry expected much from the publication of the Russian documents to enable them to counter the war-guilt accusations of the entente powers. In his speech on the theme of 'Revisionism and War Guilt' at the celebratory meeting for the publication of the first volume in German on 28 June 1931, Hoetzsch sought to emphasise the scholarly nature of the project and avoid anything in the sense of revisionist propaganda.[53] But the German publishers had been led to expect more and in December 1931 complained that the first volume was 'unfortunately a justifiable disappointment for those circles concerned with challenging the war-guilt clause, because it contains (and this is our view also) not one really new or weighty document which could convince our enemies and the neutrals of the error of their opinions'. Hoetzsch's rather limp reply was only that at least it did not contain anything about any offensive plans by Germany.[54] He was valued at this time at a high level in the Soviet Union for his work and met prominent Soviet personalities, visited factories, collective farms, and the Dnieper Dam project, which impressed him enormously. On 1 May 1931 he was invited to take a place on the reviewing rostrum on Red Square, standing only a few yards from the Soviet leaders themselves.[55]

In August 1933 Hoetzsch again travelled to Moscow to discuss the publication of the following volumes of wartime documents. By this time in Germany, since Hitler's accession to power, anti-Soviet tendencies had become more pronounced. Hoetzsch, like many other intellectuals, wrote in praise of the new beginnings in Germany. But increasingly he was unable to reconcile these views with his unchanged conviction of the need for friendly cooperation between Germany and the U.S.S.R. However, in the new circumstances Neurath approved of Hoetzsch's continuing cooperation with the Russians; and Hoetzsch kept him and the German ambassador informed of the negotiations. The political value given to this arrangement was also evident on the Soviet side, which regarded it as a test of what residual possibilities of cultural cooperation with Germany remained. The Soviet Commission agreed with Hoetzsch's wish to speed up publication of the wartime series and avoid as far as possible overlap with the already published material on the war, as much of this had already appeared in German. Hoetzsch reported that 'The negotiations, in spite of all the technical difficulties, were far easier (than the earlier ones) as the Russian side was conciliatory and willing to negotiate in every respect'. Tomsky, chairman of the State Printing House, took part in the negotiations, and the agreement was put before the Central Committee of the Party for approval.[56]

The following six half-volumes (6–8 of the Soviet series III) on the period from the outbreak of war until the entrance of Bulgaria into the war in October 1915 appeared in Russian in 1935 (now printed in Leningrad) and in German between 1934 and 1936. This was one of the last examples of Soviet-German cultural cooperation to survive into the Hitler period. The Soviets published an additional two wartime volumes (9 and 10) in 1937 and 1938 on the period October 1915 to April 1916, but the Germans were not interested in these. Over six thousand documents had been published in this third series covering the war period and the year 1914.

Apart from this major series and the publications in *Krasnyi Arkhiv*, the only other significant collection of documents from the imperial Russian Foreign Ministry to appear in the 1930s was a curious volume containing 180 documents on Russian policy in Bulgaria between 1885 and 1896 which revealed the underhand methods by which agents of the tsarist government and the tsar Alexander III himself sought to influence the situation in the

Russian interest.[57] The collection was compiled on the orders of the Bulgarian Communist Party leaders, G. Dimitrov and V. Kolarov, and selected by P. Pavlovich, a Bulgarian Communist. The documents were followed by an article on Russia and the eastern question in the decade before the 1875 Balkan crisis written by A. Popov on the basis of other unpublished documents discovered in the Foreign Ministry archives by Pavlovich. The period chosen is significant at this late date as it still emphasised the imperialist nature of Russian policy towards Bulgaria rather than its liberationist character. By 1940 if not earlier, with Stalin's criticism of Engels' views on tsarist foreign policy, such publications were no longer possible. Indeed in the post-war period the major collection of documents published by the Soviets on tsarist foreign policy from the mid-nineteenth century was specifically focussed on the 'objectively' liberationist character of tsarist policy in Bulgaria, now that it was in the Soviet sphere of influence, once again 'liberated'.[58]

While continuing work on the subsequent volumes of Pokrovsky's project for April 1916 to November 1917 (which never appeared), the Soviet historians gave precedence in the late 1930s to beginning publication of material from the second series, now to consist of twenty-four volumes from 1900 to 1913. Volumes 18 to 20 appeared between 1938 and 1940 containing more than two hundred documents in each of six half-volumes covering the period May 1910 to October 1912. No explanation was given for beginning towards the end of the second series, and the caution of Soviet historians at this time is probably shown by the fact that none of the volumes had an introduction. But it is evident that the series still found particular favour as they now appeared in a larger format, on much better paper, and generally with a higher quality presentation. Also they were printed in increased print runs of five thousand copies, and as late as 1940 volume 20 ran to a surprising fifteen thousand copies. In spite of the Stalinist purges and the fact that Pokrovsky's writings were being severely criticised, a very high standard was maintained in the selection and editing of this series. But E.B. Pashukanis, one of the members of Pokrovsky's commission for the publication of documents, and Y.A. Berzin, Pokrovsky's successor as chairman, were shot in 1937–38. Pashukanis had also been a contributor to *Krasnyi Arkhiv*, and one of his fellow contributors and pupil of Pokrovsky, G.S. Fridlyand was also labelled as an 'enemy of the people' among the 130 historians arrested at the time.[59] The continued publication of the series contrasted with the fact that only two significant

collections of documents on tsarist foreign policy were published
in the last six years of *Krasnyi Arkhiv* from 1935–41.[60]

It is remarkable that the agreement with Hoetzsch still remained
effective through this period, although the German translations
now followed much later. He was allowed to visit Moscow for the
last time in October 1934 to continue negotiations on the documentary publication, presumably now on the pre-1914 material of the
Soviet second series.[61] But Hoetzsch was unable to sustain his position in Germany, which was too closely associated with the idea of
good relations with the Soviet Union. In May 1935 he was
brusquely informed that his position at the University of Berlin
would not be renewed for the following academic year, and this
was followed up with vicious attacks on him as a 'friend of Bolshe-
vism'.[62] This naturally put in question the cooperation for publication of the Russian documents. However, Goebbels' Propaganda
Ministry, having pondered the matter for many months, concluded
at the end of December 1936 that the links should not be broken,
though any introduction had to pass the censorship and the volumes should only be advertised in the specialist journals.[63] For the
Soviets also in terms of their general foreign policy at this time, as
Jonathan Haslam concludes, 'it made good sense to mend fences
with the Germans'.[64] As a result, until 1939 Hoetzsch remained in
contact with the Soviet commission through the historian A.S.
Yerusalimsky.[65] Yerusalimsky (1901–64) was a graduate of the Institute of Red Professors and with the purge of Berzin, he became at
the age of only thirty-six the effective chairman of the commission
and chief editor of the documentary publication.[66] So in spite of the
twists and turns of Soviet-German relations, while the publication
of the Soviet second series (18–20) continued in Moscow, the typescripts for the volumes continued to be passed through the German
embassy to Hoetzsch to prepare the translation.

In the early months of 1941 the Soviets transferred to Hoetzsch
the Russian typescript for the as yet unpublished volume 21 part
1 (October to December 1912). But while the Soviets were making
their edition ready for publication, and while Hoetzsch was
engaged in translation, Operation Barbarossa began. In the chaos
of the first months of the war, the Soviets dropped publication as
a nonurgent matter and never took up this series again. But Hoetzsch completed his translation and was able to see it through to
publication in a German edition in late 1941. So the fullest collection of Russian material on the period of the First Balkan War
appeared only in this German language edition and has not been

much used by historians of the period. The German translation of two halves of volume 20 of the Soviet series (March to October 1912) appeared even later for unexplained 'technical reasons' – as late as 1943 – but no mention was now made of the origin of the documents. In October 1941 Hoetzsch also had the Soviet volume 21 part 2 (December 1912 to January 1913) 'ready for the press' and possibly the Russian typescripts for later volumes.[67] But none of these ever appeared either in Russian or German. In November 1943 Hoetzsch lost his library of thirty thousand volumes and all his personal possessions when his house in Berlin was destroyed by bombing while he was in hospital. Only the manuscripts for further volumes of the Russian documentary publication survived as they had been kept in a safe.[68] In May 1944 he wrote to the military historian Schwertfeger that another volume was ready for publication and that 'further volumes are in an early or advanced stage of editing'.[69] Even after the end of the war, Hoetzsch sought to arrange a meeting with A.V. Gorbatov, the Soviet commander in Berlin in July 1945, to discuss the continuation of the documentary publication and the renewal of Soviet-German cultural relations. Although the Soviets also showed interest in such a meeting, it never took place because of the fragility of Hoetzsch's health. He died late in 1946.[70]

The Soviet series was never continued in spite of the fact that some volumes, perhaps all those for 1913, were already completed and ready for publication. We can only speculate on the reasons for this. Priorities had changed; resources were not available immediately after 1945; the cooperation with the Germans was an embarrassment; the issue of war guilt for the First World War was no longer a live political issue; the cultural atmosphere in the late Stalin years was not conducive to publication of such a collection. But even when times changed after Stalin's death, the project was not resumed (in contrast the French brought their collection to completion as late as the 1960s). That the old project was no longer favoured was evident in 1960 when publication of a new series of Russian foreign policy documents began under a commission headed by the foreign minister himself, Andrei Gromyko.[71] The preface made no mention of the 1930s project, even though it grandiosely outlined a new programme of publications from the imperial Foreign Ministry archives in five series: 1801–15, 1815–30, 1830–56, 1856–78, 1878–95 and 1895–17. The quality of this series as a documentary publication is impeccable, and it has not yet been fully digested by historians of Russian foreign policy. In

thirty-five years the collection in fourteen volumes has reached
the year 1827. We should see the documents of the early twentieth
century on the origins of the First World War in print sometime in
the first years of the twenty-second century!

The history of the publication of the Russian documents on the
origins of the war bears the impact of the time. The driving energy
of Pokrovsky, who put his authority behind the project, the politically important debate about the nature and origins of the war,
the distinctive ideological preoccupations of Soviet historians, and
the importance of Soviet-German relations, first under Rapallo
and later as a residual cultural link with Germany under Hitler, all
had an impact on the project. In these circumstances, it is remarkable that the documents in the major Soviet series were selected
and edited to such a high standard so that they still remain as the
essential starting point for examination of the Russian role in the
origins of the war.

Notes

1. *Afganskoe Razgranichenie. Peregovory mezhdu Rossiei i Velikobritaniei 1872–1885*
   (St. Petersburg, 1886).
2. I.V. Bestuzhev, *Bor'ba po voprosam vneshnei politiki Rossii, 1906–1910* (Moscow,
   1961); Caspar Ferenczi, *Aussenpolitik und Offentlichkeit in Russland, 1906–1912*
   (Husum, 1982).
3. Osobyi komitet dal'nego vostoka: kantselariya, *Dokumenty po peregovoram c
   Yaponiei 1903–4 khranyashchie v kantselarii osobogo komiteta Dal'nego Vostoka* (St.
   Petersburg, 1905).
4. V.A. Burtsev, *Tsar i vneshnyaya politika. Vinovniki russko-yaponskoi voiny po
   tainym dokumentam* (Berlin, 1910) gives the whole history of the episode, the
   documents themselves, and Lamsdorf's memorandum. Also see V.N. Lamsdorf, 'Zapiska po povodu sbornika tainykh dokumentov' *Vestnik Evropy,*
   1907, no. 4.
5. Ministerstvo Inostrannykh Del, *Reformy v Makedonii. Diplomaticheskaya perepiska (1902–1905)* 2 issues, (St. Petersburg, 1906); *Sbornik diplomaticheskikh
   dokumentov kasayushchikhsya zaklyuchenii rybolovnoi konventsii mezhdu Rossiei i
   Yaponiei* (St. Petersburg, 1907); *Sbornik diplomaticheskikh dokumentov kasayush-
   chikhsa sobytii v Persii, 1906–1911,* 7 issues, (St. Petersburg, 1911–1913);
   *Sbornik diplomaticheskikh dokumentov po Mongol'skomu voprosu (23 avg.-2
   noyabr 1912)* (St. Petersburg, 1914); *Sbornik diplomaticheskikh dokumentov
   kasayushchikhsya sobytii na Balkanskom poluostrove (avgust 1912 – iyul' 1913)*
   (St. Petersburg, 1914); *Sbornik diplomaticheskikh dokumentov, Reformy v Armenii
   (26 noyabr 1912 – 10 maya 1914)* (St. Petersburg, 1914); *Sbornik diplomaticheskikh dokumentov. Peregovory ot 10–24 iyulya 1914 predshestvovashie voine* (St.

Petersburg, 1914); *Sbornik diplomaticheskikh dokumentov (19 iyuli – 19 okt. 1914) predshestvovayshie voiny s Turtsieyu* (Petrograd, 1914).

6. S. Zarnitskii and L. Trofimova, *Tak nachinalsya narkomindel* (Moscow, 1984), pp. 7–15.

7. A. Yur'ev, 'Gosudarstvennyi arkhiv vneshnei politiki i ego politicheskoe znachenie' *Arkhivnoe Delo*, 47, 1938, p. 117.

8. Zarnitskii, p. 15.

9. *Sbornik sekretnykh dokumentov iz arkhiva byvshego ministerstva inostrannykh del*, 7 issues, (Petrograd, 1917–18).

10. M. Rabinovich, 'Publikatorskaya deyatel'nost' Nikolaya Markina' *Arkhivnoe Delo* 50, 1939, pp. 98–102; M.S. Seleznev, 'Sovetskaya publikmatsiya diplomaticheskikh dokumentov v kontse 1917 – nachale 1918 goda' *Arkheografich-eskii Ezhegodnik za 1962* (Moscow, 1963), pp. 338–46.

11. Undated memorandum by Neratov, *Krasnyi Arkhiv* 6, 1924 p. 220. Henceforth referred to as KA.

12. Yur'ev, pp. 117–9. The archive is now the Arkhiv vneshnei politiki Rossii.

13. On Pokrovsky see John Barber, *Soviet Historians in Crisis, 1928–1932* (New York, 1981), pp. 19–27; also V. Maksakov, 'M.N. Pokrovskii i voprosy arkhiv-nogo stroitel'stva' *Arkhivnoe Delo* 16 (1928), p. 11.

14. 'Tri Soveshchaniya' *Vestnik NKID*, no. 1, 1919.

15. Pokrovsky, KA 1 (1922), p. 1.

16. KA 16 (1926).

17. KA 45 (1931), p. 52; 63 (1934), p. 54.

18. For instance on the Young Turk Revolution: KA 43 (1930), pp. 3–54; 44 (1931), pp. 3–39; 45 (1931), pp. 27–52; and on the Spanish revolution of 1873–74: KA 49 (1931), pp. 3–54.

19. *Materialy po istorii franko-russkikh otnoshenii za 1910–1914 gg. Sbornik sekretnykh diplomaticheskikh dokumentov byvshego imperatorskogo Rossiiskogo Ministerstva inostrannykh del* (Moscow, 1922).

20. René Marchand, *Livre Noir*, 3 vols., Paris 1922, 1923, 1927. For some reason the correspondence with Izvolsky relating to the Liman von Sanders affair in the Soviet publication was omitted by Marchand.

21. E.A. Adamov, ed., *Evropeiskie derzhavy i Gretsiya v epokhu mirovoi voiny po sekretnym dokumentam b. M.I.D.* NKID (Moscow, 1922).

22. See the criticisms by A. Popov, *Arkhivnoe Delo* 18 (1929), p. 35.

23. E.A. Adamov, ed., *Razdel Aziatskoi Turtsii*, 2 vols. (Moscow, 1923–24); Popov, p. 36. See note 40.

24. *Konstantinopol i Prolivy*, 2 vols. (Moscow, 1925–26); German translation, 4 vols. (Dresden, 1930).

25. *Perepiska Vilgel'ma Gogentsollerna s Nikolaem Romanovym* with an introduction by M.N. Pokrovsky, Tsentrarkhiv (Moscow, 1923). Pokrovsky was evidently rather piqued that the letters had 'as a result of a most regrettable misunder-standing' at the former Main Archive (p. III) already been published in their original English in Germany in 1919 (W. Goetz, ed., *Briefe Wilhelms II an den Zaren*, Berlin, 1919 – in the original English). Pokrovsky added the incomplete telegraphic correspondence held in Moscow. Only thirty-five out of a total of 152 items in the publication originate with the tsar. Twenty-eight telegrams had been published by E.V. Tarle in *Byloe*, 1917, nos. 1 and 2 but could not subsequently be found in the Romanov archive. Other letters of the tsar appear in *Die Grosse Politik*, e.g., vol. 19, ii. no. 6247.

26. M.N. Pokrovsky, ed., *Dnevnik A.N. Kuropatkina* (Nizhnyi Novgorod, 1923); *Russkoyaponskaya voina: iz dnevnikov A.N. Koropatkina i N.P. Linevicha* with an introduction by M.N. Pokrovsky, Tsentrarkiv (Leningrad, 1926); A.M. Zaionchkovsky, *Iz dnevnikov i vospominanii po dolzhnost' voennogo ministra i ego pomoshchnika (1907–1916)* 2 vols., (Moscow, 1924); *Dnevnik V.N. Lamzdorfa (1886–1890)* edited and introduced by F.A. Rothstein (Moscow-Leningrad, 1926). A further volume of the Lamsdorf diary for 1891–92 was published in 1934; some extracts for 1894–95 in KA, 46 (1931), pp. 3–37; further extracts for 1894–96 in *Voprosy istorii* (1977), pp. 98–115, edited by I.A. D'yakonova; and finally the complete edition for the years 1894–96, edited and translated by I.A. D'yakonova (Moscow, 1991).

27. M.N. Pokrovsky, *Tsarskaya Rossiya v mirovoi voine* (Moscow, 1926) German translation, Berlin, 1927.

28. *Russkiye Finansy i Evropeiskaya Birzha v 1904–1905gg* Tsentrarkhiv (Moscow, 1926) 400 pp.

29. KA, 10, 1925, pp. 5–35 (Kokovtsov's negotiations in Paris, December–January 1905–06; 10 (1925), pp. 36–40; 11–12, (1926), pp. 421–32.

30. *Podgotovka Rossii k mirovoi voine v mezhdunarodnom otnoshenii* (Moscow-Leningrad, 1926) documents, pp. 339–92.

31. I.V. Bestuzhev, 'Bor'ba v pravyashchikh krugakh Rossii po voprosam vneshnei politiki vo vremya Bosniiskogo krizisa. Publikatsiya dokumentov' *Istoricheskii Arkhiv* 5 (1962), pp. 113–47.

32. *Arkhivnoe Delo* 2 (1924), p. 6.

33. *Diplomatische Aktenstücke zur Geschichte der Ententepolitik der Vortriegsjahren* (Berlin and Leipzig, 1921) translated into English by G.A. Schreiner, *Entente Diplomacy and the War* (New York, 1922).

34. B. von Siebert, ed., *Graf Benckendorffs diplomatische Schriftwechsel*, 3 vols. (Leipzig and Berlin, 1928).

35. 'Unprinted Documents. Anglo-Russian Relations During the Eastern Crisis', *Slavonic Review*, vols. 3–6 (1924–28, 1931). Some of this material relating to 1878–80 was copied by W.N. Medicott and published only in 1986: W.N. Medicott and R.G. Weeks, eds., *Slavonic and East European Review* 64 (1986), pp. 81–99, 237–55.

36. *Correspondence diplomatique du Baron de Staal (1886–1900)*, 2 vols. (Paris, 1926).

37. F. Stieve, ed., *Der diplomatische Schriftwechsel Iswolskis 1911–1914*, 4 vols. (Berlin, 1925). These volumes were published under a commission from the German Foreign Ministry. The list of documents gives the source only for all those previously published. The documents need to be treated with caution. Several omissions in documents in the Stieve collection are noted in the MO series. The meaning of one item to Neratov on the Straits question (7 December 1911) is completely altered by the mistranslation of a Russian double negative.

38. *Arkhivnoe Delo* 10 (1927), pp. 6–7.

39. Gerd Voigt, *Otto Hoetzsch 1876–1946. Wissenschaft und Politik im Leben eines deutschen Historiker* (Berlin, 1978), p. 236.

40. A.L. Popov, 'O plane i priemakh izdaniya diplomaticheskikh dokumentov mirovoi voiny' *Arkhivnoe Delo* 18 (1929), p. 37.

41. M.N. Pokrovsky, *Imperialistskaya voina* (Sotsekgiz, Moscow, 1934), p. 357 and as quoted by V. Maksakov in 'M.N. Pokrovskii i voprosy arkhivnoe stroitel'stva' in *Arkhivnoe Delo* 16 (1928), p. 27.

42. Kommissiya po izdaniyu dokumentov epokha imperializma. Chief editor M.N. Pokrovskii, *Mezhdunarodnyye otnosheniya v epokhu imperializma. Dokumenty iz arkhivov tsarskogo i vremennogo pravitel'stv* series III, vol. 1 (Moscow, 1931) p. X. Hereafter cited as MO.
43. Maksakov, p. 24.
44. Popov, pp. 34–48.
45. Barber, pp. 35–36.
46. M.N. Pokrovsky, *Imperialistskaya voina* (Sotsekgiz, Moscow, 1934), p. 1; A. Yerusalimskii, 'Proizkhozhdenie mirovoi imperialisticheskoi voiny 1914–18 v osveshchenii M.N. Pokrovskogo' in *Protiv istoricheskikh kontseptsii M.N. Pokrovskogo*, part 1, AN SSSR (Moscow-Leningrad, 1939), pp. 502–3.
47. Maksakov, p. 22.
48. *Arkhivnoe Delo* 19 (1929), p. 113.
49. Voigt, pp. 208–11.
50. Barber, pp. 22–23 and p. 151 note 74; Voigt, pp. 208–18.
51. Voigt, pp. 236–7.
52. MO, III, i, p. XI. In 1935 a condensed single volume collection appeared of documents selected from the first five volumes of MO for January to August 1914. It was labelled as volume I, but no further ones appeared. It was intended to make the main items of the collection accessible to a wider audience and appeared in a print run of ten thousand. It included a long interpretive introduction by the ill-fated Y.A. Berzin, Pokrovsky's successor as chairman of the Commission.
53. Hoetzsch to Schmidt-Ott, 15 June 1931 in Voigt, p. 336. The German edition appeared as *Die internationale Beziehungen im Zeitalter des Imperialismus* and confusingly numbered the series differently from the Russian version. Hereafter cited as IBZI.
54. Voigt, p. 238. Hoetzsch had complete confidence in Pokrovsky and the Soviet editors. For instance, in his introduction to volume 5 of the German edition on the July crisis, in a careful analysis of the different numberings of correspondence by the Russian Foreign Ministry and by Hartwig in Belgrade, he showed that the suspicions that some correspondence was missing were unjustified: IBZI, series 1, vol. 5, pp. IV–VII.
55. Voigt, p. 256.
56. Ibid.
57. P. Pavlovich, ed., *Avantyury russkogo tsarizma v Bolgarii* (Moscow, 1935).
58. Institut Slavyanovedenie, *Osvobozhdenie Bolgarii ot turetskogo iga*, 3 vols. (Moscow, 1964).
59. Barber, pp. 139–40; Yur'ev, p. 121–2.
60. These were correspondence relating to the German seizure of Kiaochao in 1897 in KA, 87, 1938, pp. 19–68; and to the Franco-German crisis of 1875 in KA, 91, 1938, pp. 106–49, though most of these latter were reports from the ambassador Oubril in Berlin, and only three items were from Gorchakov himself.
61. Voigt, p. 257.
62. Ibid., p. 263–4.
63. Ibid., p. 265.
64. Jonathan Haslam, *The Struggle for Collective Security, 1933–1939* (New York, 1984), p. 126.
65. Voigt, p. 269.
66. Ibid., p. 263.

67. Hoetzsch in IBZI, II, 4, i, p. ii.
68. Voigt, p. 271.
69. Voigt, p. 269, note 49. The papers of the Soviet Commission are in the Archive of Russian Foreign Policy in Moscow, and it is probable that the manuscripts of the unpublished volumes are there. I have been unable to confirm this by a visit to the archive for the writing of this chapter.
70. Ibid, p. 276.
71. *Vneshnyaya politika Rossii v XIX i XX vekakh* (Moscow, 1960–85), incomplete.

§ Chapter 3

CLIO DECEIVED
Patriotic Self-Censorship in Germany After the Great War

Holger H. Herwig

Joseph Fouché, a man for all seasons who served the Directory, Consulate, Empire, and restoration as minister of police, was once reputed to have stated that any two lines from any *oeuvre* would suffice to have its author hanged. Indeed, the efforts of various Germans, both in official and private capacities, to undertake what John Röhl has termed 'patriotic self-censorship' with regard to the origins of the Great War reflect the sentiment expressed by the great French censor a century earlier.[1] For nearly fifty years, until Fritz Fischer's *Griff nach der Weltmacht* appeared in 1961, which in many ways offered German readers the findings of the Italian author Luigi Albertini, the German interpretation of the origins of the First World War was dominated in large measure by the efforts of 'patriotic self-censors', and particularly by the historical writings of Alfred von Wegerer.[2]

Let me state at the outset that I accept the basic tenets of Fischer's research – with the notable exceptions of the allegedly decisive 'war council' of 8 December 1912 and the so-called 'bid for *world* power' in 1914. The Hamburg historian, assisted by a coterie of talented students, has convincingly documented that Vienna and Berlin opted for war in July 1914 in the belief that time was running out for both of them. In the case of Austria-Hungary, only a military strike against Serbia could retard the centrifugal forces of nationalism within the Dual Monarchy; for Germany, only preventive war with Russia would allow the Reich to secure continental hegemony before the Russian 'Great Program' of rearmament was completed by 1917. Statesmen and soldiers in both Vienna and Berlin in July 1914 assumed a 'strike now better than later' mentality. In both capitals, they accepted the 'calculated risk' of a general European war in order to shore up – and, if at all possible, to expand – Otto von Bismarck's position of semihegemony in Europe.

This essay will trace the genesis and course of the official campaign in the Weimar Republic (and beyond) to counter Allied charges of German war guilt (Article 231 of the Treaty of Versailles), and offer some suggestions concerning its impact upon subsequent German affairs. The inquiry will show that the German government as early as 1914, and especially during the period from November 1918 to June 1919, sought to 'organise' materials in order to answer questions concerning the origins of the war. Further, it will show that from June 1919 through the Third Reich, key elements of the German bureaucracy mounted a massive and successful campaign of disinformation that purveyed false propaganda through a wide range of channels. These included the War Guilt Section (Kriegsschuldreferat) of the Foreign Ministry, which disseminated its official stance on war guilt most notably through two agencies which it recruited to this end – the Working Committee of German Associations (Arbeitsausschuss Deutscher Verbände) and the Center for the Study of the Causes of the War (Zentralstelle zur Erforschung der Kriegsschuldfrage) – as well as a parliamentary Committee of Enquiry (Untersuchungsausschuss). Writers were also engaged either directly or indirectly by the Foreign Ministry to propagate its views, to organise translations of foreign studies sympathetic to the German cause, and to channel the Wilhelmstrasse's official line to German schools and diplomatic missions via newspapers and radio. Finally, some comments will be directed toward several important memoirs which were either 'ordered' by patriotic editors or watered down in their final published versions in an attempt to preserve a national-conservative version of history.

By selectively editing documentary collections, suppressing honest scholarship, subsidising pseudoscholarship, underwriting mass propaganda, and overseeing the export of this propaganda, especially to Britain, France and the United States, the patriotic self-censors in Berlin exerted a powerful influence on public and elite opinion in Germany and, to a lesser extent, outside Germany.

Their efforts polluted historical understanding both at home and abroad well into the post-1945 period. Indeed, the acrimonious debate since 1983 concerning the originality of Kurt Riezler's diaries, especially during the critical July crisis, is but the most outward symptom of this ongoing historical conundrum.

The significance of the campaign of official and semiofficial obfuscation and perversion of fact extends well beyond the history of Germany or the origins of the Great War. It raises basic questions concerning the role of the historian in society, scholarly integrity, decency, and public morality. It further illustrates the universal problem of establishing the critical record of events that are sufficiently vital to the national interest to become the objects of partisan propaganda. What is the present generation, for example, to make of the collective and concerted efforts of eminent German scholars purposefully to distort their countrymen's study of history and sociology of knowledge? Does a perverse law operate whereby those events that are most important are hardest to understand because they attract the greatest attention from mythmakers and charlatans? And is a nation well served when its intellectual establishment conspires to obstruct honest investigation into national catastrophes, upon which past, present, and future vital national interests can be reassessed? The far-reaching effects of the resulting disinformation are incalculable.

Several other, related issues require to be addressed tangentially. Nazi expansionism clearly fed upon the fertile intellectual basis laid down for it by the patriotic self-censors in the 1920s. In other words, Adolf Hitler's radical 'revisionism' was already well rooted in public and elite opinion under the Weimar Republic. Finally, the export of this propaganda to Britain, France, and the United States did its part, however major or minor, to undermine the moral and eventually the strategic terms of the settlement of 1919. No less a statesman than Gustav Stresemann clearly recognised that patriotic self-censorship served to buttress his policy of rapprochement with the West as a necessary precondition for revision of what most Germans considered to be the most onerous clauses of the Versailles *Diktat*.

Last but not least, my investigation bears directly upon the nature and meaning of the '1914 analogy', which continues to influence political science thought on the possible causes of a third world war. I suggest that the history upon which that analogy was based has been distorted. It serves no purpose to continue to believe that Europe 'slid' into war unknowingly in 1914, that no nation harbored aggressive tendencies during the July crisis, and that fate or providence alone designed this cruel course of events. Indeed, the '1914 analogy' ought to be rethought and reworked in light of the actual mindset of German political, diplomatic, and military leaders in 1914.

To sum up: Clio was, in fact, deceived in Germany as early as 1914. It is not my purpose to indict either individuals or nations. We might do well to keep before us the words of the epitaph that the historian Hans Delbrück chose for his gravestone:

> Veritatem colui
> Patriam delixi.[3]

Deployment of Illusions

On 3 August 1914, the day before the Great War officially began, the Imperial German government published a 'coloured book' to explain its stance on the origins of the conflict. Entitled the *Deutsches Weissbuch*, the tome represented a hasty sifting of the archives of the Foreign Office. On the last day of that month, Foreign Secretary Gottlieb von Jagow directed his under-secretary, Alfred Zimmermann, to entertain a more 'comprehensive publication' of documents for what Jagow was certain would become a heated debate. He instructed Zimmermann to take as his *leitmotiv* the following: 'The ring of entente politics encircled us ever more tightly.'[4] The most knowledgeable authority on the war-guilt question, Imanuel Geiss has suggested that this was already the germ cell of the postwar documentary editions. In fact, Legation Secretary Bernhard Wilhelm von Bülow, who for much of the war oversaw the holdings of the Wilhelmstrasse as political archivist and who would head its attempts at patriotic self-censorship after 1919, probably undertook already during the Great War a first 'ordering' of the documents concerning the July crisis of 1914.[5] Whatever the truth of the matter, it was only after the trauma of defeat and revolution – first in Russia, and then in Germany – that official documents saw the light of day.

Indeed, only the Independent Socialists (USPD) demanded that Germany reveal the truth concerning the origins of the war, regardless of where the blame lay. On 21 November 1918, Kurt Eisner, minister-president of the revolutionary government in Bavaria, instructed his envoy in Berlin to press the provisional government of Friedrich Ebert to publish all documents pertinent to the outbreak of the war. Two days later, Eisner provided Munich newspapers with excerpts from the reports of the Bavarian plenipotentiary at Berlin in July/August 1914 to show that the war had been orchestrated by what Eisner termed 'a small horde of mad Prussian military' men as well as 'allied' industrialists, capitalists, politicians, and princes.[6] At about the same time in Berlin, Karl Kautsky, who had recently joined the USPD, had suggested as early as 13 November that the provisional government publish documents relating to July 1914. The provisional government, composed of Independent as well as Majority Socialists (SPD), formally entrusted him with this task on 9 December. Not surprisingly, given the sensational nature of Eisner's actions and perhaps fearing that documents might be destroyed, on November 26 the Berlin regime placed all former Imperial archives under its protection.[7]

While Kautsky labored at his editorial task, the German Socialist movement in December 1918 tore itself apart in Berlin: the Independent Socialists left the Cabinet on 29 December, and on the last day of the year the most radical socialists formed the Communist Party (KPD). Kautsky was now politically isolated. It was to be a harbinger of things to come that when he completed his task in March 1919, the Foreign Ministry, desiring to brand the highly critical work with the 'stigma of treasonable socialism', opposed and delayed its publication. Kautsky was denied access to the Wilhelmstrasse's archives, and all secret documents in his possession were recalled. In July 1919, the Cabinet of Chancellor Gustav Bauer, now devoid of any Independent Socialists, went one step further and entrusted a second documentary publication to the more conservative duo of Count Maximilian von Montgelas and Walter Schücking. And while it could not formally censor and obstruct Kautsky's efforts for fear of thereby alienating the still dominant SPD, the Foreign Ministry nevertheless did all within its power to prevent the timely publication of Kautsky's volumes. The campaign of what Erich Hahn has termed 'preemptive historiography' was in full swing.[8]

That campaign was directed by what one historian has called the 'general staff of the war-guilt struggle': the 'Special Bureau v. Bülow' at the turn of the year 1918–19, and its successor in 1920, the War Guilt Section of the Foreign Ministry. Chief of this 'general staff' was Legation Secretary Bernhard W. von Bülow, a future state secretary of the Wilhelmstrasse (1930–36).[9] Aided by

five special assistants, Bülow set out to catalogue the Foreign
Ministry's holdings for ready reference: by May 1919, a special
Kartothek, or card index of seven thousand documents, in both
chronological and subject order, was ready. A special register of
names to further expedite the Bureau's work was also prepared.[10]
By and large, the final result of these endeavours is today's Politisches Archiv of the Foreign Ministry at Bonn.

Bülow was appointed to this special post by Foreign Minister
Count Ulrich von Brockdorff-Rantzau, who commenced his assignment at the peace negotiations in Paris by assuring the French that
one of his ancestors had indeed been the father of Louis XIV, and
that in his family the Bourbons had been considered 'bastard
Rantzaus for the past three hundred years'. The unctuous Matthias Erzberger, head of the Catholic Centre Party and of the German armistice commission, also favored Bülow's appointment as
he feared the damage that a possible publication of the Kautsky
documents might do abroad. In fact, Bülow's most immediate task
in 1919 was to do the spade work for the upcoming 'negotiations'
with the victorious Allies in Paris. An ardent nationalist and zealous bureaucrat, Bülow began to comb the recently published
Soviet documents concerning the tsar's foreign policy before July
1914 for incriminating materials that could be used against the
Allies at Paris, and next studied and published critiques of the
various 'coloured books' put out by Belgium, Britain, France, and
Rumania to show that they were incomplete and inaccurate.[11] Yet
his greatest task was to prepare the case against the Allied charge
that Germany (and Austria-Hungary) was solely responsible for
the Great War, and the accompanying demand for the surrender
and trial of major 'war criminals' (later, Article 228 of the Versailles
treaty) – a demand that threatened to reach into the very chambers
of the Wilhelmstrasse.

On 7 January 1919, Erzberger convened a special meeting with
representatives of the Foreign Office and the erstwhile Supreme
Command of the Army (OHL). It was decided that Bülow would
undertake research in the diplomatic records on the issue of war
guilt; Major Bodo von Harbou, a former assistant to General Erich
Ludendorff, was entrusted with similar work in the military records. On 22 January, a second meeting was called to hammer out
what was to become the official German position on the issue of
war guilt. The documentary collections of Bülow and Harbou were
to contain materials specifically designed to show that the entente
had 'for a long time systematically and jointly prepared for a war

against Germany', that they, rather than Germany, were to be accorded 'immediate guilt' for provoking war in 1914. Specifically, the researchers were instructed to amass materials that would document France's ever increasing armaments outlays before 1914, Britain's intensive training of its 'continental army' for deployment in Europe, Italy's provocations of Austria-Hungary and, above all, Russia's long-term stockpiling of financial means with which to conduct war against Germany.[12] These views were formally adopted by the Foreign Ministry's Office for Peace Negotiations (Geschäftsstelle für die Friedensverhandlungen) in February 1919. Moreover, the Office's head, Count Johann Heinrich von Bernstorff, the former German ambassador to the United States, asked Jagow, who had been foreign secretary in 1914, to prepare the pivotal position paper on the July crisis – along with the former head of his political section, Wilhelm von Stumm. At the express request of General Detlof von Winterfeldt of the General Staff, Jagow was asked to highlight therein 'France's *revanche* policy' especially with regard to the reconquest of Alsace-Lorraine. Finally, the participants agreed to contact the former Great General Staff, Prussian War Ministry, and Imperial Navy Office to compile materials designed not only to refute the expected charge that Germany had started the war, but also to demonstrate Allied transgressions against international law both before and during the war.[13]

Bülow, who had gone to assist Brockdorff-Rantzau at Paris, was of course fully aware of the delicate nature of his task. As he returned official diplomatic records to Berlin, he instructed the later head of the Kriegsschuldreferat, Hans Freytag, to lock them up in a special safe so that 'in case the entente should demand them' – as they apparently intended to reserve the right to do (later, Article 230 of the Versailles treaty) – 'they can be got out of the way easily'.[14] And in assembling his documents, Bülow might well have been aware of Fouché's *bon mot* cited at the beginning of this essay: the legation secretary in an uncharacteristically candid moment informed Freytag that 'any nation can be charged successfully' on the basis of its documents: 'I would undertake "to prove" conclusively from the archives of any nation that it, and it alone, is responsible for the war – or for whatever else you like.'[15] In keeping with this spirit of selection, Bülow divided the documents that he assembled into two categories, marked 'defence' and 'offense'.

The immediate result of these efforts was the 'professors' memorandum' of 27 May 1919. Submitted to the Allies by Hans Delbrück,

Max von Montgelas, Albrecht Mendelssohn-Bartholdy, and Max
Weber, all members of the Heidelberg Association for a Policy of
Justice, the document asserted that Germany in 1914 had conducted a 'defensive war against Tsarism', 'the most dreadful system of enslavement...ever devised before the present peace treaty'.
The memorandum certainly was based upon documents from the
'Special Bureau v. Bülow' (today, 'Weltkrieg, Vols. 1–16, Juli–
August 1914' at Bonn); most likely, it was also penned by Bülow,
well before the professors ever arrived at Paris. The academicians
managed to agree to it in less than a week – probably a record of
sorts. Their 'prestigious autographs' lent the political document
'the hallmark of independent scholarship'.[16] All four undoubtedly
signed it for patriotic reasons. Weber, in his heart of hearts at least,
knew better, and privately confessed to Delbrück that he 'shud-
dered' at the thought of 'what might be in our documents'.[17]

The initial efforts to address Allied charges of war guilt
described above had been largely inspired by the belief that Germany could hope to gain moderate peace terms on the basis of
President Woodrow Wilson's Fourteen Points only if it could
'prove' either that others had also harbored aggressive notions in
July 1914 or that it had merely reacted to external threats. Specifically, the Hamburg banker Max Warburg had made it plain in
March 1919 that Germany could not hope to obtain much-needed
credits unless it could effectively reject war-guilt accusations.
Moreover, the entire question of reparations, at least to the Germans, seemed to be legally based upon their acceptance of moral
responsibility for the start of the war. In addition, there existed
the possibility that the Allies might go ahead with their demands
that German 'war criminals' be handed over for trial, and that
German records likewise be surrendered to serve as the basis of
such proceedings.

The crisis situation in this respect reached fever pitch on two
occasions: 7 May 1919, when the Allies handed the Germans the
text of the proposed peace accord; and 16 June 1919, when Premier
Georges Clemenceau presented Berlin with an ultimatum either to
accept the offered terms or to renew the fighting. The Germans
reacted on 28 May by submitting to the Allies a second White
Book, which Brockdorff-Rantzau concurrently released for publication; its core was the famous professors' memorandum previously mentioned. Of course, these German efforts at 'revision', as
the campaign to overturn war-guilt charges was now labelled, had
virtually no effect on the Allies. The Reich had no choice but to

accept the *Diktat* on 28 June 1919. Therewith, the immediacy of the revisionist campaign momentarily passed.

The Wilhelmstrasse now changed tactics. It devised a long-term project to publish its records from before 1914 in order to buttress its rejection of Article 231 – and possibly to force the Allies to open their archives as well. In fact, Count von Bernstorff, head of the Foreign Ministry's Office for Peace Negotiations, had suggested to the Cabinet as early as March 1919 that 1870 was the place to start.[18] That suggestion gained impetus on 10 December 1919, when British and Dutch newspapers leaked excerpts pertinent to the July crisis from Karl Kautsky's collection of documents. Such a broad investigation offered the additional prospect of shifting attention from the immediate causes of the Great War to a less sensitive debate about European affairs in general over the past four decades. Consensus to proceed with this project was reached by the Cabinet on 21 July 1919.

The editors for the project – initially estimated to run for four months and to three volumes – preferably would have to be 'respectable' scholars not immediately attached to the Foreign Ministry. Two candidates were quickly approved: Albrecht Mendelssohn-Bartholdy, a specialist on international law, was hired to investigate Germany's relations with Britain and its Empire; and Johannes Lepsius, a theologian and specialist on the Turkish treatment of Armenians, was entrusted with Balkan and Middle East issues. After considerable wrangling and upon the recommendation of the historian Friedrich Meinecke, Friedrich Thimme, the former director of the libraries of, first the Prussian Upper House, and subsequently of the entire Prussian Parliament, was selected as third editor, and made responsible for all issues not assigned to Mendelssohn-Bartholdy and Lepsius. Thimme and Lepsius were paid 2,000 Mark per month and provided with research and technical staff by the Foreign Ministry. In time, Thimme became managing editor of the mammoth project. The Wilhelmstrasse, for its part, not only directed the three editors on how to prepare the materials for publication, but also attached to them a special supervisor who was to evaluate possible public reaction to the documents selected for publication. Its War Guilt Section exercised final veto power over all volumes. The Foreign Ministry officially treated the documentary project as 'secret' and 'confidential' in order to camouflage its involvement therein.[19]

The end result was simply staggering in terms of labor and productivity: in just over six years, the three editors brought out forty volumes (in 54 parts) of documents pertaining to European affairs before 1914. Published between 1922 and 1927, *Die Grosse Politik der Europäischen Kabinette, 1871–1914,* in the words of Herman Wittgens, 'established an early dependence of all students of prewar diplomacy on German materials'.[20] Obviously, this is not the place either to trace the reception accorded the documents in the 1920s or to analyse their selection in detail. Much of the critique has come about only in the past two decades on the basis of exhaustive research in Austrian, British, French, and German records by Fischer, Geiss, and others. On the other hand, since the series is still widely used today and since many of the standard works on the origins of the Great War were based upon it, a few comments on the materials collected therein are nevertheless in order.

The most obvious shortcoming of *Die Grosse Politik* stemmed from its very nature as a publication from the files of the former Foreign Office. In other words, the collection does not include the highly important, indeed critical, materials of several other, powerful planning agencies: the General Staff, the War Ministry, the Navy Office, and the bureaus responsible for economic preparations for the war.[21] This is especially unfortunate in the case of the General Staff and the War Ministry as their files were almost totally destroyed by that greatest of 'censors', the Anglo-American Bomber Command, in February 1942 and April 1945. Of course, not all materials could be published even in a forty-volume series, and there is little doubt that many documents were suppressed or even destroyed. Moreover, some of the documents published were shortened, with potentially damaging sections deleted. Fritz Klein, for example, undertook a sample probe of volume sixteen of *Die Grosse Politik,* comparing Thimme's edition of a report on 5 October 1900 by Chancellor Bernhard von Bülow to Kaiser Wilhelm II concerning Germany's policy toward China. While Thimme shortened the report considerably and added a footnote stating that Imperial Germany had absolutely no territorial designs on China, the entire document – now available at Potsdam after the return to East Germany of the records of the former imperial embassy at Peking by the People's Republic after the Second World War – shows that quite the opposite was true. Klein reached the devastating conclusion that of the eleven points of the original memorandum, six were 'prejudicially falsified', three entirely omitted, and a mere two faithfully reproduced by the editors of *Die Grosse Politik.*[22] Above all, the kaiser's incriminating marginal comments on official documents, which Kautsky gleefully stated showed the monarch in his 'underwear', remained largely unpublished; those included were usually given apologetic explanations by Thimme.

At another level, materials that might have jeopardised the Weimar Republic's relations with prominent neutrals were often not published. As a result, the 'arrogant reports' of the former German ambassador to Italy, Count Anton Monts, were suppressed on the advice of former Chancellor von Bülow. Japan formally requested that Germany not print the documents pertaining to its East Asian policies. Materials potentially embarrassing to Berlin through its former dealings with Denmark, Norway, and Sweden were also omitted. Not even the earliest period remained immune to 'ordering', as fear of contemporary 'Bismarck admirers' prompted the editors carefully to sift materials from the stewardship of the Iron Chancellor. Finally, the organisation of the 15,889 documents into three hundred subject areas rather than chronological order – again, at the express demand of the Foreign Ministry – tended to 'sanitise' the material and to make it difficult for scholars to follow the day-to-day workings of the Wilhelmstrasse.

Imanuel Geiss has shown with specific reference to the July 1914 crisis that the editors failed to include (perhaps destroyed) a number of utterly critical documents: the discussions on 5 and 6 July at Potsdam not only among German leaders but also with Austro-Hungarian representatives; the detailed analysis of the Viennese ultimatum to Serbia, missing in *Die Grosse Politik* but handed to the Baden plenipotentiary on 20 July; virtually any and all talks held by the chancellor or the state secretary and undersecretary of the Foreign Office with representatives of foreign powers in July 1914; any and all contacts between Wilhelm II and his political as well as military leaders after the monarch's return from his northern cruise on 27 July; and, last but not least, any and all notes pertaining to important telephone calls, telegraphs, or other verbal communications.[23] And according to Annelise Thimme, Mendelssohn-Bartholdy managed to defuse some potentially incriminating statements by Chancellor Theobald von Bethmann Hollweg simply by decreeing that the materials in question be returned to the family as 'private' correspondence.[24] The chancellor's two-volume memoirs offer no clues concerning the July crisis, and his personal papers were either destroyed during the Second World War or captured by the advancing Soviet armies. Of course, we will never know how much was destroyed or returned to former players as 'private' papers. What is certain is that the

present records of the Politisches Archiv of the Foreign Ministry at
Bonn contain none of the documents listed by Geiss. They can be
assumed lost forever.

His considerable efforts at patriotic self-censorship notwithstanding, Thimme later was to experience the wrath of academia.
He was denied not only an honorary doctorate for *Die Grosse Politik,* but even the Leibniz medal from the Prussian Academy –
despite a strong recommendation from Meinecke. The noted historian Erich Brandenburg, who had penned a book on Bismarck
at the behest of the Foreign Ministry, claimed that these denials
were based on the fact that Thimme was a 'creature' of the Wilhelmstrasse and as such could not be 'placed on an equal level
with an independent scholar'. By contrast, Alfred von Wegerer's
efforts on behalf of the war-guilt campaign were rewarded with
an honorary doctorate from Giessen University.[25] The labours of
Bernhard Schwertfeger and Hans Draeger for the national cause –
which will be taken up shortly – were likewise crowned with
honorary doctorates. It is quite probable that the national-conservative German historians refused to honour Thimme for two reasons: his support of the 'defeatist' policies of Chancellor von
Bethmann Hollweg during the war, and his sharp attacks on
Admiral Alfred von Tirpitz during the latter's campaign for the
presidency in 1924–25.

With the publication of its mammoth forty-volume project, the
Foreign Ministry adopted the stance that all important documents were therewith available to scholars and that access to its
files was not to be granted freely. Indeed, in 1929 the Wilhelmstrasse decreed that all materials of the past thirty years were to be
closed to historical investigation – an unfortunate precedent that
the current rulers at Bonn seem bent on repeating with their policy
of *Datenschutz.* The widely acclaimed story that the Foreign Ministry marked several of its files 'not to be shown to William Langer'
may be apocryphal, but the case of George Hallgarten is documented. In 1931, Hallgarten was denied access to the foreign relations records as his work might 'compromise' Germany's 'present
or future interests in China'. Refusing to take no for an answer,
Hallgarten reapplied for permission to use official materials, and
was finally let in. By chance, he was handed the files on German
policy with regard to Delago Bay – files that Thimme had assured
scholars did not exist. Moreover, upon returning after the Second
World War to reexamine the dossiers on China that he had been
given in the early 1930s, Hallgarten discovered that potentially

damaging documents had been removed before he was handed the materials, and later returned to their folders.[26] It is also interesting to note that the Federal Republic of Germany entrusted the supervision of the archival records in the Politisches Archiv of the Foreign Office at Bonn to Heinz-Günther Sasse, who had worked during the 1920s in the Center for the Study of the Causes of the War, one of the numerous organisations funded by the Foreign Ministry to rebut the 'war-guilt lie'.[27] Therewith, the patriotic self-censors established continuity from the Weimar Republic to the Federal Republic via the Third Reich.

Dissemination of Illusions

After the publication of *Die Grosse Politik*, the Foreign Ministry sought to assure the widest possible dissemination of the series' findings, both at home and abroad. Legation Secretary Freytag of its War Guilt Section had suggested as early as December 1919 a massive propaganda campaign to propagate the official German position on war guilt, but Bülow did not deem the moment right as the indiscriminate use of propaganda during the First World War had rendered large segments of the populace sceptical of any government-directed information. Nevertheless, Freytag clung to his plan to make certain 'that this propaganda never be allowed to die'.[28]

After various unsuccessful attempts to recruit patriotic organisations willing, able, and suitable to conduct its propaganda, the Foreign Ministry eventually decided to establish several independent bureaus under the umbrella of its Kriegsschuldreferat. These eventually functioned on both an overt and a covert level; at the public level, they disseminated the official view of the origins of the war, while behind the scenes they sought to promote those who followed the official line and to silence – indeed, eventually to hound out of office – those who put forth independent and/or unacceptable interpretations. And while much of the nation gradually had gotten over the initial shock of the harsh terms handed down at Versailles, the Allied demand in January 1921 for reparations in the amount of 226 billion Mark, with annual payments over the next forty-two years, once again came to the aid of the Foreign Ministry's 'revisionist' endeavours.[29] Foreign Minister Walter Simons and Finance Minister Joseph Wirth were quickly able to agree to make available one million Mark for propaganda purposes to the Center for the Study of the Causes of the War; an additional 200,000 Mark was released to support the efforts of German diplomatic missions abroad to distribute materials supportive of the Foreign Ministry's war-guilt stance. Mendelssohn-Bartholdy, now at Hamburg, was able to tap into this cash flow in 1923 in order to establish an Institute for Foreign Policy, publish a journal, *Europäische Gespräche,* and a 'popular' four-volume abridgement of *Die Grosse Politik.*[30]

With governmental funding secure – augmented on occasion by private contributions – the 'patriotic self-censors' were ready to spearhead the revisionist drive through a triad of dependent organisations. The 'general staff' remained the War Guilt Section of the Foreign Ministry. It was headed by Hans Freytag in 1919–20, Professor Richard von Delbrück in 1921–22, and Friedrich Stieve from 1922 until 1928. The bureau made the basic decisions as to which publications critical of the official German line were to be attacked, by whom, and in which journals; or whether they simply were to be ignored. Moreover, the Kriegsschuldreferat acted as internal censor for all publications either of the Foreign Ministry or of the parliamentary investigations. Moreover, it composed the numerous official statements of German chancellors and President Paul von Hindenburg on the war-guilt question.[31] At least under Stieve, the War Guilt Section openly conceded that historical elucidation was not its primary concern; rather, its purpose was 'aggressive polemics'. Above all, the War Guilt Section brooked no competition in its campaign of revision; when the Potsdam Reichsarchiv in 1923 threatened to compile its own documentary collection on the outbreak of the war, the Foreign Ministry secured a decree from President Ebert that it, and it alone, was entitled to undertake such endeavours.[32]

The Kriegsschuldreferat was also active in attempting to influence the publication of archival materials in other countries. In 1924, Stieve produced a four-volume collection of the reports of the erstwhile Russian ambassador in Paris, A.P. Izvolsky, designed to show that these two entente powers had nurtured 'imperialistic war aims' against Germany. The core of the publication consisted of fifty secret documents, purchased by the Wilhelmstrasse for 48,000 Mark – in reality, a bribe paid to the archivist of the Soviet embassy at Paris to smuggle the materials out.[33] To be sure, the Foreign Ministry had long encouraged the Ballhausplatz at Vienna to publish its documents on the July crisis ' in the interests of greater Germany', and by 1923 had even hired the former editor of the Austro-Hungarian Red Book on the war's origins. Legation Secretary Roderich Gooss, in fact, was now sent to Vienna to assist the Ballhausplatz in sorting its documents – in the process passing copies of the most important materials on to his employers at Berlin. In the end, Stieve provided the editors of the Austrian documents, the Kommission für neuere Geschichte Österreichs, 50,000 Mark to facilitate their work – as well as the services of Gooss and, for good measure, Friedrich Thimme.[34] And when it appeared in 1925 that the United States, at the prompting of Senator Robert L. Owen of Oklahoma, might undertake an official publication of documents pertaining to the outbreak of war in 1914, the Wilhelmstrasse instructed its embassy at Washington to make *Die Grosse Politik* readily available; Alfred von Wegerer was dispatched to the United States in order to exert 'decisive influence' on the planned American publication, which never reached fruition.[35]

To expedite this hectic activity, the War Guilt Section in 1921 had established a pseudoscholarly bureau, the Center for the Study of the Causes of the War. Headed until August 1923 by a Swiss doctor, Ernst Sauerbeck, and thereafter until its dissolution in 1937 by Major Alfred von Wegerer, it became 'a clearing-house for officially desirable views on the outbreak of the war'.[36] The Center possessed only a small staff of 'politically trained' scholars, but its directory included such notables as Count von Montgelas, Bernhard W. von Bülow, Hans Delbrück, and Hermann Lutz. The prolific Wegerer, who had come aboard in 1923 from the *völkish* "Liga für deutsche Kultur", churned out no less than three hundred articles to buttress the revisionist cause. The Foreign Ministry, at the height of the economic crisis of 1923, financed a monthly journal for the Center entitled *Die Kriegsschuldfrage, Monatsschrift für Internationale Aufklärung*, which in 1929 changed its title to *Berliner Monatshefte*. Its circulation hovered between 2,500 and 3,000 copies in 1925, then climbed to between 3,500 and 4,000 by 1931. Both journals of the Zentralstelle zur Erforschung der Kriegsursachen appeared with the 'Quader-Verlag', a publishing house financially controlled by the Foreign Ministry – much in the manner in which the latter kept the 'Deutsche Verlagsanstalt für Politik und Geschichte' solvent by having it publish the works that the Wilhelmstrasse contracted out to Bülow, Lutz, Mendelssohn-Bartholdy, Montgelas, Schücking, Schwertfeger, Stieve, and Thimme. Again, Wegerer and his Center appeared on the surface to be independent; in reality, Wegerer remained in the pay of the Foreign Ministry in the position of *Ministerialrat*, and the War Guilt Section 'supervised' the Center's publications.[37]

Unfortunately, there is no concise accounting of the subsidies paid out by the Foreign Ministry for its campaign of revision. Ulrich Heinemann has shown that Wegerer's Center received official support in the amount of 23,400 Mark in 1924–25, 34,400 Mark the following year, and 84,000 Mark by 1929–30; private contributions amounted to 5,200 Mark, 19,000 Mark, and 24,000 Mark for those respective years. These sums can best be gauged against the 120 Mark monthly wage of an average German industrial worker. Of course, these monies formed only a very small part of the overall outlays of the Foreign Ministry to the 'war-guilt lie'.[38] Nor is it possible to gain any accurate insight into the number of independent scholars and journalists engaged by the Wilhelmstrasse in a similar function. While Geiss speaks of a small army of such publicists, Heinemann tends toward a much smaller number. In the main, these writers were paid modest honorariums of perhaps several hundred Mark in order to pen three or four articles per month for leading newspapers, which, in turn, passed them on to the provincial press. Most prominent among this group were the Munich journalist Hermann Lutz and the army's specialist on Belgium, Colonel Schwertfeger; the latter was also paid by the Foreign Ministry to compile an eight-part guide to *Die Grosse Politik* for the nonprofessional reader.[39] One of the few foreign writers directly subsidised by the Wilhelmstrasse appears to have been Milos Boghitschewitsch, the former Serbian chargé d'affaires to Germany, who wrote articles for the Foreign Office during the 1920s and who apparently was paid in that most rare of commodities at Berlin, gold.[40] Again, there is no indication of how many of these pieces were purchased by the Foreign Ministry and distributed gratis at home and abroad; Geiss speaks vaguely of 'several hundred'.

Since the Center for the Study of the Causes of the War viewed itself as a scholarly bureau, it is interesting to note the absence of German university professors – with the exception of that 'outsider', Hans Delbrück. By and large, eminent scholars such as Hans Herzfeld, Paul Herre, Siegfried Kaehler, Wilhelm Mommsen, and Hans Rothfels viewed the origins of the Great War as current events rather than history, and thus hardly worthy of serious scholarly inquiry. Moreover, they continued in their fascination with the ancient world. It is striking that not a single eminent historian of the 1920s bothered to undertake serious research and publication on the origins of the war. In contrast to the post-1945 period, they left the debate by default in the hands of the Foreign Ministry and its minions. Many of the 'German mandarins' announced at their annual convention at Göttingen in 1932 that they rejected the very term 'war guilt' as being imprecise and not belonging to the vocabulary of a professional scholar; rather, the terms 'origins' and 'consequences' of war were deemed fit and proper for the *Zunft*.[41] And on the few occasions on which the senior historians addressed the issue of war guilt in popular magazines and newspapers, they basically followed Hermann Oncken's verdict that Imperial Germany had been driven by a genuine desire for peace, while France had been obsessed with the spirit of revenge, England with the encirclement of Germany, and Russia with hostility toward Berlin.

If the Center for the Study of the Causes of the War sought to conduct the revisionist campaign on a scholarly level, the Working Committee of German Associations was quite the opposite – namely, an organisation committed to spreading the Foreign Ministry's message to as many agencies and papers as possible. The Arbeitsausschuss Deutscher Verbände (ADV) was quietly founded by the Foreign Ministry in April 1921 without public knowledge or participation, and within a year claimed ties to between 500 and 600 member organisations, a figure that skyrocketed to between 1,700 and 2,000 by 1931. In the main, the member organisations were patriotic clubs such as Rettet die Ehre and the Deutsche Frauenausschuss zur Bekämpfung der Kriegsschuldlüge, but they also included the Caritas-Verband, the World Council of Churches, and the German City League. The Working Committee chose as its first president Legation Secretary Kurt von Lersner, a former head of the Foreign Office's legal section; he was succeeded in 1925 by Dr Heinrich Schnee, the former governor of German East Africa. A special business office in Berlin, initially managed by Wilhelm von Vietsch and from 1923 until 1937 by Hans Draeger (who joined Joseph Goebbel's Propaganda Ministry in 1933), conducted the day-to-day business operations of the ADV.[42]

Perhaps because of its nature as an overt mass propaganda distribution center, the ADV was rather well financed. Official support came from the parent War Guilt Section and the Press Section of the Foreign Ministry as well as from the Ministry of the Interior, the Chancellery, and the state of Prussia. Private contributions flowed in from large industrial concerns such as IG-Farben, the northwest group of the Iron and Steel Cartel, and the Hamburg

Board of Trade, with smaller amounts being raised by govern-
ment-endorsed lotteries and public solicitations. While it is generally agreed that private contributions never amounted to more
than the actual costs of printing the materials, the direct subsidies
from the Wilhelmstrasse alone rose from 20,000 Mark in 1924 to
72,000 Mark by 1928/29.[43] With this money, the ADV organised
speakers' seminars, conventions, exhibitions, rallies, and special
information weeks to spread the gospel according to the Foreign
Ministry. It is estimated, for example, that in 1925 alone, the Working Committee conducted 1,456 such undertakings in behalf of
the revisionist campaign. Moreover, it effectively penetrated the
daily press, maintaining contacts to no less than 1,500 newspapers through the thirty-five major news agencies in Berlin. A ran-
dom sample of the Weimar press during any given week revealed
that it was not at all unusual for about three hundred German
papers to publish between 1,600 and 1,700 articles distributed by
the ADV.

The latter was particularly active in providing literature sympathetic to the Foreign Ministry's 'revisionist' stance to German
schools. Not only was its journal *Der Weg zur Freiheit* much more
popular than Wegerer's *Kriegsschuldfrage*, but the Working Committee carefully cultivated close ties to teacher organisations and
schools. Among the literature that it provided for the schools were
67,000 free copies of Friedrich Stieve's highly revisionist *Deutschland und Europa 1890–1914*, as well as popular pamphlets such as
Karl Bröger's 'Versailles' (800,000 copies), a 'Merkblatt zur Kriegsschuldfrage' (500,000 copies), a calendar 'Für Freiheit und Ehre'
(100,000 copies), and the all-time bestseller 'Schuld am Kriege'
(2.5 million copies). Assured of Foreign Ministry backing, the
ADV placed its publications free of charge in hospitals, reading
rooms, libraries, reception rooms of doctors and lawyers, and
lounges at industrial plants. Nor was the foreign press ignored:
the Working Center maintained ties to at least eleven major German-American newspapers, placing about four hundred articles
with them just in the few months between January and August
1922. It was aided in these endeavours not only by the Hamburg
Board of Trade (Max Warburg, Wilhelm Cuno), but also by the
World Council of Churches, and the Vereine des Auslandsdeutschtums. And after 1924, the ADV began to turn its attention to
radio, broadcasting its views over the 'Berliner Funkstunde'; its
leaders prised this new medium because of 'the strong participation of the workers in radio'.[44]

The Wilhelmstrasse was especially interested that the Working Committee of German Associations and the Center for the Study of the Causes of the War establish contacts with foreign scholars who either were sympathetic to its official line or who were critical, for whatever reason, of their own government's role in the outbreak of the war or its settlement. In 1925, for example, the Foreign Ministry convinced Chancellor Hans Luther to provide 500,000 Mark for this purpose. Apart from distributing gratis five thousand copies of Hermann Lutz's *An Appeal to British Fair Play* to addresses in England, the Foreign Ministry and ADV either provided research materials to or subsidised the translations and/or distribution of such sympathetic works as Alfred Fabre-Luce, *La Victoire;* Alcide Ebray, *La Paix Malpropre;* Victor Margueritte, *Les Criminels;* Georges Demartial, *La Guerre de 1914;* and Edmund D. Morel, *Pre-War Diplomacy, Diplomacy Revealed, The Secret History of a Great Betrayal,* and *The Poison That Destroys.*

Perhaps of interest to readers is the care lavished upon certain American scholars by the Foreign Ministry and its agents. As previously noted, Wegerer had been sent to the United States in 1925 to assist the Senate in a possible documentary series on the origins of the war; he also used the occasion to contact eminent historians such as Sidney B. Fay, Bernadotte E. Schmitt, William Langer, Carlton J. Hayes, and Ferdinand Schevill. The immediate upshot was that the Foreign Ministry purchased 250 copies of Fay's sympathetic two-volume *The Origins of the War* and had its diplomatic representatives overseas distribute the books free of charge. The Harvard historian was invited to visit the Center for the Study of the Causes of the War in 1923, and was asked regularly to contribute to its journal, *Kriegsschuldfrage.* In time, the Foreign Ministry funded both a German and a French translation of Fay's study. By contrast, Bernadotte Schmitt's critical *The Coming of the War 1914* was never translated into German, and when the Reich's consul at Chicago in 1928 arranged a visit by Schmitt to Germany to discuss his research, Wegerer strenuously objected to a tour by this 'incorrigible' historian.[45]

The greatest attention and support was showered upon Harry E. Barnes of Smith College. In articles that appeared in *Current History, Nation, Christian Century,* and especially in his *Genesis of the World War* (1927), Barnes depicted France and Russia as the villains, Germany and Austria-Hungary as the victims of the July crisis. Wegerer's Center moved with alacrity after 1924. It provided Barnes with research materials, propagated his writings, and funded his visits to Berlin, Munich, and Vienna in 1926. The German embassy at Washington presented him with all forty volumes of *Die Grosse Politik*. Lutz put him into contact with the Serb, Boghitschewitsch, who was in the pay of the Foreign Ministry. Wegerer had Barnes's articles translated into German and published in his journal. The ADV translated Barnes's *Genesis* into German, and with the help of the Foreign Ministry not only distributed it to Germany's overseas missions but even arranged a French translation. And while the Wilhelmstrasse saw Barnes's usefulness primarily as that of a populariser, the eminent historian Hans Herzfeld went so far as to proclaim the American scholar's work 'a document in the struggle for the war guilt thesis whose noble spirit cannot be appreciated enough'.[46]

It is impossible to pinpoint the effect of this propaganda, either in Germany or overseas. Needless to say, the cumulative effect of ten years of continuous activity in this area must have taken its toll. Several German states, such as Baden, Bavaria, Sachsen-Anhalt, Württemberg, and Waldeck, openly adopted ADV materials for classroom instruction. In 1922, the Weimar federation of teachers agreed to serve the ADV, as did the federation of university professors. The administrative guardians of German universities, the rectors, also agreed to bring the Working Committee on board. The ADV, for its part, routinely organised talks at high schools and seminars at universities on the issue of the 'war-guilt lie', and this mobilisation especially of the youth could only have paved the way for their favorable reception of Adolf Hitler's 'revisionist' ideas. Likewise, the overseas distribution of materials combatting Article 231 of the Versailles treaty must have had its effects, however imprecise they may be to define. At least one generation of university students was raised on the apologias presented them by historians such as Sidney B. Fay and Harry E. Barnes in the United States, and writers such as Edmund Morel in England as well as Victor Margueritte and Alfred Fabre-Luce in France. This pollution of American, British and French historical understanding of the origins of the Great War must have helped to undermine faith in the need to maintain the irenic clauses of the 1919 treaty. It remains an open question whether it also contributed to isolationism in the United States and proappeasement thinking in England in the 1930s.

The activities of both the Center for the Study of the Causes of the War and the Working Committee of German Associations lost much of their impact and political value after January 1933.

Celebrating the fourth anniversary of his appointment as chancellor, Hitler on 20 January 1937 informed the Reichstag that he was officially 'revoking' the German signature on the document wherein a 'weak government' had been 'pressed' to accept Germany's guilt for the First World War.[47] Therewith, the semiofficial revisionist campaign was stripped of its reason to exist – or, more precisely, it was subsumed by the state. Two years later, Wegerer published his standard apologia, *Der Ausbruch des Weltkrieges*, which was to shape so many of the post-1945 histories of the July crisis. Arguing that no single nation was responsible for the outbreak of the war, Wegerer instead ingeniously suggested that a fatal entanglement of circumstances – perhaps even providence – had afflicted Europe with this curse. This convenient position was thereafter adopted by the majority of Germany's national-conservative historians, such as Karl Dietrich Erdmann, Hans Herzfeld, Hermann Oncken, Gerhard Ritter, Hans Rothfels, Theodor Schieder, and Egmont Zechlin, to name but a few. Moreover, it also made its way into the writings of Harry E. Barnes and Sidney B. Fay as well as their students in the United States, and is to be found in countless general histories and surveys still used in American universities. An inability or unwillingness to delve into the German sources – or at least the writings of Fritz Fischer and his students – perhaps accounts for this.

Furthermore, while the Second World War for many non-German scholars merely served once more to 'prove' Berlin's responsibility for the First, the tone in what emerged as the Federal Republic of Germany (1949) was set again by historians such as Erdmann, Herzfeld, Ritter, Rothfels, and Zechlin, who now adopted the line that while Hitler (rather than Germany) was to blame for the Second World War, no such blame could be attributed for the First. In reaching this stance, they seconded Wegerer, ignored Albertini, and vilified Fischer.[48] Largely overlooked in the debate – both before 1933 and after 1945 – was the work of the Reichstag investigation into both the origins and conduct of the Great War. This investigation was completely independent of the activities of the Foreign Ministry discussed previously; it came fully under the purview of the Reichstag, which had decided in 1919 to investigate the sudden and seemingly inexplicable reasons for the German collapse. While the Left thereby sought to lay the blame for the collapse at the feet of German admirals and generals and generally to delegitimate the old order, the Right joined the investigation in order to tar the major supporters of the

Weimar Republic – Democrats, Liberals, and Socialists – with the brush of defeatism and betrayal.

Parliament and the Campaign of Obfuscation

Thus united in policy if not in motive, the various political parties in the Reichstag had decided on the basis of Article 34 of the new constitution to convene a special parliamentary Committee of Enquiry to investigate the origins of the war, its possible prolongation, and the causes for defeat in 1918. The twenty-eight member Untersuchungsausschuss was formally constituted on 21 August 1919 as the 15th Committee of the German Constitutional Assembly; it conducted its work until Hermann Göring in his capacity as president of the Reichstag dissolved it after the elections of 30 August 1932, and ordered the destruction of all available published volumes of its findings. There evolved four subcommittees of enquiry: the first was to investigate Germany's responsibility for the start of the war; the second to assess whether there had been any possibility for a negotiated peace before the military collapse; the third was to tackle Allied charges that the Reich had violated international law; and the fourth was to discern the causes behind the collapse both at the front and at home in 1918. Finally, a special tribunal (Staatsgerichtshof) composed of high-court judges and parliamentary deputies was to hear cases submitted to it by the four subcommittees. The cumbersome nature of the investigative process was due, in part, to the Foreign Ministry's desire to keep documents tied up in committee and thus from public scrutiny for an indefinite period. Indeed, the eminent jurist Otto von Gierke quickly pointed out that the special tribunal was not only contrary to German law, but that its decisions would constitute *ex post facto* justice.[49]

The story of the Untersuchungsausschuss is one of official obfuscation, interminable delays, and eventual failure. Only one subcommittee investigation, namely, that dealing with Germany's role at the Hague peace conferences in 1899 and 1907, was ever completed and printed – and then only in 1927, after the Foreign Ministry had repeatedly barred its publication as being detrimental to the national interest.[50] The Wilhelmstrasse in general and Alfred von Wegerer of its War Guilt Section in particular not only decided which documents were to be submitted to the Committee of Enquiry, but also exercised veto power over the publication of its findings. Not unexpectedly, the various military bureaus refused from the start to participate in the investigations or to make any of their materials available.[51] And as the shock of defeat and revolution wore off, the composition of the Reichstag slowly shifted to the right of the political spectrum, thereby altering the proportional composition of the various subcommittees in favor of more conservative and nationalist elements.

The most sensational investigation was that of the second subcommittee, charged with evaluating the possibility of a negotiated peace in 1917–18. Former Vice Chancellor Karl Helfferich set the tone of the investigation by charging that those political parties that had supported the Reichstag's peace resolution in July 1917 had, in effect, 'stabbed the unrestricted submarine war in the back'. In addition, Helfferich accused the Social Democrats of having accepted Soviet funds in order to 'revolutionise Germany'. But the most dramatic effect was reserved for Field Marshall von Hindenburg. Having been invited by Fritz Warmuth of the German National People's Party (DNVP) – without the consent of the rest of the subcommittee – the former chief of the General Staff arrived in Berlin to 'testify' on 18 November 1919. It was a triumphant farce. The army provided an honour guard at the train station, two officers served as adjutants, and a guard detail was stationed at the Villa Helfferich where the field marshall resided while in the capital. When Hindenburg, in full dress uniform, arrived to testify on 18 November, the chamber was packed. All rose to their feet as he strode in to take his chrysanthemum-bedecked chair. There were no questions, no cross-examination. Instead, the field marshall read a brief prepared statement wherein he blamed the military defeat on the material and numerical superiority of the Allies especially after April 1917, and on the 'planned demoralisation' of the High Sea Fleet by 'revolutionary elements', presumably the Independent Socialists (USPD). Hindenburg ended his soliloquy by announcing that the 'good core' of the army, that is, its officer corps, could not be blamed for the defeat; rather, it had been 'stabbed in the back' (*von hinten erdolcht*) by certain pacifist and socialist elements at the home front. Therewith, a legend was officially born, one that was to have fatal consequences for the Republic. Unsurprisingly, the patriotic self-censors in the Foreign Ministry barred publication of even a single volume of the findings of the second subcommittee for fear of adverse reaction both overseas and among the German clergy; further, they assured that even the unpublished material would not see the light of day by

indiscriminately stamping 'secret' on twenty-eight of the thirty-
seven folders of documents. The second *enquête's* work concluded
in 1924.[52]

The third subcommittee, dealing with possible German viola-
tions of international law, was most closely supervised by the Foreign Ministry, which provided as 'expert' none other than Dr
Johannes Kriege, the erstwhile head of the legal section of the
Imperial Foreign Office. In fact, Kriege undertook numerous visits to the exiled kaiser Wilhelm II at Haus Doorn in the Netherlands, ostensibly to keep the emperor informed of his efforts.
Whatever the case, Kriege, in the words of Ulrich Heinemann,
quickly developed into 'a master of juridical pettifoggery' *(Rabu-
listik)*. With regard to the use of poison gas, Kriege argued that
whereas French weapons were illegal under the Hague convention of 29 July 1899 because their intent was solely the dissemination of gas, German equivalents were legal because they also
served as ordinary artillery shells. In particular, Germany's first
use of gas at Ypres on 22 April 1915 had been perfectly legal
because the Reich had not used 'gas shells' but rather 'gas clouds'.
Unrestricted submarine warfare was likewise deemed legal as it
had been adopted strictly as an antidote to the illegal British
'hunger blockade'. And German air attacks on London and Paris
were ruled legal insofar as France, Germany, and Russia on 18
October 1907 had not renewed the original Hague conditions for
air warfare of 29 July 1899. The admittedly brutal deportation of
Belgian workers was attributed solely to the inadequate organisation of German transports. When the Belgian government formally protested these mental gymnastics at Berlin in 1927, the
German military reacted by suggesting that the government buy
up all remaining volumes of the findings of the third subcommittee and distribute them gratis at home. The plan was eventually
realised in 1934, when Foreign Minister Konstantin von Neurath
and Defense Minister General Werner von Blomberg persuaded
the Finance Ministry to earmark 10,000 Mark for the purchase of
all remaining volumes in the series. Of more immediate impact
was that Hans Draeger of the ADV published Kriege's findings in
ten thousand copies of his *Taschenbuch zur Kriegsschuldfrage*.[53]

Whereas the Foreign Ministry had refused to hand over only
potentially incriminating documents to the Untersuchungsausschuss, the army and navy between 1924 and 1928 proved adamant
in their refusals to assist in any way the work of the fourth subcommittee dealing with the collapse in 1918. In 1920, both services

agreed jointly to plan their strategy in this regard – in sharp contrast to their inability either before or during the war to coordinate their military and naval strategies. Major Otto von Stülpnagel of the Defense Ministry bluntly warned that any opening of army archives would have 'long-range consequences' for German policies not only domestically but also with regard to the Reich's 'future world standing'. Hence it was decided that official affidavits on the strategic ramifications of the great spring offensive in France in 1918 would be handled by the former general staff chief of Army Group Crown Prince Rupprecht, General Hermann von Kuhl, and on the political and military implications of 'Operation Michael' by Colonel Schwertfeger, one of the Foreign Ministry's paid publicists; Professor Hans Delbrück was asked to submit a counteraffidavit. Kuhl, as was to be expected, reiterated Hindenburg's brazen 'stab-in-the-back' theory, and argued that the army had been quite prepared to continue the war into 1919 – had it not been for the systematic revolutionary planning of the Socialists. Delbrück countered by arguing that General Erich Ludendorff's 'total war' strategy, which had gambled all on a decisive military victory in 1918, had grievously overestimated German resolve as well as resources, and thereby had directly contributed to the collapse. By reversing the relationship between goals and means, Ludendorff had displayed a shocking degree of 'unbridled egoism, megalomania, and lack of responsibility'. When Delbrück's statements found their way into the press in 1924, Schwertfeger, Colonel Wolfgang Foerster of the Reichsarchiv at Potsdam, and the historian Hans Herzfeld viciously attacked Delbrück for his 'unfounded, superficial and misleading' interpretation. The so-called 'Ludendorff controversy' reached its climax in November and December 1924, when the Cabinet twice agreed to sustain General Hans von Seeckt's veto of the planned publication of the findings of the fourth subcommittee for fear that this might harm 'the moral fiber of the army'.[54]

With regard to the navy's role in the collapse of 1917–18, tempers reached the flash point early in 1926, when the former USPD deputy Wilhelm Dittmann repeated his charges that the fleet 'unrest' of October 1918 had, in fact, been precipitated by an 'admirals' rebellion' against the government of Prince Max von Baden. Coming close on the heels of the sensational Munich 'stab-in-the-back' press 'investigation', Dittmann's charges sparked a vitriolic exchange with the navy's official representatives, Vice Admiral Adolf von Trotha and Lieutenant-Commander Wilhelm

Canaris, as well as with its parliamentary champion, Botho-Wendt zu Eulenburg of the DNVP. Eulenburg and Canaris especially applied the *Dolchstoss* thesis to the navy, arguing that both the SPD and the USPD in 1917–18 had delivered 'the last fatal stab into the back of the fighting front'. Had the admirals not refused to provide the fourth subcommittee with the war diary of the Supreme Command of the Navy (Kriegstagebuch der Seekriegs-leitung) – which clearly revealed that naval leaders in October 1918 had planned a 'suicide sortie' against the combined Anglo-American fleets in order to uphold the honour of the officer corps as well as to assure future naval funding – the so-called 'Dittmann controversy' might well have been defused, if not resolved, right there and then.[55]

The most controversial investigation, of course, was that of the first subcommittee, charged with assessing Germany's role in the July crisis. There, after all, was the heart of Article 231 of the Versailles treaty. The Foreign Ministry was acutely sensitive to possible Allied charges that this committee was stacked with its minions, and hence the Wilhelmstrasse encouraged the Reichstag to engage 'neutral' experts. The choice fell upon the Munich publicist Hermann Lutz and the Freiburg jurist Hermann Kantorow-icz. Despite the fact that Lutz was closely associated with the revisionist campaign conducted by the Foreign Ministry, his affi-davit, completed in 1924, proved embarrassingly balanced. Lutz placed Serbia and Russia at the top of the list of those responsible for the war, closely followed by Austria-Hungary, and then by the rest of the parties involved. Lutz's evaluation of the Habsburg pol-icy of brinkmanship in July 1914 at once drew the ire of fellow investigators Max von Montgelas and Richard von Delbrück, both intimately involved with the Foreign Ministry's revisionist endeav-ours. Indeed, the Wilhelmstrasse 'encouraged' Lutz to 'revise' his affidavit; in its second form, the *Gutachten* placed Vienna in a more favourable light. Nevertheless, the Foreign Ministry again used its veto power to delay publication of Lutz's affidavit for half a decade (until 1930).[56]

The case of Hermann Kantorowicz in many ways symbolises the entire campaign of 'preemptive historiography'. Charged with investigating the legal parameters of the war's origins, Kantorow-icz submitted his affidavit in December 1923; revisions for publi-cation were completed by the spring of 1925, and galleys were set to go to press two years later. Final publication came in 1967. Kan-torwicz's original manuscript was destroyed when the Reichstag was bombed in 1945, but Imanuel Geiss managed to obtain a copy from the family's archive.

Kantorowicz attributed responsibility for the war primarily to the Central Powers: Austria-Hungary for the aggressive manner in which it had launched the Balkan War with Serbia, and Germany not only for supporting the Habsburg initiative but also for rejecting all peace efforts undertaken by England and Russia after the assassination at Sarajevo. Jew, Anglophile, pacifist, republican, and democrat, Kantorowicz was accused of 'fouling his own nest' *(Nestbeschmutzung)* and soon experienced the wrath of official Germany. In January 1927, Prussian Cultural Minister Carl Becker informed the German Foreign Ministry of widespread opposition to Kantorowicz's recent selection to a chair *(Ordinarious)* by Kiel University on the grounds that the jurist's affidavit 'would severely damage German policies' in the eyes of the world. Foreign Minister Gustav Stresemann, who had not read Kantorowicz's *Gutachten,* concurred, basing his attempted veto of the appointment upon an evaluation of the affidavit submitted to him by none other than Johannes Kriege, the former imperial official who had headed the legal section of the Foreign Office during the Great War – in other words, the very bureau that Kantorowicz had investigated. According to Friedrich Thimme, editor of *Die Grosse Politik,* Stresemann at the end of 1927 had clearly indicated the interconnection between the nagging 'war-guilt' issue and his policy of rapprochement with the West by arguing that publication of Kantorowicz's affidavit 'would render my entire Locarno policy impossible'.[57]

Yet, in one of those rare moments when academicians are willing to place the principle of academic freedom above personal interest, the law faculty at Kiel insisted on and won Kantorowicz's appointment as professor. But the Foreign Ministry was not yet done. After September 1928, Stresemann consistently delayed publication of Kantorowicz's affidavit – at first through appeals to Chancellor Hermann Müller, and thereafter by various delaying tactics involving additional counteraffidavits. In fact, Chancellor Müller and Paul Löbe, president of the Reichstag, at the height of the national furor over the Young Plan in 1929, conspired in further delays, despite threats by Kantorowicz that he would 'privately' publish his findings. Stresemann, shortly before his death in October 1929, entrusted yet another counteraffidavit to the ever-available Kriege. Concurrently, the Wilhelmstrasse denied Kantorowicz private publication of his findings; the parliamentary

Committee of Enquiry seconded this decision in February 1930. Kriege, for his part, informed Thimme that he intended to draw out his investigation as long as possible in order to stall Kantorowicz. The Finance Ministry at this point rejoined the revisionist campaign by refusing to make available to the fourth subcommittee the agreed-upon printing subsidy of 40–50,000 Mark – while at the same time the Foreign Ministry agreed fully to fund Kriege's counteraffidavit. In the meantime, Kantorowicz's career suffered irreparable damage. In 1933, his name was on the list of the first twenty-five professors to be dismissed from university posts by the Hitler regime. Kantorowicz's earlier work on *The Spirit of English Policy and the Phantom of Germany's Encirclement*, published in 1929, was among the books burned on the Nazi's pyre of ignorance in May 1933.[58]

To be sure, the vendetta conducted against Kantorowicz would not remain an isolated case. In 1932, several German historians, led by Hermann Oncken, Hermann Schumacher, and Fritz Hartung, conspired to deny the young radical scholar Eckart Kehr the Rockefeller Fellowship that Charles A. Beard had helped Kehr secure for study in the United States.[59] And as recently as February 1964, West Germany's foreign minister, Gerhard Schröder, acting upon the recommendations of Gerhard Ritter and Karl Dietrich Erdmann, formally rescinded Goethe Institute travel funds awarded Fritz Fischer for a planned lecture tour of the United States, a tour that Ritter equated with 'a national tragedy'. Apparently, the Foreign Ministry was quite prepared once more to take on the role of patriotic self-censor. It was only through the efforts of a dozen American scholars, led by Klaus Epstein, that Fischer's visit came about.[60] Ritter not only spoke of what he decried as Fischer's penchant for 'political masochism', but poured out all his bitterness in a letter to Klaus Epstein's father, Fritz, a scholar also hounded out of German academia after 1933, by referring to Fischer as 'an old Nazi who had so quickly managed to convert to democracy' after 1945.[61] Ritter's real grudge against Fischer was that the Hamburg historian with his *Griff nach der Weltmacht* had reopened the entire war-guilt issue, an issue *'that one had believed belonged to a distant past'*.[62] In that one sentence to his colleague Theodor Schieder at Köln, Ritter expressed his generation's horror that perhaps the 'patriotic sef-censorship' of the Weimar Republic had not succeeded after all. It was a fitting eulogy for this unfortunate chapter of German historiography. And the passions engendered by the 'Fischer controversy' certainly parallelled those of the

Kantorowicz and Kehr scandals both in substance and in acrimony. Careers both before and after the Second World War all too often hinged upon one's stance on the issue of 'war guilt'.

Memoirs and Historical Falsification

Last but not least, attention should be drawn to several attempts to suppress or to 'revise' memoirs after the First World War. One of the most celebrated cases involved General Helmuth von Moltke the Younger. The former chief of the General Staff had died in 1916, and his widow, with the assistance of Rudolf Steiner, the founder of anthroposophy, had prepared by the spring of 1919 a detailed memoir that promised to shed light on Moltke's role before and during the July crisis. Before the book could go to press, however, Eliza von Moltke was paid a visit by 'certain persons' who advised her not to publish her husband's papers. Steiner, in turn, was informed by the Prussian envoy at Stuttgart, Legation Secretary Hans-Adolf von Moltke, that 'Berlin did not desire' General von Moltke's memoirs in print; an unnamed general, who had served both Wilhelm II and Moltke, also sought out Steiner to caution against publication of the book.[63] These efforts were successful, and the *Erinnerungen* eventually put out by Eliza von Moltke in 1922 proved devoid of any information on the origins of the war. Moreover, Moltke's papers thereafter were so carefully 'ordered' by self-appointed patriotic censors that, in the words of John Röhl, 'they contain not a single document worth reading from the pre-War period'.[64] The same is rumored about the papers of Field Marshal von Hindenburg, which allegedly were 'ordered' by the late nationalist historian Walther Hubatsch; the Hindenburg family to date has refused to deposit them with the Federal Military Archive at Freiburg.[65]

Three important collections of papers barely escaped destruction. Those of Admiral Georg Alexander von Müller, chief of the Navy Cabinet to 1918, were earmarked for destruction upon the officer's death – an order fortunately not executed by his son, Sven. Yet when published by Walter Görlitz after the Second World War, the diaries incredibly appeared in a 'carefully expurgated version', although the authentic text is highly readable.[66]

Likewise, in the case of Kurt Riezler, Chancellor von Bethmann Hollweg's *intimus*, the papers were slated for destruction. The conservative historian Hans Rothfels, both during the Second

World War and thereafter, advised Riezler against publication in order not to reopen the debate concerning the origins of the Great War. After Riezler's death in 1965, his brother destroyed what he termed 'private' parts of the *Nachlass*, and neither the Foreign Office at Bonn nor the Federal Archive at Koblenz could persuade Walter Riezler to turn the papers over to them. It was only through the repeated pressures of historians both in Germany and abroad to secure the critical memoir that Riezler's sister, Mary White, eventually consented to publication. Not surprisingly, the Riezler materials were carefully 'ordered' by Karl Dietrich Erdmann in book form; thereafter, they remained closed to scholars at the Federal Archive at Koblenz for another eight years. Upon becoming available, the very originality especially of Riezler's notes during the July crisis was challenged in 1983. Gerhard Ritter, in the meantime, had persuaded the Bonn regime's Bundeszentrale für politische Bildung to print ten thousand copies of his apologetic account of the origins of the war, to be distributed primarily to West German schools and libraries. Eugen Gerstenmaier, the head of the West German Bundestag, thanked Ritter for his 'brilliant clarification' and expressed the satisfaction that 'therewith Fischer should really be finished off'.[67] It was all in the best tradition of the patriotic self-censors of the 1920s.

Finally, in the case of Admiral Alfred von Tirpitz, the family in the late 1960s released the papers of the former state secretary of the Navy Office to the Federal Military Archive at Freiburg only in exchange for a substantial fee. In fact, Tirpitz had caused a national scandal in 1924–25 when he published a two-volume set of documents designed to show that 'navalism' had been the right course and that others had failed to do their part to realise it. The Wilhelmstrasse had even released Friedrich Thimme from his labors on *Die Grosse Politik* so that he could attack Tirpitz's publication 'in the national interest'.[68]

A final curiosity is the case of Prince Philipp zu Eulenburg-Hertefeld. A trusted advisor to the last Hohenzollern before his tragic involvement in a national scandal in 1907–09, Eulenburg had entrusted his voluminous correspondence to Professor Johannes Haller. The latter's handling of the matter of publishing Eulenburg's materials sheds light upon the vagaries of postwar politics and scholarship. Haller at first advised against publication of the *Nachlass* after what he termed his 'dreadful' study of the diplomatic documents published by Karl Kautsky. In 1920, the aborted right-wing Kapp *Putsch* further convinced Haller that the time to publish the papers had not yet arrived. Especially the kaiser's marginal comments on diplomatic documents and his juvenile letters to Nicholas II of Russia had shocked the Tübingen historian. Yet by the late 1920s, Haller was ready to edit the memoirs, arguing that by 'clearing' Eulenburg's honour with regard to the homosexual scandal, he could lay the basis for the restoration of Wilhelm II.[69] In other words, scholarship was to be used as a tool in the fight against the Weimar Republic. The papers were not published until 1976.

It would be tedious to continue to list similar cases of suppression or revision of memoirs and diaries. Suffice it to say that these examples should provide an insight into the business of patriotic self-censorship during the Weimar Republic and thereafter. What has been entirely omitted are the cases where editors were engaged to ghostwrite memoirs – such as those of Admirals Karl Dönitz and Erich Raeder – in order to preclude public debate on vital issues of national interest.

The Revisionist Syndrome: Conclusions

The foregoing discussion of the German war-guilt campaign raises the twin issues concerning its effect, both in the short and in the long term, and the motivations that prompted the self-censors. Of course, many German publicists simply saw it as their patriotic duty to defend the fatherland against Allied charges that it had caused the war. Few, indeed, had been in a position in July 1914 to know what had transpired. Bismarck-admirers especially could hardly be expected to believe that the men of the summer of 1914 had been so unrealistic as to risk a European war against a powerful coalition with only one ally – moribund, at that – in tow. Others simply wanted to maintain the old order under the guise of a Republic that continued to call itself a Reich and to fly the imperial black-white-red colors along with the democratic black-red-gold. It was simply too hard to break with the past; the old order, right or wrong, needed to be defended against outside attacks. Nor should it be overlooked that the men who conducted the revisionist campaign had been servants of the old imperial order. Their actions during the 1920s showed clearly that they cared little for the principles of a democratic foreign policy, and hardly at all for such 'disturbing' institutions as political parties and parliaments.

Continuity, of course, could be maintained only if the senior civil servants of 1914 could demonstrate that Allied charges of war responsibility were without foundation. In short, the high bureaucracy was not interested in personnel purges in 1919. Nor were the dominant Social Democrats. In fact, the SPD never demanded that the senior statesmen and diplomats of the empire be held accountable. The resulting irony was that the Republic's Committee of Enquiry, for example, relied for many of its 'expert' affidavits upon the very men who had been in positions of power and responsibility in July 1914, men such as Gottlieb von Jagow and Johannes Kriege. By failing to clean house in 1919, by failing to confront the matter of Germany's role in the origins of the First World War brutally and honestly, and, above all, by failing to chase the patriotic censors from their temples of influence, the first leaders of the Weimar Republic did their country a great disservice. And for much of the 1920s, the lack of political experience under the empire of the parties of the center and left, compounded by their lack of republican self-confidence, rendered them ineffective not only against the self-censors but also in uncovering the causes for the war, especially through the Untersuchungsausschuss.

Conversely, the patriotic censors with their campaign of obfuscation, delay, preemptive historiography, and mass propaganda made quite certain that the issue would never be allowed to die, as Hans Freytag had foreseen as early as 1919. Max Weber, despite his signature on the 'professors' memorandum' of May 1919, in time came to lament this turn of events. 'Every document that comes to light after decades,' he sadly noted, 'revives the undignified squabbling, the hatred and anger, instead of at least *decently* burying the war and its end.'[70] As Michael Salewski has put it, the constant obsession with war guilt eventually mired the Republic in a 'revisionist syndrome'.[71]

Unsurprisingly, some of the self-censors were driven by reasons of personal interest. As Erich Hahn has suggested, the traditional elite of the Wilhelmstrasse fought for its political survival by defending its credibility – be it in 1914 or 1919 – both at home and abroad. The war-guilt issue thus served its purpose much in the way that the 'stab-in-the-back' legend served the army: as an escape from the political consequences of defeat. In other words, the consequences of the miscalculated risk of July 1914 could be avoided only by keeping the anti–war guilt campaign alive after the peace. And since the Republic very much depended on the cooperation of former imperial officials, it naturally had an interest in establishing their 'innocence'. Yet the war-guilt game was dangerous because, as Karl Kautsky had put it in 1919, it was 'not only a scholarly question for historians', but 'an eminently practical question for politicians'. For the authors of the war, the answer to the question of who was responsible amounted to a 'death sentence' as they surely would be 'cast among the politically dead..., stripped of all power'.[72] It was to be part of the genius of the patriotic self-censors that they managed through their collective efforts at preemptive historiography to escape that 'death sentence'.

In retrospect, the revisionist campaign conducted by men such as Bülow, Draeger, Freytag, Montgelas, Schücking, and Thimme, among others, retarded critical appraisal of the origins of the war until the 1960s. A certain orthodoxy on the war-guilt issue developed; Europe, in the immortal words of David Lloyd George, had simply 'slid' into the war in 1914 with roughly equal amounts of ignorance and naiveté. It simply cannot be stressed enough that by linking the war-guilt issue very early on to the campaign to 'revise' the Versailles treaty, the patriotic censors virtually precluded sober and rational investigation into the matter. Hermann Kantorowicz's affidavit might have been accepted as an academic treatise; it was political dynamite for a Gustav Stresemann pursuing rapprochement at least with the West at Locarno. Only by rejecting Article 231 outright could German leaders hope to convince the Allies that the harsh terms of the *Diktat* were, in fact, based upon a misconception. In other words, if they could undermine the charge of war guilt, these Germans felt, they could press on with treaty 'revisions' such as evacuation of occupied territories, redress of borders, above all in the East, and lowering of reparations payments. Indeed, it had been Stresemann's onetime hope that the publication of *Die Grosse Politik* would serve precisely such national interests.[73] Put differently, the Wilhelmstrasse hoped that by undermining the moral foundations of Allied charges of war guilt, it could restore the diplomatic freedom that the Reich had enjoyed before 1914 as an equal and sovereign member of the community of European nations.

Last but not least, both Bülow and Stresemann realised that the Wilhelmstrasse's campaign against Article 231 of the Versailles treaty also served a highly useful domestic purpose: the 'national alibi' constituted a convenient integration factor by rallying the political spectrum from *Vorwärts* to *Völkischer Beobachter*, that is, from Social Democrat to National Socialist, round this one great patriotic issue. In a land that had enjoyed a mere seventy years of nationhood and that remained deeply divided socially, politically, and regionally, such an integration factor was not to be overlooked. An additional domestic benefit was that the vigorous pursuance of 'revisionism' on the part of the Wilhelmstrasse might take some of the thunder out of the charges of 'defeatism' and 'softness' constantly levelled against the Republic by its rightwing detractors over the issue of 'fulfilment' of the Versailles treaty, and thereby benefit Stresemann's flexible and moderate revisionist diplomacy.[74]

Unfortunately, the events of 1932–33 were to show that this national consensus was tenuous at best; the seemingly diametrically opposed poles of extreme nationalism and national inferiority (engendered by the war-guilt charge) were to be brutally but effectively exploited by the extreme right, the real 'winners' of the revisionist campaign. In short, by delaying an open and honest discussion on the origins of the First World War for four decades, the self-censors did their part to bring about a political climate receptive to the radical 'revisionist' ideas of Adolf Hitler and his supporters.

At the risk of belaboring the obvious, I conclude this overview of how Clio was deceived in Germany by suggesting that the moral and institutional lessons to be learned have not lost any of their crispness and validity over the decades. It serves no national interest to obfuscate and derail intellectual inquiry. Miscalculated risks are rarely glossed over simply by selectively editing pertinent documents and by having paid publicists tout the desired line through government-controlled presses and publishers. 'Preemptive historiography' may succeed in the short run; over time, it is likely to be uncovered as the sham that it is. In the final analysis, it was nothing short of a tragedy that, in the words of Hermann Hesse, '90 or 100 prominent men' conspired in the supposed interests of the state 'to deceive the people on this vital question of national interest'.[75] Nor was Hesse in doubt as to the effectiveness of the campaign of 'patriotic self-censorship', informing Thomas Mann in 1931 of his opinion that 'of 1,000 Germans, even today 999 still know nothing of [our] war guilt'.[76] Little wonder, then, that Fritz Fischer's *Griff nach der Weltmacht* had such an explosive impact precisely thirty years later.

Notes

1. John Röhl, ed., *1914, Delusion or Design? The Testimony of Two German Diplomats* (London, 1973), p. 37. The literature on this topic is truly immense – there are no fewer than three thousand books extant on the events at Sarajevo in June 1914 alone. For two recent updates, see Ulrich Heinemann, *Die verdrängte Niederlage: Politische Öffentlichkeit und Kriegschuldfrage in der Weimarer Republik* (Göttingen, 1983); and Wolfgang Jäger, *Historische Forschung und politische Kultur in Deutschland: Die Debatte 1914–1980 über den Ausbruch des Ersten Weltkrieges* (Göttingen, 1984).

2. Fritz Fischer, *Griff nach der Weltmacht: Die Kriegszielpolitik des kaiserlichen Deutschland 1914–18* (Düsseldorf, 1961); Luigi Albertini, *The Origins of the War of 1914* (London, 1952–57), 3 vols. (Italian edition, *Le origini della guerra del 1914* [Milan, 1942–43], 3 vols.); Alfred von Wegerer, *Der Ausbruch des Weltkrieges 1914* (Hamburg, 1939), 2 vols.

3. 'I sought the truth; I loved my country'. Cited in Arden Bucholz, *Hans Delbrück and the German Military Establishment: War Images in Conflict* (Iowa City, 1985), p. 174.

4. Cited in Imanuel Geiss, ed., *Julikrise und Kriegsausbruch 1914*, vol. 1 (Hanover, 1963), p. 29.

5. Ibid., pp. 29–30. See also Bernhard W. von Bülow, 'Die Behandlung der Schuldfrage', *Deutsche Nation*, vol. 3 (1921), pp. 334–7; Bülow, *Die Grundlinien der diplomatischen Verhandlungen bei Kriegsausbruch* (Charlottenburg, 1919); as well as Bülow and Max Montgelas, eds., *Kommentar zu den Deutschen Dokumenten zum Kriegsausbruch* (Berlin, n.d.).

6. Jäger, *Historische Forschung*, 22–23.

7. Erich Matthias, ed., *Die Regierung der Volksbeauftragten 1918–19*, vol. 1 (Düsseldorf, 1969), pp. 139–140. For the genesis of Kautsky's orders to publish the documents, see ibid., pp. 102, 243, 258.

8. Geiss, *Julikrise*, vol. 1, pp. 30–32; Erich J.C. Hahn, 'The German Foreign Ministry and the Question of War Guilt in 1918–1919', in Carole Fink, Isabel V. Hull, and MacGregor Knox, eds., *German Nationalism and the European Response, 1890–1945* (Norman and London, 1985), pp. 47, 49; and Heinemann, *Die verdrängte Niederlage*, pp. 75–77. The Berlin project appeared in 1919 in two versions: Karl Kautsky, *Wie der Weltkrieg entstand: Dargestellt nach dem Aktenmaterial des Deutschen Auswärtigen Amts* (Berlin, 1919); and Max Montgelas and Walter Schücking, eds., *Die Deutschen Dokumente zum Kriegsausbruch 1914* (Berlin, 1919), 5 vols. The latter series was reprinted in 1922 and 1927. For the Cabinet's decision to recall Kautsky's project and to add Montgelas and Schücking as editors, see Anton Golecki, ed., *Akten der Reichskanzlei: Weimarer Republik. Das Kabinett Bauer* (Boppard, 1980), pp. 137–138. Session of 21 July 1919.

9. Jäger, *Historische Forschung*, p. 47.

10. Heinemann, *Die verdrängte Niederlage*, p. 38.

11. Ibid., p. 38; and Hahn, 'German Foreign Ministry', p. 62. The so-called 'coloured books' were hastily assembled in the wake of the July crisis and included genuine as well as falsified materials; among the major powers, there were the Austro-Hungarian Red Book, the British Blue Book, the French Yellow Book, the German White Book, and the Russian Orange Book. See the Introduction to Albertini, *The Origins of the War of 1914*, vol. 1.

12. Heinemann, *Die verdrängte Niederlage*, pp. 38–39.
13. Ibid., p. 39.
14. Cited in Hahn, 'German Foreign Ministry', p. 63, note 48.
15. Cited in ibid., p. 67. Bülow to Freytag, 31 May 1919.
16. Ibid., pp. 64–65; Geiss, *Julikrise*, vol. 1, pp. 30–31; and Heinemann, *Die verdrängte Niederlage*, p. 45. See also Hagen Schulze, ed., *Akten der Reichskanzlei: Weimarer Republik. Das Kabinett Scheidemann* (Boppard, 1971), pp. 384–5, note 10.
17. Wolfgang J. Mommsen, *Max Weber und die deutsche Politik 1890–1920* (Tübingen, 1974), p. 340. Weber to Delbrück, 8 October 1919.
18. Schulze, *Das Kabinett Scheidemann*, pp. 86–87, session of 22 March 1919; and Hahn, 'German Foreign Ministry', pp. 67, 68.
19. Annelise Thimme, 'Friedrich Thimme als politischer Publizist im Ersten Weltkrieg und in der Kriegsschuldkontroverse', in Alexander Fischer, Günter Moltmann, and Klaus Schwabe, eds., *Russland – Deutschland – Amerika: Festschrift für Fritz T. Epstein zum 80. Gerburtstag* (Wiesbaden, 1978), pp. 225–229. See also the East German accounts, largely based upon the works of Imanuel Geiss: Fritz Klein, ed., *Deutschland im Ersten Weltkrieg*, vol. 1 (East Berlin, 1971), pp. 33–34; and Hans Schleier, *Die bürgerliche deutsche Geschichtsschreibung der Weimarer Republik* (East Berlin, 1975), pp. 141–4.
20. Herman J. Wittgens, 'War Guilt Propaganda Conducted by the German Foreign Ministry During the 1920s', Canadian Historical Association, *Historical Papers* (1980), p. 231. The project appeared as Johannes Lepsius, Albrecht Mendelsohn-Bartholdy, and Friedrich Thimme, eds., *Die Grosse Politik der Europäischen Kabinette, 1871–1914: Sammlung der Diplomatischen Akten des Auswärtigen Amtes* (Berlin, 1922–27), 40 vols. in 54.
21. For the shortcomings of *Die Grosse Politik*, see especially Geiss, *Julikrise*, vol. 1, pp. 33–34; Heinemann, *Die verdrängte Niederlage*, p. 82; Schleier, *Die bürgerliche deutsche Geschichtsschreibung*, pp. 146–51; Klein, *Deutschland im Ersten Weltkrieg*, vol. 1, p. 34; and Thimme, 'Friedrich Thimme', p. 230.
22. Fritz Klein, 'Über die Verfälschung der historischen Wahrheit in der Aktenpublikation "Die Grosse Politik der Europäischen Kabinette 1871–1914"', *Zeitschrift für Geschichtswissenschaft*, vol. 7 (1950), pp. 319, 321, 328–9. Compare *Die Grosse Politik*, vol. 16, pp. 143–6.
23. Geiss, *Julikrise*, vol. 1, pp. 33–34.
24. Thimme, 'Friedrich Thimme', p. 230.
25. Ibid., p. 235; Schleier, *Die bürgerliche deutsche Geschichtsschreibung*, pp. 146–7; Alfred von Wegerer, *Die Widerlegung der Versailler Kriegsschuldthese* (Berlin, 1928); Friedrich Thimme, 'Die Auswertung der Aktenpublikation des AA für die Kriegsschuldfrage', *Die Kriegsschuldfrage*, vol. 5 (1927), pp. 387–95; Thimme, 'Das Ausland und die deutsche Aktenpublikation', *Weg zur Freiheit*, vol. 20 (1927), pp. 314–9; and Thimme, *Die Aktenpublikation des Auswärtigen Amtes: Beiträge zu ihrer Entstehungsgeschichte* (Berlin, 1924).
26. George W.F. Hallgarten, *Imperialismus vor 1914: Die soziologischen Grundlagen der Aussenpolitik europäischer Grossmächte vor dem Ersten Weltkrieg*, vol. 1 (Munich, 1963), p. vii; and Schleier, *Die bürgerliche deutsche Geschichtsschreibung*, pp. 147–8. In a letter to Thimme on 25 February 1925, Mendelsohn-Bartholdy spoke of 'destroying', 'suppressing', and 'ordering' certain potentially damaging documents. He asked Thimme to destroy his letter. Ibid., p. 149.
27. Wittgens, 'War Guilt Propaganda', p. 244.

28. Cited in Heinemann, *Die verdrängte Niederlage*, p. 56.

29. Ibid., p. 62.

30. Ibid., p. 66; and Schleiser, *Die bürgerliche deutsche Geschichtsschreibung*, pp. 144, 151. See also Albrecht Mendelssohn-Bartholdy, ed., *Die auswärtige Politik des Deutschen Reiches 1871–1914* (Berlin, 1928), 4 vols.

31. An example of the sort of speech penned by the War Guilt Section's staff was President von Hindenburg's eulogy at the unveiling of the Tannenberg memorial in September 1927: 'The charge that Germany is responsible for this greatest of all wars, we and the German people at all levels reject with one voice. Not envy, hatred, or lust to conquer forced us to take up arms. Rather, the war was the ultimate ... means with which to sustain ourselves in a world of enemies all around.' Cited in Heinemann, *Die verdrängte Niederlage*, p. 227.

32. Wittgens, 'War Guilt Propaganda', pp. 229–30; and Imanuel Geiss, 'The Outbreak of the First World War and German War Aims', *Journal of Contemporary History*, vol. 1 (1966), p. 77. This article was reproduced in German in Geiss, *Das Deutsche Reich und die Vorgeschichte des Ersten Weltkriegs* (Munich, 1978), pp. 204ff.

33. Heinemann, *Die verdrängte Niederlage*, p. 89. See also Friedrich Stieve, ed., *Der Diplomatische Schriftwechsel Iswolskis 1911–1914: Aus den Geheimakten der Russichen Staatsarchive. Im Auftrag des Deutschen Auswärtigen Amtes in deutscher Übersetzung* (Berlin, 1924), 4 vols.; Stieve, *Iswolski und der Weltkrieg: Aufgrund der neuen Dokumenten-Veröffentlichung des Deutschen Auswärtigen Amtes* (Berlin, 1924); and Stieve, *Iswolski im Weltkriege: Der diplomatische Schriftwechsel Iswolskis 1914–1917* (Berlin, 1926).

34. Heinemann, *Die verdrängte Niederlage*, pp. 90–91. The Viennese collection appeared as: Ludwig Bittner, Alfred Francis Pribram, Heinrich Srbik, and Hans Uebersberger, eds., *Österreich-Ungarns Aussenpolitik von der Bosnischen Krise 1908 bis zum Kriegsausbruch 1914: Diplomatische Aktenstücke des Österreichisch-Ungarischen Ministeriums des Äussern* (Vienna, 1930), 8 vols.

35. Heinemann, *Die verdrängte Niederlage*, p. 91. See also Herman J. Wittgens, 'The German Foreign Office Campaign Against the Treaty of Versailles: An Examination of the Activities of the Kriegsschuldreferat in the United States' (Ph.d. dissertation, University of Washington, 1970).

36. Wittgens, 'War Guilt Propaganda', p. 233. See also Ernst Sauerbeck, *Der Kriegsausbruch: Eine Darstellung von neutraler Seite anhand des Aktenmaterials* (Stuttgart, 1919); and Alfred von Wegerer, 'Die Zentralstelle für Erforschung der Kriegsursachen und die freien Kriegsschuldfrageorganisationen', in *Die Liga: Mitteilungsblatt der Liga zum Schutze der deutschen Kultur*, vols. 7/8 (1921), pp. 90ff.

37. Wittgens, 'War Guilt Propaganda', pp. 233–4; Heinemann, *Die verdrängte Niederlage*, pp. 83, 96, 98; Geiss, 'Outbreak of the First World War', p. 76; and Schleier, *Die bürgerliche deutsche Geschichtsschreibung*, p. 153.

38. Heinemann, *Die verdrängte Niederlage*, p. 97. German wage statistics are from Gerhard Bry, *Wages in Germany 1871–1945* (Princeton, 1960), pp. 51–55.

39. Heinemann, *Die verdrängte Niederlage*, pp. 98–99; Geiss, 'Outbreak of the First World War', pp. 76–77; Schleier, *Die bürgerliche deutsche Geschichtsschreibung*, pp. 151–2; and Thimme, 'Friedrich Thimme', p. 235. See also Bernhard Schwertfeger, *Die Diplomatischen Akten des Auswärtigen Amtes 1871–1914: Ein Wegweiser durch das grosse Aktenwerk der Deutschen Regierung* (Berlin, 1923/27); *Der Fehlspruch von Versailles: Deutschlands Freispruch aus belgischen Dokumenten,*

1871–1914 (Berlin, 1921); 'Geschichtswerdung und Geschichtsschreibung', *Archiv für Geschichte und Politik*, vol. 1 (1923), pp. 385–408; and *Der Weltkrieg der Dokumente: Zehn Jahre Kriegsschuldforschung und ihr Ergebnis* (Berlin, 1929).

40. Geiss, 'Outbreak of the First World War', p. 77; and Wittgens, 'War Guilt Propaganda', p. 239. See also Milos Boghitschewitsch, *Die Auswärtige Politik Serbiens 1903–1914* (Berlin, 1928–31), 3 vols.

41. Jäger, *Historische Forschung*, pp. 69ff; and Heinemann, *Die verdrängte Niederlage*, pp. 106–7.

42. Ibid., pp. 120–1; and Wittgens, 'War Guilt Propaganda', p. 235. See also Hans Draeger, *Der Arbeitsausschuss Deutscher Verbände 1921–1931* (Berlin, 1931).

43. Wittgens, 'War Guilt Propaganda', p. 235; Heinemann, *Die verdrängte Niederlage*, pp. 122–124; Dieter Fricke, ed., *Die bürgerlichen Parteien in Deutschland 1830–1945: Handbuch der Geschichte der bürgerlichen Parteien und anderer bürgerlicher Interessenorganisationen vom Vormärz bis zum Jahre 1945*, vol. 1 (East Berlin, 1968), pp. 48–55.

44. Heinemann, *Die verdrängte Niederlage*, pp. 126–9; and Wittgens, 'War Guilt Propaganda', pp. 236–7. See also Friedrich Stieve, *Deutschland und Europa 1890–1914: Ein Handbuch zur Vorgeschichte des Weltkrieges mit den wichtigsten Dokumenten* (Berlin, 1926).

45. Wittgens, 'War Guilt Propaganda', pp. 240–4; Heinemann, *Die verdrängte Niederlage*, pp. 113, 115; and Fritz Fischer, *Kreig der Illusionen: Die deutsche Politik von 1911 bis 1914* (Düsseldorf, 1969), p. 670. See also Bernadotte E. Schmitt, *The Coming of the War* (New York and London, 1930), 2 vols.; and Sidney B. Fay, *The Origins of the World War* (New York, 1928) 2 vols. The latter appeared in Germany as *Der Ursprung des Weltkrieges* (Berlin, 1930), 2 vols.

46. Wittgens, 'War Guilt Propaganda', pp. 238–9, 242–3, 245. See Harry E. Barnes, *The Genesis of the World War: An Introduction to the Problem of War Guilt* (New York, 1927); and *In Quest of Truth and Justice: De-Bunking the War Guilt Myth* (Chicago, 1928). Barnes's *Genesis* appeared in Germany as *Die Entstehung des Weltkrieges: Eine Einführung in das Kriegsschuldproblem* (Stuttgart, 1928).

47. See Jäger, *Historische Forschung*, p. 65.

48. Geiss, 'Outbreak of the First World War', p. 78.

49. The Cabinet decision to establish the Committee of Enquiry and the special tribunal is in Golecki, *Das Kabinett Bauer*, p. 199; session of 16 August 1919. See also W. Kahl, 'Untersuchungsausschuss und Staatsgerichtshof', *Deutsche Juristenzeitung*, vol. 25 (1920), pp. 2–7; Hahn, 'German Foreign Ministry', pp. 54, 55; Schleier, *Die bürgerliche deutsche Geschichtsschreibung*, pp. 154–6; and Heinemann, *Die verdrängte Niederlage*, p. 156.

50. Eugen Fischer-Baling, 'Der Untersuchungsausschus für die Schuldfragen des ersten Weltkrieges', in Alfred Herrmann, ed., *Aus Geschichte und Politik: Festschrift zum 70. Geburtstag von Ludwig Bergsträsser* (Düsseldorf, 1954), p. 137; and Klein, *Deutschland im Ersten Weltkrieg*, vol. 1, p. 25. See also *Das Werk des Untersuchungsausschusses der Deutschen Verfassunggebenden Nationalversammlung und des Deutschen Reichstages 1919–1930* (Berlin, 1927ff), 19 vols. in 25. The first subcommittee published three volumes in 1929 and 1930; the second brought out none; the third published four volumes in 1927; and the fourth managed twelve volumes between 1925 and 1929.

51. Fischer-Baling, 'Untersuchungsausschuss', pp. 124, 129, as late as 1954 still claimed, despite his intimate association with the workings of the Committee of Enquiry throughout the 1920s, that the documentary materials of 'all

bureaus' had been made available and that it was simply inconceivable that the 'correct bureaucrats' of Imperial Germany could have 'suppressed or ordered' any evidence. See also Heinemann, *Die verdrängte Niederlage*, p. 158.

52. Ibid., pp. 162–163; and Werner Hahlweg, 'Das hinterlassene Werk des Parlamentarischen Untersuchungsausschusses', in Rudolf Vierhaus and Manfred Botzenhart, eds., *Dauer und Wandel der Geschichte: Aspekte Europäischer Vergangenheit, Festgabe für Kurt von Raumer zum 15. Dezember 1965* (Münster, 1966), p. 544.

53. Fischer-Baling, 'Untersuchungsausschuss', p. 135; and Heinemann, *Die verdrängte Niederlage*, pp. 193–4, 199–203. Kriege's numerous journeys to Doorn are chronicled in Sigurd von Ilsemann, *Der Kaiser in Holland: Aufzeichnungen des letzten Flügeladjutanten Kaiser Wilhelms II* (Munich, 1967–68), 2 vols. On the Hague conventions, see Jost Dülffer, *Regeln gegen den Krieg? Die Haager Friedenskonferenzen von 1899 und 1907 in der internationalen Politik* (Berlin, 1981).

54. Heinemann, *Die verdrängte Niederlage*, pp. 179–87. For the cabinet reaction, see Günter Abramowski, ed., *Akten der Reichskanzlei: Weimarer Republik. Die Kabinette Marx I und II*, vol. 2 (Boppard, 1973), pp. 1160–61, 1213, 1222; sessions of 7 November, 4 and 12 December 1924. See also Hermann von Kuhl, *Der Weltkreig 1914–1918* (Berlin, 1929), 2 vols.; Bucholz, *Hans Delbrück*, pp. 121ff.; and Annelise Thimme, *Hans Delbrück als Kritiker der Wilhelminischen Epoche* (Düsseldorf, 1955).

55. Heinemann, *Die verdrängte Niederlage*, pp. 188–9. The first scholarly evaluation of the navy's war diary was by Wilhelm Deist, 'Die Flottenpolitik der Seekriegsleitung und die Rebellion der Flotte Ende Oktober 1918', *Vierteljahrshefte für Zeitgeschichte*, vol. 14 (1966), pp. 341–68.

56. Heinemann, *Die verdrängte Niederlage*, pp. 212–3. See also Max von Montgelas, *Leitfaden zur Kriegsschuldfrage* (Berlin, 1923); and Hermann Lutz, *Die europäische Politik in der Julikrise 1914* (Berlin, 1930).

57. Cited in Schleier, *Die bürgerliche deutsche Geschichtsschreibung*, p. 157. Stresemann's papers were also carefully 'ordered' after his death. See Gustav Stresemann, *Vermächtnis, der Nachlass*, ed. Henry Bernhard (Berlin, 1932–33), 3 vols., and Hans W. Gatzke, 'The Stresemann Papers', *Journal of Modern History*, vol. 26 (1954), pp. 49–59.

58. See Hermann Kantorowicz, *Gutachten zur Kriegsschuldfrage 1914*, ed. Imanuel Geiss (Frankfurt, 1967), pp. 7–42; Erich Eyck, *A History of the Weimar Republic*, vol. 2 (London, 1964), pp. 105–6, note; and Heinemann, *Die verdrängte Niederlage*, p. 215. Kantorowicz's earlier book was entitled *Der Geist der englischen Politik und das Gespenst der Einkreisung Deutschlands* (Berlin, 1929).

59. See Schleier, *Die bürgerliche deutsche Geschichtsschreibung*, p. 519; and Eckart Kehr, *Der Primat der Innenpolitik: Gesammelte Aufsätze zur preussisch-deutschen Sozialgeschichte im 19. und 20. Jahrhundert*, ed. Hans-Ulrich Wehler (Berlin, 1965), pp. 18–19.

60. Klaus Schwabe and Rolf Reichardt, eds., *Gerhard Ritter: Ein politischer Historiker in seinen Briefen* (Boppard, 1984), pp. 587–9. Ritter to Schröder, 17 January 1964.

61. Ibid., pp. 559, 576. Ritter to Herzfeld, 30 October 1961; and Ritter to Epstein, 15 February 1963. On another occasion, Ritter denounced his Hamburg colleague as a 'student of the arch-Nazi Erich Seeberg' and accused him of having gained his chair at Hamburg University in 1942 through the influence of Walter Frank, head of the Reichsinstitut für Geschichte des neuen Deutschlands. Bernd F.

Schulte, *Die Verfälschung der Riezler Tagebücher: Ein Beitrag zur Wissenschafts-geschichte der 50iger und 60iger Jahre* (Frankfurt, Bern, and New York, 1985), p. 145. Fischer's defenders are conspicuously silent on the matter of his alleged Nazi past; it is inconceivable, of course, that any scholar could have attained an important academic post in 1942 without the official sanction of the Nazi regime. See Karl-Heinz Janssen, 'Historischer Realismus', *Die Zeit*, 2 March 1973, p. 15. In any case, it is illuminating that an 'old-Nazi' such as Fischer should have been able to come to the position on the origins of the war that he did in *Griff nach der Weltmacht*, while a self-proclaimed anti-Nazi such as Ritter continued to tout the position of the patriotic self-censors from the 1920s.

62. Ibid., p. 562. Ritter to Schieder, 4 December 1961. Emphasis added.

63. Helmuth von Moltke, *Erinnerungen. Briefe. Dokumente 1877–1916. Ein Bild vom Kriegsausbruch, erster Kriegsführung und Persönlichkeit des ersten militärischen Führers des Krieges*, ed. Eliza von Moltke (Stuttgart, 1922), pp. vii–viii; and Roman Boos, ed., *Rudolf Steiner während des Weltkrieges: Beiträge Rudolf Steiners zur Bewältigung der Aufgaben die durch den Krieg gestellt wurden* (Dornach, 1933), pp. 99–100.

64. Röhl, *1914: Delusion or Design?*, pp. 37–38.

65. Hubatsch used these papers, which remain with the field marshall's grandson, Hubertus von Hindenburg, in *Hindenburg und der Staat: Aus den Papieren des Generalfeldmarschalls und Reichspräsidenten von 1878 bis 1934* (Göttingen, 1966).

66. See Röhl, *1914: Delusion or Design?*, p. 37; Walter Görlitz, ed., *The Kaiser and His Court: The Diaries, Note Books and Letters of Admiral Georg Alexander von Müller, Chief of the Navy Cabinet, 1914–1918* (New York, 1961), p. xiii. The papers are now at the Bundesarchiv-Militärarchiv (BA-MA) at Freiburg: N 159, *Nachlass* Müller.

67. Karl Dietrich Erdmann, ed., *Kurt Riezler: Tagebücher, Aufsätze, Dokumente* (Göttingen, 1972), pp. 8–12. The originality of especially Riezler's notes (*Blockblätter*) for the period from 7 July through 14 August 1914 has been contended: Bernd Sösemann, 'Die Tagebücher Kurt Riezlers: Untersuchungen zu ihrer Echtheit und Edition', *Historische Zeitschrift*, vol. 236 (April 1983), pp. 327–69. Karl Dietrich Erdmann, 'Zur Echtheit der Tagebücher Kurt Riezlers: Eine Antikritik', ibid., pp. 371–402, maintains that the notes for the period in question stem from Riezler's hand. See also Schulte, *Die Verfälschung der Riezler Tagebücher*, pp. 9, 146.

68. Thimme, 'Friedrich Thimme', p. 235; Annelise Thimme, 'Der "Fall Tirpitz" als Fall der Weimarer Republik', in Imanuel Geiss and Bernd-Jürgen Wendt, eds., *Deutschland in der Weltpolitik des 19. und 20. Jahrhunderts. Fritz Fischer zum 65. Geburtstag* (Düsseldorf, 1973), pp. 463–82; and Schleier, *Die bürgerliche deutsche Geschichtsschreibung*, p. 152. The papers are now at the BA-MA: N 253, *Nachlass* Tirpitz.

69. John C.G. Röhl, ed., *Philipp Eulenburgs Politische Korrespondenz*, vol. 1 (Boppard, 1976), pp. 64–65.

70. Max von Weber, 'Politik als Beruf', in *Gesammelte politische Schriften*, ed. Johannes Winckelmann (Tübingen, 1971), p. 549.

71. Michael Salewski, 'Das Weimarer Revisionssyndrom', in *Aus Politik und Zeitgeschichte: Beilage zur Wochenzeitung 'Das Parlament'*, B2/1980 (12 January 1980), pp. 14–25.

72. Hahn, 'German Foreign Ministry', pp. 56, 69; and Kautsky, *Wie der Weltkrieg entstand*, p. 13.

73. Heinemann, *Die verdrängte Niederlage*, p. 224. On the foreign policy implications of the issue, see Andreas Hillgruber, 'Unter dem Schatten von Versailles – die aussenpolitische Belastung der Weimarer Republik: Realität und Perzeption bei den Deutschen', in Karl Dietrich Erdmann and Hagen Schulze, eds. *Weimar. Selbstpreisgabe einer Demokratie. Eine Bilanz heute. Kölner Kolloquium der Fritz Thyssen Stiftung Juni 1979* (Düsseldorf, 1980), pp. 51–67. On 7 May 1932, the former head of the War Guilt Section, Legation Secretary Karl Schwendemann, crowed to Alfred von Wegerer of the effectiveness of the anti–war guilt campaign. "You see, dear Herr von Wegerer, how important our enlightenment in the war-guilt question is for the disarmament negotiations here [at Geneva in 1932]. Had the disarmament conference taken place six years ago, then certainly the French would have brought the war-guilt question into debate and perhaps still with the prospect of success'. National Archives Record Group 242, Records of the German Foreign Office Received by the Department of State, Microfilm Series T120: 3220/E547299–301, p. 300. I am indebted to Professor Don Emerson of the University of Washington for this citation.

74. Jäger, *Historische Forschung*, p. 68; and Heinemann, *Die verdrängte Niederlage*, pp. 226, 241.

75. Eckart Klessmann, 'Als politischer Zeitkritiker neu entdeckt: Hermann Hesse', in *Die Zeit Zeitmagazin*, vol. 15 (14 April 1972), p. 10. Hesse to Wilhelm Schäfer, 1930.

76. Ibid, p. 10.

Chapter 4

SENATOR OWEN, THE SCHULDREFERAT, AND THE DEBATE OVER WAR GUILT IN THE 1920S

Herman Wittgens

Contacts in 1923 between officials of the German Foreign Ministry and Senator Robert L. Owen, Democrat from Oklahoma, seemed to hold out the promise of making the United States Senate a forum in the historiographical propaganda campaign conducted against Article 231 of the Treaty of Versailles. This campaign against the so-called war-guilt article was intended to weaken the alleged moral and legal basis of the treaty, undermine confidence in it, and so create a climate of opinion favourable to the revision of the material clauses.[1]

The major themes of the German innocence campaign emerge clearly from the so- called 'Professoren Denkschrift', a salvo fired in the exchange of notes in 1919, which aimed to repulse the charge of German responsibility for the outbreak of the war. The memorandum called for an impartial commission to examine the causes of the war. It blamed Russian imperialism, French revanchism, the equivocal position of Sir Edward Grey, and Russian mobilisation for the conflict.[2] This memorandum became, perhaps unwittingly, the point of departure for Senator Owen and so many revisionists.

The purpose of this paper is to examine these contacts from 1923 to 1927 between German Foreign Ministry officials and Senator

Owen within the context of several developments. These contacts reveal the salient features of the German innocence campaign and what German officials expected from it. The Foreign Ministry exploited marginal revisionists like the senator because they uncritically based their writings and speeches on sources circulated by it. In turn, the Ministry widely distributed the works of revisionists. The relationship with Senator Owen promised raising the war-guilt question in the Senate, perhaps by convening an investigating committee which would produce what could be construed as an 'official' statement on the outbreak of the war. These activities need to be set in the larger context of German-American relations.

The United States became a prime target for war-guilt propaganda because of its key role in German foreign policy. 'German policy makers recognised very early the potential value of the United States as an ally in their efforts to break "the fetters of Versailles"'.[3] German-American understanding, based mainly on mutual financial and commercial interests, was expected to bring economic improvement and so political equality.[4] 'The United States had become the most important partner in German politics of treaty revision ...'[5] In support of this policy the German Foreign Ministry attempted to create a favourable public opinion in the United States on reparation, the Danzig corridor, disarmament, and especially the war-guilt question. Counsellor of Legation Kiep believed that '... the main goal was to achieve a favourable public opinion in the world, especially in the United States, where the government required popular support for its activities. If a major part of world opinion no longer believed in the sole responsibility of Germany for the outbreak of the World War, and so perceives an obligation to make reparations to Germany, then a favourable basis for a general settlement shall have been created'.[6]

According to the German Foreign Ministry, the enlightenment of public opinion in the formerly neutral and enemy countries was an essential basic task for achieving the revision of the peace treaty. An extensive propaganda campaign which sought to convert people directly or to extract official statements from governments was deemed premature, and it seemed advisable to wait until reaction against the treaty and the dogma of sole German guilt had gained further ground within the intelligentsia. Wegerer stated that the '... impossible demands of the Versailles Treaty as such ... the military disarmament of the Reich, the completely superfluous occupation of the Rhineland, the maintenance of the impossible Eastern frontier, and the prohibition of the union between Germany and Austria are on every occasion justified by the idea of guilt'.[7] The destruction of Article 231 was expected to ease the revision of the material clauses of the Treaty of Versailles; that is, to undo the consequences of defeat.

Between 1919 and 1921, the German Foreign Ministry shaped the institutional framework to undertake war-guilt propaganda at home and abroad. The ministry's Kriegsschuldreferat (War-Guilt Section) or simply Schuldreferat became, after a somewhat uncertain start, the official centre for the fight against Article 231. Its most important function was the release of a vast array of documentary materials, most notably *Die Grosse Politik*, which was released between 1922 and 1927, thus creating a dependency on German materials.[8]

In 1921, two ostensibly independent front organisations emerged under the direction of the Schuldreferat. The Arbeitsausschuss Deutscher Verbände (Steering Committee for National Associations) was initially an attempt by the government to assert some control over the many patriotic organisations of all political shadings which concerned themselves with the war-guilt question and other aspects of the treaty. The London Conference of 1921 had rekindled German indignation, increasingly amplified and focussed by a growing number of patriotic associations that directed their animus against the *Diktat*. Although the primary purpose of the Arbeitsausschuss was the coordination of German public opinion, it did maintain important contacts with foreign scholars and publicists. Its approximately two thousand member organisations spanned the entire political spectrum, including all political parties, labour organisations, interest groups and patriotic organisations that reached into the far right.[9]

The Schuldreferat instituted the Zentralstelle für Erforschung der Kriegsurachen (Center for the Causes of the War) to forge special links with foreign scholars and publicists. Its most important task was publication of the monthly *Die Kriegsschuldfrage* which became the most significant forum for revisionist writers. As a necessary precondition for successful propaganda in foreign countries and a support for German statesmen in their negotiations with the former enemies, the ministry hoped to create a uniform public opinion on war guilt at home. Thus, domestic and foreign propaganda reinforced each other: foreign revisionists confirmed the innocence campaign at home, and a uniform public opinion strengthened the case of the foreign revisionists.[10]

By the mid-1920s the outline of the revisionist debate in the United States had become clear. The Smith historian, Sydney B. Fay, had published his 'New Light' articles in the *American Historical Review*.[11] Regarded as a moderate revisionist, Fay was acclaimed by the Schuldreferat as the new messiah in the war-guilt question. The Chicago historian Bernadotte E. Schmitt stood outside the revisionists' camp. Harry Elmer Barnes, of Clark University and Smith College, had just arrived at his revisionist position in a series of articles in the *Christian Century* which held that war had been brought about by a Franco-Russian conspiracy and had been made unavoidable by Russian mobilisation. The articles provoked wide discussion of the war-guilt question along lines laid down by the Schuldreferat.[12] By the middle of the decade, the Schuldreferat had given wider circulation to numerous revisionists, many of them French or English.[13] Senator Owen would draw upon their writings and become firmly established on the radical side of the revisionist spectrum.

Robert Latham Owen, Democratic senator from Oklahoma from 1907 to 1925, was a lawyer, Indian agent, and banker. A prominent supporter of Woodrow Wilson in 1917, especially of his League of Nation ideas, Owen was not a reflexive pro-German. In 1918 he supported a resolution which held that the Great War had been '... an offensive war of the completely prepared German and Austrian military autocracies against the unsuspecting and inadequately prepared democracies of the world ...[14] In the same year he advocated that Germany should be forced, with a trade boycott if necessary, to accept the Treaty of Versailles. According to a 1922 memorandum for Chancellor Wirth, his sympathies were definitely not on the German side. Owen met with Chancellor Wirth and Foreign Minister Rathenau while on banking business in Paris.[15] He converted to the revisionist cause in the war-guilt question near the end of his senatorial career, likely in the summer of 1923, after he had read Marchand's *Un Livre Noir*, Siebert's collection of despatches between the Russian Foreign Office and Benckendorff, its ambassador in London, and much of the revisionist literature of the day.[16]

State Secretary von Maltzan[17] suggested to Owen that he give a speech to the Senate on the war-guilt question. The senator decided to speak for Germany when Maltzan explained to him that Germany's word was suspect in the war-guilt question. Owen allowed that the Russian materials had convinced him of German innocence and Franco-Russian guilt; moreover, he now believed that, at the time, the United States had been deceived about the nature of the war. Sharing the guilt for this deception, the senator felt obliged to help uncover the truth. In this conversation Owen brought war guilt and reparations into close relationship by declaring that the Dawes Plan was only a temporary solution until the progressive destruction of the theses of German war guilt would make possible the revision of German reparation.[18] Maltzan could not have asked for more.

On 18 December 1923, Senator Owen burst into prominence as a war-guilt revisionist with a long speech before the Senate entitled: 'The Inner Secrets of European Diplomacy Disclosed for the First Time to the American Public'.[19] According to the senator, the question of responsibility for the outbreak of the war had a direct bearing on the interests of the American people in trade, investment and the repayment of loans, all of which the current instability in Europe affected adversely. Acceptance of American ideals of international justice would permit disarmament, stabilise currencies, and usher in an era of prosperity enhanced by American loans. However, Europe still suffered from the old ideals of imperialism which had marked the foreign relations of the European powers.[20] Only the truth regarding the outbreak of the war could pacify Europe.

Owen believed that, with the opening of secret Russian and German archives, a great mass of documentation had come to light which demonstrated that the German militaristic leaders had not willed the war but tried to avoid it. Russian and French statesmen had been determined to go to war, and their mobilisation efforts were intended to be a declaration of war against Germany.[21] In contrast, Germany ardently desired the localisation of the conflict and acted as a mediator.[22] The Franco-Russian alliance of 1892 and subsequent treaties, understandings, and military conventions amounted to a conspiracy to wage war against Germany.[23] By saying that Russia could achieve control over the Straits and penetration of the Balkans only with a European war, Owen approached the classic formulation of radical revisionists.[24]

The overly long speech consisted for the most part of 'Exhibits', that is, quotations of varying length from the works of French, English and German revisionists, as well as documentary collections. All of them had been put into circulation or promoted by the Schuldreferat. Only a thin narrative held the speech together, though the following polemical point emerged strongly: France and Russia, but especially the latter, conspired against the peace of

Europe, and Germany was their victim. According to Owen, these new disclosures about European diplomacy meant that Article 231 burdened the Germans with a profound national humiliation, and they were justifiably bitter about the article and its consequences. Owen warned that it would be well for the world to consider whether European reconciliation was possible as long as the Germans were unjustly charged with a great wrong.[25] No less than '[the] preservation of the white civilisation of Europe demands that the statesmen of the world realise the importance of pursuing ways which will truly establish understanding, good will and cooperation'.[26] The speech of 18 December 1923, established the senator as a widely known revisionist.

Owen's speech was very well received by other revisionists. The Chicago historian Ferdinand Schevill recognised it as a notable work of scholarship and an act of moral liberation. Sidney Bradshaw Fay, who had made a name for himself with the 'New Light' articles and who would emerge as the most respected authority on the causes of the war, congratulated Owen on his courage, wisdom and insight, recognised his use of first-rate sources, and hoped that the speech would be the starting point for intelligent discussion of this extraordinarily important question.[27] E.D. Morel noted that '[for] the first time since that war ended a member of one of the world's legislatures has broken through this conspiracy of silence.... German militarism was a bogey of the heated fancy. French militarism is a reality and sets its iron heel on Europe at this hour'.[28] For German war-guilt propagandists, the senator's speech presented opportunities. The German embassy believed that the speech, already read into the *Congressional Record* and widely distributed by the senator, had revived the war-guilt issue with the American public.[29] A suggestion that the documents revealed in Owen's speech be combined with others into an official publication of the U.S. government was not followed up; having them read into the *Record* seems to have given them pseudo-official standing.[30] The Schuldreferat celebrated the sensational speech as an extraordinary victory because it contained nearly the entire publication of G. von Romberg's *Falsifications of the Russian Orange Book* and other materials propagated by the Schuldreferat which also took steps to focus attention on the speech.[31] The Schuldreferat initiated discussions of it in the neutral press, especially in Sweden where German guilt for the war was almost uniformly denied, and it undertook translations into German, French, Spanish and Italian.[32] It distributed thousands of

copies of the speech because it was believed to refute effectively
the allegation of Germany's sole guilt for the war.[33] With this
speech a revolution had occurred in how the war-guilt question
was judged in the political world of the United States. At the same
time, the speech became the point of departure in demands for an
official investigation by the American Senate.[34]

In spite of this initial success, Owen did not give many speeches
in subsequent years and when he did rise on the topic of war guilt,
it was mostly to read from the works of revisionists and new documentation into the *Congressional Record*.[35] Two public speeches
given by the senator, one before the German-American Steuben
Society on 4 September 1924, and the other before the Boston Foreign Policy Association on 15 April 1926, continued to harp on the
Franco-Russian conspiracy, but they seem to have had little reso-
nance in the daily press.

In early 1924, a number of Senate resolutions addressed the
need to revise the Treaty of Versailles, especially Article 231. A resolution calling upon the president of the United States to invite
signatories of the Treaty of Versailles to revise its terms was unsuccessful.[36] However, Owen indicated the direction of an inquiry:
only when the idea had been rejected that the Treaty of Versailles
was based upon sole German guilt, when it was recognised that
three or four men in St. Petersburg brought about the war, only
then would Europe find peace. Accordingly, the Senate resolved
on 16 February 1924, that the '... committee on Foreign Relations
shall cause to be prepared for Senate an authoritative and impartial analysis and abstract of all evidence ... bearing on the origin of
the World War including ... the consequences of international
alliances ... during the quarter century preceding 1914 and the
conclusions of the committee of inquiry as to those responsible for
causing or promoting the World War of 1914–1918'.[37] The resolution directed the Senate Foreign Relations Committee to appoint a
committee of inquiry, consisting of seven to nine persons trained
in historical research and not in government service. '[It] shall submit its conclusions not later than ten days before the constitutional
expiration of the Sixty-eighth Congress.'[38]

The German embassy reacted cautiously to the opportunities
presented by this inquiry.[39] The originator of the plan to establish
a committee of inquiry was a certain Mr. McGuire, who was well
known to the embassy.[40] He had approached Senator Owen
because of the latter's brave speech, and because attempts to
recruit Senator Borah, Republican from Idaho and the pro-German

chairman of the Senate Foreign Relations Committee, had failed. Borah feared quite rightly that such a committee of inquiry could produce unwelcome results, a fear shared fully by the embassy. However, McGuire was confident that his chairmanship of the committee of inquiry and the new documentation which had become available would at least relativise the accepted view of German war guilt. In the meantime, the German press should not comment on the resolution or celebrate it as an important step for Germany.[41] Instead, the press in neutral countries should boost Owen's reputation by presenting him as a pioneer in the study of the war-guilt question.[42] This resolution and others were not acted upon and lapsed.

Renewed efforts resulted in a near-identical resolution calling for a committee of investigation that would be located in the offices of the Senate Foreign Relations Committee with a mandate to print an abstract and conclusion by 1 February 1924, for the information of the Senate.[43] Counsellor of Legation Dieckhoff cautioned that Owen was rejected by his fellow Democrats, who did not want a debate of the war-guilt question because it might conclude that Wilson's policies had been based on false presuppositions. Most Republicans, notably Senator Lodge, who would not miss an opportunity to diminish the memory of Wilson, were likely to vote for the resolution.[44] Dieckhoff's appreciation of the imperatives of party politics foreshadowed the fate of the resolution which was defeated narrowly, with members voting along party lines.[45] Indeed, Ambassador Wiedfeldt doubted that even an objectively conducted official inquiry would lead to a condemnation of Wilsonian policies during those decisive years. Prospects would be much better when more time had passed. An official expert opinion which did not strongly vindicate the German case was worse than none at all.[46] Nevertheless, Owen pressed on with yet another call for a Senate inquiry into the war-guilt question.

A Senate resolution of 16 February 1925 charged the Legislative Reference Service (LRS) of the Library of Congress to 'prepare for the Senate an impartial abstract and index of all authentic important evidence, heretofore made in printed form or otherwise readily accessible, bearing on the origin and causes of the World War, omitting all inconsequential matter'.[47] The materials were to be submitted to the Senate Foreign Relations Committee on 1 February 1926. To assure acceptance of the resolution by the Senate, Cousellor of Legation Dr Baer, who was in constant close contact with Owen, suggested a speech which would bring together the issues of war guilt and French war loans. The resolution was accepted without debate.[48] This LRS compilation of all relevant materials was regarded as a second-best alternative to the miscarried investigating committee,[49] and hope persisted that this LRS report would lead to an investigating committee. In this connection, the Schuldreferat tended to stress the official aspect of the project by insisting that Senator Owen was the first official person in the United States to call for the official investigation of the war-guilt question by the legislature.[50]

If the instigator of the project had converted to revisionism, the historian directly in charge, Charles C. Tansill, had never shared the view of the origins of the war that prevailed from 1914 to 1917. At the time professor American history at American University, he had opposed intervention into the war, devoting himself since 1919 to the defeat of the Treaty of Versailles.[51] As a result of his work on the LRS project he had become convinced of French and Russian responsibility for the war.[52] During the 1920s he also acted as an adviser in diplomacy to the Senate Foreign Relations Committee and worked in the Legislative Reference Service of the Library of Congress.[53]

The entire project was understaffed, especially lacking experts in prewar history, a circumstance that considerably eased the tasks of those seeking to influence the outcome of the project. According to Wegerer, Tansill did not possess the necessary basic knowledge, but he was conscious of the difficulties and of his deficiencies.[54] Herman H.B. Meyer, the head of the LRS, was a bibliographer of wide repute, as was William Adams Slade, chief bibliographer of the Library of Congress and compiler of the bibliography for the LRS project. However, they lacked expertise in the field under consideration. Wegerer expected problems only from Professor Ellery Cowry Stowell, an assistant to Tansill.[55] The German embassy in Washington had been in continuous contact with 'the personnel in question' through reliable intermediaries. Even before Wegerer arrived in Washington, the documentary collection had been given the closest attention for some months. With the German embassy in continual contact through reliable middlemen, the Archive of the Congressional Library received all relevant materials.[56]

The project envisioned a bibliography of all available documentary material, an estimated four thousand items, and an objective five-hundred-page narrative by Tansill, covering European history from the Congress of Vienna to the outbreak of war in 1914. The project's purpose exceeded merely informing Congress.

When Ambassador Maltzan requested additional materials from Berlin, he urged that '[the] matter is of the greatest importance because the bibliography and abstract created by the Legislative Reference Service [would] be the authoritative basis for war-guilt research in the United States'.[57] There would be no progress in the war-guilt question until the undertaking begun by Senator Owen was carried through. Maltzan believed that the task was a daunting one, and the gentlemen from the Legislative Reference Service would be most grateful for any help they could get. To exploit this situation effectively, and to insure proper consideration of the German materials, Maltzan also suggested that the Foreign Ministry despatch an expert with a good command of English to the United States. The journey would have to be camouflaged as a general information tour so that the presence of a Foreign Ministry official in Washington would be regarded as purely coincidental.[58] Alfred von Wegerer, the head of the Zentralstelle, would tour the United States and establish personal contact with the most important revisionist scholars and publicists. However, his most important task was to take up contacts with the Legislative Reference Service.[59]

During his stay in Washington he was able to discuss with Tansill and Slade the literature of the war-guilt question, leaving with them books, essays and unpublished documents from the archives of the Zentralstelle.[60] Wegerer was especially concerned to stress the true significance of the remoter antecedents of the war, and to make it clear that the main causes of the conflict were the questions of Alsace-Lorraine and the Straits. Considering the July Crisis, Wegerer claimed to have removed basic errors in such matters as the alleged 'blank cheque' to Austria, the significance of Sir Edward Grey's mediation attempts, the background to the Sarajevo assassination, and the connection between Russian mobilisation and the declaration of war.[61]

According to Wegerer, the gentlemen from the Legislative Reference Service generally judged the German literature correctly. An English translation of a register of all obtainable documents on the war-guilt question had been sent before Wegerer arrived in Washington.[62] To work up the bibliography and narrative, the Legislative Reference Service researchers relied heavily upon the bibliographical sections of the *Die Kriegsschuldfrage*. Wegerer expected publication of the work of the Legislative Reference Service which would create a basis from which to enlighten both Congress and the general public about war guilt. He would not speculate on the political consequences of this work.[63]

Reporting on the Wegerer visit, the ambassador commended him for his diligence in contacting all persons of importance, his general skill and close contact with the embassy. It was in the political interest that the Zentralstelle continue the work.[64] Perhaps a permanent office should be opened in order to enliven and direct the war-guilt debate in the United States. In a warm letter Tansill thanked Wegerer for having contributed viewpoints on war guilt that would prove to be of enduring value.[65]

Although the LRS report was kept under extraordinary security in the office of Senator Borah, the chairman of the Senate Foreign Relations Committee, the German embassy gained access through confidential channels to portions of it. Dieckhoff seems to have been satisfied. The German arguments had been taken into consideration and generally given the same weight as those of the opponents.[66] Hopes that the finished project would be published and win Congress over to the German side were premature because the work of the Schuldreferat had been too successful. Inspired by the revisionist Owen, headed by the revisionist Tansill, and watched over by the German embassy through trusted intermediaries, by the Schuldreferat, and by the head of the Zentralstelle personally, the finished narrative and bibliography showed results highly favourable to the German case in the war-guilt question. The Legislative Reference Service project on the causes of the Great War was not published as a government document because it was not the 'impartial abstract and index of all authentic and important evidence' demanded by the Senate resolution.[67] There was fairly wide agreement that the report delivered by the Legislative Reference Service was very advantageous for Germany, and for that reason it was not published.[68] There was little chance that the Senate Foreign Relations Committee would identify itself with it.[69]

Because of the overwhelmingly massive documentation, Tansill, Slade and Meyer reached the somewhat surprising conclusion that the time was not yet ripe for an exhaustive inquiry into the causes of the war. Only future historians would be able to fix the guilt for the war.[70] Slade, the chief bibliographer of the Library of Congress, expressed a sense of futility about the magnitude of the task. An overbundance of source materials precluded final judgement at present. He accurately identified the source of the overabundance. The declarations of innocence by German statesmen were accompanied by the increasing output of German printing presses, which were releasing a stream of books, documents, periodical and newspaper articles. Nevertheless, Slade believed that he had presented the materials systematically, scientifically and without outside help. Only he, as chief bibliographer, was responsible for the compilation.[71] To Dieckhoff, the outcome amounted to an indirect admission that the accusations against Germany made in the Treaty of Versailles could not have been proven by facts and documents. This was a gain for Germany.[72] However, in the summer of 1926 a somewhat pessimistic Dieckhoff complained that with waning interest in the war-guilt question, the Senate no longer pursued the report of the Legislative Reference Service.[73] In time the report simply vanished.[74]

Within months of the failed Legislative Reference Service project, Senator Owen published *The Russian Imperial Conspiracy, 1892–1914: The Most Gigantic Intrigue of All Times.* He struck a pacifist note by dedicating the work to the fathers, mothers and children of France and Germany. The book's purpose was 'the reconciliation of all people, above all the German and French people, on whose reconciliation the happiness and future peace of the world depended'.[75]

The basic arguments and structure of the slim work were the same as Owen's famous speech of 18 December 1923. The common people of Russia, France and Germany desired peace, but a few imperialists in France and Russia decided in 1894 to make war on Germany. They prepared for that war with a huge buildup in armaments. Germany was encircled with a series of treaties and understandings. To weaken Germany's moral position, she was accused of having started the war, and in 1919, the Germans were forced under military threat to accept Article 231. This confession of guilt must be removed, and the world brought back to a condition of sanity, of understanding, of truth and goodwill.[76] French imperialists had desired the return of Alsace-Lorraine and control over the Saar coal basin. Russia had desired control over the Straits and influence in the Balkans.[77] Regarding the July crisis, Owen's general point was that Russia and France foisted war upon Germany, whose statesmen desired to mediate the conflict. Once war had started, the Allies waged a war of extinction against the Germans.[78]

If Owen's arguments were old, so were the sources on which he based them. For the most part, these were the writings of French and English, and, to a lesser extent, German and American revisionists. The bulk of the extensively quoted documentation was still of Russian provenance, even though the Germans had meanwhile

published the massive *Die Grosse Politik.* However, these sources
had been propagated by the Schuldreferat since the end of the
war, and their use, after so much other documentation had
become available, simply dated the book.

Recognising that the book suffered from considerable deficiencies, the embassy and Schuldreferat nevertheless set aside whatever reservations they might have had because they found it
useful. Diekhoff believed that the book reached circles closed to
'Barnes and the professors'.[79] The reviewer from the *American
Monthly* also saw the strength of the work in that it had not been
written by a professional historian, even if Owen had fallen victim
to the treacherous language of moral indignation and its inevitably unsound conclusion. Owen was an American who had
looked with horror at something which shocked him.[80] While
Stieve welcomed the book from an author noted for his clarity, his
assessment of the book was quite critical. He rejected a German
translation because the work was superficial and much behind
German research. This, naturally, did not prejudice its value in the
United States, whereas in Europe it would only invite criticism.[81]
Tansill characterised the work most charitably as a '... skillful
restatement of pertinent evidence'.[82] Whatever the reservations,
both editions, 1926 and 1927, were published with the support of
the Schuldreferat and widely distributed in English-speaking
countries. The Schuldreferat acquired through confidential negotiations with the senator 1,500 copies which were, for the most
part, mailed by Owen to important politicians.[83]

As the result of skillful introduction to important editorial
offices, the Owen book greatly stimulated coverage of the war-guilt
question in the American press. However, negative reactions to
Hindenburg's speech on the occasion of the unveiling of the Tannenberg Monument on 18 September 1927 had shown that the final
reckoning of the war-guilt question was rejected by most German
propagandists as premature, even if there had been a significant
advance of the German viewpoint. Although German innocence
would be rejected by the majority, Kiep pronounced the *Allein-
schuldthese* as no longer tenable. He cautioned that propaganda
must continue to avoid the appearance of official involvement.[84]

When Owen departed from the Senate in 1925, the mantle of
war-guilt fighter seems to have fallen on Hendrick Shipstead,
from the heavily German state of Wisconsin. Like his predecessor,
he was also a member of the Senate Foreign Relations Committee.
Between 1928 and 1931 he tabled six resolutions pertaining to war

guilt, but none of them ever came to a vote. These resolutions were quite similar, and the first serves as a model for the others: Article 231 was based on hysteria, hypocrisy, and falsifications forged in the fires of war. The latter had been disproved by scholars. The resolution asked that the Senate Foreign Relations Committee hold an inquiry '... for the purpose of determining whether in view of the new evidence and other official material the time is appropriate for the American Government, inspired by the sense of justice and fair play, to recommend to the Allied Powers either to amend this article without further delay or to announce severally their intention to disregard it, otherwise, to propose to the Allied Powers that the question of responsibility for the World War be submitted to a commission of neutrals'.[85] Subsequent Senate resolutions pursued similar aims.[86] Overtaken by the end of the session, none ever came to a vote. While the German embassy provided Shipstead with revisionist materials through third parties, it became very pessimistic about the usefulness of these resolutions, and by the end of the 1920s, they were no longer expected to yield concrete political gains. The ambassador appreciated that the temperamental senator helped keep the issue of war guilt before the American public. On the other hand, the embassy feared that the resolutions enlivened German-American circles, who put pressure upon Shipstead to table them, interjecting themselves into the war-guilt campaign, and so robbing it of its credibility, perhaps even ruining the considerable progress made thus far.[87]

In summary: the Schuldreferat valued Owen's writings and speeches because he quickly advanced a thesis of a Franco-Russian conspiracy against the peace of Europe, a thesis which rested upon the uncritical acceptance of interpretations and documentations brought into circulation by the Schuldreferat and its front organisations. The Germans seized upon Owen because he displayed the courage to discuss openly the war-guilt question and related issues when other senators, even those with a reputation of being pro-German, would not do so. A powerful legislator, he sat on the important Senate Foreign Relations Committee. Under such circumstances the Schuldreferat was willing to engage publicists who were not nearly of the scholarly calibre it claimed for itself. Why not draw nearer to Fay and Langer? Support for Owen and the like-minded betrayed impatience to bring the case before the general public. Fay and Langer would serve the revisionist cause in time, and their conclusions, wherever they were on the revisionist spectrum, were likely to be complex and differentiated.

Owen reduced complex historical problems to simple events and explanations. The embassy and the Schuldreferat were convinced that Owen, more than anyone else, had revived the debate over the origin of the Great War in the United States.

In terms of achieving specific aims, the activities of the senator and the Schuldreferat registered gains and losses. The widely distributed 'great' speech of December 1923 read much revisionist literature and documents into the *Congressional Record*, giving them a pseudo- official veneer. Senator Owen's revisionism might strike one as unsophisticated and even naive, but it reflected the materials circulated by the Schuldreferat, which made no attempts to moderate his views. Even when glaring deficiencies in scholarship were clearly evident, as with the widely circulated *Russian Imperial Conspiracy*, this did not prevent his exploitation for the revisionist cause.

The attempts to establish a committee of inquiry failed, and the bibliography and narrative produced by the LRS never became public. The Schuldreferat was able to supply materials through a variety of intermediate sources; however, it failed on the political level when the Senate Foreign Relations Committee refused to make them public. That there was only little apparent interest in the war-guilt question in the U.S. Senate does not matter. Owen, with the help of the Schuldreferat, wanted to change that. One ought not to underestimate the potential role of Senator Owen. To have the Senate or its Foreign Relations Committee appoint an investigating committee which would, on the basis of the latest literature and documentation propagated by the Schuldreferat, have debated the validity of Article 231, would at least have kept the issue before the public. One likely result of such a debate was foreshadowed by the fate of the LRS report. Quite rightly, the embassy had fears that such an inquiry might not produce a desirable report.

While one might agree with the conclusion that Owen was a skillful populariser, a meaningful evaluation of his effectiveness within the broader innocence campaign is impossible; yet, how successful was the war-guilt campaign in which he played his part?

The Foreign Ministry claimed only limited success. Doubts about effective penetration existed in those areas where Owen was supposed to have been so effective. If the so-called 'man in the street' continued to cling to wartime slogans, then the strategy of indigenous opinion makers shaping general attitudes had not succeeded. According to the Foreign Ministry, '... the supposition

that American opinion in the widest sense of the word is convinced of the myth of the *"Versailler Kriegsschuldthese"* seems not
warranted'.[88] Revisionist publications had been well received in
the journals and, increasingly so, in the press; nevertheless, the
ministry found it impossible to dispel the thought that they did
not leave a lasting imprint on broader public opinion.[89]

There were positive assessments. The French historian, Pierre
Renouvin, judged German propaganda in the United States to
have been successful because it was able to arouse interest and
doubts in the war-guilt question and widespread sympathy for
Germany.[90] In 1931, Wegerer submitted a characteristically glowing
report on the activities of the Zentralstelle which underlined the
significance of Owen's 1923 speech and judged revisionist activity
a success.[91] Looking back over the 1920s, the German ambassador
in Washington was willing '… to risk the assertion that a change in
American public opinion on the war-guilt question occurred during the last ten years, which anyone who had experienced the post-
war mood would have held to be totally impossible'.[92]

Notes

1. The earliest published sketch based on a preliminary survey of the records of
   the Schuldreferat is I. Geiss, 'The Outbreak of the First World War and German War Aims', *Journal of Contemporary History I* (1966) 3: 75–92. Most
   recently, I. Geiss, 'Die Manipulierte Kriegsschuldfrage, Deutsche Reichspoli-
   tik in der Julikrise 1914 und Deutsche Kriegsziele im Spiegel des Schul-
   dreferats des Auswärtigen Amts, 1919–1939', *Militärgeschichtliche Mitteilungen*
   34 (1983) 2: 31–60. The most recent full-length study of the Kriegsschuldreferat and its front organiations is Ulrich Heinemann, *Die Verdrängte Niederlage, Politische Öffentlichkeit und Kriegsschuldfrage in der Weimarer Republik,
   Kritische Studien zur Geschichtswissenschaft* 59, Hg. Helmut Berding, Jürgen
   Kocka, Hans-Ulrich Wehler (Göttingen, 1983).
   Unless indicated otherwise correspondence originated in Berlin or Washington; microfilmed sources belong to Microcopy T120, and they are identified by roll, serial and frame numbers; unfilmed sources are identified by
   folder; all sources come from the Politische Archiv, Auswärtiges Amt, Bonn.
2. 'Bermerkungen zum Bericht der Kommission der Alliierten und Assoziierten
   Regierungen' in: *Deutschland Schuldig? Deutsches Weissbuch über die Verant-
   wortlichkeit der Urheber des Krieges* (Berlin, 1919), 56–69. Anlagen 69–208.
3. Marshall M. Lee and Wolfgang Michalka, *German Foreign Policy 1917–1933:
   Continuity or Break* (Hamburg, New York, 1987) 69, 68–72.

4. Ibid., 72, 152. Werner Link, *Die Amerikanische Stabilisierungspolitik in Deutschland* (Düsseldorf, 1970), 44–45, 75. Michael-Olaf Maxelon,*Stresemann und Frankreich, Deutsche Politik der Ost-West Balance, 1914–1929: Geschichtliche Studien zu Politik und Geschichte,* Bd. 5 (Düsseldorf, 1972), 116, 199.

5. Werner Link, 'Die Beziehungen zwischen der Weimar Republik und den USA', in: Manfred Knapp, Werner Link, Hans-Jürgen Schröder and Klaus Schwabe, *Die USA und Deutschland, 1918–1975, Deutsch-Amerikanische Beziehungen zwischen Rivalität und Partnerschaft* (Munich, 1978), 62–66, 104, 106.

6. Kiep (embassy) to Reichskanzler, Washington, 12 December 1927. Marx Nachlass (Stadtarchiv Köln) 112/224–6. Friedrich von Prittwitz und Gaffron, *Zwischen Petersburg und Washington, Ein Diplomatenleben* (Munich, 1952), 230. Heinemann, *Verdrängte Niederlage,* 64, 68, 91. Link, *Stabilisierungspolitik,* 572, calls attention to a number of 'linkage groups' which strengthened the process of understanding. These engaged only marginally in war-guilt propaganda and Link does not mention that propaganda.

7. Alfred von Wegerer, *Die Widerlegung der Versailler Kriegsschuldthese* (Berlin, 1928), 236–7. Arbeitsausschuss Deutscher Verbände, *Anhaltspunkte für die Schuldfragearbeit, 1922* (Berlin, 1922), 3. Propagandists could cite Lloyd George: 'For the Allies German responsibility for the war is fundamental. It is the basis on which was built the edifice of the treaty and if this ... is denied or surrendered, then the Treaty is destroyed.' Bernhard Dernburg, 'Die formulierung der Kriegsschuldfrage', in Wilhelm Ziegler, *Deutschland und die Schuldfrage* (Berlin, 1923), 7.

   Alfred von Wegerer (1880–1945) followed a military career until 1920, when he resigned from the *Grenzschutz* to join the *Liga zum Schutze der Deutschen Kultur.* He worked on the staff of the *Zentralstelle für Erforschung der Kriegsursachen* from 1921, effectively heading it from 1922 until 1937, when it was shut down as a needless expense. In 1939 he found a position in the *Reicharchiv.*

8. *Die Grosse Politik der Europäischen Kabinette, 1871–1914: Sammlung der Diplomatischen Akten des Auswärtigen Amtes,* ed. Johannes Lepsius, Albrecht Mendelssohn-Bartholdy, and Friederich Thimme (Berlin, 1922–1928). Friedrich Stieve headed the Schuldreferat from 1922–28. He had been a writer in Munich before the war and press attaché in Stockholm from 1914–21. After a tour as ambassador to Riga, he headed the Culture Department 1932–39. Whatever the assignment, Stieve remained in contact with the Schuldreferat.

9. Heinemann, *Verdrängte Niederlage,* 120–54. Hans Draeger, *Der Arbeitsausschuss Deutscher Verbände, 1921–1931* (Berlin, 1931) 9–31.

10. Arbeitsausschuss Deutscher Verbände, *Richtlinien für Leiter der Angeschlossenen Verbände* (Berlin, 1922). Draeger, *Arbeitsausschuss, 1921–1931,* 65.

11. Sidney Bradshaw Fay, 'New Light of the Origin of the World War ... I, II, III ...' *American Historical Review* XV (1920): 616–39. XXVI (1921) 37–53, 225–54. Fay, who had been sceptical of the wartime version all along, called attention to the new documentation in a review of the Kautsky documents. The articles departed cautiously from wartime propaganda but did not relieve Germany of the main responsibility.

12. *Christian Century,* XLII (8 Oct.–17 Dec., 1925).

13. Only some examples can be given: Alfred Fabré-Luce used Schuldreferat materials for his *La Victoire,* which was distributed through an Arbeitsausschuss subsidiary. Memo by Stieve, 29 July 1924. Stieve to Volksbund, 23 September

1924. (Schriftwechsel m. Behördem, Erlasse, Berichte, Aufzeichnungen, Bd. 2b, 9.24–2.25) Alcide Ebray, *La Paix Malpropre* was distributed by the Schuldreferat. See Circular to Missions, 25 February 1925. Ibid. Victor Marguerite's *Les Criminels* was widely distributed in the United States. See Erlass 14 August 1925. (Ibid., 9.25–12.25). George Demartial's *La Guerre 1914* was translated into English by the Deutsche Notbund. See Notbund to Stieve, 14 August 1925. (Schriftwechsel mit Vereinen u. Privatpersonen, Bd. 7, 1.26–12.26). It was widely distributed in the U.S. General Konsulat, Chicago to Foreign Ministry, 4 August 1925. (Marguerite, Bd. 1, 10.25–3.26).

Special funds were set aside for the distribution in the United States of French authors, especially anti-French writers. Schubert to Reichsfinanzminister, *Geheimm*, 26 March 1925, and Aufzeichnung, *Streng Geheim*, Stieve für Stresemann, 9 March 1925. (Die Kriegsschuldfrage, Sonderheft, 12.23–10.28.) See also: Heinemann, *Verdrängte Niederlage*, 115. The Schuldreferat supported financially the French revisionist journal *Evolution*. Stieve to Chapiro, 6 June 1922 (Privater Schriftwechsel 22–27).

The English revisionist and subsequent publisher of the American revisionist journal *The Freeman*, Francis Neilson was in contact with the Schuldreferat as early as 1921. Delbrück to Bülow, 3 August 1921. (Andere Bearbeiter u. Organisationen, Bd. 3, 8.21–12.21). E.D. Morel's books leaned heavily on the works by the Serb Boghitschewitsch, who was supported by the Schuldreferat, which also promoted Morel's writings. Foreign Ministry to Reichsvertretung Darmstadt, 2 August 1921. (Berichte u. Erlasse, Bd. 3, 2.28–12.30). See also Martin Gilbert, *The Roots of Appeasement* (New York, 1970) 23–24.

Selig Adler, 'The War Guilt Question and American Disillusionment, 1918–1928', *The Journal of Modern History*, XXIII (March, 1951) 1:1–28. Adler does not use the records of the Schuldreferat, but the article is an excellent survey of American revisionists.

14. *Congressional Record*, 2nd Session, 67th Congress, vol. 62, pt. 1, 291–7. The resolution had been appended to a speech condemning the Allies, especially France, for violation of the Fourteen Points.
15. Memorandum, October 1938 (2788/1397A/D546616, 25–27).
16. René Marchand, *Un Livre Noir: diplomatie d'avant guerre d'après des documents des archives russes, Novembre 1910–Juliet 1914*, 2 vols. (Paris, 1922–23). B. von. Siebert, *Diplomatische.Aktenstücke zur Geschichte der Ententenpolitik der Vorkriegsjahre* (Berlin, 1921). On the specific impact of these and others, see: Ambassador Heosch to Foreign Ministry, Paris, 26 August 1925. (Schriftwechsel m. Behörden, Erlasse u. Berichte, Bd. 7, 9.25–12.25). Robert L. Owen, *The Russian Imperial Conspiracy, 1892–1914*, 5 (np. 1926, self-published).
17. Freiherr Ago von Maltzan was state secretary from 1922–24, ambassador to the United States from 1925–27.
18. They met at a breakfast in the German embassy in Washington. (Schriftwechsel mit Behörden, Erlasse u. Berichte, aufzeichnungen, Bd. 7, 9.25–12.25).
19. *Congressional Record*, 1st Session, 68th Congress, vol. 65, 18 December 1923, 355–99.
20. Ibid., 355–6.
21. Ibid., 356–7.
22. Ibid., 365, 369.
23. Ibid., 357–62.
24. Ibid., 364.

25. Ibid., 375.
26. Ibid., 377.
27. *Congressional Record*, Senate, 1st Session, 25 February 1924, 68th Congress, vol. 65, pt. 3, pp. 3064–67 and pt. 5, pp. 5256–7. See here also for additional lettes of praise which Owen had read into the record. Ibid., p. 5257.
28. Ibid., pt. 5, 5257. Morel had written this in the *American Monthly*.
29. Deutsche Botschaft Washington (Dieckhoff) to Foreign Ministry, 29 May 1924. (Schriftwechsel mit Behörden, Erlasse u. Berichte, Aufzeichnungen, Bd. 1, 5.24–7.24).
30. *Congressional Record*, Senate, 1st Session, 68th Congress, vol. 65, pt. 3, 3065. The speech became part of a series, *Beiträge zur Schuldfrage*, published by the Zentralstelle during the early 1920s.
31. *Falsification of the Russian Orange Book: Actual Exchange of Telegrams Between Paris and St. Petersburg at the Outbreak of the War* (New York, 1923). Letter, Stieve to Romberg, 23 February 1924 (Schriftwechsel m. Behörden, Erlase u. Berichte, Aufzeichnungen. Bd. sa, 7.24–9.24). The original German edition had been introduced on 30 September 1922 with great fanfare by Chancellor Wirth. See: Die Reichsregierung und die Schuldfrage, ein Interview mit dem Reichskanzler, nd. (8859/3410/E617420–4). Friedrich Stieve's *Der Diplomatische Schriftwechsel Iswolski, 1911–1914, Aus den Geheimakten des Russischen Staatsarchivs, i. A. des AA, in deutscher Übersetzung* (Berlin, 1924) was a four-volume collection inspired by the impact of the *Fälschungen*. The Falsifications were highly successful in revisionist circles everywhere, spawning a number of works. Stieve to Press Department, 20 March 1924 (8851/3408/E0615905–8).
32. Foreign Ministry (Ref. Steive) to Generalkonsulat Montreal, 29 February 1924. See also: letter, 12 July 1924, St. S. von Maltzan to Direktor v. Stauss, Deutsche Bank. (Schriftwechsel mit Vereinen u. Privatpersonen, Bd. 1, 2.24–11.24). R.L. Owen, 'Rede über die Kriegsschuldfrage' Gehalten vor dem Senat der Vereinigten Staaten von Nordamerika am 18 Dezember 1923 (Berlin, 1924). See also: Adler, 'The War Guilt Question …' 1, 15, n. 97.
33. Maltzan speaks about many thousands having been distributed in foreign countries by August 1924. Foreign Ministry to Deutsche Botschaft, Washington, 3 March 1924 (Schriftwechsel m. Behörden, Erlasse u. Berichte, Bd. 5, 2.24–6.24) mentions a request for two thousand.
34. Anlage II (n.p.), *Veröffentlichungen der* Zentralstelle *in Buch und Broschürenform*, Dr h.c.v. Wegerer. nd.
35. For example see: *Congressional Record*, 1st Session, Senate, 68th Congress, vol. 65, pt. 5, 5256–61.
36. House Concurrent Resolution 22 (Owen/Berger), 11 February 1924, *Congressional Record*, 1st Session, 68th Congress, vol. 65, pt. 5.
37. Senate Resolution 166, 16 February 1924, *Congressional Record*, 1st Session, 68th Congress, vol. 65, pt. 3, p. 2765.
38. Ibid.
39. Letter, Dieckhoff to Bülow, 21 February 1924 (Schriftwechsel m. Behörden, Erlasse u. Berichte, Aufzeichnungen, Bd., 2c, 2.25–10.29).
40. Embassy to Foreign Ministry (Stieve), 8 May 1925 (Schriftwechsel m. Bohörden, Erlasse u. Berichte, Aufzeichnungen, Bd. 6, 12.24–8.25) mentions a Dr McGuire who was associated with an Institute of Economics and who was writing an extended article on war guilt.

41. Report, *Streng Vertraulich*, 23 February 1924 (Schriftwechsel mit Behörden, Erlasse u. Berichte, Augfzeichnungen, Bd. 4, 11.22–5.24).
42. Letter, Bülow to Stieve, 4 March 1924 (Schriftwechsel m. Behürden, Erlasse u. Berichte, Aufzeichnungen, Bd. 4, 11.22–5.24).
43. Senate Resolution 225, 16 May 1924, *Congressional Record*, 1st Session, 68th Congress, vol. 65, pt. 9, pp. 8676–77.
44. Report, *Vertraulich*, German embassy (Dieckhoff) to Foreign Ministry, 29 May 1924 (Schriftwechsel m. Behörden, Erlasse u. Berichte, Aufzeichnungen, Bd. 1, 5.24–7.24). The report also mentions a general enlivening or improvement in the debate over war guilt, due in some ways to the activities of Owen. Ironically, the resolution would be defeated because Senator Lodge changed his vote. Report, Dieckhoff to Foreign Ministry, 26 Februry 1925 (Schriftwechsel m. Behörden, Erlasse u. Berichte, Bd. 4, 1.25–3.25). Dieckhoff was counsellor of legation from 1922–27, when he became director of Abteilung III. He was ambassador in Washington 1937–38.
45. Report, German embassy (Wiedfeldt) to Foreign Ministry, 6 July 1924 (Schriftwechsel m. Behörden, Erlasse u. Berichte, Aufzeichnungen, Bd. 1, 5.24–7.24).
46. Ibid.
47. Senate Resolution 339, *Congressional Record*, Senate, 1st Session, 68th Congress, vol. 66, Pt. 4, p. 3789. The Legislative Reference Service was a small section in the Library of Congress that provided informational services to legislators. The task imposed by the Senate resolution strained especially its human resources to the limit. Its successor is the Congressional Research Service. Photocopied extract from the 1925 annual report provided by the Library of Congress.
48. Report, German embassy to Foreign Ministry, 26 February 1925 (Schriftwechsel m. Behörden, Erlasse u. Berichte, Aufzeichnungen, Bd. 4, 1.25–3.25).
49. *Der Weg zur Freiheit* 5 (April 1925) 4:71.
50. Memorandum, Schuldreferat, 24 May 1925 (Schriftwechsel m. Behörden, Erlasse u. Berichte, Aufzeichnungen, Bd. 4, 1.25–3.25).
51. From an interview, Washington D.C., 14 August 1962, with Tansill by Warren I. Cohen, *American Revisionists*, 194. Charles C. Tansill (1890–1964) was educated at Catholic University and Johns Hopkins and taught mostly at American University. By the mid-1930s he had established for himself a reputation as a diplomatic historian. Ibid., 196. His friendly attitude toward Germany remained unchanged. Note by Schwendemann, 5 July 1935 (K1582/5189/K4363437–8). In a radio address in 1937 he called Hitler an inspired leader. He became obsessed with communism after the war, serving as an advisor to Senator Joseph McCarthy. He wrote several articles for the John Birch Society. *Dictionary of American Biography*, 734–5.
52. Warren I. Cohen, *The American Revisionists: The Lessons of Intervention in World War I* (Chicago, 1967), 194.
53. *Dictionary of American Biography*, 734–5.
54. Wegerer, U.S. Report, 1 December 1925 (3738/1848/E037902).
55. Ibid., Stowell had writen *Diplomacy of the War of 1914* (Boston, 1915).
56. Memorandum by Stieve on a conversation between Chancellor Luther and Professor v. Mach, 18 August 1925 (4519/2277/E134172–73). v. Mach warns of Germanophobe elements in the Library of Congress. The conversation also suggests interest at the highest level.

57. German embassy (Maltzan) to Foreign Ministry, 8 May 1925 (Schriftwechsel m. Behörden, Erlasse u. Berichte, Aufzeichnungen, Bd. 42, 3.25–6.25).

58. Maltzan to Stieve, 8 May 1925 (Schriftwechsel m. Behörden, Erlasse u. Berichte, Aufzeichnungen, Bd. 6, 12.24–8.25 (Maltzan had actually suggested Stieve. See also Stieve to deHaas (Abteilung III), 19 June 1925. (Schriftwechsel m. Vereinen und Privatpersonen, Bd. 3, 1.25–6.25).

59. Much of what we know about his work in the United States comes from his own reports to his superiors in the Schuldreferat and Foreign Ministry. Formal title: Bericht über meine Reise nach den Vereinigten Staaten von Nordamerika vom 17. September bis 26. November 1925. (3738/1848/E037899–921). It will be cited as: Wegerer, U.S. Bericht, 1 December 1925. Wegerer was not an overly modest man. Many of his reports follow a simple pattern: much has been accomplished in the war-guilt question, but much more good work needs to be done, for which additional funding is needed. He stayed in Washington for nine days.

60. Wegerer, U.S. Bericht, 1 December 1925 (3738/1848/E037903). A systematic check of the bibliography of the Zentralstelle's journal, *Die Kriegsschuldfrage*, resulted in the purchase of some five hundred items. See the introduction to the bibliography. Enclosure, Dieckhoff to Stieve, 10 March 1926. (Die Kriegsschuldfrage, Sonderheft, 12.23–10.28).

61. Wegerer, U.S. Bericht, 1 December 1925. (3738/1848/E037903–4).

62. Foreign Ministry to German embassy, 29 June 1925. (Schriftwechsel mit Behörden, Erlasse u. Berichte, Aufzeihnungen. Bd. 5. 5.25–7.25). See also Foreign Ministry to German embassy, 10 June 1925. (Schriftwechsel, etc. Bd. 42, 3.25–6.25).

63. Wegerer, U.S. Bericht, 1 December 1925. (3738/1848/E037905).

64. Letter, Maltzan to Foreign Ministry, 2 November 1925. (3728/1848/E037897).

65. Tansill to Wegerer, 1 November 1925. Attachment to Wegerer, U.S. Report. (3728/1848/E037920).

66. Botschaft (Dieckhoff) to Foreign Ministry, *Vertraulich und Geheim*. (Die Kriegsschuldfrage, Sonderhaft, 12.23–10.28). The bibliography appears to have registered general satisfaction.

67. Not all LRS compilations are published, though this one was expected to be published. Indeed, it was seen as a potential boost to the revisionist cause in Congress and at large.

68. Memorandum, Schuldreferat, June 1931. (K1852/5189/K463272–3). The work was available in Germany. Wegerer, Stellungsnahme zum Bericht, Amerikanische Historiker und der Weltkrieg, 1 October 1932. (3738/1849/E038849–54). Draeger (ADV) to Schwendemann, 28 June 1935. (K1851/5189/463435–6). Owen, the driving force behind the report, said that Tansill's book had not been published 'for reasons of diplomatic amity'. Cohen, *American Revisionists*, 194. Dr Hans Draeger, 'Amerika und die Kriegsschuldfrage', Vortrag gehalten in der Universität Jena, nd., *Der Weg zur Freiheit* 9 (February 1929) 4:54. The head of the Arbeitsausschuss repeated that the results were advantageous but were not published '... aus Gründen diplomatischen, guten Einvernehmens ...'.

69. Dieckhoff to Stieve, 29 July 1926. See also Dieckhoff to Foreign Ministry, Confidential and Secret, 1 October 1926. (Schriftwechsel mit Behörden, Erlasse u. Berichte, Aufzeichnungen, Bd. 9, 7.26–12.26).

70. For Tansill see: Report by Maltzan for Foreign Ministry, 24 February 1926. (Kriegsgreul, Bd. 1, 11.23–12.28). For Meyer see: Copy, covering letter of introduction to bibliography, Meyer to Chairman, Senate Foreign Relations Committee (Senator Borah), Enclosure, Dieckhoff to Stieve, 10 March 1926. (Die Kriegsschuldfrage, Sonderheft, 12.23–10.28). For Slade see: Dieckhoff to Stieve, 26 February 1926. (Ibid.).

71. Enclosure, Dieckhoff to Stieve, 10 March 1926. (Die Kriegsschuldfrage, Sonderheft, 12.23–10.28).

72. Report by Maltzan to Foreign Ministry, 24 February 1926. (Kriegsgreul, 11.23–12.28).

73. Dieckhoff to Foreign Ministry, 5 July 1926. (Schriftwechsel mit Behörden, Erlasse u. Berichte, Aufzeichnungen, Bd. 8, 1.26–7.26).

74. Because of the controversial nature of the report it was placed in a 'restricted' category in the Library of Congress which, since 1936, has no record of it. Frederick Lewis Honhart III, 'Charles Callan Tansill: American Diplomatic Historian' (Ph.D. Diss. Case Western Reserve University, 1972), 42. Even Tansill did not know its location. Cohen, *American Revisionists*, 194, who cites an interview with Tansill on 14 August 1962.

75. Owen, *Russian Imperial Conspiracy*, pp. 3, 4.

76. Ibid., p. 126–7.

77. Ibid., p. 32–33.

78. Ibid., pp. 59–109, 87.

79. Dieckhoff to Stieve, 29 July 1926 (Schriftwechsel m. Behörden, Erlasse u. Berichte, Aufzeihnungen, Bd. 9. 7.26–12.26).

80. *American Monthly*, August, 1927. The review had been read into the *Record*, 1st Session, *Congressional Record*, 70th Congress, vol. 69, pt. 2, 1388–90.

81. Memo by Stieve, 24 August 1927. In Stieve to Kiep, 18 July 1927, the former suggested translations into French and Spanish.

82. *American Journal of International Law*, vol. 22, 1928, 222–3, as cited in Honhart, 'Charles C. Tansill', 53.

83. Foreign Ministry (Stieve) to embassy, 27 July 1926. A subsidy of $1,000 covered acquisition and mailing costs. Distributed through missions with circular of 14 November 1926.

84. Kiep to Foreign Ministry, 3 December 1927. The Tannenberg speech, which had been written by Stieve, the head of the Schuldreferat, closed with the passage: '... With a clean heart we went forth in defence of the fatherland, and with clean hands the German army wielded the sword. Germany is at any time ready to prove this before an impartial tribunal.' Memorandum by Schubert on the origins of the passage on war guilt, 30 September 1927. (4519/2278/E134179–50).

85. S. Res. 242. *Congressional Record*, 1st Session, 70th Congress. Quoted in full and translated into German in *Die Kriegsschuldfrage*, 7 (1929) 1, p. 83. The resolution had the support of the chairman of the Senate Foreign Relations Committee, Senator Borah, with whose help the embassy was able to improve the text. Embassy (Prittwitz) to Foreign Ministry, Manchester, Mass. 25 June 1928. (Schriftwechsel m. Behörden, Erlasse u. Berichte, Aufzeichnungen, Bd. 12, 4.28–9.29).

86. For example see: S. Con. Res. 34, 18 June 1930, *Congressional Record*, 2nd Session, 71st Congress, vol. 72, pt. 10, 11073.

87. Embassy (Prittwitz) to Foreign Ministry, 10 July 1929. (Berichte u. Erlase, Bd. 3, 2.28–12.30). Prittwitz to Foreign Ministry, *Vertraulich*, 31 December 1928. (Überlassung v. Material an Behörden, Bd. 3, 12.28–4.29). In the forefront of this movement was the former American consul in Dresden and Munich, T. St. John Gaffney, and the Concord Society of Philadelphia. See: *Die Kriegss-chuldfrage* 7 (1929) 1:80–81. *Die Kriegsschuldfrage* carried these resolutions in English and German. Embassy to Foreign Ministry, 17 February 1931. (K1852/5189/K463227–28).

88. Memorandum by Leitner, *Einstellung der Amerikanischen Öffentlichkeit zu Deutschlands Anteil am Weltkriege*. German embassy to Foreign Ministry, Manchester, Mass., 10 July 1929. (Berichte u. Erlasse, Bd. 3, 2.28–12.30). This somewhat optimistic assessment was questioned by Köpke to German embassy, Washington, February 1931. (K1852/8198/K463214). A cursory check of the indices of the *Congressional Record* suggests that veterans' affairs, for example, mattered much more to the senators and their constituents.

89. 'Der Glaube an die Deutsche Kriegsschuld ist noch in den Gemütern der überwiegenden Masse des amerikanischen Volkes vorhanden, wen er auch nicht mehr in den üblen Formen der Kriegs und ersten Nachkriegszeit zum Ausdruck gelangt.' Schnee (president of the Arbeitsausschuss) in *Der Weg zur Freiheit* 6 (1.276.) 1:7.

90. Wegerer quotes Renouvin from *Revue des Deux Mondes* (April, 1931) in Stellungsnahme, Wegerer, 1 October 1932. (3738/1849/E038849).

91. Zentralstelle Tätigkeitsbericht, 1931, Marx Nachlass, 257/231–2, concluded that the most marked changes had taken place in the United States. 'Am deutlichsten trat der Umschwung in der Beurteilung der Kriegsschuldfrage in den USA hervor. Durch die grosse Rede von Senator Owen, durch die Arbeiten von Barnes, Fay, Holmes, Langer, Bausman Burgess, Bruch, Gaffney, Sheville, durch das politische hervortreten von Borah, Shipstead, Copeland und LaFolette, McFadden wurde die öffentliche Meinung in den USA zu einer anderen Auffassung in der Kriegsschuldfrage gebracht.... Selbst Poincaré hat sich über die Erfolge der deutschen Sache in den USA schon bitter beklagt.'

92. German embassy (Prittwitz) to Foreign Ministry, 14 April 1931. (K1852/5189/K473234). See also Heinemann, *Verdrängte Niederlage*, 232, on the relative success of German propaganda in the United States.

Chapter 5

HISTORY AS PROPAGANDA

The German Foreign Ministry and the 'Enlightenment' of
American Historians on the War-Guilt Question, 1930–1933

Ellen L. Evans and Joseph O. Baylen

In his essay 'The Outbreak of the First World War and German
War Aims', Imanuel Geiss presented a 'preliminary sketch of a
very complicated story, based ... on the study of about half of the
rich material of the Kriegsschuldreferat in the Political Archive of
the Auswärtiges Amt at Bonn'.[1] It is the purpose of this essay to
illustrate and evaluate the campaign of the Kriegsschuldreferat
(also known as the Schuldreferat or Referat), a subsection of the
German Foreign Ministry, to assist the American revisionists
against the antirevisionists and to show how Dr Alfred von
Wegerer, the editor of the Referat's journal, the *Berliner Monatshefte*, sought to facilitate the work of the Referat by publicising
the writings of these revisionists in the *Monatshefte* and other
media during the years immediately before Hitler's assumption of
power. The campaign waged by the Referat and Wegerer against
Article 231 of the Treaty of Versailles in the United States, even
though unsuccessful, deserves attention because, as Selig Adler
noted, the Great Depression and the crisis in the Far East were
diverting American interest during these years 'from the question
of who started the last war to the problem of how to stay out of the
next conflict....'[2]

The Referat directed and financed its work through two allied
organisations, the Arbeitsausschuss Deutscher Verbände (ADV)

and the Zentralstelle zur Erforschung der Kriegsschuldfrage.[3] While the ADV (a federation of semipolitical associations, societies, and trade unions) directed its propaganda at the German masses, the Zentralstelle (established in 1921) sought to influence the intelligentsia and especially the academic communities in foreign countries. Both organisations sponsored a periodical, but the most important and successful of the two journals was the Zentralstelle's *Die Kriegsschuldfrage* (changed in January 1930 to *Berliner Monatshefte*), established in mid-1923 under the editorial direction of Dr Alfred von Wegerer (1880–1945), a former imperial army officer.

Since Wegerer and the Zentralstelle's propaganda and periodical were financed by the Foreign Ministry, both were directed by the Referat. Wegerer was given access to the Foreign Ministry archives and this provided him with important materials to wage 'The scholarly struggle against the "*Kriegsschuldlüge*"' through his numerous publications and those who collaborated with him.[4] Indeed, under Wegerer's editorial direction, the journal maintained 'as high objective standards as might be expected from any periodical founded to disseminate one point of view....'[5] The Referat also churned out articles on the *Kriegsschuldfrage* discreetly placed in German newspapers and periodicals and disseminated the Referat point of view: (1) by the purchase of hundreds of copies of books and pamphlets critical of the Versailles settlement for distribution to important foreign academics, libraries of institutions of higher learning, and politicians and editors friendly to Germany; (2) by the subsidisation in Germany of translations of the works of foreign scholars and journalists sympathetic to the German campaign against the Versailles treaty; (3) by utilising such pro-German organisations as the Steuben Society of America to propagandise in their publications revisionist materials published in *Die Kriegsschuldfrage*; and (4) by stimulating attacks against scholars and writers who defended the Versailles settlement or continued to insist that Germany was the major culprit for World War I.[6]

Geiss rated the work of the Referat as highly effective because ' German historians lent it their great prestige' and because the few German historians concerned with studies of pre-World War I German and European diplomacy produced nothing on the subject which equalled the studies of such foreign historians as Pierre Renouvin and Benadotte E. Schmitt. Indeed, wrote Geiss, 'The defence of the German cause was mostly left either to foreigners, such as [Harry Elmer] Barnes or [Sidney B.] Fay, or to amateurs such as Wegerer or [Hermann] Lutz'.[7] This was especially true when Schmitt posed a serious threat to the propaganda of the Referat with the publication of his detailed and closely reasoned study, *The Coming of the War: 1914*, in 1930.[8]

The 'Enlightenment of America' was one of the major objectives of the Referat during the 1920s and of special concern to the Zentralstelle. It was deemed of crucial importance to influence American opinion on the German war-guilt question not only because the United States was a great power which seemed to regret its participation in the war and was therefore more likely to adopt revisionist views, but also because a change in American public opinion might assist Germany in achieving the reduction or cancellation of German reparations payments. Several possibilities were explored, including the use of German-American organisations and German travellers to the United States, but the greatest interest of the Referat was in influencing the historical research and writing of American historians, specialising in modern European history and the history of American foreign relations. From 1931 through the first half of 1933 especially, a strong effort was made to seek information about American historians and to persuade them of the merits of Germany's case, so that they might properly 'enlighten' their colleagues and students on the injustice of the Versailles treaty.

The first historian to attract the attention of the Referat was Harry Elmer Barnes, whose revisionist views were first published in articles in *Current History* and *Christian Century* and were subsequently expanded and more emphatically stated in his book *The Genesis of the World War*, published in 1927. Although Barnes was a prolific writer on many subjects, revisionism always remained his primary interest. During his later years, Barnes expanded his revisionist ideas to include an interpretation of the causes of World War II and, convinced that his 'ostracism' by other historians was an injustice, charged that the historical 'establishment' deliberately prevented publication of revisionist studies on the origins of World War II.[9]

During his sojourns in Germany in the summers of 1926, 1927, and 1929, Barnes interviewed the ex-kaiser, Alfred Zimmermann, and Leopold von Berchtold, and became friendly with Dr Wegerer, the director of the Zentralstelle since 1922. While Wegerer publicised Barnes's book and regularly published Barnes's articles in the *Berliner Monatshefte*, Barnes reciprocated by contributing the introduction to the English translation of Wegerer's book, *A Refutation of the Versailles War Guilt Thesis*, in 1931.[10]

The Referat purchased and distributed copies of Barnes's book and, when a French translation was published, the German ambassador in Paris ordered 150 copies for distribution in France.[11] A subsequent article by Barnes, 'The Greatest Fraud in All History', in the June 1932 issue of the *Berliner Monatshefte*, was of great interest to the Referat because it explicitly denounced reparations payments. Thus, in July 1933, the Referat purchased five hundred copies of the article for distribution to German embassies and consulates in thirty-six cities throughout the world.[12]

Barnes had originally become interested in the war-guilt question as a result of his reading Sidney Fay's three articles, 'New Light on the Origins of the World War', in the *American Historical Review* during 1920–21. Fay incorporated these articles, which advanced the 'divided-guilt' thesis and were the first scholarly arguments advanced by a professional historian for revisionism in the United States, in his two-volume work on *The Origins of the World War* (New York, 1928).[13] The German Foreign Ministry and the Referat were delighted with Fay's study; here was a far more scholarly and documented treatment of the subject than Barnes's polemic. In February 1929, the German consulate in New York purchased one hundred copies of Fay's study for shipment to Berlin and, on receipt of the consignment, the Referat immediately despatched copies to fifty-seven German embassies and consulates throughout the world.[14] Meanwhile, the Wilhelmstrasse found a publisher for a French edition of Fay's study, and in February 1931, copies of the French edition were despatched to thirty-one embassies and consulates.[15] In April 1931, Fay wrote to Wegerer to congratulate him on the tenth anniversary of the Zentralstelle and solicited Wegerer's advice on the possibilities of the publication of his (Fay's) book in the Soviet Union.[16]

Although Fay knew Wegerer, his closest contact in the German Foreign Ministry was Hermann Lutz, a writer who worked for the Referat from 1919 to 1937, while serving for much of that time as a member of the allegedly independent Reichstag inquiry commission on the war-guilt question.[17] Lutz saw Fay frequently during their respective visits in the United States and Germany and regularly reported the substance of their conversations to the Foreign Ministry. Thus, in April 1931, Lutz informed the Referat of Fay's remark that Barnes was no longer held in great esteem by American scholars and that although Barnes's book had shocked American public opinion, it had really enhanced the sales of Fay's study.[18]

But the Referat's satisfaction with the progress of revisionism in the United States was dealt a severe blow by the publication of Bernadotte Schmitt's book, *The Coming of the War: 1914* (New York and London, 1930). Schmitt had previously published several reviews of studies on the origins of the war in such prestigious periodicals as the *Journal of Modern History* and *Foreign Affairs* that were deemed anti-German by the Referat.[19] Since Schmitt had previously written an unfavourable review of Wegerer's book and a devastating critique of Barnes's work,[20] his approach to the war-guilt question was already apparent to the Referat and the Foreign Ministry. In fact, Lutz had met Schmitt in Berlin in 1928 and tried to persuade Schmitt to postpone publication of his book until he had seen some documents from the German archives hitherto not available for study.[21]

The Referat sedulously collected reviews of Schmitt's book and carefully noted those which were unfavourable to Schmitt's study. While Lutz wrote a review of the book for the *American Historical Review* [XXXVI (April, 1931), 594] and Wegerer reviewed the work for the *Weltwirtschaftliches Archiv*, the German embassy in Washington posted William L. Langer's critical review of Schmitt's book in the *New York Herald Tribune* to the Referat,[22] and the *Berliner Monatshefte* reprinted Parker T. Moon's unfavourable review of Schmitt's study in *The New York Times* in which Moon charged that 'where there is conflicting testimony he [Schmitt] puts the evidence against Germany in the text and evidence for Germany in the footnotes'.[23] At the same time, Fay informed Lutz that Schmitt's study was being 'severely critised' by many American historians.[24]

In November 1931, Lutz reported to the Referat that Schmitt had told him that his publishers had arranged for a French translation of his study. Lutz was convinced that the French 'court' historian Pierre Renouvin had facilitated the publication of Schmitt's study in French and that the French government intended to make use of the book for propaganda purposes.[25] Like Schmitt, Renouvin[26] was a special target of the Referat. In April 1931, Renouvin published an article, 'Les Historiens américains et les responsibilités de la guerre', in the *Revue des Deux Mondes*, II, 8 (15 April, 1931), 886–903, in which he discussed a recent poll of American historians indicating that of 215 historians queried, only eight stated that the Central Powers were solely responsible for the war and ninety-nine believed that the Central Powers were 'preponderantly' to blame for the conflict. Renouvin not only deplored the results of the poll and attributed it to a concerted German effort to influence American public opinion on the war-guilt question, but also compared the Schmitt and Fay studies and declared that Schmitt did indeed make a good case for the view that the Central Powers had 'imposed war' on Europe.

It was perhaps the Referat's concern over the effect of Schmitt's book on the *Kriegsschuldfrage* which motivated it to consider an organised campaign through the Zentralstelle and the Arbeitsausschuss Deutscher Verbände (ADV) to sustain the revisionist cause in the United States. Thus, in February 1931, a conference between Ministerial Director Dr Gerhard Köpke[27] of the Referat and Ministerial Director Hans Dieckhoff,[28] on behalf of the ADV, resulted in the draft of a proposal by Dieckhoff for 'the Enlightenment of America on the *Kriegsschuldfrage*.'[29]

Dieckhoff's proposal (approved by Köpke) stated that it would be an error to assume that there had been a 'mass swing of public opinion' in favour of revisionism because of the publications of 'a few esteemed historians', and contended that the 'improvement in public opinion in the United States concerning Germany during the last ten years' indicated that the American people accepted the revisionists' view of Germany's war guilt. In fact, on the basis of his personal contacts with Americans in the Carl Schurz Foundation[30] and his study of several American 'school books', he was convinced that 'the older generation clings to the assertions of war propaganda as if to dogma' and that it was absolutely necessary to prevent these prejudices from being passed on to the younger generation. Hence, Dieckhoff recommended that the Referat direct its *'special attention to American history books, study these carefully and work toward altering them'*. The essential factor in 'the Enlightenment of America', observed Dieckhoff, was not the activities of such German-American organisations as the Steuben Society[31] and the support of German-American activities by such prominent personalities as Thomas St. John Gaffney and Senator Shipstead,[32] but the need to influence the *'Anglo-American segments of the population*, which are, understandably, extraordinarily difficult to approach'. These Americans, he added, had been 'awakened ... to certain aspects of the *Kriegsschuldfrage*' by Emil Ludwig's book *July 1914* (New York and London, 1929) and there was need for other German popular writers, also well-known in the United

States, such as the novelists Gerhard Hauptmann or Rudolf Herzog,[33] 'to present the [German] case on the causes of the war'.

Dieckhoff also recommended that the Referat recruit American writers interested in Germany's 'burdens after the war' and the war-guilt question and provide them with travel and materials to work in Germany. He did not believe that Americans, 'who are not keen on tradition and history', should be approached with 'a pure presentation of the war guilt problem'. On the contrary, since 'a strong interest in Germany's present economic and cultural situation exists', an attempt should be made 'to bring the *Kriegsschuldfrage* closer to wider circles [in the United States] from this standpoint'. Finally, Dieckhoff concluded with a warning against linking the war-guilt and reparations issues because this might prejudice the cause of revisionism in the United States.

A copy of Dieckhoff's proposal was despatched to the German embassy in Washington in March 1931, with an accompanying letter from the Referat.[34] The letter discussed the impact of the books by Barnes, Fay, and Schmitt in the United States and stated that although revisionism had made greater progress in the United States than in any of the other former enemy countries, it must not be assumed that American public opinion was convinced of the 'untruth' of the Versailles war-guilt thesis.

In reply to the Referat's request for an opinion on Dieckhoff's proposal, the German ambassador, Friedrich Wilhelm von Prittwitz,[35] despatched a response which dealt with each of Dieckhoff's suggestions and recommendations. Prittwitz agreed that there had been no great change in American public opinion on the war-guilt question, but pointed out that to change the American view of the *Kriegsschuldfrage*, 'We should remove anti-German history books from the schools'. Much had already been done, wrote Prittwitz, but 'the [American] federal system impedes change, and the choice of books is often left to individual teachers or principals. Consequently, we have to act only on a local basis.... [Hence] every German traveller to the United States should give some attention to this matter'. He also agreed that teachers, especially in the universities, should be approached by official German consular officers or representatives, especially through personal connections. Similarly, Prittwitz commented favourably on the use of such German writers as Ludwig, Herzog, and Hauptmann and on the employment of some American writers, but remarked that since most good writers in the United States were controversial figures it might be better to make greater utilisation of newspapers and magazine articles for propaganda purposes. As for German travellers in the United States, he believed that they could be well utilised, but should be cautioned to avoid behaving like propagandists for the German cause.[36]

In his comments on Prittwitz's despatch in May 1931, Dieckhoff again emphasised his opinion that the war-guilt question had little to do with the current attitude of Americans to Germany. He was convinced that Americans were generally indifferent to the war-guilt question and that if the issue of revision of the Versailles treaty was pressed too hard, the American reaction would be anti-German. Consequently, he did not recommend renewed efforts to influence *mass* opinion in the United States, but only efforts to eliminate the anti-German bias of history books in the United States.[37]

Several weeks later, on 9 June 1931, Dr Traugott Böhme, head of the Foreign Ministry's Auslandsschuldreferat, produced a memorandum dealing specifically with the subject of American schoolbooks.[38] Böhme began by noting that, because of the decentralised educational system in the United States, Germany could affect history textbooks only by influencing their *authors* and that almost all of the books had been written 'by university professors'. Propaganda societies like the Steuben Society, wrote Böhme, were not suitable for this sort of work because even 'Well-known professors friendly to Germany think that previous efforts by the Steuben Society were actually harmful'. Moreover, remarked Böhme, the American Historical Association was obliged on purely scholarly grounds to defend publicly such prominent historians as David S. Muzzey, Albert Bushnell Hart, and Edward Channing[39] against attacks by the Steuben Society for their anti-German bias. It would be most beneficial, advised Böhme, to provide American historians with 'objective information and translations of important German works on the war-guilt question'. He specifically recommended the translation of Eugen Fischer's *Die 39 Tage*[40] and the wide distribution of Fay's book.

Böhme also suggested the establishment of a German-American Historical Conference as a counterpart to the Anglo-American Historical Conference established at the beginning of the last decade. He pointed out that the German-American historian, Dr Carl Wittke, had participated in a meeting which had discussed the possibilities of a German-American Conference, and there had been such lively interest in the idea that it was agreed to consider the project at the forthcoming annual meeting of the American Historical Association in December 1931.[41] Prominent historians of German descent should be enlisted to support the proposal and strong emphasis should be placed on the purely scholarly nature of the projected organisation.

During the following spring and summer of 1931, the Referat utilised several opportunities to 'enlighten' American historians on the *Kriegsschuldfrage*. In May, Professor Herbert Kraus[42] of the *Seminar fur Völkerrecht und Diplomatie* apprised the Foreign Ministry of the arrangement for Professor Thomas Jefferson Wertenbaker,[43] 'Dean [sic] of the History Department' at Princeton University, to serve as an exchange professor at the University of Göttingen. Wertenbaker, wrote Kraus, could be won over to the German position on the war-guilt issue and was especially important because 'he has great influence, stretching beyond Princeton, especially in the southern states, where he and his wife are from'. Kraus therefore advised the Foreign Ministry to send some pertinent publications to Wertenbaker which were strictly scholarly and not propaganda. The current director of the Referat, Dr Max König, immediately complied with this suggestion[44]

Another American historian contacted by the Foreign Ministry in the summer of 1931 was Professor Michael Hermond Cochran of the University of Missouri.[45] On 1 June, the German consul in St. Louis informed the Foreign Ministry that Cochran (a 'solid scholar *par excellence*' who has 'a really sincere admiration and friendliness for Germany') and his wife were sailing for Germany and suggested that, since he was travelling with very limited funds and was being partly financed by the Carl Schurz Foundation, the Foreign Ministry do whatever possible for Cochran and his 'attractive wife'. Free theatre tickets and other such gifts might be welcome, wrote the consul, but cash probably not, for political reasons. Above all, Cochran should be introduced to officials in the Referat.[46] The consul's suggestion was acted upon and Cochran met with Foreign Ministry and Referat personnel and especially Wegerer in Berlin.

Cochran had come to Berlin ostensibly for research on a proposed third volume to Ernest Flagg Henderson's *Short History of Germany* (New York, 1916), 2 vols. He spoke 'tolerable' German and, even though he declared that the war-guilt question was not his specialty, was a regular reader of the *Berliner Monatshefte*. Nevertheless, Cochran soon made the war-guilt issue his interest when, after his return from Germany, he published *Germany Not Guilty in 1914* (Boston, 1931), with the subtitle *Examining a Much-Prized Book*. The 'much-prized book' was Schmitt's *The Coming of the War: 1914*, which had been awarded in 1930 both the Pulitzer Prize in history and the George Louis Beer Prize.

Cochran's work, which included a foreword by Harry Elmer Barmes, was a highly polemical examination and refutation of Schmitt's arguments. Although the language of the book was hardly scholarly, it was documented and was clearly intended as more than a journalistic exercise. In 1927, Cochran had published an article in *Current History* based on his doctoral dissertation at Harvard ('German Public Opinion and the Origin of the World War') which was moderate and balanced in its arguments.[47] The review of Schmitt's study which he had contributed to the *Berliner Monatshefte* (March 1931) was, however, quite polemical.[48] If the Foreign Ministry had expectations of Cochran's book, it soon had good reason to be disappointed. Thus, when the German embassy in Washington forwarded a copy of Cochran's book to the Foreign Ministry in December 1931, an accompanying note stated: 'It is regrettable that the author occasionally strikes a very aggressive note, by which the scholarly character of the book suffers.' Worse yet was the remark that the book had up to that time attracted little public attention.[49]

Two months later, in February 1932, the German consulate in St. Louis forwarded five copies of Cochran's book to the Foreign Ministry and several newspaper reviews, including one from the *Kansas City Star* which featured the copy of a postcard from the ex-kaiser Wilhelm II to Cochran warmly congratulating him on his book. The consul had reported that Cochran denied that he had sent a copy of his book to the kaiser or that he had requested a statement from him and declared that he had even refused an offer to visit Wilhelm II at Doorn. Indeed, added Cochran, 'Many of the people who were duped during the war are angry at me and my book, but they would not buy it anyway. The truth is that this is a highly technical book, written for the historians in the hope that they would see the light. I am much more worried about what the Germans will say of the ex-kaiser's approval than I am about the Americans'.[50]

During 1932 Cochran sought to obtain additional documentary material from Germany, particularly from the unpublished records of the Reichstag's commission on the causes of the war, with which to reply to his critics. But although he was promised copies of these and other materials by the Referat, they were slow in reaching him. Finally, in October, the Referat informed the St. Louis consulate that the first 'four series, in twelve volumes' of the

Reichstag commission's report were being forwarded to Coch-ran.[51] However, it was too late and indeed could do little to sal-vage his reputation.

Since by general consensus, the Foreign Ministry was con-vinced that Cochran's book had failed to counter Schmitt's study, the adverse effects of Schmitt's work continued to cause concern. In the spring of 1932, *Reichsgerichspräsident* Dr Walter Simons[52] informed the Referat that Bernadotte Schmitt was scheduled to speak at a Round Table Conference (an annual event sponsored by the Institute of Politics at Williams College) in Williamstown, Massachusetts, during the forthcoming summer, and suggested that a German spokesman attend the conference.[53] In considering Simon's suggestions, *Legationsrat* Dr Karl C. Schwendemann of the Referat discovered that Schmitt was scheduled to speak at the conference on 'The Peace Treaties and the Map of Europe'. After unsuccessfully attempting to determine privately ('*unter der Hand*') what Schmitt was planning to say at the Williamstown con-ference, Schwendemann decided to provide a German or Ameri-can respondent.[54] First, the German embassy in Washington attempted to persuade Fay to speak against Schmitt and, if this were not possible, to enlist the services of William L. Langer.[55] On forwarding a copy of the program of the Williamstown confer-ence to the embassy in Washington, the German consul in Boston, Werner von Tippelskirch, a personal friend of Fay, reported: 'Fay … so far as I know him, would not shrink from an armed conflict with Schmitt.'[56]

In July, the Washington embassy relayed to Berlin Tippels-kirch's report that 'after some difficulty' he had contacted Fay who stated that he would be unable to attend the Williamstown con-ference, 'at least during the first half of the session'. Fay thought that Schmitt would 'in all probability' keep strictly to his subject and might touch on the origins of the war only in passing, if at all. Moreover, Fay assumed that since the great majority participating in the conference supported his position of the war-guilt question, anything that Schmitt might say on the issue would be taken '*cum grano salis*'. 'In order to prevent the possibility of our interests suf-fering from the uncontradicted assertions of Herr Schmitt', wrote the consul, he had alerted the German economist, Professor Erwin von Beckerath, who was scheduled to speak on Germany's eco-nomic condition, and Count Eberhard Joachim von Westarp, who was coming to Williamstown from New York, to be prepared to refute Schmitt's assertions.[57]

The Round Table Conference duly met at Williamstown from 29 July to 25 August, 1932, but the expected confrontation of Beckerath and Westarp versus Schmitt did not occur. Schmitt spoke exclusively on the subject of 'The Peace Treaties and the Map of Europe' and even conceded that the frontier settlements of the Paris Peace Conference were somewhat unfair to the former Central Powers. While Count von Westarp spoke on the subject of 'Limitation of Armaments' and managed, in the open discussion which followed his talk, to present the German point of view on the peace treaties, Beckerath spoke on behalf of German interests in Upper Silesia and other issues. The war-guilt question was not mentioned, and it seems to have been deliberately avoided in the proceedings of the Williamstown meeting.[58]

Nevertheless, the Foreign Ministry continued to keep a sharp eye on Schmitt. In 1933, the German consulate in Chicago sent a detailed report on Schmitt's speech at the Chicago Council on Foreign Relations in March. During May, Schmitt and Count von Westarp debated 'The Versailles War Guilt Thesis' at a Cincinnati hotel and the German consulate in Cleveland noted that the German-Americans of Cincinnati heartily applauded Westarp.[59]

In September 1932, shortly after the Williamstown conference, the Referat received a lengthy report from the counsellor of the German embassy in Washington, Rudolf Leitner,[60] which was apparently an additional commentary on Dr Böhme's memorandum of 9 June 1931 on American history textbooks and their authors. In this interesting paper on 'American Historians and the World War', Leitner declared that 'It is not really surprising that only a few courageous individuals have arrived at an objective treatment of the events of the war, while the majority, especially the older historians, who were under the most severe pressure in the war, cling to the official versions of the course of the war'. On the other hand, wrote Leitner, the American public and press for the most part favoured a calm assessment and consideration of the arguments of all views on the war-guilt question. To Leitner, the anti-German attitude of the 'older historians' was the result of the intense social and economic pressures and war propaganda to which they were subjected during the war. In this environment, explained Leitner, it was easy for such a 'mediocre (*mittelmässiger*)' historian as William Roscoe Thayer[61] to utilise 'excessive patriotism' to rise to the presidency of the American Historical Association. Nevertheless, since the war, the older historians had attempted to justify what they had written and said during the war by rejecting new evidence on the war-guilt question and by accepting Pierre Renouvin's recent book *The Immediate Origins of the War (28th June–4th August 1914)* (New Haven, 1928) and Bernadotte Schmitt's conclusions on the war-guilt issue.

However, added Leitner, it was 'to the honour of the American historical profession' that the number of objective and 'scientifically irreproachable works on the World War' published by American historians was increasing. While he commended Barnes for his early attempts to set the record straight, Leitner did not consider Barnes's work as 'entirely satisfactory' and thought that it was definitely 'put in the shade' by Fay's study and the works of Professors Joseph V. Fuller,[62] Charles A. Beard,[63] William L. Langer, Edward Chase Kirkland,[64] and, above all, M.H. Cochran, who sought to expose 'the inadequacies and absurdities' in Schmitt's study. Unfortunately, declared Leitner, Cochran's work was considered 'embarrassing, uncomfortable, and even undesirable by the older clique of historians ...' and, like Fay's book, had not received 'the strong applause it deserved in ... the American historical profession'. Worse yet, most of the young historians of the rising generation could find little hope for academic advancement 'if they look critically at the war historiography handed on from posterity'. Yet it was the work of these historians, 'motivated by inner honesty and historical decency ...' and steadily increasing in number, which will prevail in the American historical profession 'as is already the case with the American public and press which have detached themselves from that which during the war was declared to be the truth'.[65]

On receiving Leitner's estimate of the position of American historians on the war-guilt question, the Referat requested Wegerer to comment on it, and on 1 October 1932, he responded in a 'position paper' which sought to justify the Referat's work in the United States and was a subtle plea for continued support of the Referat's activities. Wegerer concurred with Leitner's opinion that 'the older historians' still clung to the official version of the origins of the world war propagated during the war and that, in contrast to this, the American public and press favoured 'an objective conception of events'. The Zentralstelle, averred Wegerer, also attached 'special importance' to the works of Renouvin and Schmitt and especially the fact that their books were being promoted by Professor Charles Seymour[66] at Yale University. Although both works had 'Unquestionably ... worked strongly against the conceptions about the war advocated by ... Barnes and Fay', their influence should not be overestimated. In fact, remarked Wegerer, in a recent issue of the *Revue des Deux Mondes* (cf. *Berliner Monatshefte*, IX [June 1931], 603),[67] Renouvin stated that 'German industriousness' had succeeded in arousing not only interest and doubt in American public opinion, but strong sympathies for the German case in the United States.

Wegerer believed that more credit should be given to Barnes as 'the pioneer who gave the initial and decisive impetus to undermining and partially overcoming the views of the older [American] historians on the war-guilt question'. In fact, Barnes's work was far more important than the revisionist works of Professor John William Burgess[68] and William M. Sloane.[69] Wegerer attributed the rejection of Barnes's revisionism 'in some circles' to the fact that Barnes had dared, 'as a relatively unknown historian', to advocate the German viewpoint in opposition to the anti-German position of the American historical establishment.

Turning to other 'sympathetic' historians, Wegerer noted the 'excellent reputation' of Charles Austin Beard, 'who particularly sees through the conduct of the British at ... the outbreak of the war', and attached great importance to William L. Langer's recently published scholarly study of 'the background history of the World War'. Wegerer hoped that the two volumes published by Langer on the period 1870–1902 would be expanded to include a third volume on the outbreak of the war – all the more so because there was good reason to believe that on such basic questions as the Russian general mobilisation in 1914 he had assumed 'an even more decided viewpoint than that advocated in German research' on the war-guilt question.

Unlike Leitner, Wegerer was convinced that Cochran's *Germany Not Guilty in 1914* did not 'sufficiently cancel out the harmful effects of the work by Schmitt' because Cochran's style of writing was coarse, his arguments cumbersome, and his conclusions extended 'beyond what his arguments seem to warrant'. Although 'We were able to induce Mr Cochran to make considerable improvements in his work during his visit to Berlin last year', wrote Wegerer, 'it was not possible to eliminate all the shortcomings of his book.'

In addition to the 'sympathetic' historians mentioned in Leitner's report, Wegerer listed the following group of historians who were 'for the most part ... known to the *Zentralstrelle*'. Among the older historians, wrote Wegerer, Professor John Franklin Jameson,[70] formerly editor of the *American Historical Review*, had assumed a view of the war-guilt question which 'accords entirely with scholarly research' and in his editorial direction of the *AHR* brought 'understanding to revisionism'. Similarly, Professors William E. Lingelbach[71] at the University of Pennsylvania and Ferdinand Schevill[72] at the University of Chicago, also of 'the older generation', had expressed their advocacy of revisionism in various publications.

Among the 'younger historians' Wegerer recommended Professor Ernst C. Helmreich at Bowdoin College as 'A very valuable person in connection with the war-guilt question ...' who had published his views in the *Berliner Monatshefte*.[73] He also listed Professor Charles C. Tansill at American University as the author of a report, written on the initiative of the isolationist Senator Robert L. Owen[74] in 1926, and an article in the June 1931 issue of the *Berliner Monatshefte* which 'very clearly expressed a conception of the war-guilt question ... favourable to us'.[75]

In concluding his 'position paper', Wegerer suggested that 'to counteract the regressive conceptions of the war-guilt question ... disseminated by the American edition of Renouvin's book and ... the work of ... Schmitt ...' it would be necessary to establish closer contacts with American historians. To achieve this objective, the work of the Referat could be facilitated: (1) 'by identifying for it, on the basis of local knowledge, historians who have a special interest in the [war-guilt] question or are strongly caught up in the conceptions of the opposing group ...'; (2) by acquainting 'the older historians' with the results of the most recent research on the war-guilt question by the publication of articles 'by scholars who are either ... German or agree with the German point of view' in such important American journals as the *American Historical Review, Foreign Affairs, Political Science Quarterly*, and *Current History*; (3) by attracting public support through the publication of 'proper' historical articles in such popular magazines as *The New Republic, The World Tomorrow, Review of Reviews, The Nation*, and *American Mercury*; (4) by undertaking to present lectures and papers on the origins of World War I at the annual Round Table Conference in Williamstown; (5) by providing 'appropriate publications' on the origins of the war to interested American libraries, clubs, and organisations; and (6) by arranging for his (Wegerer's) personal visit to the most renowned American universities.[76]

Some of Wegerer's opinions on the American historians mentioned in his report were in part derived from the results of a questionnaire on the subject of guilt which the Zentralstelle had posted

during the previous year (1931) to seventy historians throughout
the world and had published in the June 1931 issue of the *Berliner
Monatshefte*. Ten of the historians discussed in Wegerer's commentary were among those who responded to the questionnaire,
which presented the following three questions: '(1) Do you think
Germany planned the Great War with premeditation and brought
it about designedly and intentionally? (2) Are you of the opinion
that Germany imposed the war upon the Allied and Associated
Governments? (3) Do you assent to the opinion that the affirma-
tion made by the Allied and Associate Governments at Versailles
regarding the responsibility of Germany for the war was arrived at
on the basis of material which was incomplete, tendentious and, in
part, even falsified?' In reply to the first and second questions, the
Americans queried rendered sixteen 'nays', three 'yeas', and three
'undecideds'. On the third question, the Americans responded
with nineteen 'yeas', zero 'nays', and three 'undecideds'. The following replies were received from the American 'experts': Barnes:
'No, no, yes'; Beard: declined to state 'yes' or 'no', but rendered an
implied 'no' to the first question and a 'yes' to the third and
remarked that all of the belligerents must share the blame for the
war: Binkley: 'No. *Formell Ja*, yes'; Fay: 'No, no, certainly'; Gaffney:
'*Keinesfalls! Ganz im Gegenteil! Ganz bestimmt!* '; Langer: 'No, no,
yes.'; Lingelbach: 'Emphatically no! No (although he did declare
war so quickly), yes'; Schevill: 'Essentially no, no, yes'; Schmitt:
refused to render a 'yes' or 'no' to the first and second questions
and referred Wegerer to his book, and on question three, stated
that the German and Austrian documents were as 'tendentious' as
the documentary sources of the other powers; Seymour: declined
to state 'yes' or 'no' and objected to the wording of the questions
and especially to the use of the word 'imposed'; Tansill: 'Definitely
no, definitely no, also yes' and praised the work of *Die Kriegsschuldfrage* (i.e., the *Berliner Monatshefte*).[77]

In accord with Wegerer's recommendation, the Foreign Ministry despatched a copy of his commentary of 1 October 1932, to
the Washington embassy and requested that copies be distributed
to German consulates throughout the United States with instructions to obtain the views and comments of the consular officials on
the opinions of historians in their districts. The replies from the
consuls in Cleveland, Denver, Seattle, St. Louis, Los Angeles,
Chicago, San Francisco, New Orleans, and New York, received
between 15 November 1932 and 10 June 1933, expressed considerable scepticism and lack of enthusiasm for Wegerer's plan of

campaign in the United States.[78] Thus, the consul in Cleveland did not advocate contacting historians *en masse* through the mails because 'behind each unsolicited communication with enclosure of book or brochure stands the ghost of propaganda'. He was convinced that personal contacts would be a more important and lasting method of altering opinion on the war-guilt question. The consul in Denver reported that although historians in his district were generally friendly and receptive, they would not be interested in receiving unsolicited materials on the *Kriegsschuldfrage*. Similarly, the consul in Seattle noted little academic interest in the war-guilt question and World War I, but much interest in the reparations issue.

The consul in St. Louis reported that he had discussed the entire war-guilt issue with his friend, the prominent Republican politician Charles Nagel,[79] who informed him that no intelligent person could accept the sole guilt of Germany and that while the books of Fay and Cochran were admired, Barnes was considered 'too much of an advocate to be a judge' of the *Kriegsschuldfrage*. For his part, the consul cautioned against 'overdoing' propaganda and advised that it would be best 'to plant the seed' of a new point of view on the war-guilt question and let Americans reach their own conclusions.

The consul in Los Angeles responded merely by submitting long lists of academics in the social sciences, historical societies, and libraries who might be interested in the war-guilt question, but suggested that any material posted to these individuals and organisations should be in English. The consul in San Francisco was more helpful. He reported that although he knew of no academic in his district who specialised on the war-guilt question, there were a number of specialists in modern European history who might be contacted. He especially mentioned Dr O.A. Wedel,[80] a specialist in diplomatic history at the University of Arizona, who would be pleased to receive material on the *Kriegsschuldfrage*. The consul also listed, as very friendly to Germany, the renowned medievalist James Westfall Thompson at the University of California, and stated that the Slavic specialist, Dr R.J. Kerner,[81] professor of modern European history at Berkeley, might be interested in the war-guilt question because he had written on the Slavic question and had served on the American peace delegation in Paris during 1919. The consul also mentioned that the former director of the Hoover Library, Dr Ralph Haswell Lutz,[82] at Stanford University might be receptive to material on the war-guilt question, even though he did not write from the German point of view.

The consul in New Orleans submitted a lengthy report in which he denigrated Southern universities as 'extended colleges' and noted that, since most of the professors were educated in the North, most historians in the Southern states were 'revisionist-inclined'. A major exception, declared the consul, was Dr Thad W. Riker,[83] professor of modern European history at the University of Texas, who had studied at Oxford and was decidedly pro-English.

On receiving the consular reports from the United States, Ministerial Director Hugo Mundt[84] of the Referat requested Wegerer on 18 March 1933, to comment on the reports from the consulates. Wegerer replied on 1 April that the reports not only proved that 'we are on the right track', but indicated quite clearly that German efforts to correct American thought on the war-guilt question would fail if an intense propaganda campaign were launched in the United States on behalf of revisionism. He agreed with the consuls in Cleveland and St. Louis that personal contacts should be exploited and that most of the work on behalf of revisionism should be left to American historians. Unfortunately, added Wegerer, since the recent change in the German government, American periodicals were not publishing many articles favourable to Germany. He urged that every effort be made to reverse this trend.[85]

In June, the consul in New York City finally responded in a lengthy letter to the Referat in which he commented on the historians and the state of history in his district and the United States. Thus he reported that the most widely circulated European history textbook in the United States was published in 1924 by Professor Carlton J.H. Hayes[86] of Columbia University and that, as revised in 1931, Hayes's book lacked the anti-German bias of other American history textbooks and especially the 'exceptionally anti-German' textbook by Professor Charles D. Hazen,[87] also at Columbia. Noting that Renouvin seemed to have the greatest influence among historians dealing with the war-guilt question in American universities, the consul explained that he had detected three schools of thought on the war-guilt question among American historians: (1) those who espoused the German cause represented by Barnes (whose reputation had suffered) and by Cochran ('who is so much for Germany that he does more harm than good'); (2) those who held the middle position, led by the highly respected Professor Fay, which included Dr Raymond J. Sontag[88] at Princeton, who asserted in his book *European Diplomatic History 1871–1932* (New York, 1933), that 'to fix responsibilities [for the war] is impossible', William L. Langer at Harvard, Parker T. Moon at Columbia, and such 'younger experts' as Oron J. Hale[89] at the University of Virginia, Ralph Lutz at Stanford, and Robert C. Binkley[90] at Western Reserve University; and (3) those who took the anti-German position, represented by Bernadotte Schmitt.[91]

An additional letter from the Washington embassy reached the Referat at the end of June 1933, which emphasised the need to avoid the appearance of propaganda and stated that it doubted the wisdom of sending vast amounts of printed material to American academics and scholars. Indeed, because there existed a 'lively mistrust' among the older historians of foreign attempts to inform and enlighten, any materials disseminated should be among the younger historians. Basically, the embassy recommended that the task of 'enlightenment' on the war-guilt question in the United States should be left to interested and friendly American historians.[92]

In reply to the implication from the embassy in Washington that the Zentralstelle was much too aggressive and zealous in its efforts to 'enlighten' American historians, Wegerer informed the Referat that his correspondence with American historians had never been conducted by the Zentralstrelle, but only by him personally, as from one historian to another. In fact, the Zentralstelle had never made itself conspicuous, and only those historians known to himself, such as Fay, Barnes, and the British historian Sir Charles Raymond Beazley,[93] who had visited Berlin, knew about the Zentralstelle. Any material and information which he had distributed – such as comments, scholarly works, and brochures – could not be considered propaganda because they were provided 'in the form of a·personal favour' to interested historians. Moreover, he did not consider the *Berliner Monatshefte* overly propagandistic. In fact, foreign scholars were eager to publish their work in the *Berliner Monatshefte* as a means of becoming known and respected in Germany.[94]

Unfortunately for Wegerer, the Zentralstelle's campaign to 'enlighten' American historians on the war-guilt question and revisionism did not long survive the great changes which occurred in Germany after 1933. In March 1936, Wegerer was forbidden by the Reich Ministry of Propaganda to publish anything concerning the United States' entry into the world war lest it prejudice the work of the Gerald P. Nye committee in the United States Senate

probing the reasons for that involvement. Wegerer appealed the
ban and pleaded that he had no fewer than five articles (including
one by Barnes and one by Tansill) pertaining to the subject ready
for publication in the *Berliner Monatshefte*.[95] But permission to publish these articles was denied.[96] It was clear that the work of the
Referat was being phased out of existence.

Thus ended an interesting attempt on the part of elements in
the German Foreign Ministry to influence American historians
and, through historical writing in the United States, the American
public to accept the German version of the *Kriegsschuldfrage*. The
project failed because of interdepartmental disagreements within
the Foreign Ministry and the fact that German embassy and consular officials in the United States were sceptical of Wegerer's
campaign and refused to commit themselves to his projects.
Indeed, it is quite apparent that the Wilhelmstrasse's career diplomats differed with the semiprofessionals over the efficacy of public opinion and deemed the use of propaganda to achieve certain
objectives in foreign policy as distasteful. Besides, as Selig Adler
has observed, by 1929–30 'The Germans had largely won the battle of history, and they were ready to pass from the "injured inno-
cent" role of the twenties back to the "fire-eating"'.[97] Moreover,
after 1933 Hitler preferred to destroy the Versailles *Diktat* by deeds
rather than words. Yet the National Socialist regime concluded
that, if Americans were to be convinced of anything, it was not
that Germany had been unjustly accused of provoking the First
World War, but that the Third Reich should be accepted as a
power in Europe which did not threaten the interests and security
of the United States.[98]

Notes

1. Imanuel Geiss, 'The Outbreak of the First World War and German War Aims',
   in Walter Laqueur and George L. Mosse, eds., *1914: The Coming of the First
   World War* (New York: Harper Torchbook, 1966), p. 71n. The first three paragraphs of this paper are based largely on Dr Geiss's excellent survey of the
   Kriegsschuldreferat in pp. 72–74 of his essay.
2. Selig Adler, 'The War-Guilt Question and American Disillusionment, 1918–
   1925', *Journal of Modern History* XXIII (1951), 23.
3. Geiss, 'The Outbreak', pp. 71–72. On the relative effectiveness of the Referat's
   campaign, see Adler, 'The War-Guilt Question', p. 6.

4. Geiss, 'The Outbreak', p. 72. In addition to his editing of the *Berliner Monatshefte für Internationale Aufklärung*, Wegerer published his well-known work, *A Refutation of the Versailles War Guilt Thesis* (New York, 1931). For biographical information on Wegerer, see Harry Elmer Barnes's introduction to this pp. 3–4; and notice in the *American Historical Review* LIV (1949), 990.

5. Geiss, 'The Outbreak', p. 74 and note.

6. Ibid., p. 73; and Wolfgang J. Mommsen, 'Zur Kriegsschuldfrage 1914', *Historische Zeitschrift* CCXII (1971), 608–14. On the activities of the Steuben Society, see Sander A. Diamond, *The Nazi Movement in the United States, 1924–1941* (Ithaca, 1974), p. 58.

7. Geiss, 'The Outbreak', pp. 73–74.

8. (New York and London, 1930), 2 vols.

9. Harry Elmer Barnes (1889–1968), Ph.D., Columbia University (1918), taught at Smith College from 1923 to 1929. Barnes's first pronouncements on the war-guilt issue in 1924, 'Seven Books of History against the Germans', *New Republic* XXXVIII (1924), part II, 10–15; and 'Assessing the Blame for the World War: A Revised Judgement Based on All the Available Documents', *Current History* XX (1924), 171–195, were followed by the publication of his book, *The Genesis of the World War* (New York, 1927). The *Berliner Monatshefte* published in English Barnes's article entitled 'Thoughts on Armistice Day', IX (1931), 1027–32, and his polemic, 'The Greatest Fraud in All History', X (1932), 515–532. For an extensive study of Barnes and other American revisionists, see his pamphlet, *The Struggle Against the Historical Blackout* (n. p., 1947); Warren I. Cohen, *The American Revisionists: The Lesson of Intervention in World War I* (Chicago, 1967); Adler, 'The War-Guilt Question', pp. 16–19; and Richard T. Ruetten, 'Harry Elmer Barnes and the "Historical Blackout"', *The Historian* XXXIII (1971), 202–5.

10. On Barnes's relationship with Wegerer, see Barnes's introduction in Wegerer, *A Refutation of the War Guilt Thesis*, pp. 3–4. See also reviews of Wegerer's book by Bernadotte Schmitt in the *American Historical Review* XXXVI (1931), 594–7.

11. German embassy in Paris to Legationsrat Karl C. Schwendemann in Schuldreferat 13 Jan. 1931. Records of the German Foreign Ministry (Auswärtiges Amt), National Archives Microcopy T-120 (hereafter cited as NA T-120), roll 1849, serial No. 3738, frames EO38846–47.

12. Seattle consulate to Schuldreferat, 6 Aug. 1932; Quaderverlag to Schuldreferat, 9 May 1933; Schuldreferat memoranda, 12 May and 10 July 1933, NA T-120/1849/3748/EO38855–57.

13. Sidney Bradshaw Fay (1876–1967), Ph.D., Harvard University (1900), taught at Smith College (1914–29) and Harvard (1929–46). See Fay's three articles in the *American Historical Review*, 'The Origins of the War', XXV (July 1920), 616–39; 'New Light on the Origins of the War, I', XXVI (Oct. 1920), 37–53; and 'New Light on the Origins of the War, II', XXVI (Jan. 1921), 225–54.

14. New York consulate to Schuldreferat, 29 May 1929. NA T-120/1849/3738/EO38894.

15. Schuldreferat memorandum, 19 Feb. 1931. NA T-120/1849/3738/EO38913.

16. Sidney B. Fay to Dr Alfred von Wegerer, 17 April 1931. NA T-120/1849/3738/EO38919.

17. Hermann Lutz (1881–?) wrote *Die europäische politik in der Julikrise 1914* (Berlin, 1930) for the Reichstag Commission and contributed the section on 'The German Case' to the article on 'War Guilt' in the *Encyclopedia Britannica*,

1929 edition, XXII, 350–354. See also Hermann Lutz to Max König, 6 Dec. 1936. NA T-120/1849/3738/EO39372.

18. Lutz to Schuldreferat, 10 Sept. 1929. NA T-120/1849/3738/EO39187.

19. Bernadotte E. Schmitt (1886–1969), Rhodes Scholar (1905–08) and Ph.D., University of Wisconsin (1910), taught at the University of Chicago (1925–39). See the obituary of Schmitt in the *American Historical Review* LXXIV (1969), 1765–66; and Schmitt's pamphlet *The Origins of the First World War* (London, 1966).

20. See Schmitt's review article, 'July, 1914', *Foreign Affairs* V (1926), 132–47.

21. Lutz to Schwendemann, 4 Nov. 1929. NA T-120/1849/3738/EO39165.

22. William L. Langer (1896–1977), Ph.D., Harvard University (1923), was one of the few historians to regard Barnes's book favourably and was for some years friendly with Barnes. Barnes denounced Langer as a defector from the revisionist camp because he opposed isolationism and supported the American entry into World War II and, in the post-World War II years, referred to Langer as a 'court historian'. See Arthur E. Goddard, ed., *Harry Elmer Barnes: Learned Crusader* (Colorado Springs, 1968), p. 362. Since Langer's study of *The Franco-Russian Alliance, 1890–1894* (Chicago, 1930) and article on 'Russia, the Straits Question, and the European Powers, 1904–1908', in *English Historical Review* XLIV (1929), 59–85, were critical of Russia and his *European Alliances and Alignments, 1871–1890* (New York, 1931) was an objective study of European diplomacy during the two decades after 1870, the German revisionists hoped to use it to vindicate the German position on the war-guilt question.

23. Parker T. Moon (1892–1936), Ph.D., Columbia University (1921). Moon's review of Schmitt's *Coming of the War: 1914*, in *The New York Times Book Review Magazine* (16 November 1930), p. 6, was reprinted in the *Berliner Monatshefte* IX (1931), 77–79.

24. Lutz to Schwendemann, 16 Jan. 1931. NA T-120/1849/3738/EO39407–08.

25. Lutz to Schuldreferat, 4 Nov. 1931. NA T-120/1849/3748/EO39414–15.

26. Pierre Renouvin (1893–1974), professor of the history of the Great War at the University of Paris and director of the French War Library and Museum, was an active opponent of revisionism and the author of *Les Origines immédiates de la guerre (28 juin–4 août 1914)* (Paris, 1925; 2nd. rev. ed., 1927).

27. Dr Gerhard Köpke (1873–?). An official in the Foreign Ministry since 1904, Köpke worked in its propaganda section, Information Department for War Aims, during World War I, and after the war in several branches of the Foreign Ministry including the Kriegsschuldreferat until his retirement in 1936.

28. Hans Heinrich Dieckhoff (1884–1952), counsellor of the embassy in Washington (1922–26) and director of the British and American Affairs section in the Foreign Ministry (1930–36), was appointed ambassador to the United States in May 1937.

29. Hans H. Dieckhoff, 'Draft in Reference to the Enlightenment of America on the *Kriegsschuldfrage*', [? Feb. 1931]. NA T-120/5189/K1852/K463207–12. Italics indicate Dr Köpke's underlining of passages in the text.

30. Established in 1930, the Carl Schurz Memorial Foundation (later the Carl Schurz Association) sought to promote German-American fellowship and close cultural ties with Germany.

31. The Steuben Society of America was established in New York during 1919 as 'a civic and fraternal organization of American citizens of Germanic extraction'. Until 1930, the Society published a monthly newspaper, *The Progressive* (originally titled, *Issues of Today*), which served as a conduit for Referat

propaganda. See Diamond, *The Nazi Movement in the United States*, pp. 58 and note, 59.

32. Thomas St. John Gaffney (1864–1944), an Irish nationalist and Anglophobe, was active in Republican Party politics and had served as a consular official in Germany prior to 1917. Hendrik Shipstead (1881–1960), Farmer-Labor Party senator from Minnesota (1923–46) and outspoken isolationist and Germanophile.

33. Emil Ludwig (1881–1948), biographer of Bismarck and Wilhelm II. Gerhart Hauptmann (1862–1946), awarded the Nobel Prize for literature in 1912. Rudolf Herzog (1869–1943) was the author of *Deutschland, mein Deutschland* (Berlin, 1929; Leipzig, 1931).

34. Schwendemann to the German embassy in Washington, ? Feb. 1931. NA T-120/5189/K63214–15.

35. Friedrich Wilhelm von Prittwitz and Gaffron (1884–1955), German ambassador to the United States (1928–33).

36. Prittwitz to Schuldreferat, 14 April 1931. NA T-120/5189/K1852/K46239–41.

37. Dieckhoff's memorandum, 8 May 1931. NA T-120/5189/K1852/K463239–41.

38. Dr Traugott Böhme's memorandum, 9 June 1931. NA T-120/5189/K463242–44. Dr Traugott Böhme (1884–?), Ph.D., University of Berlin (1909), held teaching positions in the United States and Mexico (1913–28) before returning to Germany as director of the Auslandsschuldreferat (1928–37) in the Kulturabteilung of the Foreign Ministry.

39. David Saville Muzzey (1870–1965), Ph.D., Columbia (1907), taught at Columbia University (1923–40). Albert Bushnell Hart (1854–1943), Ph.D., University of Frieburg (1883), taught at Harvard (1886–1926). See Hart's pro-Allies book, *The War in Europe: Its Causes and Results* (New York and London, 1914, reprinted in 1915). Edward Channing (1856–1931), Ph.D., Harvard University (1880), taught at Harvard throughout his career.

40. Eugen Fischer (1881–1964), German historian and author of *Die kritischen 39 Tage von Sarajewo bis zum Weltbrand* (Berlin, 1928).

41. Carl Frederick Wittke (1892–1971), Ph.D., Harvard University (1921), taught at Ohio State University (1916–37). The report of the annual (1931) meeting of the American Historical Association in Toronto includes no mention of any proposal for the establishment of a German-American historical conference or society.

42. Herbert Kraus (1884–1965), a specialist on the history of the German foreign service, had recently lectured on the constitution of the Weimar Republic at Princeton University.

43. Thomas Jefferson Wertenbaker (1879–1966), Ph.D., University of Virginia (1910), taught at Princeton University (1910–47) and specialised in Southern history.

44. Herbert Kraus to Schuldreferat, 19 May 1931. NA T-120/5189/K1852/K463259; Dr Max König to Kraus, May or June 1931. NA T-120/5189/K1852/K463262; T.J. Wertenbaker to König (undated, 1931). NA T-120/5189/K1852/K463288.

45. Michael Hermond Cochran (1893–1943), Ph.D., Harvard University (1924), taught throughout his academic career at the University of Missouri.

46. St. Louis consulate to Schuldreferat, 1 June 1931. NA T-120/5189/K1852/K463274–79.

47. See Michael H. Cochran, 'New Phase of the War Guilt Controversy', *Current History* XXVI (1927), 71–76; and 'Historiography and War Guilt', *Political Science Quarterly* XLIII (1928), 76–89.

48. See Cochran's review of Schmitt's study in the *Berliner Monatshefte* IX (1931), 248–62.
49. German Embassy in Washington to Schuldreferat, 30 Dec. 1931. NA T-120/1849/3738/E038862.
50. Quoted in letter from St. Louis consulate to Schuldreferat, 11 Feb. 1932. NA T-120/1849/3738/E038867–68.
51. Hugo Mundt to St. Louis consulate, 10 Oct. 1932. NA T-120/1849/3738/E038867–70.
52. Walter Simons (1861–1937), served as foreign minister (1920–21), president of the Reichsgerichts and Reichsstaatsgerichts-hof (1922–29).
53. Dr Walter Simons to Schwendemann, 21 April 1932. NA T-120/1849/3738/EO39438–39.
54. Schwendemann to Gesandtschaftsrat Dr Hufer, 29 May 1932. N A T-120/1849/3738/E039450.
55. German embassy in Washington to Schwendemann, 9 July 1932. NA T-120/1849/3738/EO39450.
56. Consul Werner von Tippelskirch to German embassy in Washington, June 28, 1932. NA T-120/1849/3738/EO39449.
57. Count Eberhard Joachim von Westarp (1884–1945), served on the imperial General Staff in World War I and with the German High Command during World War II. He was a relative of the leader of the German Nationalist Party, Count Kuno von Westarp (1864–1955). See German embassy to Schuldreferat, 27 July 1932. NA T-120/1849/3738/EO39452–53.
58. See John Bakeless, ed., *Report of the Round Tables and General Conferences at the Twelfth Session, The Institute of Politics Publications, Williams College, Williamstown, Massachusetts, Published for the Institute of Politics by the Yale University Press* (New Haven, 1932); and *The New York Times*, 28 July–26 Aug. 1932.
59. German consulate in Cleveland to Schuldreferat, 8 Mar. and 3 May, 1933. NA T-120/1849/3748/EO39465–71.
60. Rudolf Leitner (1891–?), served as vice-consul in Chicago (1923–37) and counsellor of the German embassy in Washington (1931–36).
61. William Roscoe Thayer (1859–1923), A.B., M.A., Harvard University (1881, 1886), taught at Harvard University (1888–89). The Germans' prejudice against Thayer was undoubtedly the result of his wartime anti-German pamphlets and his presidential address to the American Historical Association in 1919 which was a polemic against 'history ... made in Germany' and the 'German psychology'. See William R. Thayer, 'Fallacies in History', *American Historical Review* XXV (Jan. 1920), 179–90.
62. Joseph Vincent Fuller (1891–1932), Ph.D., Harvard University (1921), taught at the University of Wisconsin (1925–32) before joining the Department of State as senior historian and chief of the Research Section. He was the author of *Bismarck's Diplomacy at its Zenith* (Cambridge, Mass., 1922).
63. Charles Austin Beard (1874–1948), Ph.D., Columbia University (1904). Although Beard was more concerned with the question of the American entry into the war than with the war-guilt question, he was generally considered a revisionist. See Beard's 'A Bankruptcy Fire-Sale', *The American Mercury* XI (1927), 283–7; also Cohen, *The American Revisionists*, pp. 181–7; Adler, 'The War-Guilt Question', pp. 13–14.
64. Edward Chase Kirkland (1894–1975), Ph.D., Harvard University (1924), taught at Brown University (1924–30) and at Bowdoin College from 1930 until retirement.

65. Report of Rudolf Leitner to Schuldreferat, 8 Sept. 1932. NA T-120/5189/ K1852/K463323–27.

66. Charles Seymour (1885–1963), Ph.D., Yale University (1911), a firm antirevisionist, taught at Yale after 1911 and later served as president of the university (1937–50). See his article on 'The Alleged Isolation of Germany', *Yale Review* VI (1917), 521–35.

67. See Renouvin's 'Les Historiens Américains et les Responsibilitiés de la Guerre', *Revue des Deux Mondes* II, 8 *per.* (15 April 1931), 886–903.

68. John William Burgess (1844–1931), honorary Ph.D., Princeton University (1883) Ph.D., University of Leipzig (1909), taught at Columbia University (1912–28). After becoming involved in the war-guilt question, Burgess presented the pro-German arguments in such works as *The European War of 1914: Its Causes, Purposes and Probable Results* (Chicago, 1915).

69. William Milligan Sloane (1850–1928), Ph.D., University of Leipzig (1876), taught at Columbia University (1896–1928). Like Burgess, Sloane attempted to present a favourable view of the German cause during World War I and endured ostracism because of his prior connections with Germany and his views on the war.

70. John Franklin Jameson (1859–1937), Ph.D., Johns Hopkins University (1882), served as managing editor of the *American Historical Review* (1895–1901 and 1905–28), president of the American Historical Association in 1906, and director of the Department of Historical Research at the Carnegie Institute (1905–28).

71. William Ezra Lingelbach (1871–1962), Ph.D., University of Pennsylvania (1901), taught at the University of Pennsylvania (1900–46). In 1924, Lingelbach contributed an article, 'Assessing the Blame for the World War', to a symposium on the causes of the war in *Current History* XX (1924), 452–62, which was sympathetic to Barnes's point of view.

72. Ferdinand Schevill (1868–1954), Ph.D., University of Freiburg (1892), taught at the University of Chicago (1893–1936). Immediately after the outbreak of World War I, Schevill wrote a pamphlet, *Germany and the Peace of Europe* (Chicago, 1914), which was published 'under the auspices of the Germanistic Society of Chicago', and was regarded by Barnes as one of his mentors. See Goddard *Harry Elmer Barnes*, pp. 305, 553.

73. Ernst Christian Helmreich (1902–   ), Ph.D., Harvard University (1932), taught at Bowdoin College after 1931. Parts of Helmreich's doctorial dissertation, which dealt with the Balkan Wars of 1912–13, were published in the *Berliner Monatshefte* X (1932), 388–90, in which he referred to Cochran as a 'careful historian', but regretted that Cochran's 'intemperance of style' had ruined his case. Ibid., p. 390.

74. Charles Callan Tansill (1890–1964), Ph.D., Catholic University (1915) and Johns Hopkins University (1918), taught at American University (1919–39). As technical adviser to the Senate Commitee on Foreign Relations (1918–28), Tansill helped prepare a report on the causes of World War I for the pro-German Senator Robert Latham Owen (1855–1947) of Oklahoma that placed the major blame for the war on France and Russia. See Robert L. Owen. *The Russian Imperial Conspiracy, 1892–1914* (Baltimore, 1926; New York, 1927), pp. 9–10; Cohen, *The American Revisionists*, p. 194. On Tansill's Germanophile attitudes after 1933, see Dieckhoff's memorandum for the Foreign Ministry, 9 Aug. 1935. NAT-120/-5189/K1852/K463436–41.

75. Wegerer's report to Schuldreferat, 1 Oct. 1932. NA T-120/5189/K1852/ K463329–333. This report is also in NA T-120/1849/3738/EO38849–54.
76. Ibid.
77. Alfred von Wegerer, 'Ausländische Sachverständige zur Versailler Kriegss-chuldthese. Antworten auf drei Fragen', *Berliner Monatschefte* IX (1931), 519–87, and especially 539, 572–85.
78. See consular reports to the German embassy in Washington in NA T-120/-5189/K1852/K463352–74.
79. Charles Nagel (1849–1940), a Republican politician of German descent who studied at the University of Berlin and served in Congress (1881–83) and as Secretary of Commerce and Labor (1909–13).
80. Oswald Henry Wedel (1894–1956), Ph.D., Stanford University (1927), taught at Stanford (1924–27) and for the remainder of his career at the University of Arizona.
81. James Westfall Thompson (1869–1941), Ph.D., University of Chicago (1895), taught at the University of Chicago (1895–1932) and the University of California (1932–39). Robert Joseph Kerner (1887–1956), Ph.D., Harvard University (1914), taught at the University of California from 1928 until his death in 1956.
82. Ralph Haswell Lutz (1886–1968), Ph.D., Heidelberg University (1910), taught at Stanford University (1915–52) and was the author of *The Fall of the German Empire 1914–18* (Stanford, 1932).
83. Thad Weed Riker (1880–1952), B.Litt., Oxon (1908) and D. Litt., Oxon. (1935), taught at the University of Texas (1909–1952).
84. Hugo Mundt (1874–1935), served as German consul in St. Louis (1921–33) and later as Legationsrat in the Foreign Ministry.
85. Mundt to Wegerer, 18 Mar. 1933; Wegerer to Mundt, 1 April 1933. NA T-120/ 5189/K463376–80.
86. Carlton J.H. Hayes (1882–1965), Ph.D., Columbia University (1909), taught at Columbia University (1907–42) and later served as American ambassador to Spain (1942–45). The book mentioned by the German consul in New York is Carlton J.H. Hayes and Parker T. Moon, *Modern History* (New York, 1923; revised and enlarged 1930).
87. Charles Downer Hazen (1868–1941), Ph.D., Johns Hopkins University (1893), taught at Columbia University and wrote anti-German pamphlets during the war. His textbook was *Europe Since 1815* (New York, 1910, 1923, 1924, 1929, and 1931). Barnes's very critical review of Hazen's book, 'Birth Control for Clio' *New Republic* XXXVIII (5 Mar. 5 1924), 49–50 provoked a bitter quarrel between the two men. See Cohen, *The American Revisionists*, pp. 62–64; and Adler, 'The War-Guilt Question', pp. 2, 16.
88. Raymond James Sontag (1897–1972), Ph.D., University of Pennsylvania (1924), taught at Princeton University (1924–41) and the University of California (1941–65).
89. Oron James Hale (1902–91), Ph.D., University of Pennsylvania (1930), taught at the University of Virginia since 1928. He published *Germany and the Diplomatic Revolution: A Study in Diplomacy and the Press, 1904–1906* (Philadelphia, 1931).
90. Robert Cedric Binkley (1897–1940), Ph.D., Stanford University (1927), taught at Smith College (1929–30) and Western Reserve University (1930–39), and published a review of Cochran's book in the *Journal of Modern History* IV (1932), 319–22.

91. New York consulate to Schuldreferat, 10 June 1933. NA T-120/5189/K1852/-K46404–08.
92. German embassy in Washington to Schuldreferat, 26 June 1933. NA T-120/5189/K1852/K463402.
93. Sir Charles Raymond Beazley (1868–1955), British historian at Birmingham University, published such revisionist works as *The Road to Ruin in Europe* (London, 1932) and was well acquainted with Wegerer and Barnes. Adler, 'The War-Guilt Question', p. 23.
94. Wegerer to Schuldreferat, 20 June 1933. NA T-120/5189/K1852/K463397–98.
95. Wegerer to Schuldreferat, 7 Mar. 1936. NA T-120/5189/K1852/K463463–64.
96. Schuldreferat to Wegerer, 12 Mar. 1936. NA T-120/5189/K1852/K463466–67.
97. Adler, 'The War-Guilt Question', p. 21.
98. On the German government's concern with the image of Germany in the United States during the 1930s, see Diamond, *The Nazi Movement in the United States*, pp. 88–250; Leland V. Bell, *In Hitler's Shadow: The Anatomy of American Nazism* (Port Washington, 1973).

Chapter 6

AUSTRIA AND THE GREAT WAR
Official Publications in the 1920s and 1930s

Ulfried Burz

Although there was much controversy over Article 231 of the Treaty of Versailles and Article 177 of the Treaty of St. Germain, which attributed sole guilt for the outbreak of war in 1914 to Germany and Austria-Hungary respectively, it did not spur either German or Austrian historians to take a prominent part in the 'war-guilt debate'.[1] The pioneering research was left to foreign historians such as H.E. Barnes, S.B. Fay, G.P. Gooch (who very early on disputed the sole guilt of Germany), P. Renouvin, B.E. Schmitt, and L. Albertini.[2] A possible reason for the behaviour of the German historians only became apparent as late as the Göttingen Historical Conference of 1932. The general feeling then was that the term 'war guilt' was unscientific because moral concepts such as guilt and atonement had no place in the vocabulary of historians, which should rather be concerned with cause and effect.[3]

But even questions about the causes and effects of the war could motivate only a few German historians to research the outbreak of the war.[4] Apart from Friedrich Thimme and Paul Herre, and to a very limited extent Richard Fester, Fritz Kern and Georg Karo, it was mainly historians of the war veterans' generation like Hans Herzfeld, Siegfried Kaehler, Wilhelm Mommsen and Hans Rothfels who answered the repeated calls of Berhard Schwertfeger for cooperation between historical science and research into the war-guilt question in order 'to free their own Fatherland of this great stigma and to restore it to its rightful place amongst the civilised nations of the world'.[5] Only Erich Brandenburg, Hans Delbrück and Hermann Oncken published broader-based essays about the war-guilt question.[6]

The paucity of the response to the repeated calls for history to make its services available to the fatherland can perhaps be explained by the close connection between the German Foreign Ministry and the Zentralstelle *für* Erforschung der Kreigsursachen (Central Agency for Research into the Causes of the War) founded in April 1921. The Zentralstelle was for a short time only under the management of the Swiss Ernst Sauerbeck, who symbolised its neutrality. Although Sauerbeck officially stood down only in August 1923, since December 1921 the Zentralstelle had been effectively under the control of the former General Staff officer Alfred von Wegerer, an employee of the German Foreign Ministry with the rank of *Ministerialrat*. Under the management of Wegerer, who was not a professional historian, it quickly attracted international attention thanks to the journal *Die Kreigsschuldfrage*. This publication was the main resource of German research into the war-guilt question, and relied on a small group of experienced journalists and a few historians. The refusal of the Zentralstelle to connect their public arguments against the Allied-imposed guilt with the 'stab in the back myth' (thus opposing prevailing views in right-wing circles) also contributed to the low participation rate of German historians. The latter had problems both with access to sources and their temporal proximity to the subject. They also feared being drawn into politics at a time when the potential for instability in foreign policy was considerable.

Austrian historians' avoidance of prewar diplomatic history has a slightly different explanation. In 1915 nearly all historians had insisted on an indissoluble alliance between the Hapsburg monarchy and the German empire. A secretly written 'Memorandum from German-Austria', signed by 855 German-speaking university teachers in Austria, was sent to politicians and high-ranking military staff. The authors demanded 'that as close and as enduring an economic fusion as possible between Austria-Hungary and the German empire appeared to be required. This could be achieved by as far-reaching a rapprochement as possible, and by presenting as common a front as possible to the outside world. Moreover, this rapprochement should be such that a lasting community of interests develops from it'.[7] After 1918 the wish to be united with Germany was expressed in many articles and various models of *Mitteleuropa*.[8]

In 1918 it proved to have been a fatal mistake that there had been no comprehensive historical work on the subject of Old Austria. The wrestling over the complex term 'Austrianism' proved to be more a journalistic question than a scientific one. Few people showed interest in defining this 'Austrianism'.[9] Only at the end of 1917, when it was already too late, had new scientific approaches begun, in, for example, the *Neue Österreichische Biographie*, managed by Oswald Redlich, Anton Bettelheim, Gustav Winter, August Fournier, Vatroslav Jagic, and others. Wilhelm Bauer's initiative, a journal called *Österreich*, which he started with the financial help of the Foreign Ministry, involved all German-speaking Austrian history university teachers (except Ludo Moritz Hartmann) in a project which also came too late.[10] After the breakup of Austria-Hungary, none of those who regretted its demise wished to start a scientific historical discussion about it. The leaning towards Germany remained, and many Austrian historians retained their wartime idea of 'Greater Germany' until the Anschluss of 1938.[11] But the new mother country, the Republic of Austria, did not develop organisations like the Zentralstelle, and there were no clubs or associations whose activities could be compared to those of the Arbeitsausschuss Deutscher Verbände.[12] Moreover, most historians worked as civil servants, and their financial situation immediately following the war was strained. Their jobs were also publicly downgraded.

Shortly after the Anschluss with Hitler's Germany, Ludwig Bittner, one of the editors of the semiofficial Austrian work *Diplomatische Aktenstücke*, wrote an address to the readers of the *Berliner Monatshefte*:

> The fight against the war guilt lie was not effectively supported by any Austrian government despite the sonorous words of recent days. It was left to private researchers who fought the battle on their own account in independent works and in publications in Germany – above all the *Berliner Monatshefte* – always aware that they might be hindered by the raised eyebrow of an emissary of the former enemy countries. It was no thanks to the people in government at the time that Austria too had a share in the intellectual

undermining of the imposed peace treaties and thereby prepared the brilliant deeds of liberation of recent years.[13]

Bittner's strong criticism of 'the non-German states that call themselves German', and his exaggerated praise of Hitler as 'the greatest Austrian' and 'the greatest German of all time', are rendered somewhat grotesque when one recalls that the sense of mission of the Austrian government of 1934 was based on the idea of being 'the better German state'. This attack on 'the un-German state' came from a long-serving guardian of the Haus-, Hof- und Staatsarchiv, an institution in which the most important materials for the reconstruction of Austrian social, cultural and political history were stored. The reconstruction of the outbreak of the Great War on the basis of the official Austrian files shows, however, that the pan-German Bittner's criticism of Austrian governments is not entirely sound.

In the immediate aftermath of the Great War, only official commissioners of the Allied forces were allowed to use the archives and to have access to the diplomatic correspondence and official files. Only 'absolutely trustworthy researchers', and then only 'if a vital interest of our Republic were involved', as Oswald Redlich put it, received permission to use the archives.[14] The subsequent history of the production of the official and semiofficial histories shows that scientific endeavours were disadvantaged in the interests of current policy.

Roderich Gooss, who was made responsible for the publication of the official Austrian files, did not know, in December 1918, whether his work would turn out to be 'scientific' or 'political'. Amongst the problems he faced was the absence of Count Hoyos's notes about the mission to Berlin at the beginning of July 1914. Although a search had been undertaken in the spring of 1918, these notes had not been found.[15] Gooss's remarks have to be seen in the context of both internal and external politics in Austria at the time. So far as the external situation is concerned, the Anschluss question was a central theme for Austrian policy from the country's unwilling acceptance of the Treaty of St. Germain throughout the whole of the interwar period. In comparison, as the instructions for the Austrian delegation to St. Germain show, the war-guilt question took second place.

Concerned about the possibility that the Allies would attempt to extract reparations if there was any extended discussion of war guilt, the Austrians had prepared a line which reflected Austria's extremely limited negotiating position. The responsibility of the Austro-Hungarian monarchy for the outbreak of the war from the ultimatum to Serbia 'which revealed the intention to go to war' and in the reaction to the mediation attempts of Sir Edward Grey was not to be denied, but it 'must be said with all emphasis that this regime which was responsible for the war was not a German-Austrian regime but the regime of the old Austro-Hungarian monarchy whose foreign policy at that time was controlled by a Magyar clique'.[16] While Hungary was unmistakably condemned, the Austrians were prepared, if required to take a position on the question of the sole responsibility of Germany, to adopt a far more defensive line:

> As far as Germany's guilt is concerned one might possibly say that the view that Germany pushed Austria-Hungary forward is wrong, and could be refuted from the available material ... one may say that the German-Austrian government is determined to publish the whole material and that the work is in progress but not yet concluded.[17]

Otto Bauer, Secretary of State for Foreign Affairs, explained to his envoy in Berlin, the historian Ludo Moritz Hartmann, why nothing of foreign-political importance should emerge from the publication of the diplomatic files:

> With regard to the publication of the documents about the outbreak of war I have many reservations. I am not sure that the impression, that the guilt rests not with Hungary but almost exclusively with Austria, is not politically useful at the present moment. But even if one dismisses these reservations – which I am determined to do – it is obvious given the way the government is currently conducted that I cannot undertake the publication without the consent of the Staatsrates, and it is questionable whether this will be granted. In any case I will have the whole thing prepared as soon as possible so that the publication, if the Staatsrates agrees, can follow in about a fortnight.[18]

Bauer evidently wanted to hold in reserve a possible admission of Austria's war guilt for use in a move similar to the one made by Kurt Eisner, the new president of Bavaria, who a few days previously on 21 November 1918 had demanded that the German government release papers about the origins of the war so that 'the peace negotiations can be carried on in an atmosphere of mutual trust'.[19] For Austria the publication of the documents would mean that a great reckoning could be made with the military, the warmongers and the profiteers, and those who constituted the extreme right wing of Austrian politics.

Six months later, in June 1919, internal politics were still relevant but Bauer's decisions were more closely geared to the achievement of his foreign policy objectives. Gooss had finished his work and wanted to publish it in Berlin. Bauer prevented this, writing to Wedel, the German ambassador in Vienna: 'A publication in Berlin is in my view not desirable because it would give our opponents the opportunity to represent the whole thing as a Berlin intrigue': 'printing and publication in Vienna would make it clearer that the publication has come from us and not from Berlin'. He added that 'an immediate publication seems to me only to have a point if Germany refuses to sign the peace treaty. If however the Treaty between Germany and the Entente is achieved, then an immediate publication could be of no real use to Germany any more whereas it could harm German Austria'.[20]

What Bauer wished to avoid was giving the impression that Berlin might have tried to put pressure on Vienna over the publication of the files. It would appear, moreover, that the interests of Germany were more important to the Austrian foreign minister than were those of Austria.

The Treaty of Versailles was signed on 28 June 1919. Once Austria did not have to be concerned with Germany's interests, she could start to make her own contribution to the war-guilt question. Gooss's work *Das Wiener Kabinett und die Entstehung des Weltkrieges* offered an interpretation of the period from the murder of the heir to the throne to Germany's declaration of war against Russia. This was in contrast to the German official publications which were simply reproductions of diplomatic sources. Gooss's foreword stated: 'Our work offers an interpretation based on an analysis of the sources of the events which can be regarded as a direct cause of the war, and the diplomatic actions that arose from them; it is not an exhaustive account of the causes of the war.' He continued:

> These latter span whole decades, and involve the Chancelleries of all the Powers involved in the war. On this it will only be possible to pronounce with complete clarity when the political and military archives of all the States concerned are freely available for an objective study on the basis of the scientific principles of historical research.[21]

Gooss's comments on the deficiencies of his work were probably decisive in persuading A.F. Pribram to publish details of Austria-Hungary's secret treaties from 1879 to 1918. This work, published

in 1920, led to a change in the way that the prewar diplomacy of
Austria-Hungary and Germany was assessed.[22] In January 1919
another historian, Heinrich Friedjung, who in 1909 had been
involved in a sensational court case with a potentially explosive
political background, gained access to the still restricted archives.
The results of his research were published between 1919 and 1922
in the three-volume work *Das Zeitalter des Imperialismus*.[23]

Gooss, Pribram, and Friedjung constituted the small select
group of researchers who received permission to use relevant
archive materials in the immediate aftermath of the war. Gooss
was entrusted with the task of organising the printing of *Supplements and Additions* to the Austro-Hungarian Red Book of 1914. In
1930 he produced a notable treatment of the outbreak of war, evaluating a multi-volume report produced by an investigating committee of the German parliament. In this Gooss put to good use
the documents on the foreign policy of Austria-Hungary selected
by Bittner, Pribram, Srbik, and Uebersberger and published in
1930. Gooss's three-hundred-page evaluation ended with a twelve
point conclusion embodying insights which are still the subject of
learned discussion.[24]

Konsul Bischoff, a colleague at the Haus-, Hof- und Staatsarchiv,
was extremely critical of Gooss's *Supplements and Additions* to the
Red Book. In a memorandum, he deplored the attempts to present
the world with 'an unvarnished picture of the diplomatic antecedents of the war' so far as Austria-Hungary was concerned,
which 'the form of publication chosen does not only fail to achieve
but even sabotages'. In Bischoff's opinion, the most serious mistake
was that the *Supplements* seemed to have 'historically completed a
political collection of documents' which gave the impression 'that
we had concluded the investigations into our war guilt and wanted
to present the world with our confession'. Reflecting on the warguilt clause in the Treaty of St. Germain, he complained that 'when,
before which forum, and with what means, we can attempt a revision of this judgement, is not known to us today. We are not
allowed to prepare for this appeal, except on the basis of the historical documents'.[25]

Bischoff's hopes and ideas for the creation of a work 'in a completely objective and scientific form' were to be realised only in
part, and not for several years. The edition of the files produced by
Bittner, Pribram, Srbik, and Uebersberger were only a partial fulfilment of Bischoff's desire for a comprehensive reconstruction of the
diplomatic history of the previous fifty years. Because of pressure

of time and considerations of finance, the selected papers covered only the period from 1908 to the outbreak of the war. From 1923 there was renewed discussion of the question of a wide-ranging edition of the files. Bittner, not yet director of the archives, reported to the chancellor on the possible existence of files looted from the registry of the Bosnian department of the former joint Finance Ministry, which might show that the Serbian envoy in Vienna, Jovanovic, had warned the heir to the throne before the trip to Sarajevo. Some time later, statements were taken on the matter from the former valet Andreas Morsey, from the head of the military chancellery Freiherr von Bardolff, and even from Archduke Franz Ferdinand's former hairdresser Karl Mellich. In the spring of 1925 a Hungarian delegate announced an interest in initiating a joint Austro-Hungarian project analogous to the German publication *Die Grosse Politik*.[26] The momentum necessary to tackle this, however, was lacking.

The question of the Vienna files was brought to the fore again by an article concerning the Reichsarchiv and the announcement of the publication of the letters of Tisza, the former prime minister of Hungary, which appeared in the *Neuen Wiener Tageblatt* of 26 March 1925. At the beginning of the following month the head of the Haus-, Hof- und Staatsarchiv, Mitis, produced a report answering the queries of the Federal Chancellery about the possible consequences of releasing the files. Mitis stated that 'the complete neglect of our funding by the Finance Ministry' had led to a situation 'in which we are completely cut off from the historical literature of the world and it is only with the greatest efforts and often only by chance that we can get to know fundamental works at least in quotation'. The first essential was that the necessary secondary literature should be acquired. Mitis was aware of the difficulty of deciding who should be in charge of the publication of files; in suggesting names, he acknowledged that representatives of the opposition parties would have to be involved for internal political reasons.[27]

In mid-October 1925 Chancellor Ramek was questioned about publication of the diplomatic files by the member of parliament Leutner at a parliamentary financial committee. Although Ramek recognised that 'from the point of view of the Austrian Federal government and also from a foreign policy point of view there are no formal obstacles',[28] it was more than six months later that the business of publishing began. It was probably German Secretary of State von Schubert who provided the decisive impetus – 'in order at last to demolish the tale of the war guilt of Germany and Austria'[29] – during a visit Ramek made to Berlin; only a few days after his return the Federal Chancellery demanded a report on the subject. Bittner's answer dealt with the motives for the publication of the files and included a discussion of appropriate organisational measures. He referred to the significance of publication abroad and its effects on the general public, and developed the idea that

> given the ever-growing power of war-guilt propaganda, it is not impossible that an international forum, perhaps even the League of Nations, will be entrusted with the task of initiating publications from all the States concerned regarding the prehistory of the war, which might force the Austrian Federal government into such a publication under much more unfavourable circumstances.

Bittner proposed that in order to overcome the financial difficulties 'some limitation would have to be placed on the extent. We will have to content ourselves with publishing the documents from the last decisive years, I imagine from about 1908 ...'. He suggested handing over the publication to the Commission for the Modern History of Austria, through which 'any ill-feeling could to a large extent be headed off'. It was of great importance that 'the preliminary preparations should be carried on very quickly and as inconspicuously as possible'.[30] He believed that, given the opinions of the staff, this could be guaranteed only by requiring all of them to take a pledge of secrecy.

The project was finally set in motion in May 1926. Strict guidelines were laid down for the staff: 'The greatest care to be taken in respect of secrecy. Everyone to take to heart the magnitude of his responsibility. The work must all be done behind closed doors.'[31] These instructions were to be conscientiously followed until publication took place. Under the direction of the Federal Chancellery, the Foreign Ministry provided the necessary infrastructure for obtaining information about publications concerning Austria and the outbreak of the Great War which had appeared overseas. In August 1926 Bittner travelled to Berlin for an exchange of ideas with Friedrich Thimme, the editor of *Die Grosse Politik*.

The Austrian project received from Germany both ideological and financial support. At the beginning of December 1929 Bittner informed Minister Felix Frank that 'The German government has already bought three hundred copies, and wishes to distribute them to various newspapers'.[32] Behind the scenes, the Austrian government provided support. Chancellor Seipel succeeded in getting extra manpower for the archives, but, as he wrote to Finance Minister Kienböck, 'As it concerns a very confidential matter, into which apart from you only the Minister of Education, the Secretary General for Foreign Affairs, and a few leading officials of the chancellor's office are initiated, no reference could be made to this in the application to the Council of Ministers'.[33]

The publication of the *Diplomatische Aktenstücke* brought varying reactions. That of Thimme merits special attention because it acknowledged certain weaknesses in *Die Grosse Politik*:

> In many respects I regard the Austrian publication of documents as being substantially superior to the German one. In the German publication, of course, I had above all to keep in mind the objective that through the method of publication the enemy States would be forced to make public their material too. Even today my opinion is that this would not have been possible if we had presented our publication purely chronologically and without footnote comments, which showed time and again, on important points of comparison, how compromising was the material already made available from the opposite side.[34]

The German files had been gathered into three hundred chapters so as to support the propagandistic contention of Secretary of State von Jagow in 1915 that Germany had been surrounded and had merely reacted defensively to international political actions. The documents in *Die Grosse Politik* were not always complete; the omission of certain passages served to obscure and to tone down the concepts prevailing in the making of German foreign policy. Last but not least, only Foreign Ministry documents had been included, with the result that the chain of command and spectrum of consultation within the German empire was not as accurately represented as would have been the case had material from the Prussian War Ministry and the General Staff been utilised.[35]

The chronologically arranged Austrian publication had qualities of its own. The presence in the archives of individuals from the 'successor states' did nothing to reduce the secrecy in which the work was done. Yet, according to Chancellor Schober in 1929, Italian representatives had in the course of the decade 'borrowed in succession all the boxes of the Political Archive of the Austrian Foreign Ministry, copied hundreds of complete boxes and others with selected material, while the Austrian archive administration was not in a position to state in detail which pieces were copied'.[36]

Schober's story is part of a circular addressed to all Austrian missions in November 1929. The letter ended with comments which point the way for future discussions regarding the problem of the First World War. These comments, however, were formulated in such a way that even now they have not been conclusively proved or disproved. Schober wrote:

> Finally, the publication of documents brings still more evidence that Austria-Hungary and Germany, even after the break with Serbia, were seriously endeavouring to localise the war, in that they did everything in their power to hold back Bulgaria and Turkey from attacking Serbia, and that moreover they continually offered guarantees for the maintenance of Serbia as a sovereign state, even after its defeat, until in the end all these attempts at localisation failed as a result of the premature Russian mobilisation.

The *Diplomatische Aktenstücke* encouraged many Austrian and German historians to undertake new research into the problem of the outbreak of the First World War. In 1933 Uebersberger published the history of the Salonika trial, in which one of the organisers of the assassination of Franz Ferdinand, Dimitrijewitsch, was put on trial. In the same year General Sarkotic, the former general of Bosnia-Hercegovina, published under the auspices of the ADV a book about the Banja-Luka trial which proved that Serbian officials had been agitating in southern Slavic provinces of the Habsburg monarchy.[37] Members of Bittner's group were encouraged by the positive reception given by other experts, and brought out two further important works. Fritz Reinöhl was entrusted by the Foreign Ministry with writing a book about Pan-Serbian intrigues before and after the outbreak of the First World War, which was published by the Vienna Reischsarchiv in 1944, and which can be seen as a sequel to the 1933 files about the Sarajevo trial.[38] In 1945 Uebersberger, Bittner and Alois Hajek published a book on Serbian foreign policy from 1908 to 1914. They used files which in 1941 had been looted from Belgrade. What happened to the third volume of the second series, covering 26 May to 6 August 1914, which was printed and announced as to appear in several issues, is still a mystery.[39]

Conclusion

Research into the causes and outbreak of the First World War should have been an important topic so far as establishing Austria's historical identity was concerned, but the reasons for its neglect, even after 1945 and after the Fischer debate, are manifold. One of the few Austrians expert on the subject of the First World War, Fritz Fellner, has recently suggested, as a possible explanation, that the Austrians were content to bask in the known admiration of the Anglo-Saxons for the artistic and cultural achievements of *fin-de-siècle* Vienna.[40] However that may be, the subject of the First World War has been the preserve of foreign, and principally British, experts. Two British historians, F. Roy Bridge and the lately departed John Leslie, have concerned themselves particularly with Austria's position during the crisis of July 1914.[41] Both agree that Austria's decisions tipped the balance, but offer different explanations. Leslie fixes on Austrian readiness for military conflict on the Poland-Ukraine issue, which placed strains on relations between Austria-Hungary and Russia. The war with Serbia was in his view simply a route to the real adversary, Russia.[42] Bridge maintains that, in 1914, 'not internal pressure but the external threat from Serbia and indirectly from Russia led to the decision for war'.[43] It is still not certain whether Vienna and Budapest had calculated the risks of a big European war or had simply taken a huge political gamble. The role of the Ballhausplatz requires further and more intensive discussion in order to determine whether it too easily became a puppet on the strings of German policy,[44] or whether Austria-Hungary was given international help to fulfil her potential for suicide.

Notes

1. L. Bittner, 'Österreich-Ungarn und Serbien', in *Historische Zeitschrift* 144 (1931), 78.
2. L. Albertini, *The Origins of the War of 1914* (Milan, 1942–43); H.E. Barnes, *The Genesis of the World War* (New York, 1925); S.B. Fay, *The Origins of the World War* (New York, 1928); P. Renouvin, *La Crise Européenne et la Grande Guerre 1914–1918* (Paris, 1939); B.E. Schmitt, *The Coming of the War, 1914* (New York, 1930).
3. U. Heinemann, *Die verdrängte Niederlage: Politische Öffentlichkeit und die Kriegsschuldfrage in der Weimarer Republik* (Göttingen, 1983), p. 107.
4. M. Dreyer and O. Lemcke, *Die deutsche Diskussion um die Kriegsschuldfrage 1918–19* (Berlin, 1993), pp. 23–29.
5. B. Schwertfeger, 'Geschichtswerdung und Geschichtsschreibung', in *Archiv für Geschichte und Politik* (1923), p. 389, quoted in Heinemann, p. 106.

6. E. Brandenburg, *Von Bismarck zum Weltkrieg* (Berlin, 1924); H. Delbrück, *Der Friede von Versailles* (Berlin, 1930); H. Oncken, *Das deutsche Reich und die Vorgeschichte des Weltkrieges* (Leipzig, 1933); F. Tönnies, *Die Schuldfrage: Russlands Urheberschaft nach Zeugnissen aus dem Jahre 1914* (Berlin, 1919).

7. Quoted in G. Ramhardter, *Geschichtswissenschaft und Patriotismus: Österreichische Historiker im Weltkrieg 1914–1918* (Vienna, 1973), p. 41; see also 'Propaganda und Aussenpolitik', in A. Wandruszka and P. Urbanitsch, eds., *Die Habsburgermonarchie 1848–1918*, vol. vi (Vienna, 1989), pp. 496–536.

8. R.G. Plaschka, H. Haselsteiner, A. Suppan, A.M. Drabek, B. Zaar, eds., *Mitteleuropa-Konzeptionen in der ersten Hälfte des Jahrhunderts* (Vienna, 1995).

9. See, for example, R. Kralik, *Allgemeine Geschichte der Neuesten Zeit von 1815 bis zur Gegenwart* (Vienna, 1915–23).

10. H. Dachs, *Österreichische Geschichtswissenschaft und Anschluss 1918–1930* (Salzburg, 1974), pp. 130–2.

11. R. Luza, *Austro-German Relations in the Anschluss Era* (Princeton, 1975); A. Low, *The Anschluss Movement 1918–1938. Background and Aftermath: An Annotated Bibliography of German and Austrian Journalism* (New York, 1984).

12. Heinemann, p. 106.

13. L. Bittner, 'Die deutsche Sendung Österreichs', in *Berliner Monatshefte* 16 (1938), 340.

14. Redlich to Bauer, 17 July 1919, Österreichisches Staatsarchiv (ÖSTA), Archiv der Republik (AdR), Auswärtiges Amt (AA), Neues Politisches Archiv (NPA), Karton 5.

15. See F. Engel-Janosi, 'Zur Geschichte des Österreichischen Aktenwerkes über den Ursprung des Ersten Weltkriegs', in *Zeitgeschichte* 5 (1977–78), 41. On Hoyos, see F. Fellner, 'Die Mission "Hoyos"', in Fellner, *Vom Dreibund zum Völkerbund: Studien zur Geschichte der Internationalen Beziehungen 1882–1919* (Vienna, 1994), pp. 112–41.

16. See F. Fellner and H. Maschl, eds., *Die Briefe Franz Kleins aus der Zeit seiner Mitwirkung in der Österreichischen Friedensdelegation, May–August 1919* (Salzburg, 1977), p. 47.

17. Ibid.

18. Quoted in Engel-Janosi, p. 39.

19. P. Dirr, *Bayrische Dokumente zum Kriegsausbruch und zum Versailler Schuldspruch* (Munich, 1925), p. 46; also, pp. 4–5, 54–56.

20. Bauer to Wedel, 19 June 1919, ÖSTA, AdR, BMfAA, NPA-Präs, Karton 3.

21. R. Gooss, *Das Wiener Kabinett und die Entstehung des Weltkrieges* (Vienna, 1919), p. iv.

22. A.F. Pribram, *Die politischen Geheimverträge Österreich-Ungarns 1879–1914* (Vienna, 1919); *Austrian Foreign Policy 1908–1918* (London, 1923).

23. On the Friedjung trial, see H. Uebersberger, *Österreich zwischen Russland und Serbien* (Cologne, 1958), pp. 50–53.

24. R. Gooss, *Das Österreichisch-Serbische Problem bis zur Kriegserklärung Österreich-Ungarns an Serbien* (Berlin, 1930), pp. 300ff, and summaries 1, 5, 6, 7.

25. Memorandum by Bischoff, 16 March 1921, Haus-, Hof- und Staatsarchiv (HHStA), Direktionsakt, Z1. 1123/1926.

26. Bittner to Bundeskanzleramt, HHStA, Kur., SR XII.

27. Mitis to Bundeskanzleramt, 10 April 1925, HHStA, Kur. Aktenpublikationen 1, SR XII.

28. 'Bericht über die Frage der Veröffentlichung von diplomatischen Akten zur Vorgeschichte des Weltkrieges. Erstattat vom Direktor des Haus-, Hof- und Staatsarchivs Dr L. Bittner am 24 April 1926', OStA, AdR, BMfAA, NPA, Karton 305.

29. So Peter (Bundeskanzleramt, Auswärtige Angelegenheiten, Abt. 13/Pol.) Schubert zit. in einem Amtsvermerk an Bittner, 30 April 1926, HHstA, Bittner, Direktionsakt, Z1. 1123/1926.

30. As above, note 28.

31. Bittner Papers, HHStA, Karton 9.

32. Bittner to Frank, 5 December 1929, HHStA, Kur. SR XII.

33. Seipel to Kienböck, 6 April 1929, ibid.

34. Thimme to Professor Kretschmayr (Chef der Österreichischen Archivverwaltung), 30 April 1930. Ibid.

35. F. Klein, 'Uber die Verfälschung der historischen Wahrheit in der Aktenpublikation *Die Grosse Politik*', in *Zeitschrift für Geschichtswissenschaft* 7 (1959), 318–30.

36. Schober to Austrian missions, 19 November 1929, OStA, AdR, NPA, Karton 305.

37. H. Uebersberger, ed., *Der Saloniki-Prozess* (Berlin, 1933); S. Sarkotic von Lovcen, *Der Banjaluka-Prozess* (Berlin, 1933); see also E. Brandenburg, *Der Sarajevo-Prozess* (Berlin, 1933).

38. See also F. Reinöhl, 'Das angebliche Wiener Geheimdossier', in *Berliner Monatshefte* 13 (1935), 628–30.

39. *Serbiens Aussenpolitik 1908–1918* (Vienna,1945); see F. Würthle, *Die Spur führt nach Belgrad: Die Hintergründe des Dramas von Sarajevo 1914* (Vienna, 1975).

40. F. Fellner, 'Austria-Hungary', in K.M. Wlson, ed., *Decisions for War, 1914* (London, 1995), pp. 9–25.

41. F.R. Bridge, *From Sadowa to Sarajevo: The Foreign Policy of Austria-Hungary 1866–1914* (London, 1972); *Great Britain and Austria-Hungary 1906–1914* (London, 1972); *The Habsburg Monarchy Among the Great Powers 1815–1918* (Oxford, 1991); J. Leslie, 'The Antecedents of Austria-Hungary's War Aims: Policies and Policy-Makers in Vienna and Budapest Before and During 1914', in *Archiv und Forschung: Das Haus-, Hof- und Staatsarchiv in seiner Bedeutung für die Geschichte Österreichs und Europa* (Vienna, 1993), pp. 307–94. See also S.R. Williamson, *Austria-Hungary and the Coming of the First World War* (New York, 1990); and 'Confrontation with Serbia: The Consequences of Vienna's Failure to Achieve Surprise in July 1914', in *MOStA* 43 (1993), 168–177.

42. Leslie, 'Österreich-Ungarn vor dem Kriegsausbruch. Der Ballhausplatz in Wien im Juli 1914 aus der Sicht eines österreichischen Diplomaten', in R Melville, ed., *Deutschland und Europa in der Neuzeit: Festschrift für Karl Otmar von Aretin*, vol. 2, (Stuttgart, 1988), pp. 668–75.

43. Bridge, 'Österreich-Ungarn unter den Grossmachten', in Wandruszka and Urbanitsch, op. cit., p. 336.

44. M. Rauchensteiner, *Der Tod des Doppeladlers: Österreich-Ungarn und der Erste Weltkrieg* (Cologne, 1993), pp. 51–61, 113–21.

§ Chapter 7

THE PURSUIT OF 'ENLIGHTENED PATRIOTISM'
The British Foreign Office and Historical Researchers
During the Great War and Its Aftermath

Keith Hamilton

Access to public archives and the value of their contents are matters of obvious concern to all serious historians. They were subjects
to which Charles Webster, the newly appointed professor of modern history at the University of Liverpool, turned his attention in
the inaugural lecture which he delivered on 10 December, 1914.
Just four months after the outbreak of hostilities between Great
Britain and Germany, and at a time when liberals and socialists
were reaffirming and redefining their objections to a secret diplomacy which they held in large part responsible for the war, Webster argued that a truly national foreign policy could succeed
only 'if it be that of a nation instructed and informed'. And, he
continued, 'no text books or pamphlets will supply it with the
information that it needs, unless the preliminary work of scientific
investigation be also adequately carried out'. That, in his estimation, required a greater readiness than had hitherto been displayed
by British historians to utilise the records of the nineteenth-century Foreign Office. 'No country', Webster declared, 'can afford to
neglect the study of its own foreign policy, without taking the risk
that its ideals will be misunderstood and misconstrued. We must
hope for an enlightened patriotism'.[1]

There was in all this an echo of older liberal arguments in favour of providing an expanded parliamentary electorate with an 'education for citizenship'.[2] If diplomacy were to be more democratically controlled, then its future masters would require a better understanding of foreign affairs. But Webster's appeal for the 'creating of a new science of diplomatic' was directed primarily towards his fellow historians. He thus condemned as hardly 'better than ingenious speculation or unashamed bookmaking' histories of British foreign policy based upon press reports, and upon parliamentary papers whose purpose was generally 'rather to conceal than explain what actually took place'. He also singled out for criticism H.A.L. Fisher, the then vice-chancellor of Sheffield University, who in 1912 had told the Royal Commission on the Public Records that it was his impression that 'the grains of information' which were derived from research in the Foreign Office archives were 'very few and far between and for the most part unimportant'. Almost everything that was 'really important', he had added, came out of memoirs and published state papers.[3]

Fisher's object, however, had not been to deny the value of archival research, but to demonstrate the futility of the existing restrictions upon access to official records. Thus, at a time when departmental archives were still closed to the general public for almost the whole of Queen Victoria's reign, Fisher proposed the introduction of a fifty-year equivalent of the present thirty-year rule. In support of his case he cited a review by Professor James Headlam which implied that Germany had benefited from the liberality of the Prussian authorities in allowing researchers to use their archives, and that other countries must follow its example. German historians, who were hardly the most impartial in Europe, had, Fisher complained, 'got the Prussian point of view in the Prussian documents'.[4]

The contention that the British government was less generous than its continental counterparts in its treatment of researchers was not a new one. An interdepartmental committee, which had been set up in 1908 to consider a relaxation of the rules relating to the opening of public archives, had sought to refute the charge. It had also recommended that all departments should accept a uniform date up to which their records should be open to the public, that every ten years the master of the rolls should promote consultations with a view to advancing this date by a decade, and that permits to inspect archives outside the time limit 'should be granted to all *prima facie* competent and responsible persons engaged in historical or biographical research'.[5] More interesting, however, in view of the oft-repeated assertion that the pre-1914 Foreign Office gave little consideration to explaining its policies to the public,[6] was the stand taken by Eyre Crowe, its representative on the committee, in urging his colleagues to accept the idea of providing scholars with freer access to departmental correspondence. With this in mind, he advocated the establishment of a 'Research or Historical Section of the [Foreign Office] Library'.[7] 'We have', he claimed in a memorandum of 17 November 1908, 'nothing to lose as a nation, and a good deal to gain, by the widest possible publicity being given to our transactions with foreign countries.' Then, after proposing that researchers be admitted to the Foreign Office records up until what might 'be described as the Bismarck era in foreign politics', he concluded:

> I would ... further suggest that no difficulty should be placed in the way of any distinguished historian of British nationality or any young historical talent vouched for by some recognised authority such as the historical faculty of any of our foremost universities, obtaining, as a personal privilege accorded by the Secretary of State, and under specially devised rules and safeguards, access to our papers even of a much more recent period, provided it be understood that the actual text of anything proposed to be published must be submitted for the censorship of the Secretary of State and then on publication being authorised, the original notes, abstracts or copies, of Foreign Office papers are handed over to him. It is a great pity that so little original historical work is at present done in this country, and any encouragement which could be offered in this direction by the Secretary of State would, I feel sure, be a benefit to this country and to the world at large.[8]

Already in his celebrated memorandum of 1 January 1907, Crowe, a senior clerk with charge of the Foreign Office's Western Department, had attempted to explain the growth of Anglo-German enmity.[9] It was, perhaps, with an eye on the dangers inherent in having recent history written from the German documents, that Crowe now anticipated Webster's inaugural lecture by a full six years.

As a result of the interdepartmental committee's report, Sir Edward Grey, the foreign secretary, agreed to the Foreign Office's papers being made available to the public up until the end of 1837, and to scholars with permits having restricted access to departmental correspondence up until the end of 1860. But Crowe's suggestion that some historians be allowed to peruse documents of an even later date was not enthusiastically received by others in the Office. Although his colleagues recognised that there was 'much to recommend it', they were reluctant to take on either the task of having to deny to some scholars privileges which were granted to others, or the onerous duty of censorship. Any radical change in the relationship between diplomacy and academia had therefore to await the onset of the war of 1914–18 and the ensuing debate upon its origins.[10]

Few events have stimulated a greater interest in the history and methods of diplomacy than the outbreak of the First World War. Hardly had it begun before the British government, like those of other belligerent states, tried to explain its recent conduct by publishing a selection of its diplomatic correspondence. The British White Paper (or Blue Book) of 6 August 1914 was soon followed by the production of a popular edition which contained parliamentary statements and an introductory narrative of events.[11] A News Department was also established in order to place the dissemination of information about foreign affairs on a formal and systematic basis.[12] But the White Paper was hastily prepared by Miles Lampson, an assistant clerk in the Parliamentary Department of the Foreign Office, and it contained errors which left the British authorities open to the charge of having deliberately falsified their records.[13] It certainly did little to stem the rising tide of criticism of Britain's prewar diplomacy, which found its clearest expression in the works of E.D. Morel and his associates in the Union of Democratic Control (UDC).[14] Moreover, in the early stages of the conflict Grey's officials seemed capable of displaying a remarkable inflexibility in their handling of matters pertaining to the archives and historians.

This was particularly apparent when in December 1914 John Holland Rose of Christ's College, Cambridge, who wished 'to undertake a defence of British foreign policy down to 1870–1', requested access to the Foreign Office's correspondence relating to the Franco-Prussian War. Quite apart from the fact that the relevant papers were still in the Foreign Office library, where it would have been difficult to accommodate Holland Rose, there was the danger of setting an inconvenient precedent if he were allowed to consult the archives ten or eleven years beyond the usual time limit. And in any case, the librarian, Edward Blech, doubted if the archives contained 'much valuable information on the point in question'.[15] Holland Rose was, however, fortunate in being able to secure the assistance of the former Conservative prime minister,

Arthur Balfour. The latter appears to have had a clear grasp of the need for more 'enlightened patriotism', and after his intervention in March 1915, Holland Rose was provided both with a desk on the second floor of the library and the papers he required. 'A general conception of the German policy which has led up to the present catastrophe is of public importance', Balfour informed the permanent under-secretary, 'and Rose would do it well'.[16]

During the next three years politicians and diplomats alike were to discover that the British public required more than a better understanding of Germany's past policies. The mobilisation of Britain's manpower for total war, signs of a growing disillusionment with a struggle in which it at times seemed impossible to achieve a decisive victory, and the emergence of a new and subversive diplomacy by which the Bolshevik leadership in Russia endeavoured to influence, not just governments, but peoples, persuaded David Lloyd George to expound Britain's war aims along radical-populist lines. Woodrow Wilson's appeal for 'Open covenants of peace, openly arrived at', and the Soviet decision to disregard the mores of the 'old diplomacy' and to publish the secret treaties of the Allies, also provided further encouragement to those who hoped to reform the international system and to democratise diplomacy. It was thus hardly remarkable that during the last year of the war the Foreign Office should have given fresh consideration to whether or not more of its records should be made available to outsiders. Britain's diplomats could afford neither to ignore their critics at home, nor to neglect the accusations of their enemies abroad.

Renewed Foreign Office interest in public access to its archives was prompted by the appearance in the *Quarterly Review* of January 1918 of an article by John Marriott, who, in addition to being the author of several popular histories, was a lecturer at Worcester College, Oxford, and the Conservative member of parliament for Oxford City. he, like Webster, emphasised the importance of equipping the public with a proper knowledge of the 'science of politics and the art of diplomacy'. But he also complained of the existing date limits on archival research, which 'discouraged and baffled' serious students of British diplomacy, 'while the people who look up to them are not fed'.[17]

Marriott's article was drawn to the attention of the Foreign Office by Lord Sanderson, who had served both Lords Salisbury and Lansdowne as permanent under-secretary. After a conversation with Alwyn Parker, Blech's successor as librarian, Sanderson

drafted a memorandum on 18 March 1918 in which he recommended that the general public should be admitted to the archives
up to 1856, and that scholars should be allowed to inspect them,
'subject to revision of any notes or extracts made by the student',
up until 1877. He thought that so much had been published on the
period before 1856 that there was no great risk of 'inconvenient
revelations'. Sanderson's main concern was, however, with ensur-
ing that historians should have access 'under special permit ... to
comparatively recent correspondence'. A cautious and rather conservative bureaucrat, Sanderson was perturbed by what he
regarded as an increasingly distorted impression of British foreign
policy which was being presented to the public. He observed:

> A number of publications have recently appeared containing reviews
> of our foreign policy, and..the majority of them, though there is
> every sign of their being carefully compiled, suffer from the fact
> that the writers, in the absence of authentic English documents,
> have accepted assertions of somewhat imaginative foreign publi-
> cists. The details are scarcely in themselves worthy of contradiction
> or qualification, but the cumulative effect is considerable.[18]

Sanderson's proposals were from the first seen as a means of bet-
tering the public image of the Foreign Office. If put into practise,
Parker thought they would 'create a good impression in parliament and elsewhere'. Crowe, who since 1912 had been an assistant
under-secretary, was quick to recall his own suggestions of 1908.
To these he added two more specific recommendations: that the
archives be generally thrown open to about 1875, 'thus bringing
into public light whatever historical material there is in the
archives concerning the three great wars of 1864, 1866, and 1870–1';
and that students with special permits be allowed access to documents 'up to say 1890, so as to include the period of our colonial
squabbles with Germany down to the Zanzibar-Heligoland treaty'.
Lord Hardinge, who in 1916 had returned to his former post of
permanent under-secretary, did not wholly support these ideas.
Yet he too backed the notion of opening the archives to 1875, 'since
it would expose Bismarck's schemes of aggression'. Apparently,
both Crowe and Hardinge felt that in a propaganda war with Germany the British government would find advantage in opening its
diplomatic correspondence to the public.[19]

Sanderson was less confident about what historical researchers
might uncover. He had explained in his memorandum that difficulties might arise if historians were allowed to view the papers

relating to Salisbury's 'very intricate negotiations with the Austrian, Russian and Turkish governments prior to the meeting of the Congress of Berlin', and unrestricted public access to the archives up to 1875 would, he feared, result in 'inconvenience'. A 'wholesale publication of a perverse selection of the correspondence respecting the French annexation of Savoy and Nice might', he warned Parker, 'even now have an undesirable effect in France'. There was likewise the possibility that knowledge of Queen Victoria's sympathy for the claims of the duke of Augustenburg to Schleswig-Holstein in 1864 might be used by the Germans to excite ill feeling against Britain amongst the Danes. Crowe personally doubted whether there was 'any real harm in letting the simple truth be spoken either about Nice or about 1864'. Nonetheless, he, like Hardinge, was ready to fall in with Sanderson's views.[20]

Balfour, who had succeeded Grey as foreign secretary, was similarly 'inclined to favour a liberal extension of both the free and the restricted period' for access to his department's records.[21] But enthusiasm within the Foreign Office for the adoption of this course was soon dampened by a letter from Henry Maxwell Lyte, the deputy keeper of the public records. The latter was not personally opposed to admitting the general public to the archives down until the end of 1860. Nor did he believe that documents after this date should be completely inaccessible. He was, however, of the opinion that the standard intermediate period for which scholars required a permit should be abandoned, and that access 'to particular groups of [post-1860] documents should be regulated by the Secretary of State, on the merits of each case, after careful enquiry'. After all, he argued, a permit-holder might 'lack discretion, impartiality, or even honesty', and 'be acting on behalf of a foreign client with some other object than the advancement of historical knowledge'. There was, he insisted, 'no antidote to the mischief of garbled documents except their publication in an authentic shape', and, almost by way of an afterthought, he suggested that the Foreign Office consider publishing 'a selection of diplomatic papers subsequent to the Treaty of Paris [of 1856]'.[22]

Other departments were also apprehensive lest a unilateral move by Balfour should reveal any of their past correspondence with the Foreign Office. The Colonial Office was, for instance, disturbed about the possibility of papers relating to such contentious issues as Gibraltar, the Falkland Islands, and the Newfoundland fisheries, becoming available to foreign governments.[23]

Nevertheless, Hardinge considered Maxwell Lyte's suggestions to be 'very sensible', and during the next six years they were in effect applied.[24] In 1919 the Foreign Office archives were opened to the public up to 1860, scholars were able to secure permission to see documents beyond that date for specific projects, and in 1924 the government sanctioned a further extension of the time limit and decided to proceed with what eventually became the eleven volumes of the *British Documents on the Origins of the War*. But long before these decisions were taken the Foreign Office had established new links with the academic world through the acquisition of a Historical Section. This came into being, not as a result of Crowe's proposal, but in response to a joint initiative by the Admiralty and the Foreign Office library, both of which wished to ensure that Britain's representatives at any future peace conference should be fully informed on all topics with which they might have to deal. By February 1918 the section, which was placed under the direction of the distinguished Cambridge historian, George Prothero, had a staff of fifteen and had begun work on the production of its peace handbooks, amongst which was Webster's monograph on the Congress of Vienna.[25]

A more significant development from the point of view of publicity and diplomacy was the creation in April 1918 of a Political Intelligence Department (PID) within the Foreign Office. This drew most of its staff, which included Arnold Toynbee, Lewis Namier, and Alfred Zimmern, from the Intelligence Bureau of the former Department of Information. Its object was to relieve the administrative departments and to provide the government with up-to-date information on current issues.[26] But from the start Headlam-Morley, its assistant director, was keen to ensure that the staff of the PID should be able to address a wider audience. He had begun the war in the Propaganda Bureau at Wellington House, where he had completed a study of the immediate origins of the conflict, and he was anxious that he and his colleagues should not be debarred as civil servants from continuing to write articles, books and pamphlets on matters relating to foreign policy.[27] In a memorandum of 26 July 1918, he took up this issue and the whole subject of relations between the Foreign Office and the public. Conscious of the way in which recent developments had led the eclipse of the Foreign Office, he explained:

> Under modern conditions an office such as the Foreign Office cannot hold its own unless in some way or another it takes the public

into its confidence more than it has done in the past. The form of government to which we are tending is one in which the real power will be in the hands of the great public offices, but they will be subjected to a much more vigorous and constant criticism than they have had in the past. We have already had experience of this with regard to the Foreign Office. The only way of meeting this criticism, much of which is and will continue to be very ignorant, and therefore particularly liable to be captured by clever and unscrupulous people who have particular party interests or whose knowledge is very one-sided, is that we should do all that we can to build up a sound opinion, and this can only be done by providing to the educated and interested members of the public full information. The information I have in mind is not inspired guidance as to the political decisions of the goverment, but the information which the government has before it when it makes its decisions.

It was no longer sufficient, Headlam-Morley contended, for the Foreign Office to continue communicating with the public solely through speeches, parliamentary papers, and press communiqués. The public had come to regard the department as aloof, and that aloofness, he insisted, 'must tend to diminish the weight and authority of the Office'.[28]

Such arguments were probably calculated to appeal to officials who during the past four years had witnessed a steady decline in their influence over foreign policy, and whose department had been increasingly by-passed by Lloyd George and his colleagues in the war cabinet.[29] Sir William Tyrrell, who had once been Grey's private secretary, and who, as an assistant under-secretary, had been made director of the PID, was impressed by Headlam-Morley's case. Hardinge too was favourably disposed, and he thought that the 'prolific production of educative material' should, 'with careful supervision', be permitted to continue.[30] Yet what Headlam-Morley had in mind was more than just an occasional article or pamphlet. He was interested in the production of a number of popular studies of the diplomacy of the war. The PID was, for example, preparing a work on the Brest-Litovsk treaties, which, though it did not touch directly on the actions of the British government, was based upon information which anyone outside the Foreign Office would find difficult to procure. In the meanwhile, Headlam-Morley had been putting together a collection of peace notes, which, he thought, might be published with a suitable introduction. Publications of this kind, even if they were 'completely unofficial', would, he suggested, enable the Foreign

Office 'to give the public a good understanding of important points of controversy'.[31]

The end of the war and the PID's involvement in the peace-making at Paris provided Headlam-Morley with a fresh opportunity to press his case for the greater involvement of the Foreign Office in the enlightenment of the public. The presence of academics, diplomats, and politicians in the French capital encouraged a fruitful exchange of views on the nature of international relations, and at the end of May 1919 Headlam-Morley threw his intellectual weight behind Lionel Curtis's proposal for the creation of two coordinated associations in Britain and the United States for the study of foreign affairs. He was pleased both by the idea of specialists continuing to engage in the discussion of international issues and by the prospect of the publication of a regular yearbook covering recent developments. Others among the Foreign Office delegation at Paris were, however, doubtful about the value of what was to become the British (later the Royal) Institute of International Affairs.[32] Moreover, the fact that it recruited its members from both the left and right in British politics, and that it soon included supporters of the UDC, did not endear it to the higher echelons of the department. Hardinge thought it to be composed of a 'very motley crowd', and Lord Curzon, the new foreign secretary, could not see what was to be gained from his people 'meeting with our avowed and most envenomed critics'.[33] Nevertheless, no objection was raised against Headlam-Morley and two of his colleagues in the PID contributing to a six-volume study of the peace conference which was being edited, under the auspices of the institute, by the Cambridge historian, Harold Temperley.[34]

Headlam-Morley in the meantime had begun to worry over the fate of the PID, which, given Treasury strictures, seemed unlikely to survive the conclusion of the peace conference. In a lengthy memorandum of 28 October he sought to demonstrate the advantages of making the PID permanent, and in doing so he again stressed the role that it could play in influencing public opinion in an age when foreign policy was becoming 'more and more the immediate concern of the people and parliaments'. He also raised the possibility of the PID advising on the publication of Foreign Office records and the further opening of archives. His case was a simple one. For the past five years Britain's prewar foreign policy had been submitted to the 'closest analysis and criticism from friendly and unfriendly quarters', and, he contended, the treatment of this matter was of 'real and urgent importance both as

concerns public opinion in this and other countries, and, in particular, America'. Yet, if it were decided to proceed with the official, or semiofficial, publication of documents, he thought that a
new form should be found which would be more intelligible and
accessible to the general public than the customary White Papers
or Blue Books.[35] It was evidently a task in which he felt the PID
and outside academics could assist. In any event, he responded
sympathetically to a suggestion from Temperley that, since Cambridge University salaries were not what they had been, and dons
were getting into the habit of going up to London once a week,
'some to direct companies, others to lecture at the London School
of Economics etc.', they might also 'sit in the Foreign Office one
day a week reading the official information and commenting on
it'.[36] Headlam-Morley thought it 'most important' that the government should continue to have the help of those who had been
working for it through the war, and, he asked Temperley, 'What
about you yourself?'[37]

Government spending cuts determined the early demise of
both the PID and the Historical Section, and another five years
were to elapse before Temperley found gainful employment in the
Foreign Office. Official parsimony also triumphed over popular
enlightenment when the Treasury refused to fund the publication,
in one volume of English translations, of the latest German and
Austrian documents on the origins of the war. Headlam-Morley
was bitterly disappointed by this decision. 'I cannot', he minuted,
'imagine anything more important ... than that the full information as to these matters, which are of the highest political importance, should be placed before the intelligent public at once'.[38]
Indeed, he had hoped that this particular volume would be one of
a regular series of translations of foreign documents which the
government would sponsor. Headlam-Morley did, however, manage to retain a position in the Foreign Office for himself, and in
March 1920 he was appointed historical adviser to the department. This allowed him to continue in his efforts to persuade his
colleagues of the value of educating the public, while 'at the same
time getting people to regard the Foreign Office as a Department
anxious to help in this important work'.[39] His advice would also
be sought on how best to respond to outside applications for
access to the departmental records.

Where bona fide scholars were concerned, Crowe, who succeeded Hardinge as permanent under-secretary in 1920, continued
to favour the elastic approach towards late nineteenth-century

records that he had previously advocated. In certain special cases the Foreign Office had already demonstrated that it was even prepared to open its archives for the years immediately preceding the outbreak of the war. Sir Sidney Lee, who had been commissioned to write his life of King Edward VII, had been allowed in 1914 to view some of the Foreign Office correspondence on the conclusion of the *entente cordiale*, and in 1920 he was provided with further material relating to the late king's involvement in diplomacy.[40] Professor Charles Oman was also permitted to quote from previously unpublished documents in his semiofficial account of the war crisis of 1914.[41] And George Arthur, who was engaged on his biography of Lord Kitchener, was provided with access to prewar correspondence of Sir Edward Grey.[42] A better test of official attitudes towards historical researchers, however, was offered by the application of Sir Adolphus Ward, the master of Peterhouse, for the assistance of the Foreign Office in the preparation of what became *The Cambridge History of British Foreign Policy*. After a delay of nearly two months, Curzon agreed to allow the editors of the proposed work, or contributors selected by them, to have access to Foreign Office papers for the period 1861–85, on condition that 'all notes, extracts and transcriptions of correspondence' were inspected and approved by Foreign Office officials, and that proofs were submitted to the department before publication.[43]

This was a generous concession to scholarship. It also proved to be a riskier business than had originally been anticipated, since it soon emerged that the chapter of the work which would deal with British foreign policy between 1907 and 1914 was to be written by one of the coeditors of the study, George Peabody Gooch. The latter was clearly not the sort of 'distinguished historian' whom Crowe had envisaged admitting to the Foreign Office archives for the most recent period. His scholastic ability was not in question, but his political judgement was. As a Liberal member of parliament between 1906 and 1910, Gooch had been a severe critic of Grey's diplomacy in the Near East and in Persia, and as a coeditor of *The Contemporary Review*, he had demonstrated his sympathy for both the UDC and a negotiated peace.[44] Certainly, his past record did not inspire Curzon's staff with any confidence in his future researches. 'When history merges into politics', Crowe minuted, 'his [Gooch's] judgement becomes rash and nebulous'.[45] Headlam-Morley was even more scathing in his criticism of a fellow historian. After a long conversation with Gooch on 20 July

1920, during which they discussed what assistance Gooch could expect from the Foreign Office, Headlam-Morley wrote:

> Mr. Gooch's whole mind is influenced by three characteristics; firstly he is primarily a student with no real grasp of the nature of the responsibilities which fall upon a man of action; he is therefore constitutionally unable to understand or sympathise with a statesman who may have deliberately to do a minor injustice or adopt a course of action which obviously has many inconveniences attending on it in order not to sacrifice greater and more important objects. Secondly he was a member of parliament during this period and in parliament was closely associated with the Liberal group who were very critical of Sir Edward Grey's conduct of affairs; as this was the only period in which he has been active in politics, the impressions then formed remain stronger than they would with a man in whose political career they had been only a passing episode. Thirdly, he reads everything – especially everything which appears in Germany – and I know by experience how difficult it is to keep one's mind unbiased if one is constantly studying German political literature. The result of these characteristics will be that what he writes will leave the impression that the moderate and sane criticism of British policy is on the whole just.

There was then in Headlam-Morley's view the danger that Gooch's writings would leave people 'with the feeling that after all it was errors of judgement made by Sir Edward Grey that were very largely responsible for the state of things out of which the war inevitably arose'.[46]

Headlam-Morley's fears were exacerbated by the fact that since the end of the war an enormous amount of confidential material had become available from the Russian and former enemy archives. Moreover, while no adequate treatment of British policy before 1914 had yet been published, German historians had begun their work on demolishing the Versailles treaty's confident assertion that the war had been 'imposed' upon the allied and associated powers 'by the aggression of Germany and her allies'. The result, in Headlam-Morley's estimate, was that 'among neutral and impartial observers, slowly but surely the tide [had] set against this country to a far greater extent than [was] probably realised'. In these circumstances, Headlam-Morley proposed that since nothing could be done to prevent Gooch from writing his chapter, the Foreign Office should do all it could to help him state the British case 'strongly and firmly'. The department had, he thought, two options open to it: either to anticipate Gooch's chapter by a publication of Britain's prewar documents; or to allow Gooch access to its records 'under proper control'.[47] In the end a compromise was achieved, and Gooch and his associates were afforded the assistance and advice of present and former officials of the Foreign Office.[48]

Nevertheless, in permitting the contributors to *The Cambridge History* to have access to archives up to 1885, the Foreign Office set a precedent, and this affected the publication in an expurgated form of the peace conference handbooks. These for the most part dealt with geographical and historical subjects.[49] But some of them also touched upon current issues, and in doing so drew attention to matters which the Foreign Office and other departments sometimes regarded as politically sensitive. Worried lest the Argentinian government should be encouraged to reassert its claims to the Falkland Islands, the Colonial Office insisted on the deletion from the original handbook on the subject of all references to the international controversies that had preceded the final British seizure of the islands. This was despite the fact that the manuscript contained nothing that could not be found in other printed sources.[50] The Foreign Office similarly declined to sanction the publication of the handbook on Persia, which had been compiled by E.G. Browne, the eminent Persian scholar and orientalist. The latter had a very different view of developments in Persia to that upon which Grey's policy had been founded, and the Foreign Office wished to avoid giving his opinions an official imprimatur.[51] Even Webster, who had already published his *Congress of Vienna*, found himself in trouble with the Office when he tried to have included in this new edition passages from the handbook which made practical suggestions on how the Paris Peace Conference might be organised. Headlam-Morley feared that anyone reading these recommendations could base upon them a very severe criticism of the actual procedure adopted at Paris, for it was 'most instructive to note how the experience gained at Vienna was in fact completely disregarded in nearly every point'.[52]

Oddly enough, far fewer objections were raised against the publication of the handbook prepared by E.L. Woodward on the Congress of Berlin, which was largely based upon confidential Foreign Office papers. In a minute of 6 May 1920 Headlam-Morley pointed out that since Ward and his collaborators had been granted permission to inspect correspondence up to 1885, the publication of this handbook would establish the 'general point ... that material from the confidential archives might be used'. He hastened to add that this would be conditional on no reference or quotation being made which 'might be inconvenient at the present time to the government, or be capable of interpretation as being seriously discreditable'. Moreover, Stephen Gaselee, the new Foreign Office librarian, required that before the publication of *The Congress of Berlin*, all specific references to confidential papers should be omitted from it. Their inclusion might, he predicted, lead other 'historical workers' to apply to see the documents. With Crowe's backing, Gaselee also insisted on the excision from the manuscript of the noun 'Einkreisungspolitik'. He informed Prothero that 'we do not admit there was any such thing', and he urged its replacement by 'the Franco-Russian alliance'.[53]

Where earlier periods were concerned, Gaselee was altogether more generous in his attitude towards historians. He was, for instance, to suggest in February 1921 that the Foreign Office should assist researchers by making public some of the department's confidential print (selections of printed correspondence that were circulated to missions abroad) up to 1860. Unbound sets of the print might, he thought, be presented to the copyright libraries, Liverpool University Library, John Rylands Library at Manchester, and, if stocks were large enough, the Library of Congress. Such diplomatic philanthropy might well have preempted more recent schemes for the commercial publication of volumes of the print. But Crowe was with good reason reluctant to adopt Gaselee's plan. He recognised the dangers inherent in encouraging researchers to rely on the print, which only partially covered events. 'The incompleteness of the papers alone, which will hardly be understood by the casual student, is calculated', Crowe minuted, 'to produce erroneous impressions.'[54]

Under Crowe it soon became the established practise to allow genuine scholars conditional access to the Foreign Office records up to 1870, and to make available certain specific manuscript collections beyond that date.[55] The policy reflected the desire of Curzon and his officials both to meet the wishes of British historians and to influence opinion in Europe and North America. This was apparent in the department's response to the request which it received in August 1920 from Lawrence Steefel, who was then a postgraduate student at Harvard preparing his doctoral thesis on the Schleswig-Holstein question, for admission to Foreign Office correspondence of the early 1860s. Headlam-Morley, who had already stressed the importance to Britain of maintaining American goodwill, was particularly well disposed towards this application. 'On general grounds', he noted, 'it is certainly desirable, and I think may be very important, that we should encourage younger American historians who are taking up European History to come to London and thereby to get them to approach these questions from a point of view sympathetic to this country.' Besides which he considered the Harvard history school to contain some of the 'best friends' England had in the United States and their influence on American public opinion to be significant. Crowe was less certain. It was quite possible that Steefel might produce a book with a strong anti-British bias, and then, he observed, the Foreign Office 'would be reproached rightly for allowing access to our confidential correspondence to a foreigner before opening it to our own subjects'.[56]

Fortunately for Steefel, Headlam-Morley's advice prevailed, and the young American was allowed both to see the papers he required and to retain his notes, minus a few deletions.[57] Long before the appearance in 1932 of Steefel's seminal study of the Schleswig-Holstein question,[58] however, the Foreign Office had agreed to extend the period of access to its documents. Even by the autumn of 1919 the department was finding it difficult to close its eyes to the flow of revelations from the continental archives.[59] Neither the doctored version of Karl Kautsky's collection, *Die Deutschen Dokumente zum Kriegsausbruch*,[60] nor the Austrian *Diplomatische Aktenstücke zur Vorgeschichte des Krieges 1914*, could be said to have established the 'innocence' of the Central Powers. Nevertheless, they did cast doubt upon the claim made by the British and French governments in December 1918 that there was no point in setting up a neutral commission to enquire into the causes of the war 'since Germany's responsibility ... [had] long since been incontestably proved'.[61] Moreover, both Otto Hamman's *Zur Vorgeschichte der Weltkriege*, which was published in 1918, and the reminiscences of Freiherr von Eckhardstein, the first volume of which appeared in the following year, seemed to demonstrate that the growth of Anglo-German antagonism in the last two decades of the nineteenth century could not be blamed entirely upon the authorities in Berlin.[62]

Hamman's work was especially interesting to British historians because it included the texts of an exchange of notes between Bismarck and Salisbury in November 1887, in which the former had proposed, and the latter had rejected, an Anglo-German alliance.[63] What, however, was potentially more embarrassing from the British point of view was the claim of Eckhardstein that in August 1895 Salisbury had, during a conversation with the Emperor

William II, proposed a partition of the Ottoman empire: a statement that could be used to show both the extent of Britain's imperial ambitions, and the lengths to which the British had been prepared to go in promoting discord between their neighbours. Early in September 1920, the question was taken up in *The Times* by Sir Valentine Chirol, the former correspondent of the newspaper in Berlin. Besides challenging the veracity of Eckhardstein's account, he advised the Foreign Office, if it possessed the materials for doing so, to answer the allegation.[64] Headlam-Morley agreed, and although he failed to unearth any record of Salisbury's conversation with the emperor, he rebutted Gaselee's contention that since Eckhardstein's allegations had not aroused very much comment, 'it would be better to say nothing publicly'. There was, he reminded Gaselee, a large and important number of people in all countries who were following these matters with critical attention, and it was by them 'that the books and articles [were] written by which in the long run general opinion [was] moulded – in other countries perhaps even more than in this'. He wondered if Sanderson, who had been able to shed some light on the background to Salisbury's conduct, could be persuaded to write an article for the *Quarterly Review*. But Sanderson, who in fact thought it 'quite possible' that Salisbury could have encouraged the German ambassador in London 'to discuss eventual claims of the various Powers to a share' in Turkey, declined to do so. His eyesight was impaired, as it had been since 1904, and he did not feel capable of the prolonged study that an article would entail.[65]

Another consequence of the recent German publications was that they revealed significant gaps in the records of the Foreign Office. The fact that it had been necessary to seek Sanderson's advice was indicative of this. The trouble was that Salisbury had conducted much of his political business through private correspondence, and on his departure from office he had taken his papers with him. The Foreign Office thus found itself in the unfortunate position of having no copies of the Bismarck-Salisbury correspondence which had appeared in Hamman's book. One suggestion, which was made by Gaselee, was that the department should try to incorporate into its record those of Salisbury's letters which had been printed in German and Austrian works. An unsuccessful attempt was also made to persuade Lady Gwendolen Cecil, Salisbury's daughter and biographer, to allow the Foreign Office to have copies of her father's diplomatic correspondence.[66] There was, as Gaselee later admitted to the king's private secretary, 'for certain years ... more material for the historian of the future at Hatfield than at the Foreign Office'.[67]

What Headlam-Morley found more puzzling than the paucity of the archives for the Salisbury period was the absence from the library of original copies of many of the telegrams that had been published in the White Paper of August 1914. It is possible, as Miles Lampson suggested, that the scribbled copies of such telegrams, which would have been made by the resident clerks, had been destroyed by the Foreign Office printers. Nevertheless, this did not explain why the 'white copies', which were usually made by the printers and entered in the records, were missing. And for Headlam-Morley, who discovered this gap in the archive, it was a 'matter of the highest importance' that the originals of these documents should be preserved, for they could 'never be sure that it might not become necessary for the British government either to publish the full correspondence in its original form or at least to allow careful comparison of the published despatches and the originals'. If only the printed copies were available, he predicted, 'conclusions detrimental to the faith of the government might be drawn'.[68]

The problem of the missing papers was not resolved. But during the next two years it became increasingly apparent that the Germans had become adept in the use of open diplomacy, and that the British Foreign Office was in danger of losing the debate on the origins of the war. The publication in 1921 of Siebert's collection of Russian documents, *Diplomatische Aktenstücke zur Geschichte der Ententespolitik der Vorkriegsjahre*, seemed to add credence to German claims that they had been victims of a policy of encirclement, and the appearance in the following year of the first volumes of the German foreign policy documents, *Die Grosse Politik der europäischen Kabinette 1871–1914*, heralded a fresh assault upon the war guilt issue. Then in the autumn of 1922 a further challenge was posed to the honesty of the British Foreign Office by von Romberg's account of the falsification of the Russian Orange Book of 1914.[69] Therein Romberg revealed the full text of a telegram sent from St. Petersburg on 27 July 1914 to the Russian ambassador at London, only a part of which had subsequently been communicated to the Foreign Office.[70] This allowed the *Daily Herald* to claim that the communication, which had been published in the British White Paper, had been emasculated in order to present Russia's diplomacy in a more favourable light. The newspaper was mistaken in its interpretation, but Headlam-Morley, who invited its editor to examine the original document, was unable to convince him that there had been no tampering with it. Headlam-Morley wanted to write a short article about this and other questions, and so 'carry the war into the enemy's camp'. Crowe declined, however, to sanction this course. 'The incident', he minuted on 30 October, 'shows the necessity of great caution in discussing with these wild Herald people and similar crooked minds what are the internal affairs of this office.'[71]

One alternative to the Foreign Office's simply ignoring its critics was that which Headlam-Morley had long since suggested: the publication of a fresh volume of British documents on the origins of the war. This idea was also supported by Lord Grey, the former foreign secretary. In an interview with Headlam-Morley on 6 December 1922, he said that he would have preferred to have seen a general publication of British documents immediately after the war. He even observed that he would have liked an 'impartial tribunal to supervise it', and he went on to argue in favour, not just of a new volume on the war crisis of 1914, but a work which would 'go back to 1906 or 1904'. Grey thought that it might be possible 'to pick out the essential documents' bearing on Anglo-German relations, and that to these might be added 'an authorised translation of such of the new Russian documents as bore directly on English policy'.[72] Grey was evidently anxious to defend his own past actions and diplomacy. Others amongst his former colleagues in Asquith's Liberal cabinet were similarly eager to rebut the accusations of their critics. Asquith was himself engaged in writing *The Genesis of the War*, and Winston Churchill was preparing the first volume of *The World Crisis*.

Many of the memoirs and recollections which had so far been published by participants in the war crisis of 1914 and the ensuing conflict had cited, and quoted from, hitherto confidential papers. Indeed, it was with the object of enabling public figures, like Churchill, to defend themselves against criticisms based upon misleading and partial quotations from such sources, that Lloyd George's government ruled in January 1922 that former ministers should be permitted to use official documents to vindicate their actions, provided that this did not jeopardise the current public interest.[73] A problem arose, however, when Churchill, prompted thereto by Asquith, wrote to Headlam-Morley in December 1922 to explain that he could not remember what had passed during August and September 1912 with regard to the Anglo-French naval conversations and to ask if the historical adviser could let him know 'what actually happened'.[74] Headlam-Morley, who, with the approval of both Curzon and Crowe, had previously assisted Asquith, would personally have liked to have been able to provide Churchill either with copies of the records he desired, or a statement on the contents of relevant correspondence. He was, in any case, pleased to have the opportunity to correct some of the factual errors in the proofs of Churchill's chapters. As he explained in a minute of 11 January 1923, it was 'of serious public importance that if former ministers ... [wrote] books they should be free from obvious errors of fact and they should be warned as to the interpretations which may be put by hostile critics on the attitude they assume'.[75]

Crowe was equally aware of the advantage of letting the truth be known under conditions which the Foreign Office could to some extent control. Nevertheless, he was irritated by the impropriety of Churchill's having addressed himself, not to the secretary of state, but directly to an official of the department.[76] Another important point of principle was also at stake, for Churchill had sought information from a department of which he had never been head. 'Prima facie', Crowe wrote to the prime minister in January 1923, 'it seems somewhat dangerous to set the precedent of letting ex-ministers call for official statements on any subject that may have arisen during the time they were in office in order to earn money by publishing such information.'[77] Bonar Law, who had succeeded Lloyd George in the previous autumn, agreed with Crowe. As a result, Headlam-Morley had to request Churchill to address himself directly to the prime minister, who might have to take a cabinet decision upon the matter.[78] Indeed, when the publication in the press of extracts from Churchill's forthcoming book led to questions in the Commons, the cabinet agreed on 21 February 1923 to constitute under Curzon's chairmanship a committee to consider the use of official material in publications.[79]

The issue of former ministers and ex-public servants divulging cabinet and departmental secrets was not nearly so serious a problem for the Foreign Office as it was for the service ministries and the cabinet secretariat. British diplomats of the prewar period perhaps felt that they had less need to defend their conduct than did the soldiers and sailors of the Great War, and the prospective financial rewards may well have been less tempting. They also seem to have had more respect for the Official Secrets Act than did ex-ministers for their privy councillors' oath. Nevertheless, Curzon was willing to make an example of any minor delinquent. 'If we cannot cut off the head of a poppy', he protested, 'that is no reason why we should not decapitate a daisy.'[80] And Curzon readily took to task Sir George Buchanan, the last British ambassador to imperial Russia, when in March 1923 he contributed four articles to *The Times* without first having cleared them with the Foreign Office. Yet no obstacle was placed in the way of Buchanan's proceeding with the publication of his rather unexciting memoirs.[81] The Foreign Office similarly sanctioned the manuscript of the first two volumes of Sir James Rennell Rodd's *Social and Diplomatic Memories*, though much to the regret of the former British ambassador at Rome, he was compelled to omit an account of the part which he had played in 1897 in frustrating French ambitions on the upper Nile. 'It reveals', Crowe noted, 'a piece of history which it would be far better not to give the world as yet.'[82]

Other pieces of history were likewise to remain reserved for the gaze of the select few. When in March 1923 Godfrey Davies, a lecturer at Pembroke College, Oxford, who was later to become better known for his work on Stuart England and the Duke of Wellington, applied to the Foreign Office for permission to use the archives of 1885 relative to the Penjdeh crisis, access was refused. But Davies, who used his father, the Conservative member of parliament for Cirencester, as an intermediary, persisted in harassing the Foreign Office. He accused the government, wrongly it would seem, of being the 'most illiberal in Europe in granting access to its state papers',[83] and complained of the way in which statesmen and former diplomats were able to publish information 'obtained during official employment, of as late as, and even much later than, 1885'. Finally, in a letter which his father transmitted to Crowe, Davies denounced

> ... a system which is based on an arbitrary rule, fixed by departmental officials, which permits the gratification of family pride or love of money, and which denies facilities to students of history whose researches need not in any way hamper the control of foreign policy, and whose works might help to remove the reproach that the English people are singularly ignorant about relations of their own nation to other Powers.

This exercise in academic undiplomacy gave offence in the Foreign Office and did Davies's cause no good.[84] His application and subsequent letters, nevertheless, revived the debate within the Office on future access to the archives. Thus, while there was no sympathy for the idea of granting Davies any kind of exceptional privilege, there was general agreement that 1860 was too early a date to close the records to the public. Curzon suggested that it might be best to introduce a fifty-year closure rule, advancing this automatically by ten years every decade. But Crowe and Gaselee reminded him of the principle, established in 1909, that the records of all government departments should be open to the same date. Anticipating resistance from both the Colonial and the Home Offices to any advance beyond 1860, Gaselee argued that the matter should be postponed until the publication of the next batch of Queen Victoria's letters, which was due to cover the period between 1861 and the mid-1870s. The appearance of this series would, he reckoned, provide the Foreign Office with a 'lever to use upon other departments'.[85]

Gaselee reaffirmed his position on this point when in November 1923 Zimmern, in a review of the third volume of *The Cambridge History of British Foreign Policy*, speculated upon the possibility of the archives being opened until 1901. In Zimmern's opinion, such access should surely be granted 'to responsible inquirers like Mr. Gooch, who could be trusted not to transgress the limits of discretion in matters affecting individuals'. Gaselee made it quite clear that the Foreign Office had no intention of opening its records to so late a date. But Headlam-Morley, who had not participated in the discussion on Davies's application, was glad to learn that a further extension of the period of access was in the offing. 'My own feeling', he minuted on 30 December, 'is that up to 1871, or perhaps 1874, there is no reason why our archives should not now be freely opened.' For the subsequent periods he thought it necessary to remember that since so much had been published in Germany and Austria 'practically all the important secrets' had been disclosed. 'I doubt, he concluded, 'whether there is really anything, except perhaps personal questions which it is now desirable to keep secret, down to about 1885.'[86]

Further disclosures about Britain's prewar foreign policy seemed, in any case, bound to emerge from the memoirs which Grey began to write in the autumn of 1923. Grey's failing eyesight led him to turn for assistance to the Liberal journalist, J.A. Spender, who, it was agreed, should be able to use all the documents in the Foreign Office 'which might throw light on Lord Grey's action or policy'. Grey also assured the Office that he did not intend, 'at any rate at present', to remove his private correspondence from the library, and if, as was possible, the Labour Party came to power, he would offer the new foreign secretary complete access to his papers. 'It would thus be clear', Gaselee noted, 'that we have nothing to hide and that there were no secret negotiations going on behind the back of parliament and differing from the official correspondence on the same subjects'.[87] Indeed,when in January 1924 a Labour government was formed, and Ramsay MacDonald, a leading member of the UDC, decided to be his own foreign secretary, both Gaselee and Headlam-Morley appear to have welcomed the prospect of his making more of the department's records available to the public. Headlam-Morley, who had already been through many volumes of the archives, had not found anything the publication of which would cause 'serious embarrassment'. And it was on Gaselee's advice that on 20 February the Commons were told, in answer to a question from Morel, that the prime minister was considering what course 'might be profitably adopted' with regard to the further publication of the pre-1914 British records.[88]

The new government had also to respond to renewed pressure from historians for access to late nineteenth-century diplomatic correspondence. As in 1923, the issue was raised in the Foreign Office as a result of the department's turning down the application of an established academic for admission to the archives. The applicant on this occasion was Samuel Morison, the professor of American history at Oxford, who wanted to look at the Foreign Office files on the Spanish-American War of 1898.[89] Before addressing himself to the department, he had taken the precaution of enlisting the support of Harold Laski. The latter, who, besides being a lecturer at the LSE, was a friend of the prime minister, wasted no time in making plain his position on this question. 'Our attitude to the use of archives', he wrote to MacDonald on 4 April, 'is probably more reactionary than that of any first-class state except France.'[90]

Much the same point was made by Charles Webster, who in 1922 had succeeded Zimmern as professor of international politics at the University College of Wales. In a memorandum that Laski communicated to MacDonald, Webster returned to the subject which he had taken up in his inaugural lecture at Liverpool. Thus he repeated his argument that the history of past diplomacy was essential to a proper understanding of the present. 'Access to the Foreign Office Records is', he maintained, 'a vital consideration in all attempts to make foreign policy depend upon the popular will.' Then, after contesting the liberal attitudes of the defeated powers towards the use of their archives with the illiberality of the victors, he condemned a situation which had resulted in 'much loose writing and thinking'. He continued:

> There is much unfounded suspicion about British policy both amongst foreign and domestic critics. The motives and aims of the diplomatists are often misunderstood. National prejudices are thus fostered and national rivalry and suspicion kept alive. Nor will it be believed that a new spirit of frankness amongst nations is desired by any government which pursues the same policy of concealment as was followed by governments before the War.

Like Davies, Webster also attributed 'this concealment', not to any rational motive, but to 'official inertia'. To overcome it, he proposed the adoption of a fixed period of forty years during which the records would remain closed, and after which they would be automatically opened to the public. This, he forecasted, would 'almost inevitably result in the opening to a later date of the records of other countries with further advantages to the British people and to the world.[91]

Webster's paper met with mixed reception in the Foreign Office. Crowe considered it 'neither quite accurate nor altogether convincing', and, with some justice, rejected the insinuation that Britain was less liberal than other countries in providing access to its archives. After all, as Gaselee pointed out, there had only been 'an official and partial' publication from the German archives for the pre-1914 period. Both Crowe and Gaselee were also opposed to an automatic and annual advancement of the date up to which the archives were open. A decision, Crowe felt, ought to depend on 'the special features of the particular period', and on the part played by those who were still alive and possibly occupying eminent public positions. He remained, however, favourable to the notion of throwing open the archives up to 1884, 'when a distinct period of history opened with the origin of German colonial policy and Anglo-German friction'. This was advice that MacDonald readily accepted, and on 6 May Gaselee informed Laski that the foreign secretary agreed that 'there should be a considerable extension of the open period', that the necessary negotiations with other departments would begin at once, and that it was hoped that the new period would be in operation before the end of the summer.[92]

Headlam-Morley, whom Gaselee had consulted on the 'best means, or any possible means' of fulfilling MacDonald's commitment to parliament of 20 February, personally sympathised with the idea of granting some historians restricted access to diplomatic

correspondence up to 1901. He argued in a memorandum of 29
April, as Grey had done two years before, in favour of an official
publication of documents covering the decade before the outbreak
of the war. Such a work would, he believed, have to extend over
several volumes, and, since it would be expensive, seemed bound
to meet with objections from the Treasury. He also strongly
insisted that the 'whole work be done by and in the Foreign Office,
and that no countenance should be given to proposals ... that the
publication should be entrusted to scholars with no responsibility
to the Foreign Office'. It might, he reckoned, be necessary temporarily to strengthen the staff 'by engaging one or more well-
equipped historical scholars to help in the work', but they should
be regarded as part of the Foreign Office.[93]

What Headlam-Morley may have been contemplating was the
establishment of something like the PID, or, perhaps, the former
Historical Section. He had himself been assembling material for a
new collection of British documents on the war crisis of 1914, and
was probably thinking about the preparation of earlier volumes.
He appears, however, to have been reluctant to tackle the question
of whether any new historians, who might be employed by the
Foreign Office, were to work under his editorial supervision, or to
be editors in their own right. Moreover, Gaselee added nothing to
clarify this point. He thought that the task would require the
employment for a couple of years of at least two 'historians of the
highest class', and he explained, 'they must clearly be people who
will be trusted by those who believe in us least – people who think
that we are really trying, or have tried, to hide damaging documents'. The problem was that the employment of such historians
was likely to satisfy critics of the department only if they had an
independent editorial role. There was, nevertheless, general agreement within the Office on the principle of publication. Crowe was
enthusiastic about the proposal, which, he maintained, 'ought to
be looked at not only from a political but also from an educational
point of view'. Likewise, MacDonald, who had laid aside his previous criticisms of the Foreign Office, agreed that it was time to
publish 'some *histories* about events leading up to the war and to
displace the pamphleteering rubbish that some so-called historians palmed off upon us'.[94]

The prime minister's reference to the production of *'histories'*
disquieted Headlam-Morley. He wanted, not histories, but documents for historians. By 24 May, when he drafted more detailed
proposals on the project, he had come to see it as consisting of

several 'sections', each of which would deal with a particular subject and be arranged chronologically, presumably after the fashion of *Die Grosse Politik*. They could, he suggested, be compiled in one of two forms: either as a simple collection of documents assembled under the supervision of Gaselee and himself; or as a series of volumes which would contain some explanatory matter, and which would be published by the Stationery Office or in a style similar to the publications of the Camden Society and the Royal Historical Society, with the names of those who took part in the editing appearing on the title page.[95] This, however, still left unresolved the question of editorial responsibility. Gaselee, who preferred the idea of the Stationery Office publishing the contemplated volumes, pointed out in a minute of 28 May that it was

> ... necessary to find some historian young enough to take the comparatively subordinate position indicated by Mr. Headlam-Morley, and of a political complexion ... that will make him appear a trustworthy person to possible critics, whether Mr. Morel or those of the more extreme left in England or scholars and politicians of ex-enemy countries – principally of course Germany abroad.

It seems not to have occurred to Gaselee that the employment of a young historian in a subordinate position was unlikely to inspire confidence in the Foreign Office's honesty of purpose. But the point was grasped by Crowe, and when Gaselee suggested that R.B. Mowat might be too costly to employ as he had a wife and six children to support, the permanent under-secretary minuted that if the services of 'really able and competent men' were to be acquired, they must be offered 'reasonable remuneration'.[96]

Crowe had other proposals to make with regard to the arrangements of the documents. He had long favoured encouraging research on the Bismarckian era, and still thought it desirable to start any historical survey of prewar diplomacy in 1884 'when Bismarck plunged into the colonial and persistently anti-British policy'. The Boer War also constituted for him an important link in the chain of events which led to the crisis of 1914. 'It was largely the danger then appearing of a possible Franco-German-Russian coalition against Great Britain which', in his estimation, 'made the British government seek an accommodation with France which would eliminate all immediate causes of conflict between us and that country and would then leave France without any temptation to show hostility to us in case we were seriously threatened by Germany.' Nevertheless, Crowe conceded, 'especially if considerations of expense [were] strongly urged', that it would be judicious to follow Headlam-Morley's suggestion to begin the series in 1904, leaving the previous twenty years to be handled subsequently.[97]

With these matters still unsettled, MacDonald consulted his friend, G.P. Gooch. The latter's contributions to *The Cambridge History* had, despite Headlam-Morley's initial misgivings, been favourably received in the Foreign Office. MacDonald approached Gooch not, however, with a view to offering him the post of editor, but to seek his advice on the worthiness of Mowat and Basil Kingsley Martin, both of whose names had been put forward by Gaselee in connection with the project.[98] Gooch's response was not encouraging. He was sceptical about the suitability of both individuals for such editorial work, and in his opinion there 'were better men such as Temperley or Webster, if they were available'.[99] The latter might indeed have been an ideal choice. But shortly after MacDonald made his enquiry of Gooch, Webster fired a journalistic salvo at the Labour ship of state. In an article entitled 'The Labour government and secret diplomacy', which appeared in *The Nation and the Athenaeum* of 21 June, Webster expressed his surprise that the Labour government had done so little to substitute 'open' for 'secret' diplomacy. He then urged the government both to accept his ideas for making the Foreign Office records more available to the public, and to proceed quickly with the publication of the British documents relating to the origins of the war. The government, he suggested, might show its good faith by appointing a distinguished historian, who had 'no official position, such as Dr. Gooch or Mr. Temperley, to share the responsibility' for such a project with Headlam-Morley.[100]

The article provoked a strong reaction in the Foreign Office, not because of the advice which it contained, but because Webster was publicly kicking at a door which it was assumed he knew to be already open. Gaselee took 'great exception' to Webster's conduct, and Crowe backed a suggestion that he should have withdrawn from him 'any special facilities' that he might enjoy at the Office for his researches.[101] The irony was that Webster, who must surely have been one of the first people to associate the names of both Gooch and Temperley with the publication of the British documents, appears by his criticism of the Foreign Office to have virtually debarred himself from any part in the exercise. When at the end of July 1924, Gaselee complained of the slow progress in appointing an editor, Crowe minuted tersely: 'I hope we shall be spared Mr. Webster. He is a terror.'[102]

Webster's article led to further questions in the Commons concerning the prewar Foreign Office records. This time parliament was informed that the Foreign Office had under consideration 'a substantial advance' in the date up to which its archives would be open. The date which MacDonald's officials had in mind was the end of 1878.[103] The Foreign Office had, however, as in 1918–19, to overcome the reluctance of other ministries to open up their archives. The Treasury refused altogether to accept any further extension of the open period; the War Office wished its records always to be closed for at least fifty years and would not budge beyond 1874; and the Colonial Office required both that the self-governing dominions be consulted and that the files relating to Gibraltar and the Falkland Islands remain closed.[104] These were conditions which the Foreign Office was prepared to accept, and after all the dominion governments had assented it was settled in December 1924 that the Office would proceed with its plan.[105] While discussions were continuing on this matter, MacDonald on 11 August wrote to Gooch, whom he had originally assumed would not want to take on the job, to invite him to edit the British documents. Gooch, after rejecting MacDonald's notion of an historical narrative with documents, accepted the offer, and, on his advice, Temperley was invited in September to share the work.[106] But the Foreign Office still had to reckon with the equivocation of the Treasury, which displayed its customary reluctance to fund such a project. Nothing was settled by mid-October 1924, and with a general election pending Gaselee suspected that the Treasury was deliberately delaying matters 'on the chance of there being a change of government and so a chance of defeating the scheme'.[107] Indeed, not until 27 October, two days before the defeat of MacDonald's government at the polls, did the Treasury give its sanction.[108]

The formation of a Conservative government and the appointment of Austen Chamberlain as foreign secretary did not lead to the abandonment of the planned publication. Nevertheless, the historical fraternity had doubts about the government's intentions, and in November the whole subject of the documents was taken up in the correspondence columns of *The Times*. Already on 24 October there had appeared in the newspaper an account, extracted from the recently published memoirs of Admiral Tirpitz, of an interview between Lord (then Sir Charles) Hardinge and the German emperor at Cronberg in August 1908.[109] Hardinge had wanted to correct what he felt to be a misleading report, and with the Foreign Office's permission, he published in *The Times* of 10 November his own record of the interview.[110] This and *The Times* leader on the issues raised, prompted Sidney Lee to write to the newspaper to point out that German accounts of what had happened at Cronberg had long been circulating on the continent and in America and that it might already be too late to 'correct' them. 'The authentic, if incomplete, evidence which Germany is freely placing at the disposal of historical study must', Lee argued, 'inevitably ... tend to give the German interpretation of prewar events historical authority all the world over.' The same point was made by R.W. Seton-Watson in *The Times* of 15 November. He was 'convinced', he added, that the 'present official attitude [was] merely one of traditional departmental caution'.[111]

The latter charge, albeit an old one, was not wholly fair. The Foreign Office had in many respects been far more open in its attitude towards historians than other government departments. And, as Crowe explained in a minute of 19 November, he had for years been pressing on successive foreign secretaries a far less modest system of publication than that which had been agreed upon. It was other government departments and the principle of interdepartmental unity which had impeded the granting of more generous access to the archives, and it was the political heads of department who had been slow to respond to the arguments of their officials. Even MacDonald had, after endorsing the principle of publication, left the matter in abeyance, and Treasury quibbling delayed any formal announcement of the employment of Gooch and Temperley. In November the Treasury was still discussing the details of Temperley's employment, and had it not been for a threat from *The Times* that it would soon take up the whole issue of publication, it is doubtful if Chamberlain would have shown the urgency that he did in deciding to confirm the department's intention to proceed with the British documents.[112] He did so in an open letter to Seton-Watson of 28 November.

Chamberlain's letter, which appeared in *The Times* on 3 December 1924,[113] was nevertheless insufficient to satisfy those historians who continued to clamour for the adoption of a system whereby his department's post-1878 records would be automatically opened for additional years. Temperley, who supported this proposal, also reminded the Foreign Office of the danger in permitting historians 'to form their judgment during the next two years purely on German or Bolshevik versions of certain incidents or conversations'. In truth, however, there was little that the Foreign

Office could do at this stage to counter the influence that the publication of the German documents was having upon the writing of recent history. Favourable consideration could, as Temperley suggested, be given to the requests of historians to see post-1878 documents. But even if Gooch and Temperley were to work at the rapid pace that they had optimistically predicted, it would be another three years before the published British documents reached 1914.[114]

It was this prospect that led the editors to propose in February 1925 that the collection of documents which Headlam-Morley had already compiled on the war crisis of 1914 should be published, both as part of the series, and in advance of the other volumes. This, Headlam-Morley hoped, would counteract the claims of hostile critics with regard to the White Paper of August 1914, and show 'how little there was to produce'. There was also, however, the possibility that if the published documents of this critical period were assembled by a member of the Foreign Office, the department would again be accused of garbling, or suppressing, essential documents. After all, Chamberlain had made the point in his letter to Seton-Watson that the reputations of the editors, both of whose politics were to the left of centre, offered 'the best guarantee of the historical accuracy and impartiality of their work'. It was a difficulty that was finally overcome by Gooch and Temperley checking the genuineness of the volume and giving it their imprimatur.[115]

The editing of the *British Documents* was to give rise to numerous problems before the work was completed in 1938. Decisions had to be taken with regard to the publication of departmental minutes, the inclusion of papers originating in other ministries and offices, and the consultation of foreign governments on documents recording communications from them. The latter issue was particularly troublesome since it affected Britain's relations with its former allies, and the endeavours of Chamberlain and his successors to reconcile current policy interests with the principle of editorial freedom provoked Gooch and Temperley to make threats of resignation.[116] French objections and Yugoslav procrastination also delayed the publication of the first of the volumes (volume xi of the series) until December 1926.[117] Its appearance was for Headlam-Morley the culmination of the best part of eight years' work. Ever since the establishment of the PID he had been campaigning for the Foreign Office to take the public more into its confidence. He shared Webster's belief that the democratic control of foreign policy required an educated electorate. Moreover, he was, like his colleagues in the department, genuinely alarmed by the impact on opinion at home and abroad of diplomatic histories based mainly upon available Austrian, German and Russian sources. As Hubert Montgomery, the chief clerk of the Foreign Office, explained in December 1925, 'the primary object of the present publication was to clear the Foreign Office of the totally unfounded charge that they had engineered the War'.[118]

The department's concern with more open government had, however, predated the outbreak of the war. Crowe had argued in 1908 that the Foreign Office had 'nothing to lose' in admitting scholars to archives of a recent date.[119] And after the war he continued to believe that a 'country like England ought to show some largeness of spirit in dealing liberally in regard to national historical work'.[120] Tyrrell, Crowe's successor as permanent under-secretary, was also convinced that the Office had 'nothing to conceal or be ashamed of'. [121] They and their associates were confident, perhaps overconfident, that once the truth was known neither Grey nor his officials could be held responsible for a war whose origins they assumed to be essentially European. The public reception of volume xi may well have confirmed them in their views. Chamberlain was so fascinated by its contents that he sat up until 2 A.M. in order to finish reading it, and all the leading newspapers reviewed the work. But no attempt was made to revive old controversies, and there was almost complete lack of correspondence in the press upon the subject of the documents. Headlam-Morley was thus to conclude that the public knew that things were all right, 'that Sir Edward Grey and the Foreign Office each did their best in their own way, and that they told the country the truth in 1914'.[122]

Headlam-Morley was equally certain that the British publication would not alter opinion in Germany. The 'general German attitude' would, he predicted in January 1927, 'remain … that the real cause of the war was the Russian mobilisation which was unnecessary, and that the British government knew of this but did nothing to prevent it'.[123] During the previous eight years the German public had, after all, had ample time in which to digest the Wilhelmstrasse's version of events. Webster too had learned from the recent past and had decided that 'enlightened patriotism' was not enough. In the inaugural lecture which he delivered at Aberystwyth on 23 February 1923, he condemned the writing of history for the 'glorification of national prejudices', and extolled the virtues of training men and women 'to be members of the community of nations'. It was, he maintained, the 'function of knowledge or reason to dig as it were a channel for the immense and potent forces that lie within humanity', and he warned his audience that unless an outlet were found for the 'new and formidable masses of energy' liberated by the war, they would 'overwhelm the world'.[124] German historians had, however, already taken up Webster's earlier prescription with a vengeance, and faith in their defence of the fatherland remained unshaken by the appearance of the *British Documents*. It was Germany's misfortune that their pursuit of 'enlightened patriotism' encouraged, and ultimately served, the purposes of blind nationalism.

Notes

1. C.K. Webster, *The Study of 19th-Century Diplomacy* (1915), pp. 9–12.
2. D.A. Reeder, ed., *Educating our Masters* (Leicester, 1980), pp. 1–33.
3. Webster, *19th-Century Diplomacy*, pp. 13–16, 29; *Royal Commission on Public Records* [Cd. 6396], 'Minutes of Evidence', pp. 78–79, H.C. (1912–13), xliv. 228–9.
4. 'Minutes of Evidence', pp. 78–9; review by J.W. Headlam of Alfred Stern's *Geschichte Europas seit den Verträgen von 1815 bis zum Frankfurter Frieden von 1871*, i (Berlin, 1894), in *Eng. Hist. Rev.* x (1895), 593–6. Prior to 1909 the Foreign Office correspondence had been open to the general public up until the end of 1780, and scholars with permits had restricted access up to the end of 1850.
5. *Royal Commission on Public Records* [Cd. 6395], 'Appendices on the 1st Report', pp. 62–64, H.C. (1912–13), xliv. 140–2.
6. See for example: P. Taylor, 'Publicity and Diplomacy: The Impact of the First World War upon Foreign Office Attitudes Towards the Press', in D. Dilks, ed., *Retreat from Power: Studies in Britain's Foreign Policy of the 20th Century* (London, 1981), i. 42–63.
7. Public Record Office, FO 370/81, L50296/50296B, minute by Crowe, 23 March 1918.
8. FO 370/16, L40126/16761/B, memo. by Crowe, 17 Nov. 1908.
9. G.P. Gooch and H.W.V. Temperley, eds., *British Documents on the Origins of the War, 1898–1914* (hereafter cited as *B.D.*) (11 vols. in 13, 1926–38), iii. 397–420.
10. Under pressure from Sir E. Davidson, the department's chief legal adviser, Grey insisted on the removal from those Foreign Office files that were to be opened to the public and scholars of all the law officers' reports. Papers relating to the Newfoundland fisheries were also withheld from inspection in 1909. (FO 370/16, L4012/16761/B, minutes by Crowe, Brant, Davidson, Langley, Hardinge and Grey; FO 370/23, L21311/7526/B, Campbell to P.R.O., 11 June 1909; L45765/7526/B, Campbell to P.R.O., 24 Dec. 1909).

11. J.W. Headlam, *The History of Twelve Days, July 24th to August 4th, 1914: Being an Account of the Negotiations Preceding the Outbreak of the War, Based on the Official Publications* (1915), pp. vii-xi.
12. Taylor, 'Publicity and Diplomacy', pp. 48–52.
13. One of the most notorious of these errors, which began with the misattribution of an enclosure and ended with the deliberate falsification of the French Yellow Book, is described in *B.D.*, xi. no. 319. For further details see FO 370/202, L3624/792/402, undated memo. by Headlam-Morley; FO 370/209, L6230/152/402, minute by Lampson, 17 Nov. 1925.
14. C.A. Cline, E.D. *Morel, 1873–1924: The Strategies of Protest* (Belfast, 1980); M. Swartz, *The Union of Democratic Control in British Politics During the First World War* (Oxford, 1971); K. Robbins, *The Abolition of War: The 'Peace Movement' in Britain, 1914–19* (Cardiff, 1976), pp. 27–47.
15. FO 370/67, L82607/82607/B, Holland Rose to F.O., 13 Dec. 1914, and minutes by Parker, Blech, Langley, and Nicolson; Parker to Holland Rose, 18 Dec. 1914.
16. FO 370/73, L38322/38322/B, Holland Rose to Balfour, 3 Feb. 1915; Balfour to Nicolson, 20 March 1915; Nicolson to Balfour, 1 Apr. 1915.
17. J.A.R. Marriott, 'Modern Diplomacy', in *Quarterly Rev.* ccxxix (1918), 222–38.
18. FO 370/81, L50296/50296/B, memo. by Sanderson, 18 March 1918, and minute by Parker, 23 March 1918; L58040/50296/B, Sanderson to Parker, 30 March 1918.
19. FO 370/81, L50296/B, minutes by Crowe and Hardinge, 23 March 1918.
20. Ibid., memo. by Sanderson, 18 March 1918; L58040/50296/B, Sanderson to Parker, 30 March 1918; minute by Crowe, 1 Apr. 1918.
21. FO 370/81, L50296/50296/B, Langley to Maxwell Lyte, 4 Apr. 1918.
22. Ibid., L66263/50296/B, Maxwell Lyte to Langley, 12 Apr. 1918.
23. The Colonial Office had been consistently more cautious than the Foreign Office in admitting students to its records. Before 1919 only in exceptional cases was access permitted to post-1837 documents (FO 370/41, L39928/34954?B, Colonial Office to F.O., to Oct. 1911; minute by Brant, 12 Oct. 1911; FO 370/57, L3166/3166/B, Colonial Office to F.O., 20 Jan. 1913; FO 370/81, L70398/50296/B, Colonial Office to F.O., 20 Apr. 1918; L9377/50296/B, Colonial Office to F.O., 25 May 1918).
24. FO 370/81, L66263/50296/B, undated minute by Hardinge; Parker to P.R.O., 18 Apr. 1918.
25. FO 370/84, L30550/30550/E, Hardinge to Prothero, 14 Feb. 1918; L50425/30550/E; G.W. Prothero, 'Instruction to Historical Writers', in S. Gaselee, ed., *A Select Analytical List of Books Concerning the Great War* (1923), pp. ii-iv.
26. FO 371/4363, PID 74/74, circular from Hardinge, 5 May 1918; M.L. Dockrill and Z. Steiner, 'The Foreign Office at the Paris Peace Conference in 1919', in *International Hist. Rev.* ii (1980), 55–86.
27. Headlam-Morley had had access to confidential Foreign Office correspondence when he was preparing his *Twelve Days* but he was not permitted to cite or quote from it: FO 370/179, L1149/20/45, memo. by Headlam-Morley, 11 Feb. 1922; J.W. Headlam-Morley, *A Memoir of the Paris Peace Conference, 1919*, ed. A. Headlam-Morley and others (1972), pp. ix-xlii.
28. FO 371/4366, PID 263/263, memo. by Headlam-Morley, 26 July 1918.
29. R.M. Warman, 'The Erosion of Foreign Office Influence in the Making of Foreign Policy, 1916–18', in *Historical Journal* xv (1972), 133–59.
30. FO 371/14366, PID 263/263, minutes by Tyrrell and Hardinge.

31. Ibid., memo. by Headlam-Morley, 26 July 1918; FO 370/84, L82065/82065/E, Headlam-Morley to Parker, 4 May 1918.
32. Headlam-Morley, *A Memoir*, pp. 132–3; M.L. Dockrill, 'The Foreign Office and the proposed Institute of International Affairs, 1919', in *International Affairs* lvi (1980), 665–72; FO 371/4383, PID 806/618, minute by Headlam-Morley, 31 Dec. 1919.
33. FO 371/4383, PID 806/618, minutes by Tilley, Hardinge, and Curzon, 17 and 18 Dec. 1919.
34. Ibid., PID 618/618, R.A. Leeper to Headlam-Morley, 27 Oct. 1919, and minutes by Headlam-Morley, Tilley and Hardinge. Objections were, however, raised against the proposal made by Headlam-Morley in June 1924 that Toynbee, who was to edit the Institute's *Survey of International Affairs* should be provided with the 'historical resumés', which were made from time to time in the Office, and the 'annual reports' of British missions abroad. 'I am', noted Gaselee, 'a little alarmed by the prospect of a series of annual volumes now beginning. Are the Institute to have a lien on us forever?' (FO 370/203, L2421/2421/402, Headlam-Morley to Tyrrell, 11 June 1924, and minutes by Gaselee, Tyrrell, and Crowe).
35. FO 371/4382, PID 619/587, memo. by Headlam-Morley, 28 Oct. 1919.
36. Temperley to Headlam-Morley, 28 Oct. 1919, University of Ulster at Coleraine, Headlam-Morley MSS.
37. Ibid., Headlam-Morley to Temperley, 18 Nov. 1919.
38. P.M. Taylor, *The Projection of Britain: British Overseas Publicity and Propaganda, 1919–39* (Cambridge, 1981), pp. 13–15; FO 370/101, PID 811/811, Treasury to F.O., 19 Feb. 1920, and minute by Headlam-Morley.
39. FO 370/125, PID 889/889, Director of Military Intelligence to F.O., 27 Apr. 1920 and minute by Headlam-Morley, 1 May 1920.
40. FO 370/129, L1010/1010/406, Gaselee to Hardinge, 15 Sept. 1920, and minute by Hardinge; L1534/1010/406, Lee to Gaselee, 11 Dec. 1920; Gaselee to Lee, 17 Dec. 1920.
41. C. Oman, *The Outbreak of the War of 1914–18* (London, 1919). There appears, however, to be no record in the Foreign Office library files of permission having been granted to Oman to quote from confidential correspondence. Headlam-Morley wrote in 1922 that he did not know 'how it came about that in this case an exception was made to the general rule' (FO 370/179, L1149/20/405, memo. by Headlam-Morley, 11 Feb. 1922).
42. FO 370/103, L51511/51511/19, Malcolm to Drummond, 26 Feb. 1919; F.O. to Arthur, 10 Apr. 1919.
43. FO 370/116, L678/678/34, editors of *Cambridge History* to Balfour, 1 Aug. 1919; Tilley to editors, 1 Oct. 1919.
44. F. Eyck, *G.P. Gooch: A Study in History and Politics* (London, 1982), pp. 135–293.
45. FO 370/116, L678/34, Ward to Gaselee, 7 Apr. 1920, and minutes by Headlam-Morley and Crowe; Gaselee to Ward, 5 May 1920.
46. Ibid., minute by Headlam-Morley, 21 July 1920.
47. Ibid.
48. Gooch was in the end responsible for writing chapters v, vi and vii of volume iii, covering the period 1902–19 (*The Cambridge History of British Foreign Policy, 1783–1919*), ed. A.E. Ward and G.P. Gooch [3 vols., Cambridge, 1922–23], iii. 294–509. The editors received assistance from both Crowe and Sanderson. This included the drafting by Sanderson of a memorandum on the origins of

the Anglo-French entente of 1904 (FO 370/149, L399/399/406, Gaselee to Ward, 8 March 1921). Algernon Cecil, who wrote a chapter on the nineteenth-century Foreign Office, was aided by Sanderson, Crowe, and Gaselee (FO 375/135, L1054/1054/402, minute by Gaselee, 9 June 1921; L1427/1427/402, minutes by Headlam-Morley, 19 July 1921, and Crowe, 21 July 1921).

49. FO 370/84, L192644/30550/E, memo, by Prothero, 20 Nov. 1918, and minute by Hardinge.

50. Gaselee noted that it had been 'considered desirable to let sleeping dogs lie very quiet in the matter of the Argentine claims to the Islands' (FO370/122, L6836/6/405, Prothero to Gaselee, 22 July 1920, and minutes by Gaselee and Sperling; Gaselee to Prothero, 26 July 1920).

51. Ibid., L922/6/405, minute by Oliphant, 13 Sept. 1920; Gaselee to Prothero, 15 Sept. 1920.

52. Headlam-Morley had, however, no objection to Webster publishing his observations elsewhere, and although they were omitted from the H.M.S.O. publication of 1920, they were included in the 1934 edition of the book: FO 370/ 121, L174/6/405, Prothero to Gaselee, 29 and 30 Apr. 1920, and minutes by Headlam-Morley, Gaselee and Crowe; Gaselee to Prothero, 13 May 1920; C.K. Webster, *The Congress of Vienna, 1814–15* (1934, repr. 1963), pp. 15, 198–209.

53. FO 370/121, L174/6/405, minutes by Headlam-Morley, 6 May 1920, Crowe, 12 May 1920, and Gaselee, 13 May 1920; E.L. Woodward, *The Congress of Berlin, 1878* (Historical Section Handbook no. 154, 1920).

54. FO 370/135, L316/316/402, minutes by Gaselee, 19 Feb. 1921, and Crowe, 25 Feb. 1921.

55. FO 370/203, L2308, 'Foreign Office Confidential Papers and Information: Control over Unauthorised Publications', memo by R.C. Dickie, 2 March 1923, and annexes.

56. FO 370/116, L758/758/402, Curtis to Sperling, 3 Aug. 1920, and minutes by Headlam-Morley and Crowe.

57. Ibid., Gaselee to Williams, 9 Aug. 1920; L1144/758/402, minute by Parker, 13 Oct. 1920.

58. L.D. Steefel, *The Schleswig-Holstein Question* (Cambridge, Mass., 1932).

59. FO 371/4382, PID 588/588, memo. by Randall, 15 Oct. 1919.

60. On the origins of Kautsky's collection, see J. Droz, *Les causes de la Première Guerre mondiale: Essai d'historiographie* (Paris, 1973), pp. 12–15. The Foreign Office was aware that Kautsky might be compelled to omit certain documents that he wished to publish and contact was made with him through the British military mission at Berlin with a view to preventing this (FO 371/4384, PID 670/670, Grande to Russell, 3 Nov. 1919; Malcolm to Hardinge, 22 Nov. 1919)

61. FO 371/4359, PID 53/53, Weekly Secret Cable to Dominion Govts., 28 Dec. 1918.

62. H. von Eckhardstein, *Lebenserinnerungen und politische Denkwürdigkeiten* (3 vols., Leipzig, 1919–21).

63. FO 370/119, L594/403. Prothero to Gaselee, 7 June 1920, and enclosures.

64. *The Times*, 11 and 13 Sept. 1920.

65. FO 370/128, L982/982/20, minutes by Gaselee, 28 Sept. 1920, and Headlam-Morley, 30 Sept. 1920; notes by Sanderson, 15 and 16 Sept. 1920; Sanderson to Hardinge, 9 and 13 Oct. 1920.

66. FO 370/119, L921/921/403, minutes by Headlam-Morley, 14 July 1920, Crowe, 27 July 1920, and Gaselee, 28 July 1920; Curzon to Gwendolen Cecil, 20 Aug. 1920; Curzon to Crowe, 14 Oct. 1920, and enclosures; minute by

Headlam-Morley, 16 Oct. 1924, FO 370/122, L656/6/405, Gaselee to Prothero, 12 and 17 Aug. 1920; Prothero to Gaselee, 15 Aug. 1920.

67. FO 370/173, L2556/673/407, Gaselee to Stamfordham, 9 Aug.1922.

68. FO 370/144, L210/210/405, minutes by Headlam-Morley, 2 Feb. 1921, Gaselee, 4 and 18 Feb. 1921, and Lampson, 15 Feb. 1921.

69. C.G.W. Romberg, ed., *Die Fälschungen des russischen Orangebuches: Der wahre Telegramwechsel Paris-Petersburg bei Kriegsausbruch* (Berlin, 1922).

70. For Headlam-Morley's explanation of the handling of this communication see *B.D.*, xi, no. 206.

71. FO 370/171, L3627/3627/405, extract from the *Daily Herald* and minutes by Headlam-Morley, 24 and 31 Oct. 1922, Crowe, 31 Oct. 1922, and Gaselee, 4 Dec. 1922.

72. FO 370/194, L3894/3894/405, memo. by Headlam-Morley, 6 Dec. 1922.

73. J.F. Naylor, *A Man and an Institution: Sir Maurice Hankey, the Cabinet Secretariat and the Custody of Cabinet Secrecy* (Cambridge, 1984), pp. 117–23.

74. FO 370/179, L20/30/405, Churchill to Headlam-Morley, 26 Dec. 1922.

75. Ibid., minutes by Headlam-Morley, 30 Dec. 1922, and 3, 8 and 11 Jan. 1923; notes by Headlam-Morley on draft chapters of *The World Crisis*; minute by Gaselee, 2 Jan. 1923.

76. Ibid., L20/20/405, Crowe to Bonar Law, 10 Jan. 1923.

77. Ibid.

78. Ibid., minute by Crowe, 10 Jan. 1923; Headlam-Morley to Churchill, 12 Jan. 1923.

79. CAB 27/217, Committee on the Use of Official Material in Publications; Churchill to Bonar Law, 3 March 1923. Although Maurice Hankey, the cabinet secretary, sought the opinions of government departments on this question, the committee never in fact met.

80. Curzon's remark was occasioned by the publication, without prior permission, of the recollections of Captain Peter Wright, a secretary and interpreter of the Supreme War Council, and subsequent discussions on whether or not to prosecute Wright for breaching the Official Secrets Act (P.E. Wright, *At the Supreme War Council (1921)*; FO 370/149, L668/668/406, minutes by Crowe and Curzon, 12 Apr. 1921.

81. FO 370/187, L883/883/405, minutes by Parker, 2 March 1923, and Crowe, 15 March 1923; Curzon to Buchanan, 15 March 1923; *The Times*, 15, 16, 17 and 19 March 1923. The articles were based on extracts from G. Buchanan, *My Mission to Russia and Other Diplomatic Memories* (2 vols. London, 1923).

82. FO 370/190, L2350/2303/405, minute by Crowe, 5 June 1923; Rodd to Curzon, 8 June 1923.

83. FO 370/187, L930/930/405, G. Davies to T. Davies, 25 Feb. 1923; Vansittart to T. Davies, 8 March 1923. At the time of Davies's application the archives of the Quai d'Orsay were open to the end of 1852.

84. Ibid., L1494/930/405, enclosure in T. Davies to Crowe, 13 Apr. 1923; minute by Gaselee, 2 May 1923.

85. The principal objection of the Home Office to the opening of departmental archives to a later date was the possibility of the names of 'agents and informers' who might still be alive thereby becoming known to the public (ibid., L930/930/405, minutes by Gaselee, 12 and 15 March 1923; minutes by Curzon, 5, 13 and 15 March 1923; minute by Crowe, 15 March 1923).

86. *The Nation and the Athenaeum*, 24 Nov. 1923; F.O. 370/187, L4779/1178/405, minutes by Gaselee and Headlam-Morley, 30 Dec. 1923.

87. FO 370/197, L5021/5021/405, minute by Gaselee, 14 Dec. 1923.
88. FO 370/202, L792/792/402, notice of parliamentary question, 14 Feb. 1924; minutes by Gaselee and Headlam-Morley, 15 Feb. 1924, and MacDonald, 16 Feb. 1924. The answer was given by Arthur Ponsonby, MacDonald's parliamentary under-secretary (Hansard, *Parliamentary Debates*, 5th ser., clxix, xol. 1715, 20 Feb. 1924).
89. Morison's request was turned down on the ground that it would be a 'serious departure' from Foreign Office practice (FO 370/203, L1399/1399/402, Morison to MacDonald, 1 Apr. 1924, Montgomery to Morison, 14 Apr. 1924).
90. Ibid., L1484/1399/402, Laski to MacDonald, 4 Apr. 1924.
91. Webster also argued that telegraphic intercepts, law officers' reports and departmental minutes should be available for use by historians (ibid., 'Notes on Public Access to the Foreign Office Records', by Webster).
92. Ibid., minutes by Gaselee, 19 Apr. 1924, and Crowe, 28 Apr. 1924; Gaselee to Laski, 6 May 1924.
93. FO 370/202, L792/792/402, Gaselee to Headlam-Morley, 26 Feb. 1924; memo. by Headlam-Morley, 29 Apr. 1924.
94. Ibid., minutes by Gaselee and Crowe, 30 Apr. 1924, and MacDonald, 1 May 1924.
95. Ibid., L2157/792/402, memo. by Headlam-Morley, 24 May 1924.
96. Ibid., minutes by Gaselee, 28 May and 4 June 1924, and by Crowe, 4 June 1924.
97. Ibid., minute by Crowe, 29 May 1924.
98. Ibid., MacDonald to Gooch, 5 June 1924.
99. Ibid., L2766/792/402, Gooch to MacDonald, 9 June 1924.
100. FO 370/203, L2571/1399/402, extract from *The Nation and the Athenaeum*, 21 June 1924.
101. Ibid., minutes by Gaselee, 25 June 1924, Bland, 27 June 1924 and Crowe, 4 July 1924.
102. FO 370/202, L3140/792/402, minutes by Gaselee and Crowe, 29 July 1924.
103. FO 370/203, L2660/1399/402, notice of parliamentary question and minute by Gaselee, 30 June 1924; *Hansard*, 5, clxxv, cols. 614, 1298, 26 June 1924 and 2 July 1924.
104. FO 370/203/L2947/1399/402, Colonial Office to F.O., 17 July 1924; minute by Gaselee, 20 July 1924; Gaselee to Colonial Office, 23 July 1924; L2745/1399/402, Parkinson to Gaselee, 2 July 1924; L4505/1399/402, minute by Gaselee, 1 Dec. 1924.
105. Ibid., minute by Gaselee on Jellicoe to J.A. Thomas, 30 Oct. 1924; Gaselee to Stamp, 2 Dec. 1924.
106. FO 370/202, L2157/792/402, MacDonald to Gooch, 5 June 1924; L3330/792/402, MacDonald to Gooch, 11 and 15 Aug. 1924; Gooch to MacDonald, 13 Aug. 1924; minutes by Gaselee, 18 and 20 Aug. 1924, and Crowe, 22 Aug. 1924; L3617/792/402, minute by Gaselee, 9 Sept. 1924.
107. The Treasury's attitude was all the more resented in the Foreign Office because Gooch had offered to work without remuneration (FO 370/202, L3617/792/402, Gaselee to Treasury, 15 Sept. 1024; Gaselee to Stationery Office, 29 Sept. 1924; minute by Gaselee, 16 Oct. 1924).
108. Even then the Treasury still objected to paying Temperley a salary of £750 p.a., which Gaselee had thought appropriate: FO 370/202, L4200/792/402, Treasury to F.O., 27 Oct. 1924).
109. *The Times*, 24 Oct. 1924.

110. Ibid., 10 Nov. 1924.
111. Ibid., 12 and 15 Nov. 1924.
112. FO 370/202, L3140/792/402, minutes by Gaselee, 29 July 1924, Selby, 7 Aug. 1924, and MacDonald, 8 Aug. 1924; L4376/792/402, Temperley to Gaselee, 8 Nov. 1924, and minute by Gaselee; L4411/792/402, minutes by Headlam-Morley, 17 and 19 Nov. 1924, Crowe, 19 Nov. 1924, and Chamberlain, 21 Nov. 1924.
113. *The Times*, 3 Dec. 1924.
114. Temperley, who had recently attended the Anglo-American Conference of Professors of History at Richmond, Virginia, advocated a system whereby 'carefully selected' British and American historians would be permitted to use the Foreign Office records in the period 1878–1903, and to see, though not necessarily use, those of the years 1903–14 (FO 370/209, L342/152/402, memo. by Temperley enclosed in Howard to Crowe, 5 Jan. 1925).
115. Ibid., L820/152/402, minutes by Gaselee, 19 Feb. 1925, Headlam-Morley, 23 and 24 Feb. 1925, and Crowe, 24 Feb. 1925.
116. Eyck, pp. 329–405.
117. Headlam-Morley was by March 1926 thoroughly exasperated by French objections to his volume, which in their eyes 'passât sous silence quelques uns des faits les plus notoires qui établisent la responsabilité de l'Allemagne et ses alliés dans la guerre mondiale' (FO 370/239, L1483/24/402, note from the French embassy, 23 Feb. 1926, and minute by Headlam-Morley).
118. FO 370/309, L6205/152/402, minute by Montgomery, 10 Dec. 1925.
119. Five years after the war Crowe was still insisting that it was 'important to demonstrate that we have nothing to hide' (FO 370/203, L1478/1478/402, minute by Crowe, 8 Apr. 1924).
120. FO 370/202, L792/792/402, minute by Crowe, 30 April 1924.
121. FO 370/202, L3617/792/402, Tyrrell to Stamfordham, 15 Sept. 1924.
122. FO 370/241, L80215/24/402, minutes by Headlam-Morley, 6 Jan. 1927, Tyrrell, 10 Jan. 1927, and Chamberlain, 10 Jan. 1927.
123. Ibid.
124. C.K. Webster, *The Study of International Politics* (1923), pp. 23–24, 29.

 Chapter 8

THE IMBALANCE IN *BRITISH DOCUMENTS ON THE ORIGINS OF THE WAR, 1898–1914*
Gooch, Temperley, and the India Office

Keith Wilson

G.P. Gooch and H.W.V. Temperley selected for publication, and were allowed to publish (as an appendix in volume iii of *British Documents*) not only E.A. Crowe's Memorandum on the Present State of British Relations with France and Germany of 1 January 1907, but also the minute on it in which the foreign secretary stated that 'the part of our foreign policy with which it is concerned involves the greatest issues, and requires constant attention'. They did not select for publication in any later volume Sir G.R. Clerk's Memorandum on Anglo-Russian Relations in Persia of 21 July 1914, which the same foreign secretary had commissioned, of which he said that it 'very ably dealt' with the issue, and which was not far short in length of the memorandum by Crowe. The omission of the Clerk memorandum, which certainly dealt with a 'part of our foreign policy', is all the more difficult to understand as the commissioning of it is mentioned in minutes that were published in volume x(ii).[1]

In their foreword to volume iv, Gooch and Temperley stated:

> The chapter on Persia contains two important papers, the 'Curzon despatch' from India of September 21, 1899, previously printed only in part, and of which the most important passage is now given in full (pp. 356–63), and a despatch from Lord George Hamilton of

July 6, 1900, stating the policy of the Home Government (pp. 363–5). There is also a valuable Foreign Office Memorandum on Persia of October 31, 1905 (pp. 365–74). Another of October 14, 1903 (Chapter xxvii pp. 512–22) deals with Afghanistan.

The whole diplomatic transactions are therefore related in considerable detail, and evidence is supplied from the British representatives at St. Petersburg and Tehran, and in India, as well as from the Foreign Office direct.

The first paragraph of the above, supplemented as it was by the later remarks, 'The India Office and Government of India have given consent to the publication of certain parts of the Curzon despatch of September 21, 1899 (pp. 356–63) which the Editors considered vital to their purpose' and '(the Editors) wish also to thank Sir Robert Holland and others at the India Office for their assistance ...', created, and was designed to create, a most misleading impression. The impression given was that, with the consent and help of the India Office and Government of India, the Curzon despatch, previously printed without its most important passage, was now made available in full. In fact, as has been noticed,[2] paragraphs 28 to 39 inclusive of the original Curzon despatch, omitted by whoever edited it from Command Paper 3882 (Persia no. 1, 1908), remained absent from Gooch and Temperley's version. As for the idea promoted by the second paragraph, that with the printing of four documents, only one of which (and actually only part of it) emanated from the Indian authorities, 'the whole diplomatic transactions' were 'therefore related', this was tendentious and mischievous in the extreme. Of another paragraph left out of another memorandum printed in *British Documents* volume iv, Professor Ian Nish wrote simply: 'This paragraph is unfortunately omitted from the text as printed in B.D.iv no.127.'[3] He was being decidedly kind. It was indeed unfortunate for the historian without access to the archives. Luck, however, had nothing to do with it.

There is a lack of balance in *British Documents*, and the picture of British 'foreign' policy which rests upon *British Documents* is also unbalanced. Historians of British 'foreign' policy have only recently, as a result of fuller access to the archives, begun to redress the balance. Whether it will ever be fully redressed is moot, for, as what follows will illustrate, views formed in advance of seeing all the relevant documentation do tend to withstand later exposure to new primary material.

For one thing, Gooch and Temperley were only allowed to glimpse a very small proportion of Committee of Imperial Defence (CID) material. What Prime Minister Asquith described as 'the *arcana imperii* ' were not disclosed to Gooch and Temperley, as they were to those present at meetings of the CID. Gooch and Temperley, indeed, were not even allowed to see the minutes of the meeting at which Asquith used this phrase, at which he said, of the secretary of state for India, that he 'is probably more or less directly or indirectly connected with most of our problems', and at which he also said that the 'most solemn obligations of secrecy and of confidence' taken by those present at the deliberations of the CID enabled that body to be, in its discussions, 'perfectly open and frank'.[4] It is, however, the efforts made by Gooch and Temperley to gain access to the records of the India Office, and their failure in this, which best makes the point about the unrepresentative, incomplete, and unbalanced nature of their thirteen-volume work.

<hr>

It was on 7 February 1927 that Headlam-Morley, the director of the Historical Section of the Foreign Office, wrote informally to Sir Arthur Hirtzel, permanent under-secretary of state at the India Office, in connection with the wishes of Gooch and Temperley to include the 'Curzon despatch' of September 1899 in their first volume. Headlam-Morley told Hirtzel that the selection of the documents which the editors published was left to their discretion, subject to the necessity of asking for the assent of foreign governments in the case of confidential documents emanating from them; however, 'It would clearly not be right that the Foreign Office should permit the publication of this document without informing and consulting the Government of India from whom it emanates'.[5] The response of the officials at the India Office was mixed. L.D. Wakely, the secretary of the Political and Secret Department, minuted:

> If open diplomacy is being made the rule in other matters of the same period, I can see no objection from the point of view of India to the publication of this despatch. It is nearly thirty years old. The details of circumstance and personality are quite different, for the most part, from those of today; and the despatch affords no reasonable ground for charges against the policy of the Government of

India or H.M. Govt. of aggressiveness or other nefarious qualities –
unless it be the charge of being unduly suspicious of other peoples'
proceedings, which if the victims can prove so much the better.
Rather contradictorily, however, he went on to remark on 'a rather
extraordinary parallelism' between the general lines of the despatch and the general line 'of the discussions of the present
moment in regard to Russian penetration in Afghanistan and
Central Asia'. From this point of view, he wrote, 'the despatch
might attract considerable attention, and commentators will
draw opposite inferences, necessary to their tastes'. Even so, he
was not convinced that this would do any harm. Sir M. Seton,
deputy under-secretary, was categorical. He strongly deprecated
the publication of the despatch, not only for the reasons given by
Wakely, 'but also because I do not think the public has any claim
to be told about our suspicions in 1899 of the two Powers that
were our Allies in 1914'. Having re-read the despatch 'less hur-
riedly', Wakely came round to Seton's view: he did find that he
would object to the publication of certain passages. He also noted
that a 'comparison of the published and unpublished versions
reveals very fully the machinery of editing and publication, and
shows that it included here and there more or less material alterations of wording, besides mere omissions'. He supposed that this
was common knowledge, and perhaps it was, but only to the man
in the corridors of the India Office.[6]

On 16 March Hirtzel replied to Headlam-Morley in the negative, stating that the document in question was the property of the
secretary of state for India and only came into the possession of
the Foreign Office in the course of interdepartmental correspondence; moreover, 'it is not a diplomatic document in the ordinary
sense of the term. The Government of India has no foreign relations, and a communication from them to the Secretary of State in
Council is merely a communication from one part of the administration to another. For both these reasons the despatch in question
does not appear to Lord Birkenhead to be covered by the authority given by Sir A. Chamberlain; and as he thinks its publication is
undesirable in itself he regrets he is unable to permit it'.[7] Only a
month had passed since Sir H. Montgomery of the Foreign Office,
when dealing with a threat from Gooch and Temperley to resign if
documents were suppressed, or unduly delayed, by some foreign
government, had minuted: 'I think it is time that we made it clear
that foreign governments are not the only black sheep.'[8]

At the Foreign Office Headlam-Morley was disappointed with what he regarded as the India Office's 'peremptory decision', and regretted that Lord Birkenhead's 'definite refusal' left the Foreign Office with no opportunity to present what he considered 'a strong case' for publication. He believed that, had a liaison officer been appointed with the India Office, as had been done with other departments when the project was being set up in 1924 (the oversight, or blind-spot, was that of Gaselee, the Foreign Office librarian[9]) no problem would have arisen. His colleagues disagreed. Montgomery asked for the views of the heads of the Eastern and Northern Departments of the Foreign Office. Speaking for the former, Oliphant wrote: 'As regards Persia, (the views of the political Department) are (1) that the India Office views cannot well be ignored or overridden (2) that politically it would be entirely inappropriate to publish any new material out of Lord Curzon's Despatch to the India Office or to call attention to the subject of Persia even by republishing the 1908 White Paper etc.' For the Northern Department, Palairet wrote: 'I agree with Mr Oliphant entirely. I should deprecate the publication or re-publication just now of anything which is, like Lord Curzon's despatch, likely to lead to controversial discussions in the press about Russia's designs on India and Persia. It will only give the Bolsheviks a fresh text for a sermon against our "imperialism". But the final decision rests of course with the India Office.' Montgomery concluded that the Foreign Office was 'in no way bound to press a party when the undertaking [of Ramsay MacDonald to Gooch and Temperley] cannot be held to bind (in this case the India Office) to agree to the publication of a document to which they on their part take strong objection when we ourselves share their views as to the undesirability of such publication'. The matter was then referred to the foreign secretary, who had no time to form a personal judgement. Chamberlain could say only: 'Speaking generally, I desire the broadest possible publication. If I.O. refuses, I.O. must defend this refusal.' Headlam-Morley interpreted this as a decision that the Foreign Office 'shall not, at any rate at this stage, approach the India Office with a view to getting them to reconsider the decision conveyed in Sir Arthur Hirtzel's letter'.[10]

On 26 March Gaselee informed Gooch and Temperley of the attitude of the India Office. On 8 April Temperley expressed his willingness to defer the matter until Persia became more of a live issue, which it would be in connection with the volume dealing with the 1907 agreement with Russia. Temperley raised a number of awkward questions, and made it clear that he did not acquiesce in the India Office's decision:

> ... question of publicity would arise which we should be unable to avoid, and in which we should apparently have to contrast the India Office disadvantageously not only with the Foreign Office but with foreign Governments. The suggestions of the India Office appear more extraordinary in that they wish to delete references apparently, for instance, to the despatches from Lord Salisbury to Sir Mortimer Durand. One would rather like to know what the whole situation is, what despatches or telegrams the India Office claim and do not claim to be their property. Are the despatches of Lord Salisbury there alluded to, their property, for example? Do they intend to refuse us access to their despatches and telegrams if we ask it? If so, we should have to announce that fact in public at once ...
>
> I should wish, therefore, for it to be understood that we do not at present acquiesce in the decision of the India Office in this matter, and that we should like to know how they propose to proceed in general as regards the future ...[11]

Gaselee, who personally considered 'of doubtful validity' the India Office's claim that despatches from the Government of India to the secretary of state for India were 'a domestic concern' of their own, tried to reassure Temperley that if any 'doubtful cases' occurred they would be taken up personally with Sir A. Hirtzel, who was 'a perfectly reasonable creature'.[12]

Not until October 1927 did Gaselee write to the India Office, asking on Chamberlain's behalf whether the secretary of state for India was prepared to designate an officer with whom Gooch and Temperley could consult personally in the course of the work upon which they were engaged, and pointing out that officers of this kind had been appointed at the Admiralty, the War Office, and the Colonial Office, 'with whom such informal communications have proved most satisfactory'. The India Office ignored the request, which had to be repeated a month later. Only on 29 November was P.J. Patrick, principal of the Political Department at the India Office, assigned to the job. Even then his superior, Wakely, rather ominously stated that 'it will no doubt be necessary for him [Patrick] at times to refer to higher authority for decisions'.[13]

During part of this particular delay Gaselee was occupied with a similar matter which was to parallel the progress of *British Documents*. On the day after he had written to the India Office, the secretary of the Historical Section of the Committee of Imperial Defence, E.Y. Daniel, had sent to him some correspondence generated by General F.J. Moberly's official *History of Operations in Persia, 1914–1919*. In September Sir Denys Bray, the foreign secretary to the Government of India had written a note reacting to what he had already seen of the manuscript. He doubted the wisdom 'of publishing in detail accounts of our dealings with neutral countries like Persia and Afghanistan during the war'. Maintaining that 'it is surely very dangerous for us to lay bare to the world our negotiations during the war with various Persian Governments and personages', he added that 'it is not altogether edifying for India or Persia or Afghanistan to read the recommendations of the Government of India and the decisions thereon (sometimes adverse) by His Majesty's Government'. He suggested either 'a very strict bowdlerisation of the whole' or, as he preferred, the restriction of the work as a confidential document for official use only. Forwarding Bray's note, Daniel made it clear that he personally was decidedly in favour of the latter course. Having consulted all those in the Foreign Office who were concerned from both an historical and a political point of view, Gaselee agreed that Bray's arguments were 'quite unanswerable'. He added:

> It is likely that before long the Russian Soviet Government will publish the secret archives of the old Russian Foreign Office relating to Persia, as they have already published those relating to Constantinople and the Straits. Such publication might not include a great number of British despatches, but would include reports from Russian Ambassadors and representatives abroad, notes of conversations with British diplomatists, appreciations prepared in the Russian Foreign Office, and minutes by Russian Foreign Ministers. If this were to happen, it would be a distinct disadvantage to us to be saddled with a published and therefore expurgated official version of our part in Persia during [and] immediately after the war. I think if General Moberly keeps in view the probability of a Russian publication of secret documents it may help him in dealing with his subject.[14]

By March 1928 volume iv of *British Documents* was in galley stage. The editors wrote to Gaselee a letter revealing just how little India Office material in Foreign Office files they had dared to include, and placing themselves in the hands of the Foreign Office so far as getting even that small amount past the obstacles to its publication:

... As regards the India Office several questions arise. We have endeavoured wherever possible to avoid quoting India Office documents. We have frequently been satisfied with the final result or decision as embodied in a Foreign Office despatch or telegram, and thus avoided any direct quotation of an India Office opinion.

In certain Foreign Office Memoranda (e.g., galley 154–5 Russia and Afghanistan) reference is frequently made to India Office points of view. The general result, however, is that it is the attitude of the India Office rather than its ipsissima verba that we quoted. There are other occasions, e.g., doc. 2 from bottom on p. 157, dated F.O. 11th December, 1905, where the India Office is so briefly mentioned that it seems rather a question whether the matter is worth submitting to them. A number of these documents seem to be in reality Foreign Office papers, with brief references only to the India Office. And it seems to be a real question whether submission to the latter is needed at all.

Under the circumstances we think it would be desirable for the Foreign Office to indicate to us the specific documents they propose to submit. We are likely to be influenced a good deal in future volumes by the Foreign Office point of view in this matter and should be glad of their assistance.[15]

On 8 June Patrick recommended the omission of any material that could be said to have a bearing on the present state of British relations with Afghanistan. In addition to the question of what it was desirable to omit 'on political grounds', he claimed that the question of principle raised in Hirtzel's letter of 16 March 1927 remained unanswered: 'what class of documents can legitimately be described as *diplomatic documents?* It would be useful to know whether, in the opinion of the Foreign Office, despatches of the Government of India or letters from the India Office to the Foreign Office are diplomatic documents or whether as interdepartmental correspondence they should be excluded.'[16] Gaselee stated the Foreign Office view:

'diplomatic documents' ... means correspondence between the Foreign Office and representatives abroad. Inter-departmental correspondence is on the same footing as minutes: we do not regard these as coming entirely within our promise that everything can be published. India Office to Government of India is entirely 'domestic' to yourselves, and you have every right to withhold it if you wish to. India Office to Foreign Office is partly domestic, partly diplomatic.

He reminded Patrick of Chamberlain's minute on Hirtzel's letter, and advised him not to put the India Office's rejections in the form

of absolutely final and peremptory decisions, but rather to present
them as reasoned objections, 'possibly open to further discussion'.[17] Patrick wrote to Hirtzel that he was firmly opposed to the
publication of any of the extracts over which the India Office had
control, except perhaps those in a Foreign Office memorandum of
14 October 1903, 'which are concerned with ancient history'. As
the foreign secretary was not authorising the Foreign Office to
draw a firm distinction between diplomatic documents and interdepartmental or intradepartmental documents, however, he was
not sure what to reply to Gooch and Temperley. He did not think
they would be satisfied by a statement that 'our present relations
with the U.S.S.R. in Persia, Afghanistan, and Central Asia are such
as to preclude the publication of documents in which views and
recommendations are expressed which are applicable to the present situation'.[18] It fell to Hirtzel to state the formal position
adopted by the India Office:

> The Secretary of State for India in Council has never been asked for,
> and has never given, permission to publish the recommendations
> and documents belonging to this office. If such is desired, formal
> application should be made to him by Gooch and Temperley.
>
> As matters stand, each document must be considered on its mer-
> its. It would be necessary to know (1) the object of publication:
> what is the thesis which the particular document is intended to
> support or refute (2) what other documents bearing on the subject
> it is proposed to publish.
>
> It must be further borne in mind (a) that the Government of
> India is not in the position of an Ambassador. It is a great Govern-
> ment, de jure subordinate in matters of foreign policy, but possess-
> ing de facto a degree of authority which places its operations in an
> altogether different category from those of H.M.'s representatives
> in foreign countries (b) that although the control of foreign policy is
> in the hands of the Foreign Office, the execution of it, so far as Per-
> sia, Afghanistan, Thibet is concerned, is largely in the hands of the
> Government of India, and it is on India – for the security and peace
> of which the Government of India and the Secretary of State in
> Council are solely responsible – that the consequences of that pol-
> icy fall in the first instance.[19]

The resolve of the India Office was bolstered by the cabinet secretary, Hankey, whom Gooch and Temperley had said in March
they would approach directly about Committee of Imperial
Defence papers. Hankey told Hirtzel on 19 June that he personally
thought it would be a great mistake to publish many of the

extracts, and better to publish none of them. With utter disingenuousness he said, 'I do not understand what it has to do with the
origins of the war'. After receiving Hirtzel's advice, Hankey
intended to raise with the prime minister the question of principle
'as to whether we are going to allow CID minutes and so forth, to
be quoted in this publication'.[20]

Before Hirtzel replied, Wakely wrote:

> Looking at this particular proposal by itself, the objections to pub
> lication seem to me very strong, and it is difficult to think that suf
> ficient grounds could be shown for setting them aside in the
> interests of a general policy of publication. The position is no doubt
> quite different in regard to purely European pre-war international
> politics: circumstances in Europe have entirely changed, and the
> political mentality of European nations may be considered to have
> advanced far enough to make publicity possible and desirable.[21]
> But what is good for Europe is not necessarily good for Asia. It is
> hardly possible to say that the order of ideas illustrated by these
> extracts is entirely a thing of the past.
>
> In any case political opinion in Persia would seize upon them; I
> do not see that these revelations of Anglo-Russian rivalry in Persia
> have any particular bearing on the origins of the war; the publication
> of scrappy extracts would only whet the appetites of commentators.
>
> It would seem desirable (but this is not our business) that CID
> reports as such should be excluded from publication. But as regards
> the whole matter we are really not in a position to judge properly
> without fuller information as to the policy underlying the proposed
> publication and the manner in which it is being carried out. One
> obvious consideration is that a policy of publicity qualified by
> numerous reservations of papers that are withheld from publica
> tion will carry so little conviction that it seems hardly worth enter
> ing on it at all.[22]

Hirtzel's reply of 30 June to Hankey was entirely at one both
with Wakely's note and Hankey's original attitude. Of Gooch and
Temperley, Hirtzel wrote: 'I have no knowledge of the circumstances in which the Foreign Office threw open its doors to these
gentlemen; but we have not thrown open ours, and the Secretary
of State has refused permission to publish a number of documents emanating from this Office and from the Government of
India. I have no reason to suppose that he will modify that attitude.' He ended:

> Memories in the East are long, and questions do not easily die – we
> are still ploughing the same sands as twenty or even fifty years ago.

Present policy is interpreted by Persians and Afghans in the light of
past policy. And if Persian and Afghan dovecotes are fluttered by
indiscreet publication India is the first to suffer.[23]

In the meantime, in connection with the contents of volume iii and
the preface to that volume, Gooch and Temperley had taken up
the general question of omissions with the Foreign Office and foreign secretary. On 12 June they had written to Gaselee, saying that
their editorial good faith and independence had been questioned
in certain quarters owing to omissions already made at the request
of foreign governments. There had been a recent public challenge
from Professor E. Halevy, an adviser to the French government
over its publication of documents: 'He suggests quite plainly that
the British Foreign Office are in a position to control the Editors
and would, under certain circumstances prevent the publication
of documents of a purely British character, and have in fact already
done so.' The difficulty raised by this and other criticism, they
wrote, was a very real one:

> For historians differ from statesmen in this respect. No one believes
> that a historian would willingly omit any passage from a document
> and the proper historical course is that followed in the Grosse Poli-
> tik, i.e., the publication of documents entire. The fact that we have
> consented to certain omissions reveals a keen desire on our part to
> meet the wishes of the Secretary of State, but it is in the eyes of his-
> torians a concession to political expediency.

Gooch and Temperley insisted that they must make their public
position quite clear and explicit, and wished to utilise the preface
to volume iii for this purpose, and to say there that they would
resign if attempts were made to insist on the omission of documents which they considered vital or essential.

An interview between the editors and the foreign secretary was
arranged for 3 July. Headlam-Morley was relatively sympathetic
to the editors' position. He thought that in substance their contention was sound and that they must state clearly the conditions
on which they undertook the work entrusted to them, namely
'that they should be given a free hand in the selection of documents to be published and that they could not continue the work
if in any way this condition were violated'. Gaselee was less

enthusiastic, but concentrated in the memorandum he wrote for the foreign secretary on issues raised by other departments of state approached by Gooch and Temperley:

> The Editors have direct contact with the India Office and the Committee of Imperial Defence and have asked both of these for permission to publish documents which will come in later volumes of the series. We have acted strictly on a former minute of yours when questions connected with the India Office were being considered: 'Speaking generally, I desire the broadest possible publication. If India Office refuses, India Office must defend the refusal.' We have informed the India Office and Sir Maurice Hankey accordingly and both are willing to take upon themselves the task of imparting to the Editors their refusal to publish certain documents and the reasons for doing so.
>
> The India Office in the course of their correspondence with us raised the point of the definition of the expression 'diplomatic documents'. Mr Ramsay MacDonald gave the Editors a pledge that they should be allowed to publish all diplomatic documents without restraint and you in effect continued this permission. Now what is a diplomatic document? In the narrowest sense it is a communication between the Secretary of State and a British representative abroad. Is interdepartmental correspondence in the same category? I think not quite, for it is part of the machinery by which a governmental decision is arrived at, and the same may be said about Foreign Office minutes on papers. We are naturally anxious to let the Editors publish as much as possible of both classes, but have a right to withhold if we think it desirable.
>
> Among the papers under consideration by the CID and the India Office there are some which I think quite certainly do not come into this category, such as a memorandum drawn up for the CID on British policy in the Near East, and, in the other case, correspondence between the Secretary of State for India and the Viceroy. These I think are properly regarded by their own Offices as domestic and quite impossible to include in the term 'diplomatic documents'.

Gaselee doubted whether Chamberlain would wish to raise these questions of relations with the India Office and CID at the forthcoming interview, but he thought it 'quite likely that the Editors will bring them up to strengthen their case against government censorship generally'.[24]

In a memorandum submitted on the day before the interview was due to take place, Gooch and Temperley reminded the foreign secretary, more accurately than Gaselee had just done,[25] of the terms of his announcement of their appointment. The announcement, they pointed out, 'suggests only two limitations on the classes of documents to be published (a) they were to be "official documents" (b) they should bear "on the general European situation out of which the War arose"'. They added that the determination of what documents were relevant in accordance with (b) 'is one on which the Editors would naturally maintain their own judgment', and that they had not been informed, at the outset, by the foreign secretary, that it would be necessary to submit certain documents to foreign powers. They continued:

> The series is stated to be 'edited for the Foreign Office' but the announcement did not define the documents as Foreign Office or diplomatic ones. If therefore an accurate account of vital negotiations could not be compiled from Foreign Office papers the Editors would feel justified in saying that their task was rendered impossible if access to other necessary papers were denied them.

Later on, they maintained that no question had as yet been raised in connection with memoranda prepared in the Foreign Office or with interdepartmental correspondence, and forecast that

> When they are as in other cases the Editors will determine their attitude by their interpretation of the terms 'historical accuracy and impartiality'. They will be prepared to consider any special objection to the publication of any particular document, and they would wish to meet the views of the Secretary of State whenever possible but they could not agree to a suppression of any document or part of a document that they considered essential to the presentation of the truth ... The material contained in the document itself must determine the decision. Papers communicated to the Foreign Office by another department have also to be considered on their merits as they may in some cases be essential to the explanation of the policy pursued in foreign negotiations.[26]

At the interview, which took place on the afternoon of Tuesday 3 July, and at which Montgomery and Gaselee were also present, the foreign secretary took the line, despite the brave effort of the editors, that 'departmental minutes, and to some extent interdepartmental correspondence, were not official documents suitable for publication'. Chamberlain went on to maintain 'that in the East political problems have not been completely changed and cut off from the past as in the West by the Great War. With respect to Persia and Afghanistan and our relations with Russia over these countries, the old questions are still alive and the publication of documents of twenty years ago may still be extremely dangerous'.

With regard to Committee of Imperial Defence material, Chamberlain stated that the authority of the prime minister was absolute. With regard to the India Office, which Temperley said 'appeared to be reluctant to let anything at all be published', the foreign secretary said that whilst he could not override 'the authority of a brother Secretary of State', he was willing 'to appeal to Lord Birkenhead to be as merciful as possible'.[27]

Chamberlain was as good as his word. On 12 July he wrote to Lord Birkenhead and appealed to him to give Gooch and Temperley 'the greatest latitude that you feel is consistent with your duty to the State':

> You will understand what would be my position, and incidentally that of the Government, if, having announced this publication to the world and having begun it, the editors threw up their task on the ground that they were prevented from presenting a true picture of British policy.

Birkenhead was unmoved even by this. Although he instructed his officials to draw up a 'civil answer',[28] neither he nor they had any intention of yielding any ground. The answer was sent on 18 July. It began:

> I am afraid that Ramsay MacDonald left you a very uncomfortable legacy, and I will gladly do what I can to prevent trouble arising for you in respect of my sphere, though I am little disposed to be dictated to by a couple of dons who (from what you tell me) seem to think more of their professional reputation than of the public interest.

Birkenhead accepted Chamberlain's suggestion regarding machinery; he would instruct his people to act in the spirit desired by the foreign secretary, and would get Sir Robert Holland, a retired member of the Council of India, to liaise with Gaselee. First, however, the air had to be cleared a little, and this Birkenhead proceeded to do:

> So far as I know no undertaking to disclose India Office documents has ever been given, nor am I prepared to give one wholesale. That I must make plain. Those of our papers that have passed in the Foreign Office in the ordinary course of correspondence must, you will agree, be regarded as still our property for the present purpose, and therefore as not covered by Ramsay MacDonald's undertaking.

I am ready to consider (in consultation with the Government of India who may have views of their own) the disclosure of any particular document on its merits, but in doing so I conceive that I have to ask myself two questions (1) is publication in the public interest? (2) is the document directly or indirectly connected with the origin of the war?

As regards (1) what you have told the Editors about the general difference between western and eastern problems seems to me to be absolutely sound. In the east these problems go on for ever; eastern memories are long; and eastern politicians read past policy into the present and the future ... we cannot disclose past fears and hopes and aspirations without creating in the minds of the Persians and Afghans suspicions which must unfavourably affect our present relations.

But if the Editors will be reasonable in such matters, and will take our word on questions of eastern mentality of which they can have no experience, there should be no great difficulty.

The other question is perhaps not so easy. But is it not possible to mark off in advance certain spheres which quite certainly had nothing to do with the genesis of the war? In Afghanistan and Thibet (as in Persia almost down to 1907) Russia was the only enemy, and I cannot see that our hostility to Russia before 1907 had anything to do with German hostility to both of us in 1914 ...[29]

Birkenhead sent copies of Chamberlain's letter and his reply to it to the Viceroy of India, Lord Irwin. He drew the latter's attention to one thing in particular: 'You will notice that I have kept the way open for the Government of India to express their views on the disclosure of any particular document affecting them that Temperley and Gooch desire to publish.'[30] It really was just as well that Temperley, for one, had, even in the days before his interview with Chamberlain, not been optimistic about his and Gooch's chances of success as regards the India Office: on 28 June he had told Professor C.K. Webster that whilst he thought the editors might beat Chamberlain's fight to censor their preface, 'over there [the India Office] I think we shall fail'.[31] Nevertheless, Temperley did not improve the editors' chances by taking the line he took at an interview with Sir A. Hirtzel on 18 July. As Hirtzel put it in a letter to Holland, Temperley's main points seemed to be

1) that because the Anglo-Russian agreement made it easier for Russia to go to war with Germany therefore it was necessary to show the genesis of that agreement and

2) as many documents were partly published or mentioned,
unless the rest follow, certain microscopic and malevolent historians in the USA and France will challenge the editors.

He talked a good deal about resignation, and throughout took
the attitude of one who was asked to make concessions to us. He
was emphatic in saying that the argument that the publication of a
certain document was contrary to the public service would not be
accepted by him.[32]

At the Foreign Office, Gaselee considered Birkenhead's statement
of the position to be 'very sound'. He jibbed only at the proposal
that certain areas should be ruled out in advance, thinking that
'any such actions would precipitate the resignation of the Editors
at once, and they would contend that among the despatches referring to, for example, Afghanistan, there must be some, even if only
one or two, related distantly to the Anglo-German problem'. Headlam-Morley's was a more mature view:

From the point of view of the Editors we must keep in mind that
the 'general situation out of which the war arose' includes not only
Anglo-German but Anglo-Russian relations. They can therefore
claim the right to publish all conversations and negotiations which
took place directly between the British and the Russian Governments and were an essential part of the events leading up to the
Entente of 1907, whether they had to do with Persia, Afghanistan or
Thibet. These negotiations were in fact an essential part of the relations between the European Powers just as were those connected
with the Far Eastern question.

Searching for a general principle which might be laid down, he
suggested the publication be confined to those direct negotiations.
The trouble was that the result would be to eliminate 'a large
amount of the material as between the Foreign Office and India
Office about Persia', and the difficulty was that 'there are a certain
number of despatches and private letters which technically
belong entirely to the Foreign Office ... as well as Foreign Office
memoranda, which refer to the questions which are dealt with in
fuller detail in the correspondence between the Foreign Office and
the India Office'. Montgomery thought that 'we shall not be able
to go the whole way with Lord Birkenhead's suggestion, but that

a measure of agreement with the editors could well be reached on the general lines suggested' by Headlam-Morley.[33]

On reading the above minutes, Chamberlain thought it best that Gaselee, Headlam-Morley and Sir M. Hankey should confer and present a joint report on principle to the prime minister, Birkenhead, and himself, as a basis for a communication to Gooch and Temperley. This proposal was approved by the prime minister, who had been consulted separately by Hankey about CID papers.[34]

The report, entitled 'The Publication of *British Documents on the Origins of the War*', was finished on 4 August 1928. As it effectively set the guidelines for official historians, and as hitherto only extracts from it have been made,[35] it is printed in full as an appendix to this chapter. Although almost entirely the work of Headlam-Morley,[36] such was the negative input already received from the India Office and other quarters, of which Headlam-Morley had to take account, that it effectively dashed any hopes Gooch and Temperley may still have retained as regards utilising material in departments other than the Foreign Office.

The comments of the officials at the India Office on the report will not surprise any reader who has reached this point. Patrick was somewhat startled to learn (from paragraph 27) that Gooch and Temperley were claiming 'to burrow in the archives of other Departments besides the Foreign Office', and relieved to note that the Foreign Office were apparently not disposed to accept this contention. Wakely wrote:

> We need not feel compelled to admit without question the argument that appears in paragraphs 30, 31 – that, because the Anglo-Russian agreements of 1907 are an essential part of the story, the negotiations leading up to them are also essential; and the argument is still less conclusive if it is extended to cover the inclusion of incidental documents dealing with local problems. The fact of Anglo-Russian agreement is no doubt vital; but the subject-matters of the agreement, unless they concern other European Powers or bear on the European situation otherwise than through the mere fact of Anglo-Russian agreement, seem really to be irrelevant to the purposes of this publication. This appears to be recognised, to some extent at any rate, in the general principle of paragraph 34 – we might push the argument somewhat further (Thibet, Afghanistan) than the general principle as stated appears to do.[37]

Although Temperley attempted to exert some pressure on the India Office, telling Holland on 3 September, for example, that before his appointment every government department and foreign government had already given their consent to publication,[38] it did no good. Birkenhead, who by this time had received the Viceroy's reply of 23 August to his letter of 19 July, a reply which 'entirely agreed' with the line of the secretary of state for India, and in which Lord Irwin expressed gratitude for keeping Afghanistan and Thibet out of it, and for 'reserving the last say in the matter for yourself and us',[39] told Holland on 11 September to tell Temperley that he had reserved the right to consult the Government of India. Efforts by the editors to see Holland earlier rather than later were staved off, so that Holland might have time to study the report.[40] When the prime minister asked for the views of Birkenhead on the report Seton suggested, successfully, that the views of the Viceroy must first be ascertained.[41] Seton drafted Birkenhead's letter to Irwin of 4 October, saying that he was disposed to accept the report. However,

> The question raised in paragraphs 27–29 is important, and I am certainly not prepared to turn these investigators loose on the India Office secret papers. The principle laid down in paragraphs 34–35 can be accepted, but their application in points of detail will be important. The Anglo-Russian agreements of 1907 are certainly an essential part of the story, but the subject-matter of the agreements, unless they concern other European Powers or bear on the European situation generally seem to me to be irrelevant ... Holland is at present conferring with Temperley, and trying to educate him in the elements of Asiatic policy.[42]

Seton also wrote to Birkenhead's private secretary on 11 October, saying:

> We find it difficult to see that the publication of the details of Anglo-Russian controversies, which were satisfactorily settled seven years before England and Russia took the field as allies, can be needed to throw light on the causes of the war, but we should not oppose our uninstructed view of such matters to that of professional historians if the documents could be published without offending Persian or Afghan susceptibilities and increasing certain difficulties that still exist.

He suggested summaries of Indian foreign policy instead, as one way of stopping Temperley from resigning and publishing his reasons for so doing.[43]

On 7 November the Viceroy's reply was sent to Viscount Peel, who had replaced Birkenhead on 1 November. Irwin accepted the report as it stood. He added that 'the difficulties involved in preventing the two historians running amok among the Departmental archives were evidently even greater' than he had supposed.[44] In December the India Office insisted on omissions from volume iv.[45] At the same time, the minds of the India Office and of the Government of India were put at rest by the following communication from Gaselee to Holland:

> ...we think that there should not only be no question of communicating now with the editors on the lines of paragraphs 34 and 35 of the confidential printed memorandum, but that the paragraphs themselves ought not to be communicated to them at any time in future without the express approval of our two Secretaries of State. The memorandum was not written for communication to the editors but for the guidance of the government departments concerned, and if (as we hope will not be the case) it became necessary to communicate to the editors the principles of these two paragraphs then it should be done in such a form that they would not appear to be an extract from a larger memorandum. In short, we think that the editors should not know, now or ever, of the existence of the confidential memorandum at all.[46]

The editors' campaign for greater access had rebounded upon them. The poetic justice of the situation was that it had led to the production of yet another secret document relevant to their enquiries, the mere existence of which was to be kept a secret from them. They were, as a matter of public policy, to be kept in ignorance of the reasons why they would fail to penetrate the archives of the India Office and Committee of Imperial Defence, and those of the Foreign Office beyond a certain point.

[The fate of General Moberly was, if anything, even worse. The proof of his book had been sent to the India Office in September 1928. On 26 February 1929 Colonel J.C. Freeland, for the military secretary at the India Office, replied to Daniel at the Committee of Imperial Defence that he was directed to inform him that the secretary of state for India 'regrets that he finds himself unable to approve (chapters ix, x and xi)': 'Much of the material contained in them is, from a political point of view, of so highly secret a nature that the inclusion of it in a volume issued even "For Official Use Only" appears to him to be open to the gravest objection.' Freeland went on:

> From every point of view, it would appear unnecessary for a military history to contain précis of documents showing the course of discussions preliminary to the issue of orders, and the value of the volume for military purposes would not suffer if all such passages

were omitted and replaced by brief statements regarding the instructions sent to Persia. These statements should, of course, be carefully written so as to eliminate political matters unsuitable for publication. I am, therefore, to say that Lord Peel suggests that these three chapters should be re-written accordingly, and the others chapters of the volume should be similarly revised ...

Moberly protested that, since Bray's note, all the chapters in their final form had, 'after approval by the Foreign and Political Department and the General Staff in India, been passed and approved officially by the Foreign Office, the Army Council and Admiralty and all but the last three by the India Office'. The Committee on Official Histories took the view that there were only two courses open to it – either to bowdlerise the volume, or to issue it as 'Confidential' in this country and as 'Secret' in India. The following exchange took place at their meeting on 26 March 1929:

> J.C. *Walton (I.O.):* the India Office favoured bowdlerisation, felt that a good deal could be omitted ... it contained the whole of our policy in Persia ten years ago ... Any leakages would be very unfortunate. *Lord Eustace Percy (Chairman and President of the Board of Education):* if the whole of the political matter was eliminated nobody would understand what we were doing in Persia at all. *Walton:* agreed.[47]]

On the late appearance of volume iv in 1929, following volume vi which had been published in 1928, Gooch and Temperley sent a signed copy to Sir Robert Holland, drew his attention to their acknowledgement of his help, and expressed their 'deep appreciation' for it.[48] They were never to get into the files of the India Office, the Government of India, or, except on two occasions, the Committee of Imperial Defence. They kept up appearances, nevertheless, throughout. Their final foreword to their last volume, published in 1938, was an attempt to recapitulate what they regarded as their achievements. The paragraph on volume iv ended with the sentence, 'To complete the picture, a despatch from Lord Curzon (much mutilated in its Blue Book form) is quoted at much greater length on British policy in India and towards Russia ...'.[49] Only now that the picture of the incomplete picture is complete can we see how hollow was the ring to this.

Appendix

Report by Gaselee, Headlam-Morley and Hankey, 4 August 1928
The Publication of 'British Documents on the Origins of the War'
(I.O. L/P&S/10/1227 L5138/5/402)

1. BEFORE dealing with the particular difficulties which are the immediate origin of this memorandum, it is desirable briefly to put on record the reasons and objects for which publication was undertaken.

2. The immediate occasion was a question in Parliament on the 20th February, 1924, by Mr. Morel, who

> asked the Under-Secretary of State for Foreign Affairs whether, in view of the publication by the Russian Government of official documents from the Russian Imperial archives disclosing pre-war actions and negotiations between our Russian and French Allies, presumably withheld from His Majesty's Government and concealed from this House, of the existence of numerous falsifications, likewise revealed by the Russian Government, in the Russian Imperial Orange Book, which was officially circulated together with the official publications of other Allied Governments by His Majesty's Government at the outbreak of war, and of the recent reproduction of many of these documents in the Congressional Record of the United States, His Majesty's Government will consider the advisability of placing members of this House in a position at least as advantageous as that of members of the United States Congress for the examination of these documents, by issuing them as a White Paper, and will further consider the public advantage which would be derived from the publication of such documents as may exist in the British official records calculated to throw light upon these disclosures?

Mr. Ponsonby answered:–

> The United States Congress places material on its Record of a less official kind than that laid before Parliament by His Majesty's Government, and it is impossible to publish as a White Paper records of negotiations with which His Majesty's Government were not at the time directly concerned, and of which they have now no knowledge other than that in the possession of the public at large. In any case, action could not be taken in the manner suggested without the permission of the other Governments concerned. The same consideration applies to the suggestion in the last part of the hon. member's question. My right hon. friend the Prime Minister sees, however, the advantage of some further publication of the pre-war British records, and will consider what course might be profitably adopted.

3. The arguments for publication were irresistible. In no other way could the criticism and attacks on British foreign policy before the war be satisfactorily met. As Sir William Tyrrell wrote in a minute to the Secretary of State in December 1925: "The project was warmly welcomed by Crowe and myself as, in so far as this Office was concerned, the publication of our papers, together with the minutes, would help to destroy the belief in certain quarters of this country that the Foreign Office had plotted the late war." Moreover, the voluminous publication of the most secret documents abroad, both from the Russian and the German archives, had already completely dissipated the secrecy with which hitherto many of the most important events had been clothed, while, on the other hand, they exposed

us to this disadvantage, that everything was put forward from the point of view of foreign Governments, and there was no clear and authentic statement of British policy. Definite proposals were therefore put before the Prime Minister by Sir Eyre Crowe who "earnestly begged him for his support on the proposal," to which he attached importance, "not only from a political but also from an educational point of view."

4. The suggestion made in the Office was that while it would be necessary to get in external assistance, the publication should be made officially by the Foreign Office and that the editors should be directly responsible to the Secretary of State. Mr. MacDonald, however, determined to invite Dr. Gooch, the well-known historian, to undertake the proposed publication on behalf of the Foreign Office. There were obvious and cogent reasons for adopting this course, however contrary to precedent it might be. The publication could not fulfil its object unless external and hostile critics could be convinced that it was impartial and unbiased; had it been done under the control of the Foreign Office, there would always have been the suspicion that compromising documents might have been omitted for political purposes. As soon as this method was adopted, it was almost inevitable that Dr. Gooch would be asked to undertake the work. Not only was he a very distinguished historian, but he was probably the only historian in England who would command the confidence of German and other hostile critics. As Sir William Tyrrell minuted in December 1925: "We welcomed his appointment, as he had been one of the most persistent critics of the pre-war foreign policy of this country."

5. Mr. MacDonald, in consulting Dr. Gooch about the publication, had spoken of an "historical narrative." Dr. Gooch at once pointed out that what students of the war origins required was not a narrative written by him or anyone else, but the essential documents themselves. This of course was what the Office had contemplated. The only other request he made was that he might have a colleague, for "the scope and responsibility make it imperative that more than one editor should be appointed." He suggested Mr. Temperley, a proposal which was warmly welcomed by Sir Eyre Crowe, who said: "He has worked with and for us before and earned general respect and satisfaction."

6. An agreement having been arrived at as to the general scheme, it became necessary to refer the matter to the Treasury in order to procure their assent to the necessary expense, as well as to obtain their authorisation that the Stationery Office should undertake the printing and publication of the proposed work as a non-parliamentary publication. A letter was therefore written to the Treasury on the 15th September, 1924. In this the scope of the publication is defined as follows: "I am directed by Mr. Secretary Ramsay MacDonald to state that he has decided to make a wide publication of the correspondence of the Foreign Office bearing on the general European situation out of which the Great War arose." On the same date letters were despatched to the other Government Departments which might be concerned, namely, the War Office, the Colonial Office and the Committee of Imperial Defence, as well as to Lord Stamfordham, informing them of the scheme and asking for their co-operation (see below, paragraph 26).

7. The whole scheme had therefore in its general outline been determined before the change of Government took place in November 1924. Up to this date no official announcement had been made except a statement in Parliament by Mr. Ponsonby on the 2nd July that 'the Prime Minister has decided that there shall be some such publication, and is at present considering the plan on which it shall proceed." During the month of November letters were published in the "Times" by Sir

Sidney Lee, Dr. Seton-Watson and other historians, urging the importance of an authentic publication from the Foreign Office records. Mr. Chamberlain, in order to avoid the difficulty of waiting until Parliament met, suggested that Dr. Seton-Watson should write to him calling his attention to the matter; he would then reply announcing the project which had already been approved. In consequence of this, Dr. Seton-Watson wrote to Mr. Chamberlain on the 25th November, and Mr. Chamberlain replied on the 28th November. The essential paragraph in Mr. Chamberlain's letter (which together with Dr. Seton-Watson's letter, was published in the "Times" on the 3rd December, and a copy of which is annexed) is as follows:-

> As regards the publication of the official documents bearing on the general European situation out of which the war arose, a collection of these documents will be edited for the Foreign Office by Mr. G.P. Gooch and Mr. H.W.V. Temperley, who will, I hope, be in a position to begin serious work at a very early date. The reputation of the editors offers the best guarantee of the historical accuracy and impartiality of their work.

8. This narrative will show that there was among all concerned full agreement as to the desirability and the character of the proposed publication. It was not, as has been sometimes suggested, imposed on an unwilling Office by the Labour Government. While Mr. MacDonald strongly supported it, the initiative[+] came from the Office; the only essential change he made was his decision that the work should be entrusted to an independent editor, but this was at once accepted without demur, and at the beginning there was general agreement between the Office and the appointed editors. No attempt was made in the Office to take advantage of the change of Government to introduce any modification in the scheme, and Mr. Chamberlain at once, without any hesitation, accepted and made his own the decision arrived at by his predecessor.

9. Some matters at issue with the Treasury having been settled, the editors were able to begin work in the spring of 1925. It was clear from the beginning that they had very seriously under-estimated the amount of labour which the task they had undertaken would entail and the time that it would require. They seem originally to have held that they would be able to complete the work in about two years, although neither of them was able to give the whole of his time to it. In 1925 they contemplated three years. As a matter of fact, the first two volumes dealing with the years 1898-1904, were published in October 1927, and the third volume has just appeared. In each case some delay, which may be reckoned at about six months, was caused by difficulties for which the editors were in no way responsible, especially by the consultation with Foreign Governments (see below, paragraph 15). In addition to this, the whole of Volumes IV, V and VI are in print, and it is understood that a good deal of work has been done on the later volumes. It may be expected, therefore, that the whole series will be complete in ten volumes in two to three years from the present time.*

10. The work already produced shows that the editors have justified the confidence placed in them. In their general scope and form the volumes already prepared meet the requirements both of the Foreign Office and of historians. So far as it is possible to judge, the selection of documents has been judicious; there is no sign of any bias or partisanship, and, subject to certain quite minor points of criticism, the editing has been well done, and the brief comments and editorial notes are suitable. Though, owing to their nature, it could not be expected that these volumes would have a very wide circulation,± the very fact of their publication has

already been effective. The suggestions that the British Government did not dare to imitate the action of Germany and disclose the secrets contained in its own archives, have been silenced. The decision of the Secretary of State has been warmly approved in all responsible quarters, and there can be no doubt that the Government and the Office have been placed in a much stronger position by this publication. The whole controversy as to the responsibility of the war has been put on a more satisfactory basis. Although the first two volumes deal with some very delicate matters of diplomacy, the complete revelation of all the secrets of the Foreign Office has, it may be confidently said, increased rather than diminished the reputation of the British Government. It is worth noting that quite recently the French Government have declared their intention of publishing a similar selection of documents from the French Foreign Office. In this case, however, the procedure adopted has been different; the work has not been entrusted to independent editors, but is placed under the supervision of a large and rather miscellaneous committee, nominated by the Government.

11. It follows from this that it is of the highest importance that the work begun should be carried to a successful conclusion, and it is much to be hoped that, notwithstanding the occasional difficulties which have arisen and which are referred to in succeeding paragraphs, it will be completed by the present editors. Any serious difference which led either, on the one side, to their resignation, or, on the other, to the termination of the arrangement by the Foreign Office, would undoubtedly be very detrimental.

12. We can now proceed to the discussion of certain difficulties with regard to method and procedure which have arisen during the past three years. That such difficulties would arise was inevitable. The whole undertaking was of a completely novel character; no precedent could be found for it in the annals of this country, and, for obvious reasons, the Foreign Office was in a very different position from that of the German Foreign Office when they sanctioned the publication of their documents. From time to time important questions of principle have arisen and the discussions have sometimes assumed a serious aspect. While there has been every effort on the part of the Foreign Office, and especially of the Secretary of State, who has taken a keen personal interest in the whole matter and has gone very far to meet every request made by the editors, their attitude has on some occasions not been conciliatory. More than once they have begun a discussion by presenting to the Office something in the nature of an ultimatum, and throughout the negotiations they have again and again resorted to a threat of resignation. While they rightly rate very highly the responsibility which they have to "historians" and the general public, they do not seem to have realised the existence of an equal responsibility to the Foreign Secretary, who has invited them to undertake the work, and they have been slow to recognise the very exceptional efforts which have been made to assist them, not only by the Foreign Secretary and the Foreign Office, but by all others whose co-operation is needful, especially foreign Governments and other Departments, and they seem to be unduly sensitive to adverse criticism and doubts as to their integrity, which, in fact, whatever is done, are sure to be made by controversial writers.

13. As has already been pointed out, when Mr. MacDonald offered Dr. Gooch the appointment, he did not himself give any instructions as to the details of the work, and Dr. Gooch at this period did not specify the conditions on which he was willing to undertake it. All details were left, and probably wisely left, to be settled as they might from time to time come up. On one point, however, there was a complete

agreement on both sides from the beginning. The editors were to have a free hand in the selection of the documents which they would desire to include. There was to be no control or censorship by the Office or the Secretary of State. The editors have always represented with justice that, unless they could say that they were working with complete freedom, suspicions of undue interference for political reasons would doubtless arise, and both the Office and the Secretary of State have always fully recognised the justice of this contention. It has been carried out in practice. The editors, while they receive the fullest assistance from the Librarian and the officers of his department in tracing out all relevant documents, do not submit their proofs for approval. They are, as explained below, for certain specific purposes, read through by the Historical Adviser to the Office; it is his duty to note passages which should be submitted for approval to Foreign Governments, passages or papers which concern other Government Departments, and also minutes and extracts from private letters which, in his opinion, should not be published without express permission. He has, however, no instructions or authority apart from this to make any official criticism.** He does not submit any report or pass on the material to the administrative departments or to the heads of the Office, and members of the Office have no knowledge of any kind about the scope and character of each volume. They do not see them until they have been published.

14. This is the general principle. Experience, however, has shown that it was necessary to make certain exceptions, which have largely turned on the definition of the expression "official documents." These are as follows:–

(1) *The King:* At the same time that letters were sent to other Government Departments, the Librarian wrote to Lord Stamfordham acquainting him with the nature of the proposed publication and asking for his co-operation. Arrangements have in consequence been made by which all documents in which King Edward is referred to and all minutes written by him should be sent to Lord Stamfordham by the editors, it being understood that nothing of this kind should be published without express permission. So far as our information goes, in every case the permission has been granted and the volumes already published and those in print contain numerous minutes by King Edward. In addition, the editors have received constant assistance from the Librarian of the Royal Archives, who has communicated to them documents, copies of which were not to be found in the Foreign Office. Apart from volume XI, the work so far is confined to the reign of King Edward; in volume XI there are no minutes by the present King, and the Foreign Office records for the periods covered by this volume contain no papers bearing on the personal action or correspondence of the present King.

15. (2) *Communication to Foreign Governments:* Among the documents which the editors desired to include were a considerable number of such a character that, according to the ordinary courtesy of diplomatic intercourse, the British Government could not publish them or consent to their publication without asking the permission of some foreign Government. Among these were, *e.g.*, confidential notes and memoranda emanating from a foreign Government and the record of confidential conversations between foreign officials and diplomatists and representatives of the British Government. It was determined, after very careful and prolonged consideration, that all such documents must in the ordinary course be submitted to the foreign Government concerned. That the permission of foreign Governments should be requested had already been intimated by Mr. Ponsonby in the House of Commons on the 20th February, 1924 (see paragraph 2), and this must have been known to the editors. None the less they strongly protested against

this decision, stating that "it was quite unexpected by us." and that "no such sub-mission of documents to foreign Governments was ever mentioned to them". Their protests were based on two grounds: first, that it would inevitably cause very con-siderable delay. In fact, under the procedure adopted, it undoubtedly causes them a certain amount of technical inconvenience, and means that the publication of each volume is postponed for about six months. This is a point of comparatively small importance, on which nothing more need be said.

16. More important was their apprehension that the result would be that they might be asked to omit documents which, in their opinion, were of vital impor-tance for elucidating the character of British diplomacy and the working of the *Entente* with France and with Russia. The point was a just one, and in consequence the Secretary of State, who throughout was keenly interested in the whole matter, personally received the editors on the 30th July, 1926, and explained to them the reasons for his decision.

17. In a written memorandum they had demanded a definite assurance from the Secretary of State that they should not under any circumstances be asked to omit any document which they considered vital, and threatened, if they did not receive a definite promise to this effect, to resign. Sir Austen Chamberlain explained that it was impossible for him in advance to give the required under-taking. There were documents the publication of which, without the consent of the other Governments concerned, "would not only be justly resented as a serious breach of courtesy, but would dry up for ever those and similar valuable sources of information and means of political negotiation. It was conceivable, though exces-sively improbable, that the publication of a specific document of past years might imperil peace in the present; in such a possibility the judgment of the Secretary of State must be final." He then continued:–

If the editors will work with a full knowledge of my desire that every vital doc-ument shall be published, I will recognise that, if in any given case I have to refuse sanction for publication, I shall have no cause of complaint if the editors withdraw their names from the title-page, and I am placed in the extremely dis-agreeable position of having to explain in Parliament the cause of their with-drawal. I undertake to put all possible pressure on foreign Governments to induce them to agree to the publication of the documents about which we have consulted them, and even, in the last instance, if sufficient reason is shown, to consent to publication against their will; but you must not put me in the position of giving in advance a pledge that in certain hypothetical conditions I will con-sent to the publication of every conversation and note to or from a foreign Gov-ernment which may be found in these records, for that is a pledge which I honestly cannot give. All my interest is on the side of full publication, but my first duty is to preserve peace now and in the future. I cannot sacrifice *that* even to his-torical accuracy. What I can say is that if such a case arises I will assume full responsibility. I do not ask the editors to accept responsibility for or lend their names to any volume which they consider is not a fair presentation of the facts as disclosed to them by their inspection of our records.

18. So the matter was left. The experience of the last two years has been to show that the apprehensions of the editors were unfounded. It has been necessary to ask sixteen different Governments for their consent to the publication of specific documents; in no case has the omission of a document for political reasons even been asked for; in a few instances objection has been raised to certain passages, chiefly on personal grounds, and occasionally a foreign Government has asked

that if a document were published incorrect statements contained in it might be corrected. In all such cases a satisfactory arrangement has been come to. The whole story is indeed remarkable. The questions dealt with in these volumes are of the highest possible political importance, including as they do the whole negotiations leading up to the original Anglo-Japanese Treaty of Alliance and the revised treaty of 1905, and the very delicate negotiations regarding the Portuguese colonies; both these Governments have without demur consented to the full publication of everything contained in our records. In particular, the attitude of the French Government, which is, of course, very peculiarly concerned in the whole matter, has been most satisfactory. It cannot be doubted that the decision of the Secretary of State has been fully justified, and that it has had the result that foreign Governments, instead of looking on our publication with apprehension, have been made to feel that they themselves are associated with it.

19. The French General Staff recently refused permission asked on behalf of the editors by the War Office to publish a document on the ground that it was of military and not of political interest. The editors, while accepting the decision, insisted on making a specific reference to it in the introduction to the third volume, expressing their regret. To this the Office objected, their view being that if permission to publish a document not of vital importance were refused, it was discourteous and unwise to place the fact on record. The particular difficulty on this occasion was met by the Secretary of State, who caused a personal appeal to be made to the French Foreign Office, who, at his request, overrode the decision of the General Staff and approved publication of the document, which, therefore, appears as an appendix to Volume III. The general question was, however, discussed at a meeting between the Secretary of State and the editors on the 3rd July, 1928. The Secretary of State asked whether it was desirable for the editors to say "We were forced to omit a non-essential document; did not thus calling attention to an omitted document rather throw doubt on the whole work?". The editors did not agree with this, but they undertook that "they would carefully consider the whole question of mentioning any non-essential document of which an omission had been found to be obligatory." We are strongly of opinion that if a foreign Government has objected to the publication of a particular document, and if the Secretary of State and the editors agree that the objection is a reasonable one and that the document is not of vital importance, the editors should not be permitted to make any specific reference to the matter in their introduction. If they were to do so, the result would almost certainly be comments and enquiries which would be more inconvenient to the foreign Government concerned than the publication of the document itself, and might well be regarded by them to be both discourteous and disloyal.

20. (3) *Publication of Minutes and Signed Memoranda:* The Office have never interpreted the free hand given to the editors to publish official documents as necessarily including minutes by the permanent officials, and in the same category must be placed signed memoranda by permanent officials giving their advice or opinion on matters of policy. (There are of course a large number of signed memoranda which consist merely of a précis of correspondence, to the publication of which no objection would be raised.) In connexion with the preparation of Volume XI, the question was officially referred for decision to the Office, and Sir Eyre Crowe minuted:–

As regards minutes, I think we must maintain the rule that they shall not be published. Cases may arise when, on given papers, or in a given situation, no action is taken, but where the taking of no action indicates a policy which it is important to disclose. In such cases perhaps exceptions should be allowed.

There may be other kinds of exceptional cases. But each ought to be considered on its merits. My idea would be to let the historians see the minutes with the express proviso that they are not at liberty to publish or quote any except with specific *ad hoc* authority.

This decision was conveyed to the editors in a letter of the 16th March, 1925, by the Librarian, to which no answer seems to have been received.

21. In fact, however, the attitude of the Office has considerably changed and the procedure suggested by Sir Eyre Crowe has been greatly modified. This is largely due to the death of Sir Eye Crowe. The question whether any particular minute or Office memorandum should be published is necessarily to a large extent a personal one. It is the duty of civil servants in the Foreign Office, as in other Departments, to give the frankest and freest advice to the heads of the Office on the questions which come within their competence. In doing so they have hitherto had the fullest confidence that the opinions expressed would be regarded as strictly confidential and that they would not be exposed to the public criticism which, if known, their views might entail. On this point civil servants have the right to the protection of the Parliamentary head of the Office, just because, owing to their position, they are not able to defend themselves, and it is on the head of the Office that the official responsibility for decision depends. He, therefore, and he alone, must bear the brunt of public criticism.

22. In addition to this, the value of the services of individual members of the staff might be gravely compromised if they were publicly associated with a course of policy of which Parliament did not approve. It is easy to conceive cases in which, supposing all the confidential minutes and memoranda were published while those who wrote them were still in the service of the Crown, they would be forced to resign.

23. For these reasons, it would in our opinion have been quite impossible to publish many of the minutes and memoranda contained in the official papers, written by Lord Carnock, Lord Hardinge of Penshurst and Sir Eyre Crowe, had they still been in the service of the Foreign Office. In fact, however, this difficulty, which Sir Eyre Crowe no doubt had in mind when he wrote the minute quoted above, has to a large extent disappeared. When Volume XI was in preparation it became apparent that its value would be greatly enhanced if the minutes written by Sir Eyre Crowe himself were published. In consequence, after consulting Viscount Grey of Fallodon, the Secretary of State gave his consent to the publication of all those of political importance. This established a precedent which has been followed in later volumes; and, in fact, it may be said that in Volumes I, II and III there have been included all the important political minutes written in the Foreign Office. The editors attach great importance to the continuance of this practice. It is inevitable that they should do so. For many years public criticism of the policy of the British Government has drawn attention to the important part played in Germany and elsewhere, especially by Sir Arthur Nicolson (Lord Carnock). He, together with Lord Hardinge, have again and again been referred to as the fathers of the *Entente*, and of what is called the "encirclement" of Germany. The very candid, very able memoranda and minutes which they and Sir Eyre Crowe submitted to the Secretary of State are an essential and vital part in the history of British policy during these eventful years, and any publication from which they were omitted would give a very imperfect picture of the course of events. While recognising the great force of the considerations to which we have already drawn attention, we believe that under the very exceptional circumstances permission to publish these

minutes and memoranda should be continued. No doubt very serious criticism will be forthcoming, but we believe that on the whole the general result will be that the public will come to recognise the high public spirit, the great ability and great knowledge displayed by the permanent officials of the Foreign Office.

24. None the less, it is essential to maintain the principle that there is a distinction between papers of this kind and other official documents, and though experience shows that it will not often be necessary to use it, it is essential that the Foreign Office and the Secretary of State reserve the right to refuse permission to some particular minute or memorandum. Great discretion should be observed with regard to the publication of the minutes by anyone still in the service of the Crown, and to publication of minutes written by junior officials should be strongly discouraged; owing to changes in Foreign Office procedure, they are likely to be more frequent than they were in the earlier volumes; it should therefore be an instruction to the officer who reads the proofs on behalf of the Foreign Office that he should call the attention of the editors to any minutes or signed memoranda the inclusion of which might appear undesirable, and, if necessary, refer the matter to the Office.

25. (4) *Private Correspondence:* The editors have had access to the private correspondence of Sir Edward Grey, which is preserved in the archives of the Foreign Office, and also to that of Lord Carnock, which he has deposited there. Many of the papers which they contain are of very high political importance; they have been freely used by the editors, and we agree with them when they say that 'the publication of such papers has done a good deal to reassure the public, and, in particular, serious historical writers." They recognise, however, that these papers are in a different category from "official documents", and that they "could not insist on publication of private papers (*e.g.,* the Carnock MSS) should objection be made to them". It would certainly be most discourteous and undesirable to publish, for instance, some of the very intimate letters from Lord Hardinge to Lord Carnock without the permission of the writer. This matter should continue to be dealt with by a procedure similar to that for minutes, and in those cases in which it appears desirable, application for permission to publish should be made to the writer of the letter, if he is still alive.

26. (5) *Inter-Departmental Correspondence:* We now come to the particular question which is the occasion for this memorandum. It was from the beginning recognised that special arrangements would have to be made for dealing with those papers contained in the Foreign Office records which had been communicated by other Departments and could not properly be published without the consent of the Department concerned. In order to meet this difficulty, at an early stage, the 15th September, 1924, the Librarian of the Foreign Office addressed an official letter to the Departments which seemed most likely to be concerned; namely, the Admiralty, the War Office, the Committee of Imperial Defence and the Colonial Office, and at a later date° to the India Office, acquainting them with the project and asking them to appoint an officer with whom the editors could consult personally in the course of their work, so as to save time which would be occupied by official correspondence on each specific point. By this the principle was clearly laid down and accepted by the editors, who were informed of this action, that in regard to certain papers the co-operation of other Departments would be necessary. This system has hitherto worked satisfactorily in practice, and, in particular, the War Office have not only consented to the publication of documents belonging to their Department found among the records of the Foreign Office, but have also communicated to the editors, with permission to publish, documents of the highest importance regarding

the Anglo-Belgian military conversations in 1905-6, a series of documents which had never been communicated to the Foreign Office.

27. The editors are now apparently contending that the words "official documents" must not be limited to Foreign Office or diplomatic papers, and seem as of right to claim access to papers preserved in other Government Departments which, in their view, would be essential to an understanding of the European situation out of which the war arose. They base this claim on the fact that:–

> The series is stated to be 'edited for the Foreign Office', but the announcement did not define the documents as Foreign Office or diplomatic ones. Moreover, the Secretary of State has said that he took over the project already decided by Mr. Ramsay MacDonald. The latter was then Prime Minister as well as Foreign Secretary, so that his control extended to all Departments. If, therefore, an accurate account of vital negotiations could not be compiled from Foreign Office papers, the editors would feel justified in arguing that their task was rendered impossible if access to other necessary papers were denied them.
>
> Thus the Anglo-Belgian negotiation*** of 1906 is contained in papers at the War Office, and these are certainly essential to an understanding of the 'European situation out of which the war arose'. A denial of access to these papers would therefore have created a very serious situation. The editors are of the opinion that vital negotiations come within their sphere, irrespective of the channel through which the negotiations were conducted; and there is evidence to show that foreign critics are unlikely to accept the plea that such documents are in the charge of another Department, and therefore inaccessible. The editors gratefully recognise the willingness of the Secretary of State for Foreign Affairs to assist them in securing the co-operation of other Departments if any difficulty arises.

28. The contention in the first paragraph of this quotation cannot be accepted. It was as Foreign Secretary and not as Prime Minister that Mr. MacDonald gave his invitation to Dr. Gooch, and in writing to him on the 11th August, 1924, all that he promises is: "I will place at your disposal all the documents at the Foreign Office, and, of course, you would work with the people we have there, especially those in charge of the archives." The agreement is one then between the editors and the Secretary of State for Foreign Affairs; he, of course, could only give them access to, and permission to publish, documents belonging to his own Department, and they appear bound to accept this situation unless a further decision is made by the Prime Minister and the Cabinet. It may be mentioned in this connexion that the German work "Die Grosse Politik" is strictly confined to Foreign Office documents, and the editors have obviously not had access to the records of other Departments, and especially not to those of the General Staff, the War Office or the Admiralty.

29. None the less, we agree that the editors may justly ask that in special cases the facilities promised to them by Mr. MacDonald should be extended, and we hope that the heads of other Departments concerned will, if they receive requests from the editors, not only to publish documents belonging to them preserved in the Foreign Office archives, but also in special cases to look at some particular group of papers, grant this permission, as has already been done by the War Office. In this connexion we think it right to mention that the Prime Minister, after consulting the Secretary of State for Foreign Affairs, recently instructed Sir Maurice Hankey to inform the editors that they may have access to the proceedings of the Committee of Imperial Defence on the understanding that any summaries they may wish to publish will first be submitted to the secretary of the committee, and that the opinions attributed in the record to particular individuals shall not be

included in such summaries. The editors have also been authorised, should the necessity arise, to state publicly that they have been given access to the proceedings of the committee. If this example is followed in other Offices, then the British publication will be superior to that of the German Foreign Office, which has been very adversely criticised just because papers of other Departments are not included.

30. Quite recently, however, difficulties have arisen in connexion with (a) the Committee of Imperial Defence, and (b) the India Office. Both these Departments have raised objection to the inclusion in one of the forthcoming volumes of documents which the editors had proposed to print. The documents in both cases deal with the same subject and, to a large extent, can be dealt with together. Volume IV is entirely devoted to the negotiations leading up to the Anglo-Russian agreements concerning the relations of the two countries in Persia, Afghanistan and Tibet, which were signed at the same time in 1907. These agreements, though they deal entirely with Central Asia, in fact form a turning point in the relations of the European Powers to one another, for the conclusion of these agreements made possible the close diplomatic *entente* between Great Britain and Russia in the same way as the several treaties regarding Egypt and Morocco, Newfoundland and Siam formed the basis for the diplomatic *entente* between Great Britain and France. It was only after the conclusion of these treaties that the Triple *Entente* came into existence as a firmly established diplomatic group, which provided a counter-weight to the Triple Alliance of Germany, Austria and Italy. For this reason, the negotiations leading up to these agreements, and the subsequent working of the agreements, are one of the most important subjects with which these volumes have to deal, and one which it may be noted has been subjected, both at the time and since, to the keenest criticism, not only in Germany, but among certain groups in this country.

31. For this reason the editors have rightly considered it necessary to include a very extensive, and probably almost complete, selection of all the negotiations which took place direct between the British and the Russian Governments, as well as the confidential memoranda written on the subject in the Foreign Office, the minutes of Foreign Office officials, and the private correspondence conducted by the British representatives abroad with the Secretary of State or the Permanent Under-Secretary of State. These latter documents necessarily deal largely not only with the relations between Great Britain and Russia, but also with the local problems, especially as they appeared to our representatives in Persia, Sir Cecil Spring-Rice and Sir Arthur Hardinge. In view, however, of the great interest which the Government of India had in anything which concerned Tibet, Afghanistan and Persia, they and the India Office had to be consulted as to the whole policy of Sir Edward Grey regarding Russia and the effect which the terms of the proposed agreements would have in Asia itself. There was considerable difference of opinion on this matter between the Foreign Office and not so much the India Office as the Government of India. It may be noted that the existence of this difference has been well known, and is referred to discreetly by Lord Morley in his Reminiscences. The India Office now, on their own behalf and on that of the Government of India, raise strong objections to the publication of many of the proposed documents. This objection is supported by the contention that documents even more than twenty years old may, if published, have an unfavourable effect on our present relations, especially with Persia and Afghanistan. As Lord Birkenhead has pointed out in his letter of the Secretary of State for Foreign Affairs of the 18th July, 1928:–

In the east these problems go on for ever; eastern memories are long, and eastern politicians read past policy into the present and the future... It seems to me pretty clear that we cannot disclose past fears and hopes and aspirations without creating in the minds of Persians and Afghans suspicions which must unfavourably affect our present relations.

This view, it may be added, is also strongly supported by the Eastern Department of the Foreign Office. In effect, therefore, we have a proposal that the documents contained in this volume should be carefully considered from this point of view, and that permission to publish should be refused to any document which it might seem would prejudicially affect our present relations with the Governments of Persia and Afghanistan.

32. Obviously these representations cannot be ignored. For reasons which have been pointed out, it is for the advantage of this country that a *complete* disclosure should be made of the whole course of British policy in Europe and its relations to other European States in the years preceding the war. The time has not yet come when any such full disclosure regarding our policy in Central Asia can be made. This difference does not arise from any suggestion that our action in these countries may have been in any special way ill-advised or even discreditable to His Majesty's Government; it is simply due to the fact that here the story has not yet come to an end. The British Government are at the present day confronted by problems similar to those of the past, and to some extent have to deal with the same personalities. If the time has not come for a complete publication, it may well be held that it is very undesirable to publish a rather fortuitous and scrappy collection of documents which, while they chiefly deal, as is necessarily the case, with those questions on which special difficulty was found, and those on which there was a difference of opinion between the different branches of His Majesty's Government, were chosen, not so much because of their particular importance, but because, almost for accidental reasons, copies of them happen to have been preserved in the Foreign Office records.

33. Lord Birkenhead raises another point. It must be considered whether a document is "directly or indirectly connected with the origin of the war." This is important and must be kept in mind. The instructions to the editors were to publish everything bearing on this subject; they have not received a roving commission to dig out papers on any subject which they may find in the Foreign Office archives and publish them if they are not obviously relevant to the subject of their work. From this point of view the first three volumes are very satisfactory; they are strictly confined to papers directly bearing on the relations of the European Powers to one another. The proofs which have been received of Volumes IV, V and VI seem to show a tendency to include matter rather outside this scope. The original proof of Volume VI contained, for instance, documents extending to over 100 pages describing the Government and conditions of the Turkish Empire; this, no doubt, is of great historical interest, but much of it seemed unsuitable for inclusion, and would distract attention from other and more important subjects. Unofficial representations were therefore made to the editors, and they have cut out a good deal, but even now the mass of material on this subject may well be considered excessive. In this particular case no harm is done, but clearly the editors could not be permitted under the scope of their agreement to include matter which was not only irrelevant to the main subject of the work, but the publication of which would be for other reasons inconvenient and even dangerous. This might, for instance, be of real importance in connexion with our relations with the United States, and it

might, we think, be justly held that, on the ground of irrelevancy, the omission of some of the documents included in Volume IV concerning Tibet and Afghanistan might well be asked for.

34. The general principle seems to be that nothing outside the negotiations with the Russian Government should be included, except so much as is necessary to explain points of issue between Great Britain and Russia, and that, so far as possible, these explanations should be given in the form of editorial notes rather than by the publication of documents, in particular as little as possible should be said about inter-departmental differences. We believe that, in fact, it would not be difficult, working on these lines, to come to an agreement with the editors; they have already agreed to withdraw some of the documents to the publication of which objection had been raised; the two Secretaries of State have instructed officers in their Departments to discuss the question first of all with one another and afterwards with the editors, and it is probable that the difficulties which have arisen in this connexion will be overcome.

35. In their memorandum of the 12th July, 1928, the editors say that "the determination of what documents are relevant [to the general situation out of which the war arose] is one on which they would naturally exercise their own judgment." This is a position which cannot be accepted. In the case of a serious difference of opinion, the final decision must be reserved to the Secretary of State, and the editors should be so informed. Of course it is always open to them to resign should such a decision be adverse to their contentions. This we desire to avoid. Definite refusal to permit the publication of a diplomatic document on this ground should therefore only be given when there is a very strong case of such a kind that if it became necessary to publish the correspondence, the action taken would be generally approved.

36. In conclusion, we should like to say that, in our opinion, the differences and difficulties which have arisen are in fact not so serious as might appear from this lengthy enumeration. Hitherto a solution for each point of controversy has been reached by dealing with it on the merits of the particular case. This has been possible because there is a fundamental agreement about the general scope and purpose of the work. On the other hand, experience shows that it is not desirable to embark on a discussion of general principles with the editors, but so far as possible to limit the discussion to the special points which may from time to time arise.

August 4, 1928

+   marginal note by Hirtzel: '? from Mr Morel'.

*   Volume XI containing the documents of the weeks immediately preceding the outbreak of war (July and August 1914) was, at the editors' request, prepared for them by Mr. Headlam-Morley, Historical Adviser to the Foreign Office. The Office agreed that for this purpose he should work under their supervision and should be responsible to them and not to the Office. This volume was published on the 1st December, 1926.

±   The sales up to the present (September 1928) have been:–

Volume XI	2,159
" I.	987
" II	992
" III	650

**   From time to time he makes certain criticisms and suggestions on technical points of editing, but this is done privately and unofficially; these have been received in good part and often acted upon.

ø marginal note by Hirtzel: 'Possibly this refers to F.O. letter of 18 Oct/27. No earlier intimation seems to have been received'.

*** The word "negotiation" is incorrect; there were no negotiations between the Governments.

Notes

1. B.D.x(ii), p. 820; the memorandum itself, from F.O. 371/2076/33484, is printed in K.M. Wilson, 'The Struggle for Persia: Sir G. Clerk's memorandum of 21 July 1914 on Anglo-Russian relations in Persia', in *Proceedings of the 1988 international conference on Middle Eastern Studies* (Leeds, 1988), pp. 290–334.

2. See R.L. Greaves, 'Sistan in British Indian Frontier Policy', in *Bulletin of the School of Oriental and African Studies* xlix (1986), p. 94; the Curzon despatch can be found in full in F.O. 60/615.

3. I. Nish, *The Anglo-Japanese Alliance: The Diplomacy of Two Island Empires 1894–1907* (London, 1966), p. 318; Grierson to Sanderson, 16 June 1905, F.O. 46/673.

4. H.H. Asquith at 118th meeting of the Committee of Imperial Defence, 11 July 1912, CAB 2/2/3 p. 2.

5. Headlam-Morley to Hirtzel, 7 February 1927, I.O.L. MSS, L/P&S/10/1227.

6. Minutes by Wakely, 3 and 12 March, by Seton, 11 March 1927, ibid.

7. Hirtzel to Headlam-Morley, 16 March 1927, ibid. In the draft reply, but omitted in order to please Wakely from the letter as sent, was the following stronger passage: 'Lord Birkenhead regrets that he is unable to consent to publication. He has not been informed of the precise purpose to which it is proposed to put the despatch or the context in which it would find itself. But apart from that he considers that publication would not be in the public interest from the Indian point of view.'

8. Minute by Montgomery, 15 February, on Gooch and Temperley to Chamberlain, 10 February 1927, F.O. 370/265/L935.

9. Minute by Gaselee, 9 September 1924, F.O. 370/202/L3617.

10. Minutes by Headlam-Morley ,17, 24 March, by Oliphant and Palairet, 18 March, by Montgomery, 19 March, by Chamberlain, 23 March 1927, F.O. 370/265/L1690.

11. Temperley to Gaselee, 8 April 1927, ibid. L2264.

12. Minutes by Gaselee, 13, 19 April; Gaselee to Temperley, 19 April 1927, ibid.

13. Gaselee to India Office, 18 October; Foreign Office to India Office, 19 November; India Office to Foreign Office, 29 November 1927, L/P&S/10/1227.

14. Note by Bray, 11 September, Daniel to Gaselee, 19 October, Gaselee to Daniel, 26 October 1927, enclosures B, E and F in Appendix II to meeting of Committee on Official Histories, 9 March 1928, CAB 16/52.

15. Gooch and Temperley to Gaselee, 7 March 1928, F.O. 370/290/L1536.

16. Patrick to Gaselee, 8 June 1928, L/P&S/10/1227.

17. Gaselee to Patrick, 15 June 1928, ibid.

18. Patrick to Hirtzel, 16 June 1928, ibid.

19. Note by Hirtzel, 16 June 1928, ibid.

20. Hankey to Hirtzel, 19 June 1928, ibid.

21. This view was entirely at variance with that expressed by Headlam-Morley in a minute of 17 November 1924 in which he wrote: 'I deprecate Sir Sidney Lee's view that "from the current policy point of view the outbreak of war and its sequels have converted into ancient history all that took place before August 4, 1914". This is not the case; not to speak of the whole of our policy towards the United States and the Far East, there are many matters connected even with Turkey and the Near East, and also even with some European states, in which we are still influenced by considerations similar to those which existed before the war.' F.O. 370/202/L4411.

22. Note by Wakely for Hirtzel, 25 June 1928, L/P&S/10/1227.
23. Hirtzel to Hankey, 30 June 1928, ibid.
24. Memo by Gaselee, 29 June, including Gooch and Temperley to Gaselee, 12 June 1928, F.O. 370/290/L4422.
25. Ramsay MacDonald had used the term 'correspondence of the F.O.': Chamberlain had used the wider phrase 'official documents'. The term 'diplomatic documents' had been introduced into the discussions through India Office minutes and correspondence with the Foreign Office.
26. Memo by Gooch and Temperley, 2 July 1928, ibid.
27. Note by Gaselee, 4 July 1928, ibid.
28. Chamberlain to Birkenhead, 12 July 1928, and minute by Birkenhead, L/P&S /10/1227.
29. Birkenhead to Chamberlain, 18 July 1928, ibid.
30. Birkenhead to Irwin, 19 July 1928, ibid.
31. J.D. Fair, *Harold Temperley* (London and Toronto, 1992), p. 204.
32. Hirtzel to Holland 25 July 1928; see also Temperley to Hirtzel 21 July 1928, in which the threat was made to name the government departments which refused to allow publication of a part of a document which if not printed in full was not worth resigning over. L/P&S/10/1227.
33. Minutes by Gaselee and Headlam-Morley, 23 July, by Montgomery, 24 July 1928, F.O. 370/290/L4574.
34. Minutes by Chamberlain, 25 July 1928, ibid.
35. F. Eyck, *G.P. Gooch* (London, 1982), pp. 382–90. It was first mentioned in Butterfield's obituary of Gooch in *Proceedings of the British Academy* 55 (1969), pp. 329–30.
36. Minute by Gaselee, 15 August 1928, F.O. 370/290/L5138.
37. Minutes on the Report by Patrick, Wakely L/P&S/10/1227.
38. Temperley to Holland, 3 September 1928, ibid.
39. Irwin to Birkenhead, 23 August 1928, ibid.
40. Gaselee to Patrick, 15 September 1928, ibid.
41. Prime minister to Birkenhead, 1 October 1928, minute by Seton, ibid.
42. Birkenhead to Irwin, 4 October 1928, ibid.
43. Seton to Monteath, 11 October 1928, ibid.
44. Irwin to Peel, 7 November 1928, ibid.
45. Holland to Penson, 11 December, Penson to Holland 17 December 1928, ibid.
46. Gaselee to Holland, 12 December 1928, ibid.
47. Freeland to Daniel, 26 February, Observations by Moberly 4 March 1929, Appendix II to COH 24, CAB 16/52; minutes of 26 March 1929, CAB 16/53. Moberly's *Operations in Persia 1914–1919* was finally published in facsimile by the Imperial War Museum, with an Introduction by G.M. Bayliss, in 1987.
48. Gooch and Temperley to Holland, 21 May 1929 L/P&S/10/1227.
49. B.D. x(ii) xv.

❦ Chapter 9

TELLING THE TRUTH TO THE PEOPLE
Britain's Decision to Publish the Diplomatic Papers of the Interwar Period

Uri Bialer

The conflict between secrecy and publicity is one of the most delicate issues in foreign policy. Not long ago, absolute monarchs were able to conduct diplomacy that was really secret and could make war and peace – not to mention less cardinal decisions – without explanation. However, in the age of mass armies and of total wars, public opinion has to be mobilised and the issues of foreign policy need to be elaborated, justified and defended, even by nondemocratic governments. On the other hand, professional diplomats continue to claim that secrecy is often a crucial prerequisite for successful foreign policy. Modern international relations have thus posed a seemingly insoluble dilemma that will probably haunt governments in the future: negotiations can be flexible and successful only if they are kept secret, but they will be barren without popular consent.

A partial solution to this problem in nineteenth-century Britain was the system of Blue Books, which contained extracts from diplomatic correspondence. These, however, were issued to meet a particular situation and, generally speaking, were in the nature of *pièces justificatives*. The one conspicuous exception prior to the end of the Second World War was the publication of a series of British documents on the origins of the First World War, edited by Gooch and Temperley.[1] This was in response to the German publication

Die Grosse Politik der Europäischen Kabinette 1871–1914,[2] a collection of documents designed to shake the moral foundation of Versailles. As its title indicates, the British collection was directed to a single objective and not to a comprehensive coverage of British foreign relations.

The publication – from 1947 to the present – of such a comprehensive series covering the interwar period (*Documents on British Foreign Policy 1919–1939*) represented a major departure from British government practice. Not only did it open a new era in the history of the conflict between secrecy and publicity in British foreign policy, but it was also a landmark for historical research into interwar Britain. However, virtually nothing has been written about the genesis of the publication of these documents.[3] This is rather surprising since, as will be shown here, the decision to issue them, which was made early in 1944, was not a trivial one. The British government took more than four years to finally reach a decision. During that period debates on the subject often gave rise to bitter controversy involving not only 'historical' considerations, but also important personal and political ones. The latter were based on conflicting assessments of past, present and future British foreign policy. This essay, therefore, deals with a neglected, though not unimportant, aspect of historiography in the period following the First World War.

The story began early in December 1939, when the foreign secretary, Lord Halifax, asked the Foreign Office to check and supplement his personal diary of the events leading to the war.[4] Frank Roberts, of the Central Department of the Foreign Office, accordingly checked the records, but in the process realised that since the volume of information was so great, it was difficult to make a selection. The overworked Foreign Office therefore considered the possibility of asking the historian, E.L. Woodward,[5] to draw up a full diary of the events leading to the outbreak of the war from the material in their possession. At the time, Woodward was attached to the Political Intelligence Department (PID) of the Office, and acquired knowledge of the outline while collaborating on the Blue Book on the origins of the Second World War. It is hardly surprising that Sir S. Gaselee, keeper of the papers at the Foreign Office, gave his wholehearted support to that suggestion, minuting that 'such a document will be of inestimable value in the future'. What is more interesting is that history-conscious officials of the Office considered it a very worthy project. Thus, William Strang, the assistant under-secretary of state, wrote, 'the historian of the future will have to work from papers alone. If Mr Woodward does this work now, some parts of the truth may be saved which would otherwise be lost'. Halifax accordingly gave his consent on 6 December and asked that his diary be printed and also that a 'fuller record ... from all the material at the disposal of the Office' be prepared. Thus began the long period of Woodward's personal involvement with the project, which proved to be of crucial importance for the government's final decision to publish the diplomatic papers of the interwar period.

While Woodward was engaged in the initial work, the Germans published a new White Book containing nearly five hundred documents, going back to 1930, in which the central theme was that British policy since 1914 was anti-German. That publication led Woodward to strongly urge the Foreign Office to answer the Germans in the form of a set of British documents. The unmistakable importance of his personal initiative justifies reproducing his arguments in full. 'I am not looking at the matter as a kind of esoteric quarrel between rival sets of scholars over historical details,' he wrote to Strang on 15 December, 'there is an important practical side'.[6] As an historian with a keen interest in politics, he presented some 'lessons of history' which should not be lost upon British politicians:

> The public at large does not read those collections of documents, but – as the Germans know well – pubic opinion is influenced by them indirectly, and through countless works of *'vulgarisation'* based, ultimately, on the original documents. The Germans know this well because they have reaped a most valuable harvest in the years since 1919 for their case in sowing documents on a large scale in the most propitious fields. American opinion on the origins of the last war has been an important factor in determining the attitude of the American public towards the present war. This American opinion about the last war was influenced – to an extent which few people in Great Britain have realised – by the spate of books, articles and lectures in the USA inspired by the German publication of documents – *Die Grosse Politik*. The Germans got in first with their collection – they distributed its many volumes as widely as possible – and they used the whole force of German and German-American scholarship to spread the view of an innocent imperial Germany treacherously attacked by the *entente* powers. We made a good reply by publishing a set of documents of our own, but the Germans had a long start. Whereas they encouraged people to read these documents at second hand by issuing two different summarised 'guides' to them, we did nothing of this sort.

Wondering, if the Weimar Republic 'played tricks of this kind', what could be expected from the Nazis, Woodward was certain that 'we do not want this to happen again, we do not want the Germans to create this "atmosphere" in neutral countries – especially in the USA and, for that matter, among the *New Statesman* type in Great Britain' – favourable to the Germans' claim that they have been, as in 1914, victims of wicked British aggression: 'We do not want a peace conference in such an atmosphere.' The depth of the feelings that this historian harboured towards the subject was expressed in a very atypical way. 'You may think', the usually very reserved Woodward concluded his letter to Strang

> ... that as an historian I am exaggerating the importance of this wordy war about who killed Cock Robin. But I *know* I am right. I have watched the Germans at their game for years past and I wrote a learned book which had some effect, but it was only one book – to try to clear some of the German lies away ... so that you see that if I am a fanatic on the subject, the fanaticism does not date from 1 September 1939.[7]

In a private letter to Sir John Simon, late in 1941, he confessed that after publishing in 1935 his book on pre-1914 British foreign policy,[8] he had planned a work on post-1919 policy.[9] But he had hardly started when war broke out. Being over military age, Woodward first thought that the best thing for him to do would be to write as planned, or perhaps to lecture in the United States on British foreign policy. Later, however, he came to the conclusion that it would take a very long time to produce a book on an authoritative scale and that the most effective method of establishing a correct understanding of the facts of British foreign policy towards Germany and Europe would be for His Majesty's government to publish the relevant documents. With that in mind, and after what he later termed in a letter to Sir Charles Webster a 'wasted time' at the PID,[10] Woodward must have considered the publication of the German documents a golden opportunity to realise his own ideas of a very worthy service to his country. A few days later he was ready with practical suggestions for translating his plan into action.

At a meeting with Strang,[11] he made three proposals, which subsequently became the basic guidelines for selecting and preparing the documents. First, the main body of the collection should consist solely of records of contacts between Germany and Great Britain (and their representatives) which, with the necessary explanatory

connecting links, would paint the picture of Anglo-German relations; the collection would thus exclude, as far as possible, the
expression of opinions, forecasts or judgments of events by members of His Majesty's government, the Foreign Office, and the
diplomatic service. Secondly, it might be desirable to include
records of contacts between HMG and the other governments
intimately connected with specific developments, e.g., the Czech-
oslovak government during the crisis of 1938. Thirdly, the collection would start from the Locarno agreements of 1925. Strang
considered Woodward's general idea and his specific suggestions
'excellent'. Reginald Leeper, assistant under-secretary of state, in
supporting Strang, wrote that he could think of nobody better
qualified than Woodward to do the work: 'Having watched him
daily at work for four months [at the PID] I would pay a testimony
to his care and accuracy as an historian.' Woodward was thus formally asked to prepare a preliminary survey of Confidential Prints
with a view to the publication of a book of documents of his selection on Anglo-German relations from the time of the Locarno
agreements to March 1939.

The efficient Woodward completed his work in a few weeks and
the result of his survey was that the proposed book would contain
1,200 pages of documents.[12] However, no comment on the actual
selection of documents was needed at the time until a decision in
principle to publish them was made. In the meantime, Woodward
continued his work and by early June 1940 completed the actual
selection which was the major part of the work. He concluded his
examination of the documents convinced that 'their publication
would have the effect which we want to produce. The documents
show that over a series of years we did everything possible to meet
German wishes, to redress German grievances, to smooth down
European differences and to secure the full cooperation of Germany as a Great Power in the European Concert'. This historian
was 'struck by the resemblance between British policy since 1925
and British policy preceding the war of 1914. In each case we were
ready to make far-reaching and even dangerous concessions, and
in each case our efforts failed, because the Germans were not content with security or equality, but wanted domination'. Woodward wrote to Strang that he realised that at a time when his
country was fighting for its life, the publication of historical documents might well seem to many people a matter of secondary
importance. However, he still tried to convince the Foreign Office
that if the war was prolonged for many months, American public

opinion would be of vital importance and that anything which could be done to counteract German propaganda was worth trying. At the outbreak of war, the British government knew that the majority of Americans sympathised with the Allied cause and wanted Hitler to be defeated. However, this sympathy was based primarily on American ideas of right and justice, rather than on calculated American interests. Thus, one of the problems confronting the Foreign Office in the first stages of the war was that public opinion in the United States did not realise the extent to which American strategic and economic interests were connected with an Allied victory.[13] It is no wonder, then, that the Office looked favourably – *in principle* – on suggestions that could influence American public opinion. It, nevertheless, did not share Woodward's views as to *the urgency* of a decision; the matter thus lay dormant for almost ten months.

In mid-March 1941, when pressure of work apparently diminished temporarily, the Foreign Office began discussing the subject in order to decide whether or not to publish the collection of documents already at their disposal. As a preliminary procedure, Strang suggested consulting both Sir Robert Vansittart, who had been permanent under-secretary of state during half of the fourteen years covered by the documents, and Sir Horace Wilson, the permanent under-secretary of the Treasury, who had been a close adviser to Neville Chamberlain on all matters, including foreign affairs.[14] Vansittart urged prompt publication of the entire volume as 'it will be excellent propaganda'. He dismissed the notion of asking politicians and civil servants 'whether they mind the inclusion of this or that paper', since it 'might ruin the entire effort ... there can be no question of consulting Lord Simon [foreign secretary 1931–35] or Sir H. Wilson, why they more than Sir S. Hoare [foreign secretary 1935] and why any of them?' Some influential officials at the Foreign Office, however, held different opinions, the most important among them being Vansittart's successor, Alexander Cadogan. In mid-April, he wrote apologetically about not going into the matter at an earlier stage. However, after 'glancing' at some of the documents, he deplored immediate publication. His reasoning, which was later shared by some cabinet ministers, focused on his estimate of the impact which appeasement still had on British politics:

> Do we want to revive all the Munich controversy (to say nothing of earlier events) at this moment? What effect would the publication

of H. Wilson's records of talks with Hitler have in present circumstances? Do the British want convincing of Hitler's putridity? Will
not publication merely produce recrimination on the sense of the
stupidity of the Government in their being 'taken in' by Hitler
(though it is not quite so simple as all that)? I do feel that now we
do not want to step up controversy.

The Foreign Office was clearly divided on the issue. Against
Cadogan stood others who strongly urged publication, with Strang
prominent among them. After reading the entire collection, Vansittart, another supporter, gave a typically colourful exposition of
the arguments in favour of releasing the interwar diplomatic
papers, which is worth quoting in full:

[The collection] shows the Germans at their worst ... It should be
highly exploitable. In my opinion, the slithering out of the guarantee to the new Czechoslovakia was near knavery; but only the German dirty linen is here washed in public, as it well deserves, so here
again a good time is had by all but the Germans ... We shall have
nothing better for long to come. We are on velvet. Every foreigner
accepts the tradition that we are naive. He would perhaps be disappointed if we were not, or anyhow, if we did not look it. Here we
are playing to perfection. It is – particularly in view of what has
happened – the only convincing answer to that other, and fictitious
role – a quite incompatible one, which our enemies always try to
foist upon us – of *perfide Albion*. Every continental called us naive
for years because we could not see the storm coming. In these
papers we disappoint nobody and disarm many.[15]

The division within the Foreign Office was thus based on conflicting assessments of the value of publication versus the probable disadvantages, a divergence of opinions which later became
entrenched among British politicians. On the one hand, there was
the fear that publication of the documents would give rise to damaging criticism of HMG for being so foolish in trusting German
professions. On the other hand, there were desirable short and
long range propaganda effects and the readiness to take a certain
risk in order to remove the more dangerous impression that British policy had been Machiavellian without the saving quality of
success. It is a remarkable fact that, for quite a long time, the
apparent disadvantages clearly held sway. This was first mani-
fested when the matter was brought to the foreign secretary for a
final decision. After consulting his predecessor, Lord Halifax,
Eden decided early in July against publication. Then followed several representations, apparently the most important one by Oliver

Harvey, Eden's private secretary, who urged publication for the reasons previously expressed and who tried to convince him that it would not stir up political controversy. 'The fact that all parties in Britain are equally responsible' for the appeasement policy, he wrote, 'seems to mitigate the chances of this'. Eden then changed his mind and on 9 August came to the conclusion that, on balance, publication should be 'to the national advantage'. The issue was thus elevated from the realm of internal debates within the Foreign Office to what proved to be the much more hostile arena of the cabinet.

In consenting to publication, Eden decided to consult those politicians and civil servants who were involved in British foreign policy during the 1930s regarding documents that concerned them personally. This, in turn, created considerable obstacles in realising the project. The first was Sir H. Wilson's strong objection to the publication of four documents dealing with the Munich crisis. Harvey wrote in his diary that Wilson 'is kicking wildly at his part in the Munich proceedings',[16] but Wilson said that the reason for the objection was that publication of these documents 'may well give rise to fresh controversy' and 'raises a question of taste'.[17] Wilson was reluctant to agree to the publication of his notes on the Munich conference and of Mr Chamberlain's notes of his conversation with Hitler on 30 September 1938, also on the grounds that the records would have been prepared 'differently' had they been intended for release. At the same time, he claimed that the Berchtesgaden and Bad Godesberg meetings were covered pretty fully in Chamberlain's speech to the House of Commons on 27 September. These arguments could hardly have carried conviction within the Foreign Office. Roger Makins of the Central Department at the Office, echoed the prevalent reaction when minuting that 'by the very fact that they do not add very much to what is already known or inferred', the documents that aroused Wilson's opposition 'will draw the sting from any further criticism', while at the same time, 'they are rare among diplomatic documents for the vivid and unforced character of the style and for the manner in which they reveal the intention of the negotiators and the atmosphere in which the conversation took place'. Woodward naturally shared these views and added another consideration which militated against tampering with or amending the records (except where strictly necessary) and which also showed the extent to which his attention focused on issues beyond his pure historical profession:

Among other considerations which seem to me to make the publication of this corpus of documents [desirable] now is the possibility ... that the trend of post-war politics in Britain might well lead to a demand for the publication of documents on lines, and for reasons which we should deprecate most strongly (e.g., 'grand inquest' into pre-war diplomacy). The present 'controlled' publication should go a long way to avoid this risk of 'uncontrolled' or 'unsatisfactorily controlled' publication, but it can do so if the documents are 'cut' only for obvious reasons of state not if they [are] cut in order to avoid chances of criticism of particular points.

A reply on these lines was accordingly sent to Wilson in late September, expressing the hope that 'on reconsideration' he would agree that the decision to publish the documents as they stood was 'well founded'. Wilson, however, was not convinced, and in a letter three weeks later he again expressed serious reservations, but added that if his views were finally rejected, he would want to make a few verbal changes in the notes of the Munich conference. Eden, determined 'not to falsify history', made it absolutely clear to Wilson that no changes could be made in the documents.

Wilson's objection was relatively easy to waive. It was similarly not difficult to convince Lord Cranborne, Eden's under-secretary during the late 1930s, who, while supporting the idea of publication, confessed to the foreign secretary early in October that the 'dreadful document' [the record of Hitler's conversation with Chamberlain on 26 September] describing 'our readiness to bully and batter the Czechs and to do anything however contemptible to avoid war makes me blush and is bound to create a deplorable impression both in the U.S. and in the occupied countries themselves'.[18] This was not the case with the reservations expressed by Eden's predecessor. Halifax had tried to persuade the foreign secretary that the collection should not be released, but after meeting with him late in September, he agreed to leave the decision in Eden's hands,[19] apparently because he realised that Eden himself was hesitant about the advantages of publication. Thus, early in October, Eden wrote, very unenthusiastically, 'I did not start this business though I am ready to see it through'.[20] Harvey found out to his dismay a few weeks later that his minister 'had suddenly developed fresh qualms about publication of British documents ... A.E. is anxious about the effect on his own reputation and fears he may look like an appeaser too'.[21]

Eden could hardly avoid a definite decision when, late in November, it became clear that his predecessors in office in the 1930s all came out in favour of publication. Hoare wrote to say that he was sure Eden 'was wise'.[22] At the same time, Halifax, after thinking over his conversation [with Eden] 'revised his first opinion',[23] and Simon informed the foreign secretary that after talking to Woodward in All Souls and 'glancing' through some of the bundles of papers proposed for print, he was entirely converted to the view that 'it was a good thing to take a decision on publication on the principle that it is half the battle to get your blow in first'.[24] This must have come as a great surprise to the Foreign Office, which was aware of Simon's strong reservations on the subject.[25] In view of his previous attitude and his later very stubborn (and effective) opposition to carrying out the project, the only reasonable explanation of why Simon gave his blessing in November is that the shrewd politician must have realised that it would be much easier to exercise his influence when the matter was referred to the cabinet. And indeed, when Eden put the plan for publishing the diplomatic documents to the cabinet on 1 December, its attitude was hardly positive.[26]

In the discussion, the question was again raised of whether publication at that time might not revive old controversies and therefore tend to weaken the war effort. Churchill's reservations at that meeting were significant. He noted that while few people would read such a long publication, there was the risk that a particular document or passage might be excerpted out of context and to rake up past failures. While not objecting in principle to publication, he was against the timing and thought that it would be more advantageous 'after some success by our armed forces'. Churchill must have realised that some members of his cabinet were against publication, prominent among them Sir John Simon, the lord chancellor. He accordingly suggested that in order to give the cabinet the benefit of the view of some ministers – Simon in particular – who would have read the proposed volume by then, the decision be postponed for three months. The cabinet agreed. The Foreign Office initiative was thus blocked – at least temporarily – and Harvey described it as 'disheartening … [it] makes one despair of our government, such lack of confidence in the people, such signal failure to realise the right of the people to see their official documents'.[27]

The cabinet decision was however not definitely negative, and the Foreign Office waited for comments, especially from Simon, before raising the matter again. It proved to be a very long wait indeed. After four months, the Office discovered that Lord Simon 'was still reading the volume',[28] but on Woodward's advice, the department decided to leave the matter open a little longer, until the cabinet was less preoccupied with events in the Far East. Roberts found out later that month that Simon seemed to have 'some renewed doubts' about publication; a junior official, who, on instruction, casually approached the lord chancellor, received an answer that was evasive, but at the same time left little doubt that the minister was against publication. Eden decided to 'leave it' to Woodward: 'When he thinks the moment ripe, I am ready to approach Lord Simon or raise the matter in the cabinet.' Woodward, on his part, though naturally in favour of following 'Stresemann's preference for getting into a cold bath at once if you have to take one', recommended waiting a little before again raising the question in the cabinet. He wrote to say that the ministers had had to put up with a good deal of 'unfair' criticism in the last few months and that he therefore would not blame them if they did not show eagerness at that moment to run what some of them, including Simon, felt to be 'risks of supererogation in supplying ammunition to any silly candidate at a by-election or to the Kingsley Martin type of slapdash journalists'. His suggestion, which Eden regarded as 'very sound', was to bring up the question of the documents after some political success that would 'silence the carpers'.

Woodward soon learned that it would take much more than that to convince Simon and the cabinet. On 8 May, Lord Simon utterly surprised the Foreign Office by circulating among the cabinet a paper which, while purporting to briefly put forth the 'pros and cons in the hope that this may help the war cabinet to come to a decision' was actually a blank rejection of the idea of publishing the diplomatic papers of the interwar period.[29] His arguments did not sway Woodward and the Foreign Office. Indeed, Simon was blamed for ignoring the most important considerations. His first argument was that 'diplomatic documents can at best only recount part of history' and need to be supplemented by parliamentary speeches and a record of the tendencies of British opinion. This, of course, was not an argument against publication but a suggestion that additional material be introduced. It also overlooked the plain fact that the parliamentary speeches Simon wanted to include, which were already accessible in published form, 'had not convinced people'. His second and third arguments – which suggested that few people would read the documents because everyone knew that Hitler started the war – clearly missed the central objective of the countering of the charges that British policy towards Germany from 1925 led to the rise of Hitler and that the policy between 1933 and 1938/9 was responsible for giving Hitler a free run in Europe. His fourth argument – that publication might arouse 'biased controversy' which would adversely affect 'maximum unity' at home and with Britain's allies – could hardly carry conviction within the Foreign Office.

What the department, and many of Simon's colleagues as well, had perhaps not realised was the extent to which the ex-foreign secretary was personally sensitive to criticism of his part in formulating and executing British foreign policy in the 1930s. His private papers, which have only recently become public, clearly and unmistakably attest to this phenomenon and, no less relevant to our story, to the tactics that he constantly employed to avoid such apparently very painful criticism.[30] In a letter to a friend late in 1942, Simon wrote very frankly that he had had to put up with all sorts of ill-informed and 'unkind' criticism which was 'unpleasant to those who admire Neville Chamberlain as I did and do', and that to attempt to deal with it publicly would only give it prominence and circulation which it 'does not deserve'. He felt that the wisest reaction was to refrain from action. 'If you want to escape criticism the best thing is to say nothing, do nothing and be nothing.'[31] It is hardly surprising, then, that the lord chancellor was apparently very worried lest this silence be broken, and strove to prevent it.

Simon's behaviour forced the Foreign Office to change its tactics. Although they preferred to wait for a more appropriate moment to press the matter, they could not afford to leave the lord chancellor's memorandum unanswered. Thus, the Foreign Office presented their case in form of a cabinet paper in mid-August and forced a decision.[32] The paper was noteworthy for two reasons. First, the Foreign Office called attention to the importance of discrediting the Russian idea that British policy before the war was aimed at placating Germany and embroiling the U.S.S.R. in conflict with Germany, an idea which would have 'unfortunate ... effects upon decisions of post-war policy in regard to Germany'. Secondly, forced to request a decision in the face of a reluctant cabinet, the Foreign Office suggested that the date on which publication should take place be left to the foreign secretary's discretion. A showdown thus became inevitable, and on 7 September the cabinet debated the subject. Simon succeeded in enlisting the support of a number of ministers. Prominent among them was Sir Kingsley Wood, the chancellor of the exchequer. The latter strongly backed his ideas in a paper circulated to the cabinet. Simon's faction carried the majority; the decision reached was that the documents should be prepared for publication but then await 'further authority from the cabinet'. Woodward was naturally very frustrated and later divulged his feelings to Edward Bridges, the cabinet secretary:

> I think my temporary boss (It is odd for me to have a boss in my late middle age – never having had one all my life heretofore) realises [the necessity of publication] but his ministerial colleagues seem too busy to bother at all. I also wish I could persuade Lord Simon that his stock can not go lower but rise a little by the publication of some of his despatches. The poor man has even tried bribery on me. Last All Souls Day he asked me whether I had any ex-pupil I would care to support for a living in the gift of the lord chancellor.[33]

Woodward understood that what he termed the 'immediate aims' of the collection – disproving the thesis of the German White Book and demonstrating to the United States the danger of a German victory in Europe – had, by early 1943, clearly become much less relevant,[34] in large measure because public interest in both Britain and the United States had turned from questions of prewar policy to matters affecting the peace settlement and post-war reconstruction. However, he still felt that the 'long range' goal was not affected. Indeed, he strongly believed, and tried to convince his colleagues at the Foreign Office, that the question of the ultimate responsibility for the war – involving accusations that the policy of appeasement always implicitly meant 'surrender' to fascism, and the view that the Foreign Office failed to perform its proper functions during the interwar period – made it absolutely necessary to publish the collection of documents which he had prepared. But nothing could be done in those circumstances of late 1942.

Three important developments early in 1943, however, made it possible to raise the issue again. First, the U.S. government had by then published a book entitled *Peace and War: U.S. Foreign Policy 1931–1941*, which constituted an apologia for American policy in the face of increasing threats of aggression by the Axis Powers during the decade between the Mukden incident and Pearl Harbour. This was to be supplemented by a collection of documents. Secondly, the U.S. State Department, which for more than a century had been publishing a continuous series of diplomatic correspondence covering the main features of American foreign policy, started to produce volumes covering controversial issues – such as the Disarmament Conference – in which the British were clearly interested and about which it would have been particularly desirable that their version of events should be made known. And thirdly, during these months, there arose in both houses of parliament pressure for the publication of documents illustrating the conduct of foreign affairs before the war. While these developments made the early publication of British documents seem more necessary, they marked a change in the perspective from which publication was initially advocated. It was clear that the Anglo-German collection, which was then ready, would cover only part of the field embraced by the American documents, and the Foreign Office was naturally displeased that the only authoritative records of international relations during the prewar period would come from American sources and that compilers of textbooks would have to rely on the American view of events. That, in turn, led to the suggestion that in addition to the early publication of the Anglo-German collection, work should commence as soon as possible on a *general collection* of documents illustrating the whole spectrum of British foreign policy from 1925, the year of Locarno.

In discussions within the Foreign Office during March and April, it became apparent that such a collection, while able to show that HMG was certainly not less well informed about the Axis Powers by the Foreign Office and British mission in Berlin than was the U.S. government by American diplomatic services in Europe, could well invite other forms of criticism to which the original collection was not subject. Woodward drew the department's attention to the fact that 'if we had included all the "warning" information (e.g., some of Sir H. Rumbold's despatches) received by the Foreign Office since 1933 or some of the "warning" memoranda (e.g., those of Lord Vansittart) or minutes (e.g., those of Sir O. Sargent) written in the Foreign Office, the impression given by the *collection* would be different. The Foreign Office would come out of it with more credit, but I doubt whether this would be the case with HMG'. Thus, the Foreign Office could hardly oppose the idea of a complete documentary history of British foreign relations. Other difficulties, e.g., the controversial aspects of Anglo-French and Anglo-Russian relations, were more seriously considered. Woodward himself was of the opinion that if a decision on the more general collection were likely to be made in the near future, he would suggest postponing the separate publication of the

Anglo-German documents. However, if that decision were delayed, he would act 'on the principle *le mieux est l'ennemi du bien'* and proceed at once with the publication of the Anglo-German documents. At the end of May, Eden finally decided to take the matter to the cabinet with a view to reaching a decision to publish the Anglo-German collection 'in the near future' and to start preparing a general collection of documents from 1925 on.

While the Foreign Office was preparing a paper to circulate to the cabinet, an unexpected obstacle to the seemingly less ambitious publication of the Anglo-German collection arose.[35] On 15 July, Sir George Gater of the Colonial Office wrote to say that they strongly deplored the publication of the documents as they stood because of the documents relating to Neville Henderson's interview with Hitler on 3 March 1938 about the territories in Africa. The plan which His Majesty's government then had in mind was that as a contribution to a general settlement with Germany, the possibility should be explored of setting up a special colonial regime – in which Germany would participate – embracing roughly the areas lying south of the Sahara, Anglo-Egyptian Sudan, Italian Somaliland, the areas north of the Union of South Africa, and Northern and Southern Rhodesia. Germany would, according to this plan, receive an appropriate share of these territories; all the colonial powers concerned would make concessions and sign a convention of special undertakings with regard to the preservation of native rights, freedom of trade, a degree of disarmament, etc. The matter was not pursued following the annexation of Austria. Nevertheless, the Colonial Office considered that the publication of these documents would have 'disastrous results'. Gater elaborated: 'it would play straight into the hands of those sections in the colonies which wish to throw off Downing Street control and thus to ensure that at no future date should their fortunes be subject, as they were evidently in 1938, to the perilous vicissitudes of European politics'. 'As you know', he explained to Cadogan, 'there are plenty of critics of imperialism and when the Armistice comes we shall need every argument which we can use to establish our right to the continued control of our colonial territories.' Woodward, perceiving that if the Colonial Office imposed a veto on the publication of the 1938 proposals, they 'are thus imposing a veto on the whole plan of publication', reacted immediately with a long memorandum explaining that examination of these proposals in detail and in context would show that the facts were not entirely surprising and that the proposals neither constituted an 'old-style' political deal for the sole advantage of Great Britain, nor involved 'any disregard of native rights'.

The assessment within the Foreign Office – which Woodward shared – was that a confrontation in cabinet against the Colonial Office could only lead to an indefinite postponement of publication. It was accordingly decided to try to come to an understanding with the Colonial Office before taking any further action.[36] However, after it became clear late in September that no such agreement could be reached, Eden decided to take the matter to a higher authority.[37] Thus, just before leaving for Moscow in early October 1943, he asked Churchill to consider the objections of the Colonial Office and possibly to deal with the matter in his absence, since it was to be expected that before long questions would be asked in parliament. The prime minister agreed to 'take charge' of the matter, but asked to see the documents in question, especially the 'spicy bits'. These were submitted to him on 14 October, together with Cadogan's note that Eden wished him to add that the documents were 'untouched' and that he could not agree to any omissions and modifications since 'once that were started, all concerned would be wanting to improve their own parts'. In his reply four days later, the prime minister opined that there was no need to rush publication and said that he would prefer to wait until Eden's return from Moscow. Not only did Churchill find 'what was actually meant' in the proposed colonial agreement of 1938 to be unclear, he also thought it 'a pity that Mr Eden's name should be mixed up directly with appeasement'. No less significant were his apprehensions lest the publication of these documents harm South Africa. Churchill was very reluctant to run the risk of doing anything that General Smuts – his close and admired friend, who not only had been out with him 'in all weathers'[38] but whose advice he sought constantly during the war – would find offensive or undesirable. Accordingly, he asked the Foreign Office to solicit the view of the elder statesman. Churchill's reaction made it clear that the battle for publication was, if anything, far from being resolved in favour of the Foreign Office.

Woodward was near despair, for almost five years had passed since the question of publishing a collection of documents was first raised. He thus came to the conclusion that a different publication proposal should be presented. 'It is clear', he wrote late in October, 'that we *must* publish something and that whereas in the winter of 1939–40 our primary purpose was to contradict Ribbentrop, this purpose must be widened to include "keeping our end up" with the State Department.' His colleagues, however, were reluctant to depart from the previous intentions. Roberts, who had strongly urged publication in preparing memoranda submitted to the War Cabinet, thought 'it would look very odd, to say the least, if we now say that we have changed our minds and propose to publish quite a different set of documents'. His view, which was shared by Cadogan, was that they should continue pressing for the publication of the Anglo-German collection and at the same time obtain authority to prepare a wider collection of documents.

They were forced to change their minds, however, after 20 November, when General Smuts, to whom the documents had been sent for study, wrote deploring publication 'in the heat of the struggle'.[39] Supporting the Colonial Office claims unequivocally, the general, 'as an African and one of those concerned in African leadership', sounded a 'warning note' against publication and its possible repercussions on public opinion. 'I do not see', he added, 'why we cannot delay publication till after the war, when interest in them will be more or less of an historical character only.'

In the meantime, however, the Foreign Office realised that the powerful opposition to publication made it necessary to reconsider the whole proposition.[40] Woodward understood that the only alternative open was to advocate publication of a general series on British foreign policy in the interwar period. The publication of a series of documents on the line of the American volumes provided the only way to avoid severe criticism and opposition. Again, it was Woodward who put the case very convincingly to the Foreign Office. He explained that the scale of the undertaking necessitated that several volumes be published; the first volumes of the proposed new series would not include the critical period after 1934. Woodward thus thought the objection raised to the publication of documents covering the years 1938–39 would not apply 'and this stream could be crossed when we reached it, probably, in calmer weather', some years later. He proposed starting the series simultaneously from 1919 and from 1930 in order to keep up with the American publications – and at the same time to close the gap of the early part of the interwar period. Reluctantly, Foreign Office officials agreed and Eden concluded the deliberation in minuting that they 'could certainly go ahead with Woodward's recommendations'. The matter was discussed in cabinet on 27 January 1944, and, as expected by the Foreign Office, the publication of British diplomatic papers on the lines of Woodward's plan was finally authorised.[41] The decision became public as a result of an inspired question in parliament on 29 March.[42]

That decision was not the concluding chapter of the story. As noted, the fact that the critical period of 1938–39 would not be dealt with for quite a long time made it easier to gain approval of the cabinet. Developments after the war, however, seemed to alter the situation and led to renewed debate within the government. Early in 1947, when plans for the orderly publication of the British documents had already matured, the U.S. and the French governments decided to publish selections from German documents captured after the war. The Foreign Office felt that Great Britain would be at a disadvantage should the German version of the events immediately preceding the outbreak of war be made available to the world some years in advance of the corresponding British documents.[43] Other developments were equally undesirable from the Foreign Office's point of view. First, the number of memoirs published by foreign statesmen dealing directly or indirectly with British foreign policy was growing. Secondly, the official American series of documents, the *Foreign Relations of the United States*, was forging ahead and would probably reach the 1938–39 period well in advance of the British counterpart. Finally, other governments were publishing their own documents on the events of the period. All that, according to the feeling prevailing at the Foreign Office, had another deplorable effect – the growing belief, both at home and abroad, that His Majesty's government had something shady to hide regarding the negotiations preceding Munich. These developments led to the suggestion of publishing – out of the chronological sequence originally proposed in 1944 – a *third* series of documents covering the years 1938–39.

It is a remarkable fact, however, that the Foreign Office – which had previously been quite willing to risk possible criticism for lack of wisdom or foresight resulting from publication of the diplomatic papers – were extremely worried and hesitant when the time came to actually release the documents covering those critical years. Some difficulties were obvious, e.g., the possible reactions of the Soviet Union to certain revelations concerning activities of British diplomats and military attachés. However, this type of problem had been tackled before, when discussing the publication of Anglo-German documents. Apparently, the fact that a mere ten years separated British officials from the traumatic events of the eve of war, combined with the fact that the documents were to cover the entire field of British foreign policy –

including relations with countries which, at least technically, were friendly – lay behind the unmistakable lack of enthusiasm on the part of some Foreign Office officials for the proposed third series and behind a certain inclination to omit comparatively important documents. It was again Woodward who took an active part in internal debates on the subject. 'My own view', he wrote early in December 1947, 'may, of course, be affected by the facts that the burden of the disadvantage would not fall on me, and that as a student and observer without executive responsibility, I incline to think that we have done ourselves harm by the unusual care which we show for other people's susceptibilities.' More important, he reminded his colleagues that sooner or later all the documents of that period would be open to inspection in public archives and if it were then discovered that important documents had been left out of the collection, the credit of the series and reputation of the Foreign Office would certainly suffer.

Woodward was not alone in this opinion. Consequently, after a few months of indecision, early in March 1948 Sir Orme Sargent, the permanent under-secretary, presented to the foreign secretary, Ernest Bevin, the case favouring the third series.[44] Bevin agreed, and on 22 March 1948, so did the cabinet.[45] The documents have subsequently been published according to directives that took almost nine years to finalise.

Several concluding remarks are in order. Had it not been for external pressure – mainly the publication of documents by other countries – the British government would probably not have decided in 1944 to authorise the publication of the diplomatic papers of the interwar period. The battle for publicity was finally won largely because the government could not allow itself to be left by the Americans, their very strong reluctance to abandon secrecy notwithstanding.[46]

The evolution of Britain's decision to publish these papers brings to light the critical role of the Foreign Office in the decision-making process. Paradoxically, it was the Foreign Office, which traditionally preached secrecy, that fought for publicity.[47] There were many reasons for this unique stand. A very important one, though never expressed in cabinet papers, was the bitterness and frustration within the Foreign Office as a result of public attacks on their role in formulating and executing the policy of appeasement. It is hardly surprising, therefore, that within the framework of the anti-appeasement viewpoint the Office comes out well from the published documents.[48] Another point that should be made in this context, and which redounds to the credit of the Foreign Office, is that at no time during the long period of debate over publication did they really try to impair Woodward's freedom to choose the documents to be published. This certainly took a considerable degree of courage and integrity.

Lastly, our story highlights the centrality of Professor E.L. Woodward in the process leading to publication. That was the result of a rare combination of factors: Woodward's distinct talent for exercising influence on both large questions of policy and minor, though important, issues of implementation, and also the remarkable trust of officials in an 'outsider' historian.[49] It is clear that Woodward's extraordinary efficiency, his mastery of the indispensable tool of memoranda writing, and his obvious understanding of the dictum that politics is the art of the possible, secured him a unique position in the Foreign Office that led to his ultimate success.

———

I am grateful to Mr R. Butler of All Souls College, Oxford, for his very useful information and advice. I am indebted to Professor N. Rose and Professor M. Verete of the Hebrew University of Jerusalem and to Mr M. Gilbert for their valuable comments on an early draft of this essay.

Notes

1. G.P. Gooch and H. Temperley, eds., *British Documents on the Origins of the War, 1898–1914* (London, 1926–38).
2. The series was published in 1922–27 and edited by J. Lepsius, A. Mendelssohn-Bartholdy and F. Thimme. See on it H. Koch, ed., *The Origins of the First World War* (London, 1972), pp. 1–13.
3. The introductions to the series *Documents on British Foreign Policy 1919–1939* are very laconic on the subject. The reviews of the series are likewise devoid of any information on it. See, for example, 'The Secrets of Diplomacy', in *The Times Literary Supplement*, 12 April 1947; W. Medicott's review in the *English Historical Review* LXIII (1948), 120–5; C. Read's reviews in the *American Historical Review* LVIII (1948–9), 307–14, 854–6; and Woodward's replies to his critics in the *Times Literary Supplement*, 26 April 1947, and in the *American Historical Review* LVIII (1948–49), 782–4.

4. Foreign Office Records, Public Record Office, Kew (hereafter F.O.) 371/22987,C/ 20648/G, is the source of the following excerpts until otherwise indicated.

5. Sir Ernest Llewellyn Woodward (1890–1971) was born into a middle class London family and was educated at Corpus Christi College, Oxford. After completing his studies in 1913, he became a senior scholar at St John's. During the First World War he served in France and Salonika. Returning to Oxford he became a regular fellow of All Souls, a status he was to hold until 1944. In that year he became Montague Burton professor of international relations at Oxford, a chair that he held until 1947, when he changed it for the Regius chair in modern history. In 1951 he accepted a call to the Institute for Advanced Study at Princeton University, where he remained until his retirement. His writings include *Christianity and Nationalism in the Later Roman Empire* (London, 1916); *Three Studies in European Conservatism* (London, 1930); *War and Peace in Europe, 1818–1870* (London, 1931); *French Revolutions* (Oxford, 1934); *Great Britain and the German Navy* (Oxford, 1935); *The Age of Reform, 1815–1870* (Oxford, 1938); *British Foreign Policy in the Second World War* (London, 1962) (4 vols. London 1970–75); and as editor with R. Butler, *Documents on British Foreign Policy 1919–1939* (London, 1947–55). On Woodward, see R. Butler's perceptive description in the *Proceedings of the British Academy* LVII (1971), 497–511. His private papers, which are deposited at Worcester College, Oxford, are inaccessible for research; however, Woodward did leave a subtly reflective autobiography, *Short Journey* (London, 1942).

6. FO 371/22987, C/20489/15/18, is the source of the following excerpts until otherwise indicated.

7. It is interesting to note that his ideas concerning German guilt in instigating the First World War notwithstanding, Woodward did not regard other countries, including his own, as free from responsibility for that catastrophic event. In a revealing memorandum, written while he was doing his preliminary research at the Foreign Office, he claimed that although Germany was to blame for 'taking the lead' in the wild quest for power, 'the independent sovereign states of Europe ... tended without exception to look to the increase or maintenance of state power as their main end'. That, according to him, created the 'European Anarchy'. 'Independent Sovereign States in Europe', 24 October 1939, FO 800/325.

8. Woodward, *Great Britain*. It should be noted that Woodward was invited by the Foreign Office in the spring of 1936 to write an analysis of the philosophy of *Mein Kampf*. That had been done in order to both understand and exploit the autobiography of Germany's head of state. See J. Barnes and P. Barnes, *Hitler's Mein Kampf in Britain and America; A Publishing History, 1930–39* (Cambridge, 1980), pp. 41–42.

9. 4 December 1941. F.O. 371/26579, C/13417 is the basis for the following account until otherwise indicated.

10. 8 August 1942. Webster papers, London School of Economics 1/23. That letter includes a revealing confession by Woodward on his feelings during the early stages of war which is worth quoting: 'It is a queer thing that, in the last war (when) we were young, we saw the ablest and best of our contemporaries killed as junior officers when they should have been singled out for high military responsibilities, and in this war when we have behind us years of experience and of the exercise of judgment and authority, we cannot get into the key positions controlling policy and executive action within the sphere of our

special competence.' Webster actually did take an active part in formulating some crucial decisions during the war; see E. Hughes and P. Reynolds, *The Historian As Diplomat* (London, 1976). On historians in war, see D.C. Watt, 'Every War Must End. War-Time Planning for Post-War Security in Britain and America in the Wars of 1914–18 and 1939–45: The Roles of Historical Examples and Professional Historians', in *Transactions of the Royal Historical Society* xxvii (1978), 159–73.

11. F.O. 371/22987, C/20489/15/18 and F.O. 371/24403, C/273/88/18, are the basis and source of the following account and excerpts until otherwise indicated.

12 .F.O. 371/24403, C/1527/88/18, is the basis and source of the following account and excerpts until otherwise indicated.

13 .See Woodward, *British Foreign Policy*, I, 155–64.

14. F.O. 371/26579 is the basis and source of the following account and excerpts until otherwise indicated.

15. 30 May 1941. F.O. 371/26579, C/7366/7366/18 is the basis and source of the following account and excerpts until otherwise indicated. On Vansittart, see N. Rose, *Vansittart* (London, 1978).

16. Entry in diary on 15 September 1941, in J. Harvey, ed., *The War Diaries of Oliver Harvey 1941–45* (London, 1978), p. 43.

17. F.O. 371/26579, C/9416/7366/18, is the basis and source of the following account and excerpts until otherwise indicated.

18. 5 October 1941. F.O. 371/26579, C/11032/7366/18.

19. See F.O. 371/26579, C/10407/7366/18, C/13145/7366/18, and Harvey's entry in his diary on 19 September 1941, Harvey, *Diaries*, p. 61.

20. F.O. 371/26579, C/11032/7366/18.

21. Entry in diary, 8 November 1941, Harvey, *Diaries*, p. 61. At least one high ranking official at the office did not regard these fears as groundless. Thus, three weeks later, in deploring the idea of publication Cadogan wrote 'Does A. [Anthony Eden] realise that *he* is responsible for the great and tragic appeasement – no reacting to German occupation of the Rhineland in 1936? How lucky he is – no one has ever mentioned *that*! and *that* was the turning point'. Entry in diary on 1 December 1941 in D. Dilks, ed., *The Diaries of Alexander Cadogan, 1938–1941* (London, 1971), p. 415.

22. 31 October 1941. F.O. 371/26579, C/12127/7366/18.

23. Makins' notes on 24 November. F.O. 371/26579, C/13145/7366/18.

24. 7 November 1941, in ibid.

25. See Harvey's entry in his diary on 6 October 1941, in Harvey, *Diaries*, p. 48.

26. F.O. 371/25579, C/13362/7366/18 and C/13417/7366/18, are the basis and source of the following account and excerpts until otherwise indicated.

27. Entry in his diary on 29 November 1941, which must have been written on 1 December following the cabinet decision of that date. Harvey, *Diaries*, p. 67.

28. Roberts's minutes on 5 March 1942, in F.O. 371/30945, C/3622/2165/18; this is the basis and source of the following account and excerpts until otherwise indicated.

29. F.O. 371/30945, C/4932/2165/18, is the basis and source of the following account and excerpts until otherwise indicated.

30. See, *inter alia*, his correspondence with Lord Strabolgi in June 1940, with C.E. Roberts in November 1940, and with F. Archer in November 1943; Simon papers, Bodleian Library, Oxford.

31. Letter to G.H. Cuming Bulter, 24 July 1942, Simon papers.

32. War paper 364 (1942), F.O. 371/30945, C/8072/2165/18, is the basis and source of the following account and excerpts. See also, Harvey, *Diaries*, p. 153.
33. 31 March 1943, Cab. 103/218. On Woodward's futile efforts to persuade Simon to change his mind, see also his letter on 7 October 1942, Simon papers.
34. F.O. 371/34477, C/5025/1558/18, is the basis and source of the following account and excerpts until otherwise indicated.
35. F.O. 371/34477, C/7383/1558/18 is the basis and source of the following account and excerpts until otherwise stated.
36. See F.O. 371/34477, C/9260/1558/18. It should be noted that as early as February 1940, the Foreign Office was debating the question of whether to include in their Germany prints for departmental use the documents relating to the African issue. The fact that it was then decided *not* to print them, even for internal use, stands in marked contrast to the strong backing that the Foreign Office gave Woodward three years later to secure their publication. It is a distinct proof not only of Woodwards's status, but also of the Foreign Office's integrity; see F.O. 371/24403, C/3547/88/18.
37. F.O. 371/34478/A, C/12405/1558/18, is the basis and source of the following account and excerpts until otherwise indicated.
38. See W. Hancock, *Smuts: The Field of Force, 1919–1950* (London, 1968), p. 7. In a telegram to Roosevelt on 24 October 1942, Churchill described Smuts as 'one of the finest men in the world', Churchill papers. I am grateful to Mr Martin Gilbert for bringing this information to my attention. On Churchill's relations with Smuts, see also Lord Moran (Charles Wilson), *Winston Churchill: Struggle for Survival* (London, 1966), pp. 146–7, 317.
39. F.O. 371/34478A, C/13904/1558/18, is the basis and source of the following account and excerpts until otherwise indicated.
40. F.O. 371/34478A, C/14000/1558/18, is the basis and source of the following account and excerpts until otherwise indicated.
41. F.O. 371/39084, C/1311/G.
42. F.O. 371/39084, C/4162/G.
43. F.O. 370/1801, L/6495/1744/402, is the basis and source of the following account and excerpts until otherwise indicated.
44. F.O. 370/1704.
45. Cab. 128/12.
46. The broad subject of publicity versus secrecy in British foreign policy in the era of the two world wars could be fully analysed only by a comparative research dealing with other major decisions taken by the British government, such as the establishment of the Fifty-Year Rule concerning access to the government documents (see on this D.C. Watt, 'Foreign Affairs, the Public Interest and the Right to Know', in *Political Quarterly* xxxiv, 2 April 1963), its replacement in 1967 by the Thirty-Year Rule, and the decision concerning publication of the diplomatic papers of the period preceding the First World War.
47. It should be noted in this context, however, that the Foreign Office banned publication by Woodward during the war on the diplomatice origins of the war. In November 1943, the Ministry of Information suggested that Woodward write a book for them on the diplomatic origins of the war. The book would be commissioned by the ministry, but published under the imprint of a private publisher for distribution in newly liberated Europe. Eden decided in December to defer a decision until Woodward prepared a test chapter. When the historian had done so by March 1944, the Foreign Office was reluctant to

authorise publication of the book. Eden also had reservations about assuming even indirect responsibility for a work dealing with the very controversial issues surrounding diplomatic events before the outbreak of the war, e.g., judgements on Neville Chamberlain's policy and motives and on the views of those who criticised him. The decision to regularly publish a comprehensive collection of the interwar documents also seemed to officials to render super-fluous any special accounts of the prewar period; as Harvey put it, 'they are, in fact, what historians and publicists want to see rather than an official write-up'. Much to Woodward's regret, the decision was finally made to drop the idea of writing the book. (The above account is based on and the excerpt is taken from F.O. 371/39084, C/3357, and F.O. 370/1082.) During his service with the Foreign Office, Woodward had worked on a diplomatic history of the immediate origins of the war. This was undertaken on the secretary of state's instruction, but for internal use, not designated for publication. (See F.O. 370/1808, F.O. 371/30894, C/4308/4308/18, and Cab. 103/317–8 and Woodward's letter to Halifax on 11 November 1943, Halifax papers, King's College, Cambridge, 410/3/10, II.) The final work of 346 pages was never published, nor was it used in the introduction to Woodward's first volume of *British Foreign Policy in the Second World War* (see F.O. 370/1808 and Sargent's letter to Sir Norman Brook on 21 April 1948 in F.O. 370/1704). The present writer failed to trace it at the Public Record Office.

48. See T. Desmond Williams, 'The Historiography of World War II', in E.M. Robertson, ed., *The Origins of the Second World War* (London, 1971), p. 46.

49. A very frank, though not unique, expression of this is given in H. Grey's private letter to Sargent on 12 December 1947 in F.O. 370/1808, L/6495/1744/402.

Appendix

HAROLD WILSON AND THE ADOPTION OF THE THIRTY-YEAR RULE IN GREAT BRITAIN

In April 1924 C.K. Webster maintained that 'the public papers should be the property of the public, and it is suggested that after forty years no possible harm could result'. On the last clause the permanent under-secretary at the Foreign Office, Sir Eyre Crowe, minuted: 'This is not a sound proposition.' In April 1947 the points made by A.J.P. Taylor similarly fell on deaf ears. He described *Documents on British Foreign Policy 1919–1939* as 'no more than a glorified Blue Book', illustrated the fact that the policy of the editors was neither as open nor as independent as that even of Gooch and Temperley, and advocated the unrestricted examination of the archives (then closed after the year 1885) up to 1919 – in effect an interval of thirty years. He ended by recalling how Palmerston, in the 1860s, had objected to the revelation of material relating to 'so recent a period' as the wars with France of the 1790s; nevertheless, 'these departments are the servants of the public; and the British Government can have nothing to hide either from the British public or from the rest of the world after the individuals concerned had left their service'.

On June 1962 *The Times* published an article by H.G. Nicholas entitled 'Foreign Historians Get First Say'. This quoted President Kennedy's letter of 6 September 1961 to the State Department:

> The effectiveness of democracy as a form of government depends on an informed and intelligent citizenry. Nowhere is the making of choices more important than in foreign affairs; nowhere does government have a more imperative duty to make available as swiftly as possible all the facts required for intelligent decision.
>
> In recent years the publication of the Foreign Relations series has fallen farther and farther behind currency. The lag has now reached approximately 20 years. I regard this as unfortunate and undesirable. It is the policy of this Administration to unfold the historical record as fast and as fully as is consistent with national security and with friendly relations with foreign nations.
>
> Accordingly I herewith request all departments, agencies and libraries of the Government to collaborate actively and fully with the Department of State in its efforts to prepare and publish the record of our diplomacy. In my view, any official should have a clear and precise case involving the national interest

before seeking to withhold from publication documents or papers 15 or more years old.

Nicholas' article, which ended by pointing out that under the current British rules free enquiry was confined to 'the dangerous topicalities of the Haldane Mission of 1912', and D.C. Watt's 'Foreign Affairs, the Public Interest and the Right to Know', published in *Political Quarterly* in 1963, did make an impression, especially upon the mind of the leader of the Labour Party, Harold Wilson. It was to these articles in particular that, in paragraph 5 of a memorandum of 27 July 1965, Wilson, then prime minister, was referring. Wilson's memorandum, released into the public domain in January 1996, is printed in full below. His recommendations were adopted by the cabinet on 5 August 1965.

Memorandum by Harold Wilson, 27 July 1965 (CAB 129/122, C.(65) 114)

'The Fifty-Year Rule'

The Public Records Act, 1958, established the statutory principle that departmental records should not be available to the general public until a date 50 years after their creation. This principle has already been the subject of criticism by modern historians on the grounds that the period of 50 years is unnecessarily long and that the rule is inimical both to the public interest and to the requirements of genuine scholarship. The question has recently been examined by the Advisory Council on Public Records, under the chairmanship of the Master of the Rolls; and the Council have recommended to the Lord Chancellor:

(i) that the 'closed' period should be reduced to 40 years; and
(ii) that even within that reduced period more liberal access should be allowed to established historians.

The Scottish Records Advisory Council have made recommendations along similar lines.

2. In discussion with the Lord Chancellor I have formed certain preliminary views on these proposals; and I should welcome the opinion of my colleagues on the course which we should now pursue.

3. The justification for the present period of 50 years (which was accepted on the recommendation of the Grigg Committee on Departmental Records) is that it not only prevents the premature disclosure of confidential information which might be prejudicial to the State but also, and chiefly, preserves the constitutional principle of the collective responsibility of the Cabinet and the individual responsibility of Ministers to Parliament. For these reasons it is necessary to preserve the confidential nature of a Minister's relationship with his Ministerial colleagues on the one hand and with his senior advisers on the other hand. Moreover, it is desirable, in the interests of history as well as of current administration, to safeguard the quality of 'unselfconsciousness' in official records in the sense that, if advice is to be tendered frankly and discussed freely, neither Ministers nor their senior advisers should be subjected to the possible embarrassment of having their deliberations published while they are still active in public affairs.

4. On the other hand, 50 years is admittedly an arbitrary figure; and, after weighing the considerations mentioned above against the desirability of allowing

informed public opinion to enjoy freer access to the raw material of history, I have no doubt in my own mind that a closed period of 40 years (or less) could be adopted without any harm to the basic principles of the rule.

5. But the Council's recommendation that within the closed period more liberal access should be allowed for established historians is more debatable. I recognise that there are good arguments in favour of this proposal. Thus:

(a) Almost the whole of the advance of our Colonies, and much of that of India, towards independence has taken place within the last 40 years. If we do not write the history of this process, the newly independent Governments of those countries will; and, unless we permit access to our records, our side of the story will be liable to go by default.

(b) The same is true of large areas of international affairs, since certain other countries, particularly the United States, are considerably more generous in allowing access to their documents than we are to ours.

(c) The study of recent history is now a recognised branch of scholarship; and, while this does not in itself give scholars working in this field a right of access to material which, in the interests of proper administration, ought to remain confidential, an objective and dispassionate analysis of the recent past can, on occasion, promote a more informed public understanding of contemporary issues and contribute to the greater efficiency of current policy-making and administration.

6. On the other hand, I suspect – and this is also the consensus of view of Departments which have given much study to the matter – that the recommendation would be extremely difficult to implement in such a way as not to undermine the basic principles of a closed period. We should be faced with a number of awkward problems. For example:

(a) There would be the question whether access to Cabinet papers should be allowed within the closed period. It has always been a strictly enforced principle that access to the papers of the cabinet and its Committees within that period is not granted to any 'outside' individual; and, in so far as we conceded the more generous degree of public access which the Advisory Council have proposed, we should be departing from all previous practice.

(b) It would not be easy to devise a procedure for selecting 'established' historians which would not cause resentment and perhaps, in the long run, undo the goodwill generated by a decision in principle to allow freer access.

(c) Nor would it be easy to devise a procedure for deciding which episodes of recent peace-time history should be treated by the established historians. If the purpose of more liberal access were not to be frustrated, the decisions would have to be free from political controversy and run no risk of undermining the established convention that one Administration does not enjoy access to the records of its predecessors. In this connection we have to remember that the periods or episodes which command the greatest interest among historians are, naturally, those which are the most politically controversial. This is not the case in relation to the two Great Wars of this century, since for the major part of the time in each case Coalition Governments have been in office and there has been a truce in party conflict. It is largely this truce which has made it possible for us to write, and to publish, the Official Histories of both Wars; and it is the necessary absence of any such truce in peace-time which makes the writing of peace-time histories more arguable, particularly on any basis which involves discrimination between one historian, or one historical period, and another.

7. For these reasons, it might be wise to find other means of satisfying the desire which prompted the Advisory Council's second recommendation; and I believe that our best course would be to reduce the closed period to 30 years, rather than 40, while retaining the existing safeguards against premature disclosure, as follows:

(a) The Public Records Act, 1958 (s. 5 (4)) already allows controlled access to records which are still within the closed period of 50 years; but it clearly envisages such access as being exceptional and the provision has been so interpreted by Departments in practice. This provision and this interpretation of it should remain unaltered in relation to a closed period of 30 years.

(b) There should be no change in the arrangements whereby the Lord Chancellor has (under s. 5 (1) of the Public Records Act) already prescribed closure for specified classes of records for longer periods – up to 100 years. Generally these classes are those which contain information about individuals which could cause embarrassment or distress to living persons or their immediate descendants; or contain information whose disclosure might constitute a breach of confidence; or involve special security considerations.

Provided that we maintain these provisions in relation to a closed period of 30 years, I do not believe that a reduction of the period to that figure would undermine the essential principles of public administration which the present rule was designed to preserve; and, in terms of allowing unrestricted access (subject to the exceptions noted above) to the official documentation of a period of history which is presently closed, it would offer to historians a substantially greater concession than the Advisory Council have recommended.

8. A reduction in the closed period would involve a Bill to amend the 1958 Act (although the change could be made in Scotland without legislation). Pending the Bill, there is one anticipatory step which we might take, by Order, as an earnest of our intentions – namely to derestrict in a single operation the official records of the 1914–18 war, instead of releasing them only one year at a time by the existing process of 'creeping decontrol'. In practice, this would imply the release of all records, both Cabinet and Departmental, relating to the period of the war (other than those which will still have to be withheld indefinitely, for reasons of public policy); and it would be convenient if 'the period of the war' were interpreted as including the immediate aftermath of the war itself, *i.e.,* up to the end of 1922, the year in which the Coalition Government fell. I believe a gesture of this kind would gain us considerable credit with the professional historians and with public opinion.

9. Apart from the questions of a reduction in the closed period, I should like my colleagues to consider two supplementary, but separate, measures which we might take in the same field:

(i) On occasion the Government might think that it was in the public interest that a history of relatively recent events should be undertaken while the written records could still be supplemented by reference to the personal recollections of public men who took part in the events in question. For this purpose, we might extend the range of Official Histories (which have so far been confined to the two world wars) to include selected periods or episodes of peace-time history, on the understanding that the publication of works of this kind would need to be suspended for a time which would normally be at least equivalent to the 30-year period. In order, however, that there should be no derogation from the principle that one Administration does not enjoy access to the policy records of its predecessors, it would be necessary to arrange that any decision to commission such a history should be taken by the Government only with the consent of the Leaders of the other political parties or of some form of bi-partisan body, preferably consisting of Privy Councillors, which might be established for the purpose.

(ii) Alternatively, or in addition, we might publish, in relation to particular episodes of peace-time history, as much as possible of the relevant official documents, on the same lines as the Foreign Office series of documents on British Foreign Policy. On the basis of that precedent, the documents chosen for publication would have to be confined to the formal records illustrating the historical development and execution of policy, *i.e.*, they would have to exclude the internal minutes and records of discussions by means of which policy was formulated. Even so, the reception accorded to the Foreign Office series suggest that, if we extended the practice to the records of other Departments concerned with our external relations, we should do no damage and should, indeed, do something to put in more accurate perspective our own version of, *e.g.*, the complex progress of some of our former dependencies towards independence. It might also help to reduce the embarrassment in which we sometimes find ourselves in relation to the practice of the United States Government, who are considerably more generous in allowing access to their documents than we are to ours and whose records include a number of documents originating in this country, to which historians can obtain access in the United States but not here. It would thus, in some measure, meet the arguments set out in paragraph 5 above.

10. I should be glad if members of the Cabinet and other Ministers in charge of Departments would consider the above proposals carefully. If the Cabinet endorsed them, particularly the proposed change to a 30-year rule (both generally and as regards Cabinet records), the next step would be to discuss them with the Opposition Leaders and to seek The Queen's approval in relation to Cabinet records. Thereafter we could proceed to a public announcement and to the introduction of the necessary legislation when Parliamentary time permits.

§ Notes on Contributors

Joseph O. Baylen is Regents' Professor of History Emeritus and a member of the Advisory Committee for the British Newspaper Library. His most recent publication is a chapter on the history of the British press from 1860 to 1919 in the *Encyclopaedia of the British Press* (1993).

Uri Bialer is Professor of International Relations at the Hebrew University of Jerusalem, and a Visiting Professor at the University of Chicago. Among his publications are *The Shadow of the Bomber: The Fear of Air Attack and British Politics 1932–1939* (1980), and *Between East and West: Israel's Foreign Policy Orientation 1948–1956* (1990).

Ulfried Burz is an Assistant at the Institute of History, University of Klagenfurt, where he concentrates on the history of Austria and Carinthia in the nineteenth and twentieth centuries.

Ellen L. Evans is Professor of History, Georgia State University, and author of *The German Center Party 1870–1933: A Study in Political Catholicism* (1981). She is currently working on a comparative study of Catholic political movements and parties in Germany, Belgium, Switzerland, Austria and the Netherlands from 1789 to 1980.

Keith Hamilton is editor of *Documents on British Policy Overseas* and historian in the Library and Records Department of the Foreign and Commonwealth Office. His publications include *Bertie of Thame, Edwardian Ambassador* (1990) and (with Richard Langhorne), *The Practice of Diplomacy: Its Evolution, Theory and Administration* (1994).

Holger Herwig is Professor of History at the University of Calgary. Among his publications are *The German Naval Officer Corps: A Social and Political History 1890–1918* (1973), *'Luxury' Fleet: The Imperial German Navy 1888–1918* (1980), and *Germany's Vision of Empire in Venezuela 1871–1914* (1986).

Derek Spring is Senior Lecturer in Russian and East European History at the University of Nottingham. He is the author of articles on Russian foreign policy before 1914, and has edited and contributed to *The Impact of Gorbachev: Propaganda Politics and Film* (with Nicholas Pronay), and *Stalinism and Soviet Cinema* (with Richard Taylor).

Keith Wilson is Reader in International History at the University of Leeds. His publications include *Empire and Continent: Studies in British Foreign Policy from the 1880s to the First World War* (1987), *The History and Politics of the Morning Post 1905–1926* (1990), and *Channel Tunnel Visions: Dreams and Nightmares 1850–1945* (1994); he edited *Decisions for War, 1914*, which was published in 1995.

Herman J. Wittgens is Professor of History and Chairman of Department at St. Francis Xavier University, Antigonish, Nova Scotia.

INDEX

Abaza, Admiral, 64
Académie de Paris, 45
Acton, Lord,1, 22
Adler, Selig, 151, 170
Afghanistan, 233, 236, 237, 238, 239, 240, 242, 244, 246
Africa, 279, 280–1
Albert, Prince, 6
Albertini, Luigi, 87, 107, 178
Aexander III, Tsar, 78
Algeciras conference, (1906), 68
Alldeutscher Verband, 19
All Souls College, Oxford, 274
Alsace-Lorraine, 31, 93, 137, 139
American Historical Association, 9, 16, 158, 162
American Historical Review, 131, 154, 164, 165
American War of Independence, 49
Anglo-American Historical Conference, 158
Appuhn, Professor, 45
Arbeitsausschuss Deutscher Verbände, 88, 103–6, 130, 151–2, 156, 180
Armenia, 64, 95
Arthur, Sir George, 203
Asquith, Henry Herbert, 210, 211, 232
Auerbach, Bertrand, 40, 41–2, 45
Austria, ch. 6 passim, 279; Kommission für neuere Geschichte Osterreichs, 101
Austria-Hungary, 97, 113

Baer, Dr, 135–6
Baden, Prince Max von, 10, 111
Bailleu, Paul, 38
Balfour, Arthur James, 7, 15, 195–6, 198
Balkan War (1912), 68, 80–1
Ballhausplatz, 100, 189
Bapst, Edmond, 52
Barbarossa, Operation, 80
Bardolf, Freiherr von, 185
Barnes, Harry Elmer, 105–6, 131, 153, 157, 160, 163, 164, 166, 167, 168, 170
Barthou, Louis, 14, 45
Baschet, Armand, 33, 37, 39
Bauer, Gustav, 91
    Otto, 182–3
    Wilhelm, 180
Beard, Charles A., 114, 163, 164, 166
Beazley, C.R., 169
Becker, Carl, 113
Beckerath, Professor Erwin von, 161, 162
Bemis, Samuel, 52
Benckendorff, Count Alexander, 70, 131
Bérard, Victor, 47
Berchtold, Leopold von, 153
Berliner Monatshefte, 101, 151, 160, 165, 169, 180

Berne Copyright Convention (1886), 77
Bernhardi, Theodor von, 3, 17
Bernstorff, Count Johann Heinrich von, 93, 95
Berzin, Y.A., 79, 80
Bestuzhev, I.V., 70
Bethmann-Hollweg, Theobald von, 97, 98, 115
Bettelheim, Anton, 180
Bevin, Ernest, 283
Bidault, Georges, 57
Binckley, Robert C., 167, 169
Birkenhead, Lord, 233, 243–4, 245, 246, 247
Bischoff, 184
Bismarck, Prince Otto von, 6, 14, 30, 67, 88, 98, 207, 217
Bittner, Ludwig, 180–1, 184, 186, 188
Björko agreement (1905), 65, 68
Blech, Edward, 195
Blomberg, General Werner von, 110
Boer War, 19, 217
Boghitschewitsch, Milos, 102, 106
Böhme, Dr Traugott, 158
Bolshevik party, 64–5; revolution, 75
Bonnin, Georges, 3, 4, 17, 22
Borah, Senator, 134–5, 138
Bosnian crisis (1908–9), 70
Boston Foreign Policy Association, 134
Bourgeois, Émile, 47, 53
    Léon, 49
Bouthy, Émile, 32, 36
Brandenburg, Erich, 3, 98, 179
Bray, Sir Denys, 236, 249
Best-Litovsk, peace of, 200
Briand, Aristide, 44, 45, 46
Bridge, F.R., 189
Bridges, Edward, 277
*British Documents on the Origins of the War, 1898– 1914,*13, 18, 44, 199, 221, 223, ch. 8 passim, 265
British Museum, 8
Brockdorff-Rantzau, Count Ulrich von, 92, 93, 94
Bröger, Karl, 104
Brookes, Jean Ingram, 49
Browne, Professor E.G., 205
Buchanan, Sir George, 212
Bulgaria, 69, 76, 78–9, 188
Bülow, Prince Bernhard von, 3, 19, 96, 97
    Bernhard Wilhelm von, 90, 91–2, 93, 94, 101, 119
Burgess, Professor J.W., 164
Butterfield, Sir Herbert, 1, 22–3

Cadogan, Sir Alexander, 270–1, 279, 280
Cambon, Jules, 49

Cambridge History of British Foreign Policy,
    15, 203, 205, 213, 218
Canada, 52
Canaris, Wilhelm, 111–2
Caprivi, Leo von, 3, 14
Caritas Verbänd,103
Carnegie Institute, 52
Cavour, Count, 4, 22
Cecil, Lady Gwendolen, 208
Chadwick, Professor Owen, 1, 4
Chamberlain, Austen, 2, 219, 220, 221, 222,
    233, 234, 235, 237, 241–3, 246
    Neville, 270, 272, 273, 276, 279
Channing, Edward, 158
Charléty, Sébastian, 45
Chateaubriand, 32
Chicago Council on Foreign Relations, 162
China, 96, 98
Chirol, Sir Valentine, 208
Christian Century, 131
Churchill, Winston S., 210, 211, 274, 280
Clemenceau, Georges, 42, 94
Clerk, Sir G.R., 230
Cochran, Professor M.H., 159–63, 164,
    167, 168
Cohn, Willy, 3
Colonial Office, *see* Great Britain
Committee of Imperial Defence, 232, 236,
    238, 241, 243, 246, 248, 249
Committee on Official Histories, 249
Congress of Berlin (1878), 7, 198, 205
    of Vienna (1814–15), 46, 136, 199
Constant, Charles, 35
Corsica, 40
Courcel, Baron de, 36, 41, 46, 47, 51, 52, 53,
    55–6, 57
Cranborne, Lord, 273
Crimean War, 6
Cromer, Lord, 19
Crowe, Sir E.A., 5, 6, 7, 8, 15, 16, 17, 19–20,
    21, 22, 194, 197–8, 199, 202, 203, 206,
    210, 211, 212, 213, 215, 217–8, 220, 222,
    230, 289
Cuno, Wilhelm, 104
Curtis, Lionel, 7, 17, 201
Curzon, Lord, 7, 201, 203, 206, 211, 212,
    2134, 231–2, 234, 249; despatch of 21
    September 1899, 231–2, 234, 249
Czechoslovakia, 269, 271, 273

Daily Telegraph interview, 4
Daniel E.Y., 236, 248
Danzig corridor, 129
Davies, Godfrey, 212–3, 215
Dawes Plan, 132
Decazes, Duc Elie, 33, 34, 46
Delago Bay, 98
Delbrück, Hans, 3, 90, 93–4, 101, 102, 111, 179
    Richard von, 100, 112
Demartial, Georges, 105
Denmark, 97
Deutsche Frauenausschuss zur Bekämp-
    fung der Kreigsschuldlüge, 103
Deutsche Gesellschaft zum Studium
    Osteuropas, 75–6
Dickie R.C., 8
Die Grosse Politik, 1, 4, 11–12, 13, 15, 17, 43,
    71, 73, 96, 97, 98, 99, 101, 116, 119, 130,
    140, 185, 187, 209, 217, 266, 267
Die Kriegsschuldfrage, 43, 101, 104, 105, 130,
    137, 152, 166, 179

Dieckhoff, Hans, 135, 139, 140, 156–7
Dimitrijewitsch, 188
Dimitrov, G., 79
Disarmament Conference (1932), 278
Dittman, Wilhelm, 111
*Documents on British Foreign Policy
    1919–1939*, 22, ch. 9 passim, 289
Documents Diplomatiques Français, 13, 42,
    45, 55, 56
*Documents on German Foreign Policy
    1918–1945*, 20
Donitz, Admiral Karl, 117
Draeger, Hans, 98, 103, 110, 119
Driault, Edouard, 39, 40
Dugdale E.T.S., 13
Dunham, Professor, W.A. 49
Durand, Sir Mortimer, 235

Ebert, Friedrich, 91, 100
Ebray, Alcide, 105
Eckardstein, Freiherr von, 207, 208
École Libre des Sciences Politiques, 32–3
Eden, Anthony, 271–2, 273, 274, 275, 279,
    280, 281
Edward VII, King, 203
Eisner, Kurt, 90–1, 182
Engels, 79
Epstein, Fritz, 114
    Klaus, 114
Erdmann, K.D., 107, 114, 116
Erzberger, Matthias, 92
Esher, Lord, 15, 19
Eulenburg, Botho-Wendt zu, 112
    -Hertefeld, Prince Philipp zu, 116–7

Fabre-Luce, Alfred, 105, 106
Fair, Professor J.D., 17
Falkland Islands, 205, 219
Faugère, Pierre, 14, 30, 31, 34, 35, 36, 49,
    50, 51
Fay, S.B., 16, 105, 106, 131, 133, 141, 153,
    154–7, 161, 163, 166–9, 178
Fellner, Fritz, 189
Ferry, Jules, 38, 39
Fester, Richard, 178
Fischer, Eugen, 158
    Fritz, 18, 87, 96, 107, 114, 120, 189
Fisher H.A.L., 193
Foerster, Colonel Wolfgang, 111
Foreign Office, *see* Great Britain
Foreign Relations of the United States, 8–9,
    10, 282, 289
Fouché, Joseph, 30, 87, 93
Fournier, August, 180
France 14, ch. 1 passim; Archives
    Nationales, 32;
    Commission des Archives Diploma-
    tiques, 30, 31, 33, 35, 36, 38, 39, 40, 41,
    42, 46–8, 50–55; Commission de Publi-
    cation des Documents relatifs aux
    Origines de la Guerre de 1914– 1918,
    43, 45; Ministry of Finance, 45; Min-
    istry of Marine, 48; Ministry of Public
    Instruction, 34, 35, 38, 39
Franco-Prussian War, 30, 42
Franco-Russian Alliance, 132
Frank, Felix, 186
Frankfurt, Treaty of (1871), 30–31
Franz Ferdinand, Archduke, 185, 188
Federick the Great, 4
Freeland, Colonel J.C., 248–9

Friedjung, Heinrich, 184
Freycinet, Charles de, 35, 36, 37, 38
Freytag, Hans, 93, 99, 118
Fridlyand G.S., 79
Fuller, Professor Joseph V., 163

Gambetta, Leon, 42
Gardiner, Samuel Lawson, 51
Gasalee, Stephen, 16, 206, 208, 209, 213–4,
   215–19, 234, 235, 236, 237, 240–3, 245,
   246, 248
Gater, Sir George, 279
Geffroy, Matthieu, 35, 36
Geiss, Imanuel, 90, 96, 97, 98, 113, 151
German City League, 103
German Foreign Ministry, see Weimar
   Republic
German General Staff, 93, 96
Germany, Federal Republic of, 107
Gerstenmaier, Eugen, 116
Gibraltar, 219
Gierke, Otto von, 108
Giolitti, 4
Goebbels, Joseph, 80, 103, 169–70
Goethe Institute, 114
Gooch G.P., 2, 15, 18, 21, 22, 178, 203–5,
   213, 218, 219, 220, 221, ch. 8 passim
Gooss, Roderick, 101, 181, 183, 184
Gorbatov A.V., 81
Göring, Hermann, 108
Görlitz, Walter, 115
Göttingen Historical Conference (1932),
   103, 178
Granville, Lord, 8
Great Britain, 93; Admiralty, 199, 235, 249;
   Army Council, 249; Colonial Office,
   198, 205, 213, 219, 235, 279–80, 281;
   Foreign Office, ch. 7 passim, ch. 9 pas-
   sim, Committee on Public Records,
   5–6, Foreign Trade Department, 8, His-
   torical Section, 199, 202, 216, 232,
   News Department, 195; Home Office,
   213; India Office, ch. 8 passim; Parlia-
   mentary Blue Books, 9, 202, 265; Treasury, 219, 220; War Office, 219, 235
Greece, 69
Grey, Sir Edward, 9–10, 15, 128, 137, 193,
   203, 204, 205, 210, 213–4, 216, 222
Gromyko, Andrei, 81

Hague Peace Conferences (1899, 1907), 108
Hahn, Erich, 91, 118
Hajek, Alois, 188
Hale, Oron J., 169
Halevy, Professor E., 240
Halifax, Lord, 266, 267, 271, 273, 274
Haller, Professor Johannes, 116–7
Hallgarten, George, 98
Hamburg Board of Trade, 103–4
Hamman, Otto, 207, 208
Hankey, Sir Maurice, 238–9, 241, 246
Hanotaux, Gabriel, 31–2, 33, 36, 38, 44, 51,
   53, 54, 55, 57
Harbou, Major Bodo von, 92
Hardinge, Lord, 7, 197, 198, 199, 200, 202,
   219–20
Hart, Albert Bushnell, 158
Hartmann, Ludo Moritz, 180, 182
Hartung, Fritz, 114
Harvey, Oliver, 271–2, 273, 274
Hasse, Professor Ernst, 19

Hauptmann, Gerhard, 157
Haus-, Hof und Staatsarchiv, 46, 181, 184, 185
Hayes, Carlton J., 105, 168
Hazen, Professor Charles D., 168
Headlam-Morley, J.W., 9, 15, 21, 193,
   199–211, 213, 215–7, 221, 222, 232, 233,
   234, 240, 245, 246
Heidelberg Association for a Policy of Jus-
   tice, 94
Helfferich, Karl, 109
Helmreich, Ernst C., 165
Henderson, Ernest Flagg, 159
   G.B., 21
Herre, Paul, 102, 178
Herzfeld, Hans, 102, 106, 107, 111, 178
Herzog, Rudolf, 157
Hesse, Hermann, 120
Hesselbarth, Hermann, 14
Hindenburg, Paul von, 100, 109, 111, 115, 140
Hirtzel, Sir Arthur, 232, 233, 235, 237, 238,
   239, 244–5
Hitler, Adolf, 78, 82, 89, 106l 1–7, 120, 151,
   170, 181, 270, 271, 272, 273, 276, 279
Hoare, Sir S., 270, 274
Hoetzsch, Otto, 75, 76, 77, 78, 80, 81
Hohenlohe-Schillingsfürst, Prince, 3
Hohenzollern Candidature, 3–4, 14, 18
Holland, Sir Robert, 231, 243, 246, 247,
   248, 249
Holstein, Friedrich von, 4
Hoyos, Count Alexander, 181
Hubatsch, Walther, 115
Hüffer, Professor, 50
Hungary, 182, 185

IG-Farben, 103
Imperial Russian Historical Society, 51
India, Council of, 243; Government of,
   232, 233, 236, 237, 238, 244, 248, 249;
   Office, ch. 8 passim
Iron and Steel Cartel, 103
Irwin, Lord, 244, 247–8
Isvolsky, Alexander, 63, 69, 100
Italy, 5, 12, 40, 69, 93, 187

Jagic, Vatroslav, 180
Jagow, Gottlieb von, 90, 93, 118, 187
Jameson, Professor John Franklin, 164
Jonas, Hans, 76
Jusserand, 52

Kaehler, Siegfried, 102, 178
Kantorowicz, Hermann, 112–5, 119
Kapp Putsch, 116
Karo, Georg, 178
Kautsky, Karl, 14, 91, 92, 95, 96–7, 116,
   119, 207
Kehr, Eckart, 114, 115
Kellogg, Frank B., 8, 10
Kennedy, John F., 289
Kerensky, Alexander, 65
Kern, Fritz, 178
Kerner, R.J., 167
Kienböck, 187
Kiep, 129, 140
Kirkland, Professor Edward Chase, 163
Kissinger, Henry, 11
Kitchener, Lord, 203
Klein, Fritz, 96
Kolarov, V., 79
König, Max, 159

Köpke, Gerhard, 156
Kornilov affair (August 1917), 66
Krasnyi Arkhiv, 67, 68, 69, 70, 78, 79, 80
Kraus, Professor Herbert, 159
Kriege, Dr Johannes, 110, 113, 114, 118
Kuhl, General Hermann von, 111
Kuropatkin, 68, 69

Lai, Cardinal de, 4
Lamsdorff, V.N., 64, 69
Lampson, Miles, 195, 209
Langer, W.L., 98, 105, 141, 155, 161, 163, 164, 166, 169
Laski, Harold, 16, 214
Law, Andrew Bonar, 211
Layard, Sir Henry, 8
League of Nations, 44, 131, 186
Lee, Sir Sidney, 203, 220
Leeper, Reginald, 269
Legrelle,14, 50
Leitner, Rudolf, 162–3, 164
Lenin, V.I., 65
Leo XIII, Pope, 4–5
Lepsius, Johannes, 95
Lersner, Kurt von, 103
Leslie, John, 189
Leutner, 185
Library of Congress, 52, 135; Legislative Reference Service of, 135–139, 142
Linevich, 69
Lingelbach, W.E., 165, 166
Livre Noir, 68, 71, 131
Lloyd George, David, 119, 196, 200, 211
Löbe, Paul, 113
Locarno agreements (1925), 75, 113, 119, 269, 278
Lodge, Senator, 135
Lord, R.H., 4
Loreburn, Lord, 15, 19
Louis XIV, 33
Louis-Philippe, 30
Ludendorff, General Erich, 92, 111
Ludwig, Emil, 156, 157
Lunacharsky, 75
Luther, Hans, 105
Lutz, Hermann, 101, 102, 105, 106, 112, 153, 154–5
    Ralph Haswell, 167, 168
Lyte, Henry Maxwell, 198–9

MacDonald, Ramsay, 11, 12, 214, 215, 216, 217, 218, 219, 241, 243, 247
MacMahon, President, 33
Macedonia, 64
Makins, Roger, 272
Maksakov, 72, 74
Maltzan, Freiherr Ago von, 131, 132, 137
Mann, Thomas, 120
Marchand, René, 68, 131
Margerie, Pierre de, 44
Margueritte, Victor, 105, 106
Markin, N.A., 64, 65
Marriott, J.A.R., 21, 196
Martin, Henri, 36, 39
    Kingsley, 218, 175
Marx, Ernst, 3
    Wilhelm, 11, 12
Maury, Alfred, 36
May, Ernest R., 11
McGuire, 134–5
Meinecke, Friedrich, 95, 98

Mellich, Karl, 185
Mendelssohn-Bartholdy, Albrecht, 12, 94, 95, 97, 100, 101
Meurthe, Boulay de la, 40–1
Meyendorff, Alexander, 70–1
Meyer, Herman H.B., 136, 138
Michelet, Jules, 32
Mitis, 185
Moberly, General F.J., 236, 248–9
Moltke, Eliza von,115
    Hans-Adolf von, 115
    Helmuth von, 115
Mommsen, Wilhelm, 102
Monod, Gabriel, 31, 32, 36, 37, 40, 41, 46, 51, 57
Montelgas, Count Maximilian von, 91, 94, 101, 112, 119
Montgomery, Sir Hubert, 222, 233, 234, 242, 245–6
Monts, Count Anton, 97
Moon, Parker T., 155, 169
Morel E.D., 105, 106, 133, 195, 214
Morier, Sir Robert, 8
Morison, Samuel, 214
Morsey, Andreas, 185
Mowat R.B., 217, 218
Müller, Admiral Georg Alexander von, 115
    Hermann, 113
Mundt, Hugo, 168
Munich crisis (1938), 270–2
Muzzey, David S., 158

Namier L.B., 199
Nagel, Charles, 167
Napoleon III, 30, 32, 43
Neratov A.A., 65,66
Neurath, Constantin von, 1, 12, 78, 110
Nicholas II, Tsar, 117
Nicholas H.G., 289, 290
Nish, Ian, 231
Nitze, Paul, 11
Norway, 97
Nye, Gerald P., 169–170

Official Secrets Act, 15, 211
Oliphant, Sir L., 234
Ollivier, Émile, 43
Oman, Charles, 203
Oncken, Hermann, 103, 107, 114, 179
Oncken, Wilhelm, 3
Origines Diplomatiques de la Guerre de 1870–1871, 42, 43, 45, 55
Ottoman empire, 208
Owen, Robert L. 101, ch. 4 passim, 165

Palairet C.M., 234
Paléologue, Maurice, 13
Palmerston, Lord, 289
Paris Peace Conference (1919), 56, 205
Parker, Alwyn, 196, 197
Pashukanis E.B., 79
Patrick P.J., 235, 237, 238, 246
Pavlovich P., 79
Pearl Harbour, 277
Peel, Sir Robert, 8
    Viscount, 247, 249
Penjdeh crisis (1885), 63, 212
Percy, Lord Eustace, 249
Persia, 64, 203, 205, 234, 236, 238, 239, 240, 242, 244, 247
Pichon, Stephen, 42, 43, 46

Pick F.W., 22, 23
Picot, Georges, 36
Platzhoff, 4, 18
Poincaré, Raymond, 13, 44, 45, 53
Political Intelligence Department, 7, 9, 199, 200, 201, 202, 216, 221, 266, 268
Pokrovsky M.N., 13–14, 67, 68, 69, 70, 71, 72–3, 74, 75, 76, 77, 79, 82
Polivanov, 69
Popov A.L., 73, 79
Potsdam Reichsarchiv, 100, 111
Preobrazhensky E.V., 70
Pribram A.F., 183–4
Pritwitz, Friedrich Wilhelm von, 157–8
Propaganda Bureau (Wellington House), 199
Propaganda Ministry, *see* Goebbels
Prothero, George, 199, 206
Prussian Academy, 98
Prussian Landtag, 36
Prussian War Ministry, 93, 96

Raeder, Admiral Erich, 117
Ramek, 185, 186
Ranke, Leopold von, 30, 50
Rapallo, 75, 82
Rathenau, Walter, 11, 131
Read, Conyers, 23
Redlich, Oswald, 180, 181
Reinach, Joseph, 40, 42
Reindorff, 4, 18
Reinöhl, Fritz, 188
Renouvin, Pierre, 45, 143, 152, 155–6, 163, 164, 168, 178
Rettet die Ehre, 103
Revue des Deux Mondes, 155–6, 164
Rialle, Girard de, 38
Ribbentrop, 280
Richelieu, 31
Riezler, Kurt, 89, 115–6
Riker, T.W., 168
Ritter, Gerhard, 107, 114, 116
Roberts, Frank, 266, 275, 281
Rockefeller, John D., 52, 114
Rodd, Sir Rennell, 8, 212
Röhl, John C.G., 87, 115
Romberg C.G.W., 133, 209
Rose, John Holland, 15, 195–6
Rothfels, Hans, 102, 107, 115–6, 178
Round Table Conference, Williamstown (1932), 161–2, 165
Rousset, Camille, 35, 36
Royal Commission on the Public Records, 193
Royal Institute for International Affairs, 7, 17, 19, 201
Rumania, 66, 69
Rumbold, Sir H., 278
Rupprecht, Crown Prince, 111
Russia, 13, 93, 189, 196, 233, 234, 236, 242, 244, 249, 276, 282; Academy of Sciences, 75; All Russian Congress of Soviets, 64; Asiatic Department, 69; Central Executive Committee, 75; Commissariat of Enlightenment, 66, 75; Commissariat of Foreign Affairs, 68, 69, 72, 74, 75; Commission for Publication of Documents of the Epoch of Imperialism, 75; Committee on Far Eastern Affairs, 63–4; Communist Academy, 71; Council of Ministers, 74; Decree on Peace (8 November 1917),
64; Finance Ministry, 74; General Staff, 74; Institute of Red Professors, 80; State Printing House, 75, 77, 78; Tsentrarkhiv, 67, 69; War Ministry, 74
Russo-Japanese War, 64, 68

Saar, 139
Sablin A.A., 70
St. Germain, Treaty of, 178, 181, 184
St. Hilaire, Barthelemy, 38
St. John Gaffney, Thomas, 156
Salisbury, third Marquess of, 18–19, 198, 107–8, 235
Salomon, Professor, 45
Sanders, Liman von, 67
Sanderson, Lord, 196, 197–8, 208
Sargent, Sir O., 278, 283
Sarkotic, General, 188
Sasse, Heinz-Günther, 99
Satow, Sir Ernest, 16
Sauerbeck, Ernst, 101, 179
Sazonov, Serge, 68, 69
Schevill, Ferdinand, 105, 133, 165, 166
Schieder, Theodor, 107, 114
Schleswig-Holstein, 15, 198, 206–7
Schmidt-Ott, Dr, 75, 76
Schmitt, B.E., 105, 131, 152–3, 155, 156, 157, 159–60, 161, 162, 163 164, 166, 178
Schnee, Dr Heinrich, 103
Schober, 187–8
Schröder, Gerhard, 114
Schubert von, 185
Schücking, Walter, 91, 101, 119
Schumacher, Hermann, 114
Schurz Foundation, 156, 159
Schwendemann Dr Karl C., 161
Schwertfeger, Colonel B., 13, 81, 98, 101, 102, 111, 178
Seeckt, General Hans von, 111
Seipel, 186–7
Serbia, 69, 87, 188
Seton, Sir M., 233, 247
Seton-Watson R.W., 70, 220, 221
Seymour, Charles, 163, 166
Shipstead, Hendrick, 140, 141, 156
Siebert, Benno de, 70, 131, 209
Simon, Sir John, 268, 270, 274, 275–6, 277
Simons, Walter, 99, 161
Slade, William Adams, 136, 137, 138–9
Slavonic Review, 70
Sloane, William M., 164
Smuts, 280–1
Société de l'Histoire de France, 35
Solf, 10–11, 12
Sontag, R.J., 168–9
Sorel, Albert, 32, 33, 35, 36, 37, 38, 39, 44, 46, 47, 50, 51, 57
Southcott, Joanna, 2
Spanish-American War, 214
Spender, J.A., 213
Srbik, Heinrich, 184
Staal, Baron de, 71
Stalin, Josif, 79, 81
Steefel, Lawrence, 15, 206–7
Steiner, Rudolf, 115
Steuben Society, 134, 152, 156, 158
Stieve, Friedrich, 71, 100, 101, 104, 140
Stowell, Professor, E.C. 136
Straits, 66, 67–8, 69, 132, 137, 139
Strang, William, 266, 267, 268–9, 270, 271

Stresemann, Gustav, 1, 11, 12, 89, 113, 119, 120, 275
Stulpnagel, Major Otto von, 111
Stumm, Wilhelm von, 93
Sukhomlinov, 68
Sweden, 97, 133
Switzerland, 51
Sybel, Heinrich von, 3, 14, 30–1, 36–7, 38, 50, 57

Tansill, Charles C., 136, 137, 138, 140, 165, 166, 170
Tarle E.V., 74
Taylor A.J.P., 2, 22–3, 289
Temperley H.W.V., 15–16, 17–18, 201, 202, 218, 220, 221, ch. 8 passim
Thayer, William Roscoe, 162
Thibet, 238, 244, 246
Thierry, Augustin, 32
Thimme, Annelise, 97
    Friedrich, 1, 4, 11, 12, 15, 17, 18, 95, 96, 98, 101, 113, 116, 119, 178, 186, 187
Thirty-Year Rule, 2, 289–93
Thompson, James Westfall, 167
Tippelskirch, Werner von, 161
Tirpitz, Admiral Alfred von, 98, 16, 219
Tisza, Count I., 185
Tomsky, 78
Toynbee, Arnold, 199
Trotha, Admiral Adolf von, 111
Trotsky L., 64, 70
Tyrrell, Sir William, 200, 222

Uebersberger H., 184, 188
Union of Domocratic Control, 15, 195, 201, 203, 214
United States of America, 8–9, 49, 50, 52, 101, 105, 114, 202, 267, 273, 277; public opinion chs. 4 and 5 passim, 269–270; Senate 169–170; Senate Foreign Relations Committee 134–5, 136, 138, 140–42; State Department 10
Utrecht, Treaty of (1713), 33

Valfrey, Jules, 35
Vansittart, Sir Robert, 270, 271, 278
Vereine des Auslandsdeutschtums, 104
Versailles, Treaty of, 11, 18, 43, 45, 99, 107, 129, 134, 183, 204, 266; Article, 228, 92; Article, 230, 93; Article, 231, 43, 88, 95, 106, 112, 128–130, 133, 134, 139, 141, 142, 151, 178
Versen, Max von, 3
Victoria, Queen, 5, 193, 198, 213
Viel-Castel, Baron de, 33, 50
Vietsch, Wilhelm von, 103

Wakely, L.D., 232, 233, 235, 239, 246
Walton, J.C., 249
Warburg, Max, 94, 104
Ward, Sir Adophus, 203, 205
Warmuth, Fritz, 109
Watt, D.C., 22, 290
Weber, Eugen, 39
    Max, 94, 118

Webster, C.K., 9, 10, 16–17, 20, 21, 49, 192, 193, 196, 199, 205, 214–5, 218–9, 221, 222–3, 244, 268, 289
Wedel, O.A., 167
Wegerer, Alfred von, 56, 87, 98, 101–2, 105, 107, 108, 129, 136–8, 143, 151–5, 159, 163, 164–6, 168, 169–70, 179
Weimar Republic, 29, 88–9, 97, 99, 117, 118–9, 168; Centre Party, 92; Communist Party (KPD), 91; Defence Ministry, 111; Finance Ministry, 114; Foreign Ministry, chs. 3, 4, 5 passim, 179, Office for Peace Negotiations, 93, 95, Press Section, 103, War-Guilt Section, 88, 91, 93, 95, 99, 100, 101, 108–9, 130, 131, 132, 133–4, 136, 140–2, ch. 5 passim; German National People's Party (DNVP), 109; Institute for Foreign Policy, 100; Interior Ministry, 103; Patriotic Clubs, 103; Reichstag Committee of Enquiry, 88, 107–115, 118; Socialists, Independent (USPD), 90, 109, 112, Majority (SPD), 91, 112, 118
Wertenbaker, Professor Thomas Jefferson, 159
Werthern, Colonel von, 3
    Georg von, 3–4
Westarp, Count Eberhard Joachim von, 161, 162
Westphalia, Peace of (1648), 37
White, Mary, 116
Wilhelm II, Kaiser, 3, 69, 96, 97, 110, 115, 116–7, 153, 160, 208, 219
Wilson, Harold, 290
    Sir Horace, 270, 271, 272, 273
    Woodrow, 94, 131, 135, 196
Windsor, Duke of, 20–21
Winter, Gustav, 180
Winterfeldt, General Detlof von, 93
Wirth, Joseph, 99, 131
Wittgens, Herman, 96
Wittke, Dr Carl, 158
Wood, Sir Kingsley, 277
Woodward E.L., 2, 7, 23, 205, 266, 267–9, 270, 272–3, 274, 275, 277, 278, 279–84
World Council of Churches, 103, 104

Yanushkevich, 68
Yerusalimsky A.S., 80
Young Plan (1929), 113
Young Turk Revolution (1908), 68

Zaionchkovsky A.M., 70
Zalkind I.A., 64, 65
Zechlin, Egmont, 107
Zentralstelle für Erforschung der Kriegsurachen, 88, 99–101, 103, 105, 106, 130, 137, 143, 152–3, 156, 163, 165–6, 169, 179, 180
Zimmermann, Alfred, 90, 153
Zimmern, Alfred, 199, 213, 214
Zingeler K.T., 3